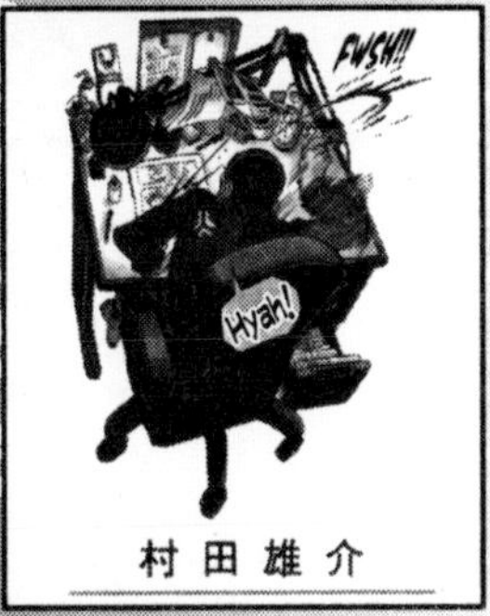
FWSH!!
Hyah!
村田雄介

Yusuke Murata

For scenes that require intensity, I feel the energy in my belly and use my entire body to draw with vigor. Naturally, drawing becomes a battle of physical strength, so I realize that when I get older I won't be able to draw action scenes. Because of that, I have to draw action scenes like crazy now, while I've still got my youth!

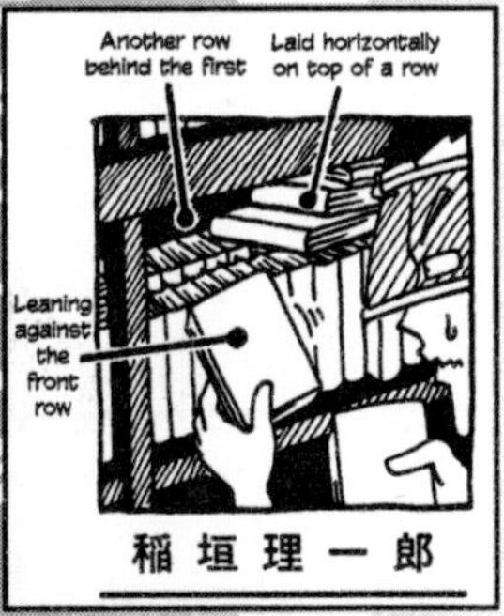
Another row behind the first
Laid horizontally on top of a row
Leaning against the front row
稲垣理一郎

Riichiro Inagaki

I'm constantly accumulating books, either for work or for my personal interests.
I threw away all my clothes, and now bookshelves cover every wall, like in the picture to the left. It looks like I'm going to have to get rid of some of the old books. Argh... I can't bear to lose any of them!!

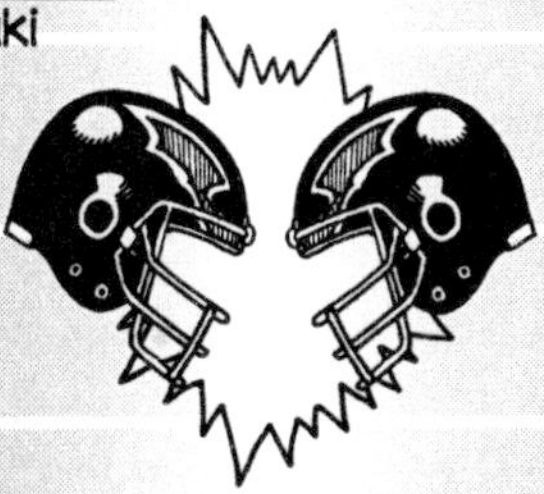

Eyeshield 21 is the hottest gridiron manga to hit the scene. A collaborative effort between writer Riichiro Inagaki and artist Yusuke Murata, ***Eyeshield 21*** was originally serialized in Japan's ***Weekly Shonen Jump***. An OAV created for Shueisha's Anime Tour is available in Japan, and the ***Eyeshield 21*** hit animated TV series debuted in spring 2005!

EYESHIELD 21
Vol 8: True Warriors Seek Out Strong Foes
The SHONEN JUMP ADVANCED Manga Edition

STORY BY RIICHIRO INAGAKI
ART BY YUSUKE MURATA

Translation & English Adaptation/Allison Markin Powell
Touch-up Art & Lettering/James Gaubatz
Cover and Graphic Design/Sean Lee
Editor/Frances E. Wall

Editor in Chief, Books/Alvin Lu
Editor in Chief, Magazines/Marc Weidenbaum
VP of Publishing Licensing/Rika Inouye
VP of Sales/Gonzalo Ferreyra
Sr. VP of Marketing/Liza Coppola
Publisher/Hyoe Narita

Printed in the U.S.A.

Published by VIZ Media, LLC
P.O. Box 77010
San Francisco, CA 94107

SHONEN JUMP ADVANCED Manga Edition
10 9 8 7 6 5 4 3
First printing, June 2006
Third printing, January 2008

www.viz.com

THE WORLD'S MOST
CUTTING-EDGE MANGA

www.shonenjump.com

Vol. 8
True Warriors Seek
Out Strong Foes

Story by **Riichiro Inagaki**   Art by **Yusuke Murata**

THE PLAYERS

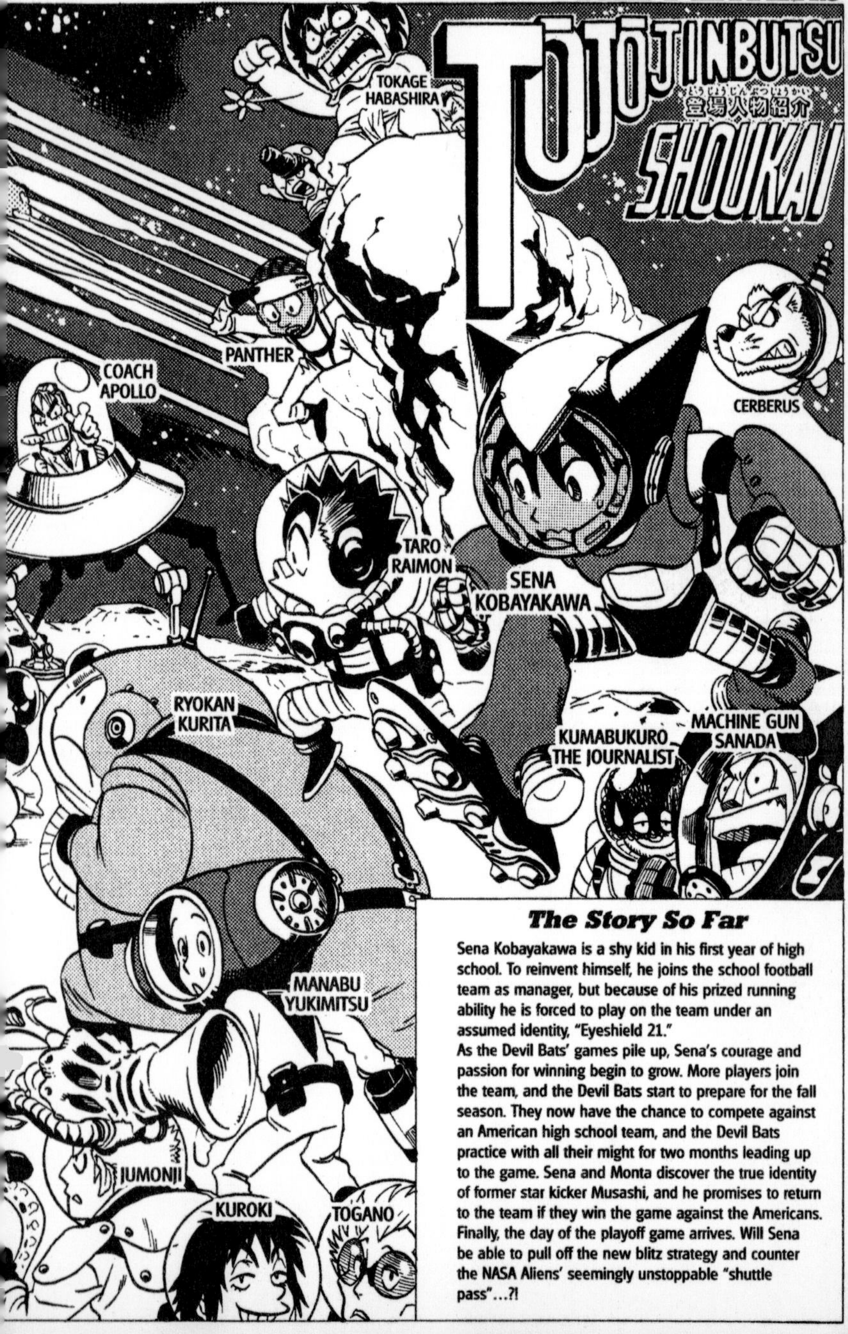

TŌJŌJINBUTSU
登場人物紹介
SHOUKAI
TOKAGE HABASHIRA
CERBERUS
PANTHER
COACH APOLLO
SENA KOBAYAKAWA
TARO RAIMON
MACHINE GUN SANADA
KUMABUKURO THE JOURNALIST
RYOKAN KURITA
MANABU YUKIMITSU
TOGANO
KUROKI
JUMONJI

The Story So Far

Sena Kobayakawa is a shy kid in his first year of high school. To reinvent himself, he joins the school football team as manager, but because of his prized running ability he is forced to play on the team under an assumed identity, "Eyeshield 21."

As the Devil Bats' games pile up, Sena's courage and passion for winning begin to grow. More players join the team, and the Devil Bats start to prepare for the fall season. They now have the chance to compete against an American high school team, and the Devil Bats practice with all their might for two months leading up to the game. Sena and Monta discover the true identity of former star kicker Musashi, and he promises to return to the team if they win the game against the Americans. Finally, the day of the playoff game arrives. Will Sena be able to pull off the new blitz strategy and counter the NASA Aliens' seemingly unstoppable "shuttle pass"...?!

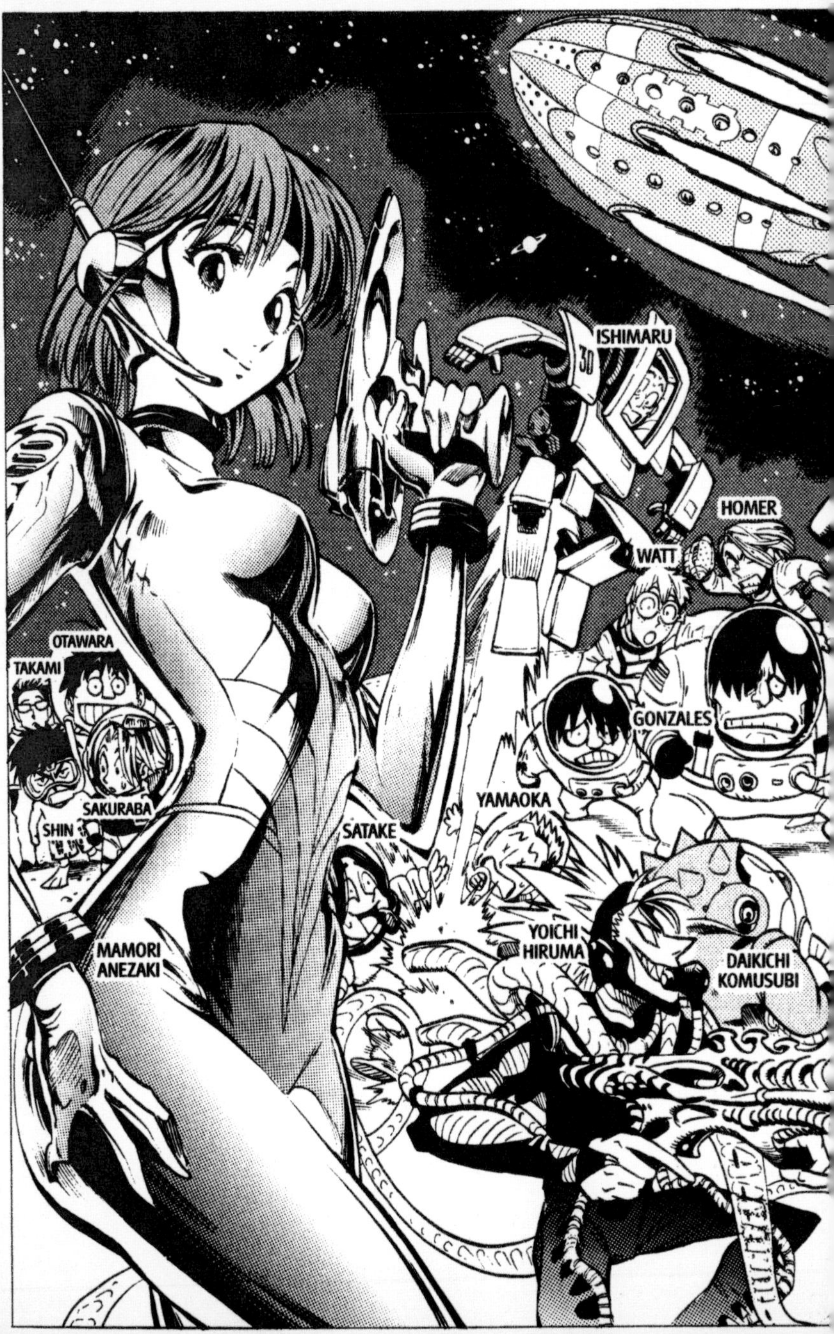
ISHIMARU
HOMER
WATT
GONZALES
YAMAOKA
SATAKE
OTAWARA
TAKAMI
SAKURABA
SHIN
DAIKICHI KOMUSUBI
YOICHI HIRUMA
MAMORI ANEZAKI

Vol. 8
True Warriors Seek Out Strong Foes

CONTENTS

Chapter 62
American Muscle

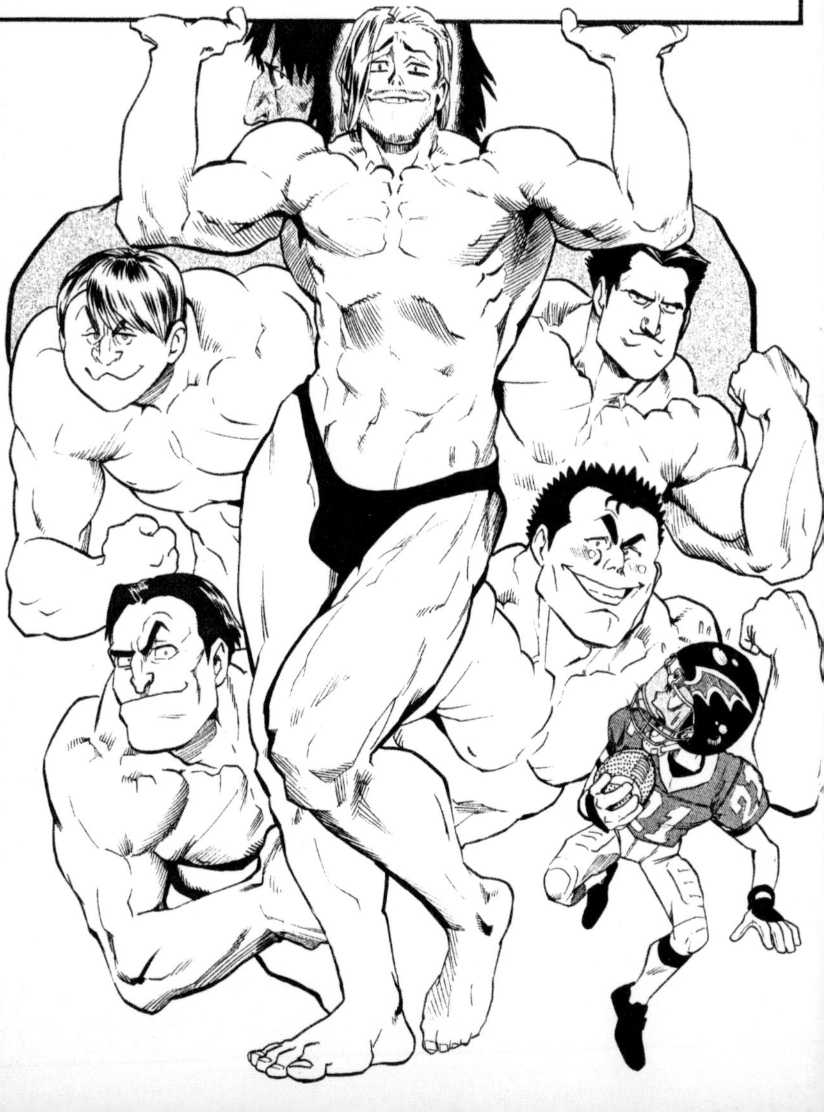

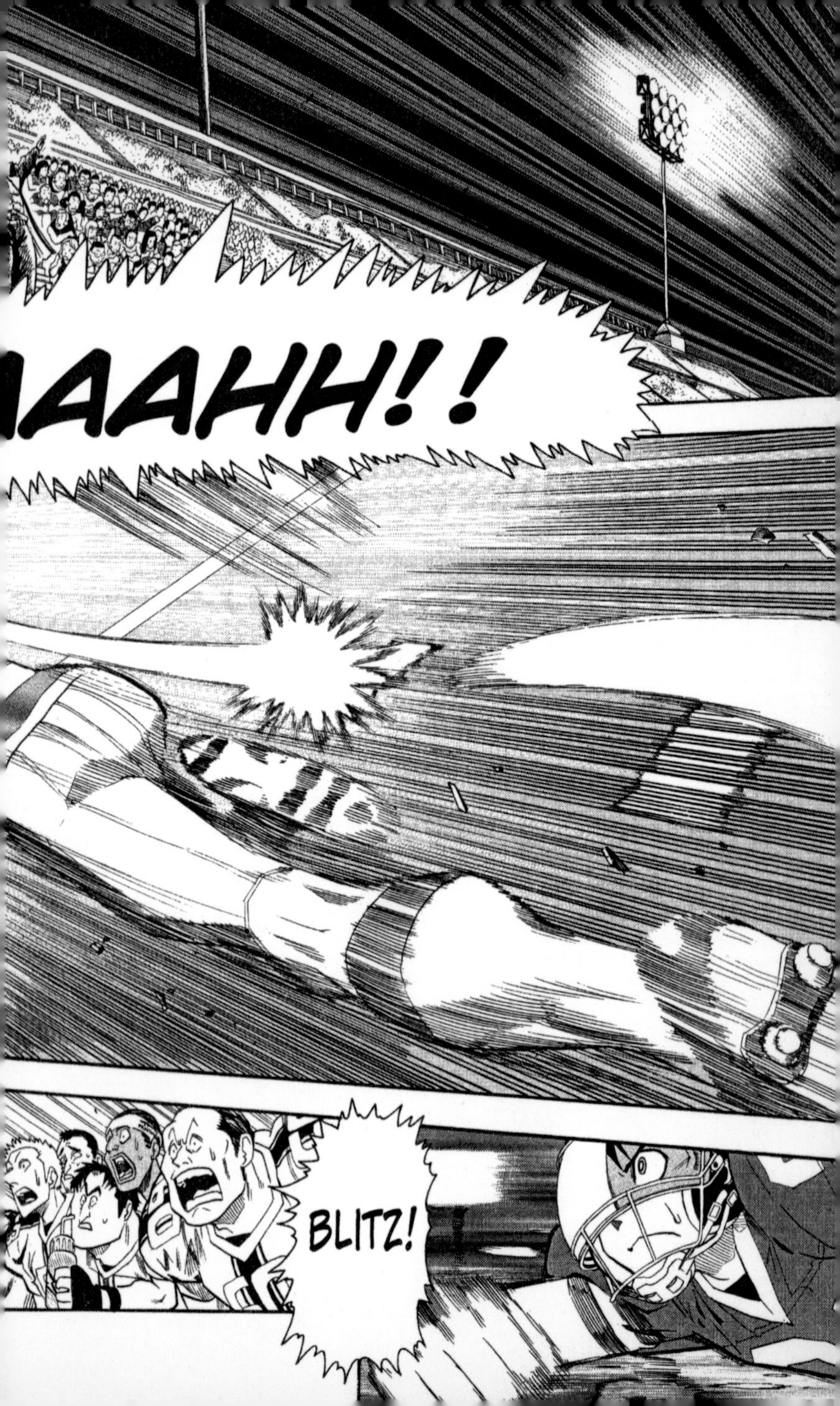
AAHH!!
BLITZ!

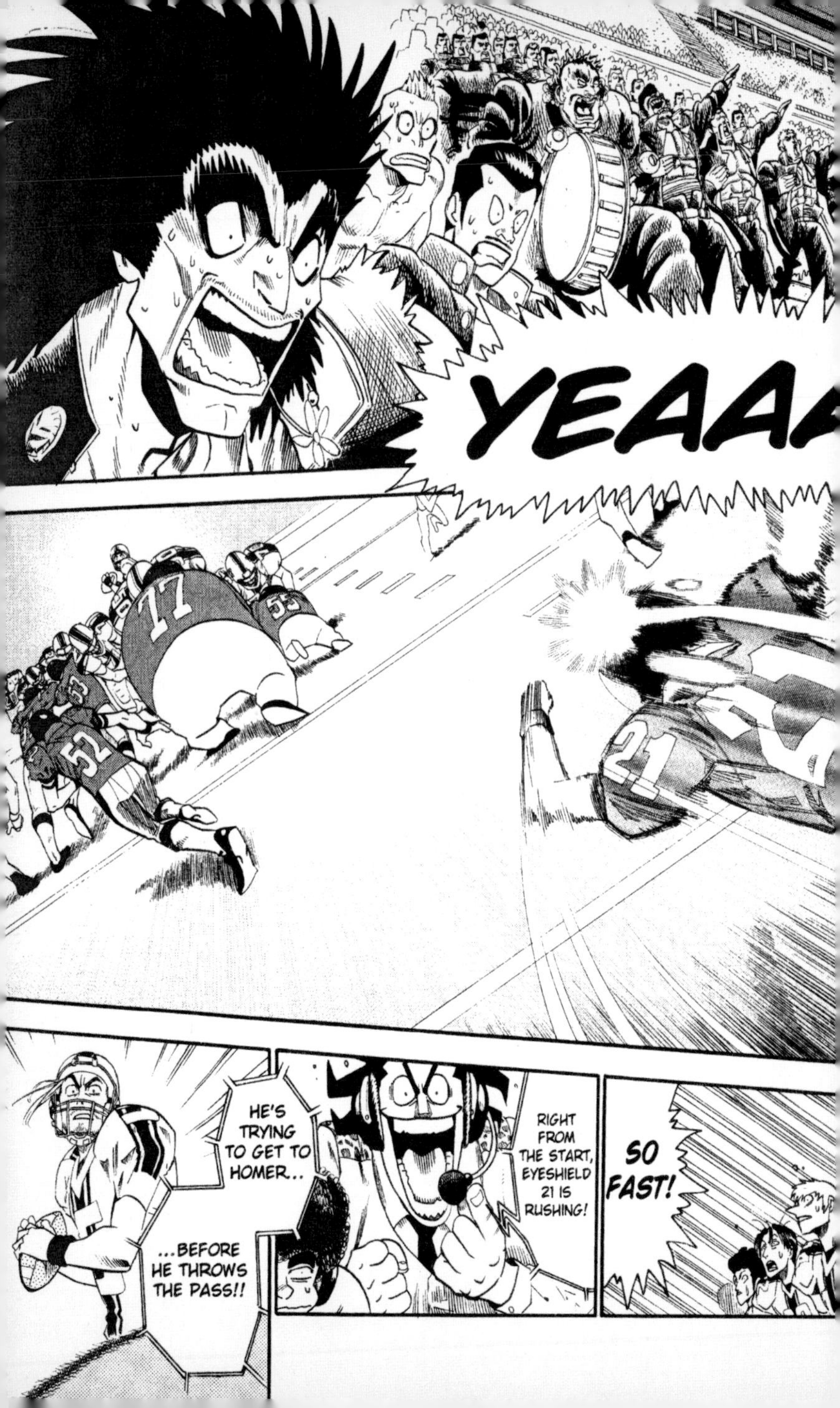
YEAAA
SO FAST!
RIGHT FROM THE START, EYESHIELD 21 IS RUSHING!
HE'S TRYING TO GET TO HOMER...
...BEFORE HE THROWS THE PASS!!

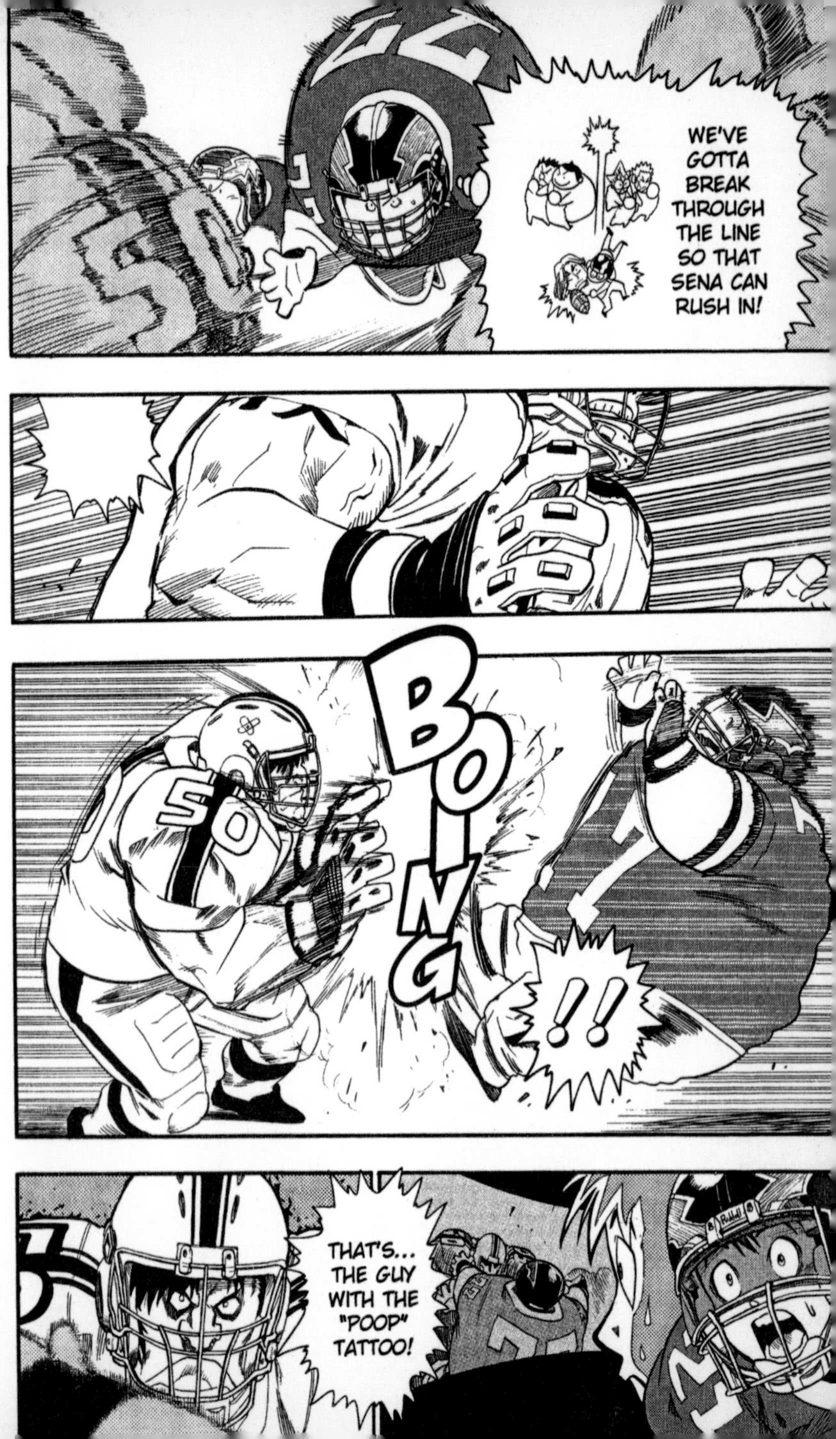
WE'VE GOTTA BREAK THROUGH THE LINE SO THAT SENA CAN RUSH IN!
BOING
!!
THAT'S... THE GUY WITH THE "POOP" TATTOO!

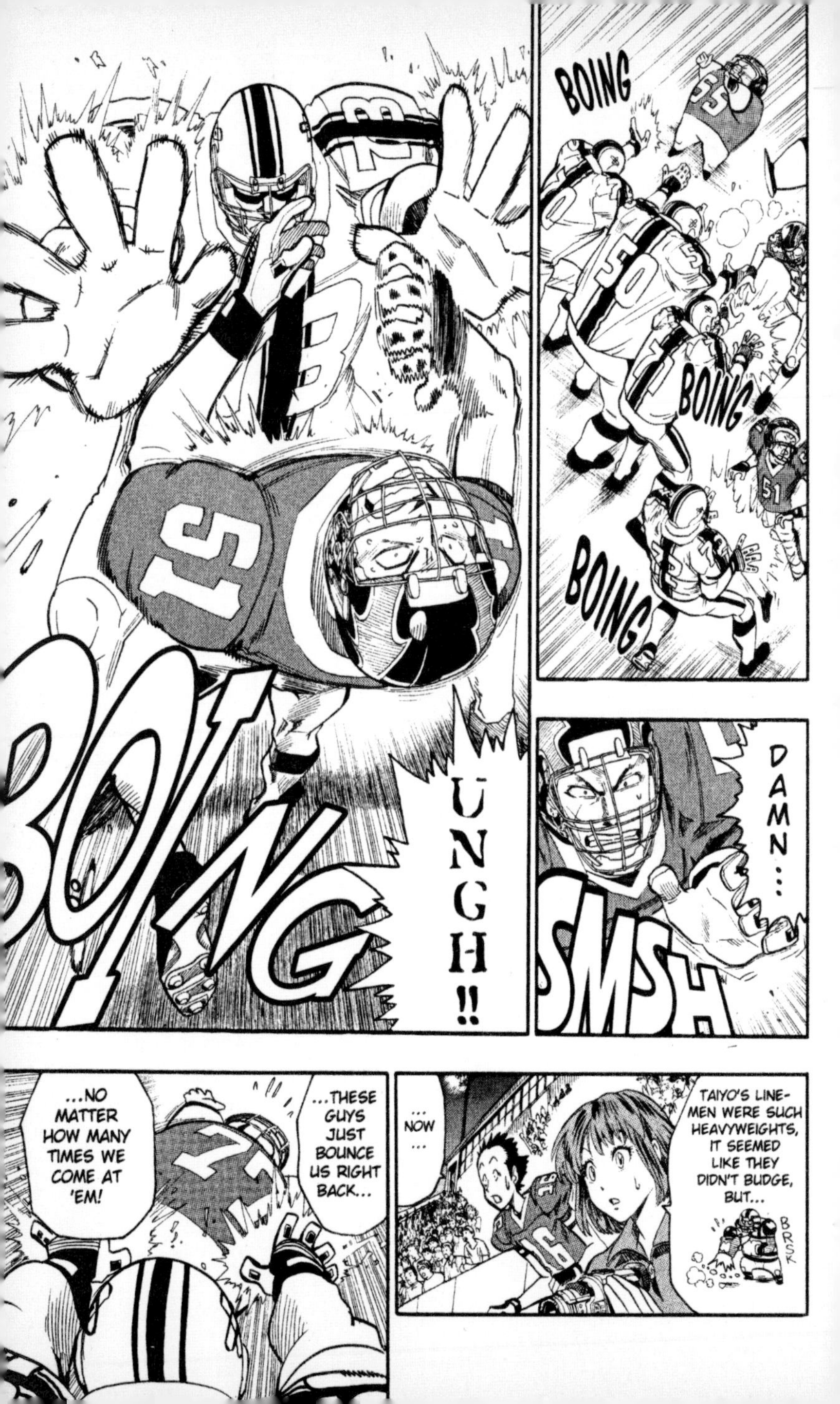

BOING
BOING
BOING
DAMN...
SMSH
BOING
UNGH!!
TAIYO'S LINE-MEN WERE SUCH HEAVYWEIGHTS, IT SEEMED LIKE THEY DIDN'T BUDGE, BUT...
...NOW...
BRSK
...THESE GUYS JUST BOUNCE US RIGHT BACK...
...NO MATTER HOW MANY TIMES WE COME AT 'EM!

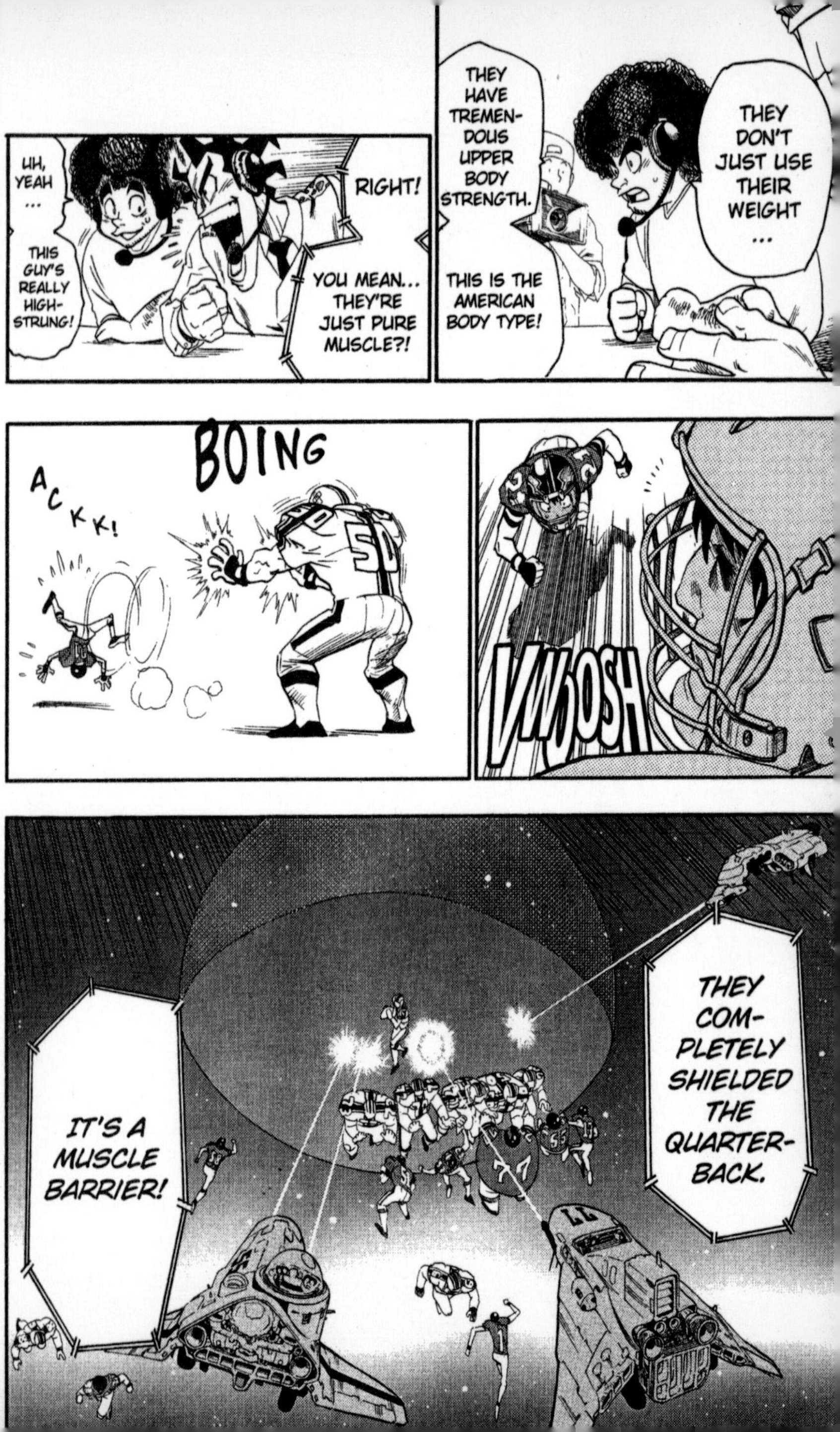
THEY DON'T JUST USE THEIR WEIGHT ...
THEY HAVE TREMEN-DOUS UPPER BODY STRENGTH.
THIS IS THE AMERICAN BODY TYPE!
RIGHT!
YOU MEAN... THEY'RE JUST PURE MUSCLE?!
UH, YEAH ...
THIS GUY'S REALLY HIGH-STRUNG!
VWOOSH
BOING
ACKKK!
THEY COM-PLETELY SHIELDED THE QUARTER-BACK.
IT'S A MUSCLE BARRIER!

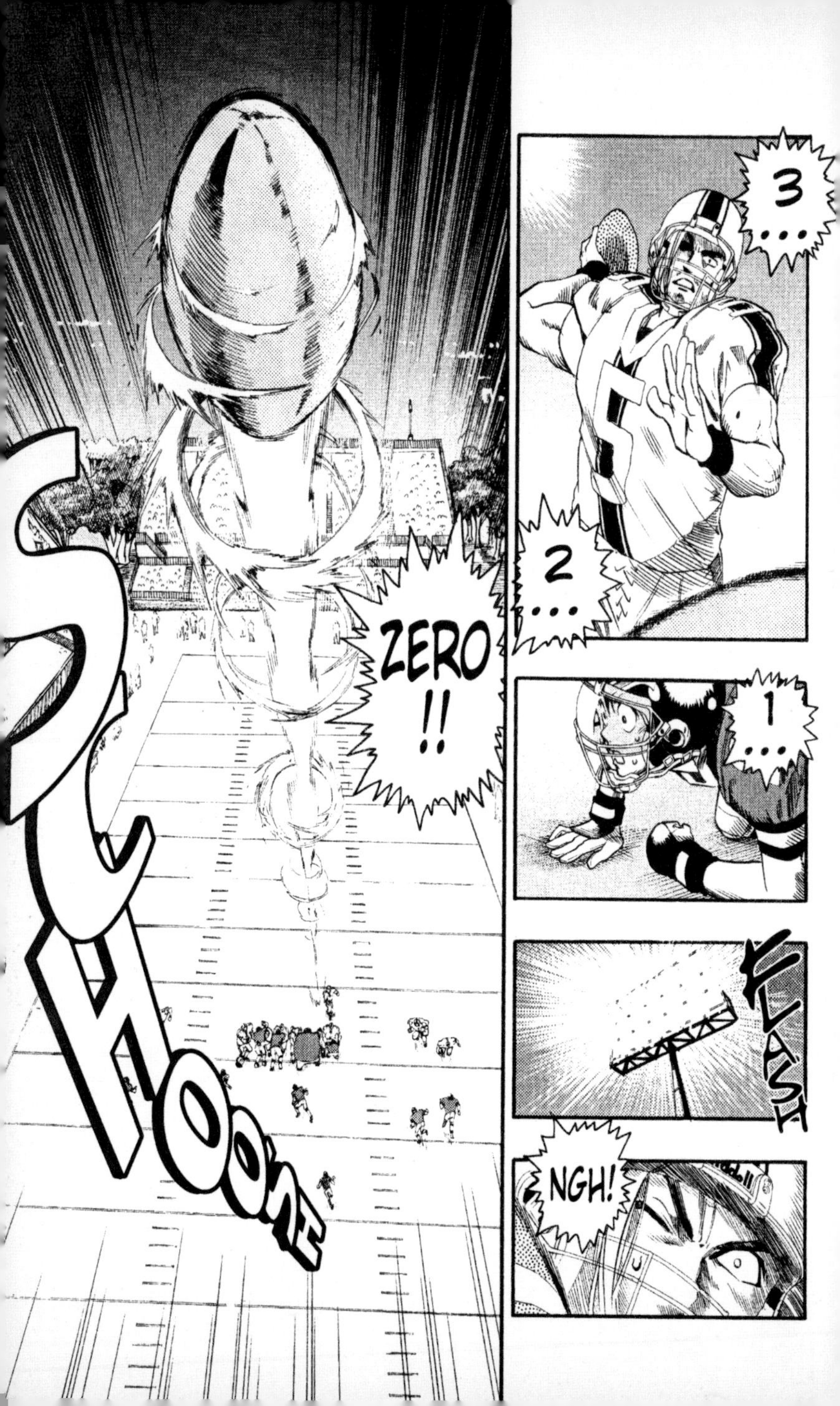
3...
2...
1...
FLASH
NGH!
ZERO!!

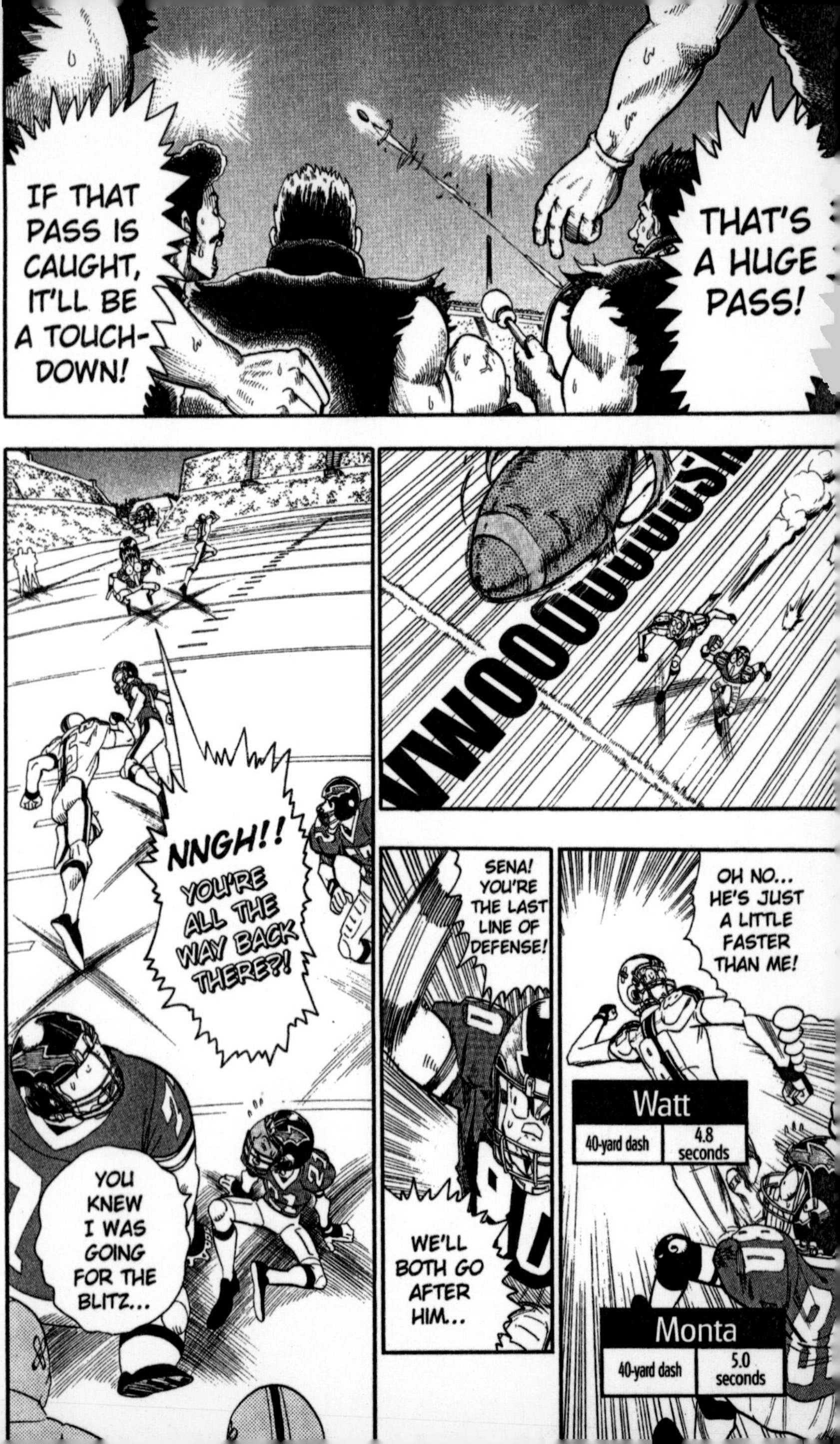
THAT'S A HUGE PASS!
IF THAT PASS IS CAUGHT, IT'LL BE A TOUCH-DOWN!
VWOOOOOOOUUUSH
OH NO... HE'S JUST A LITTLE FASTER THAN ME!
Watt
40-yard dash
4.8 seconds
Monta
40-yard dash
5.0 seconds
SENA! YOU'RE THE LAST LINE OF DEFENSE!
WE'LL BOTH GO AFTER HIM...
NNGH!!
YOU'RE ALL THE WAY BACK THERE?!
YOU KNEW I WAS GOING FOR THE BLITZ...

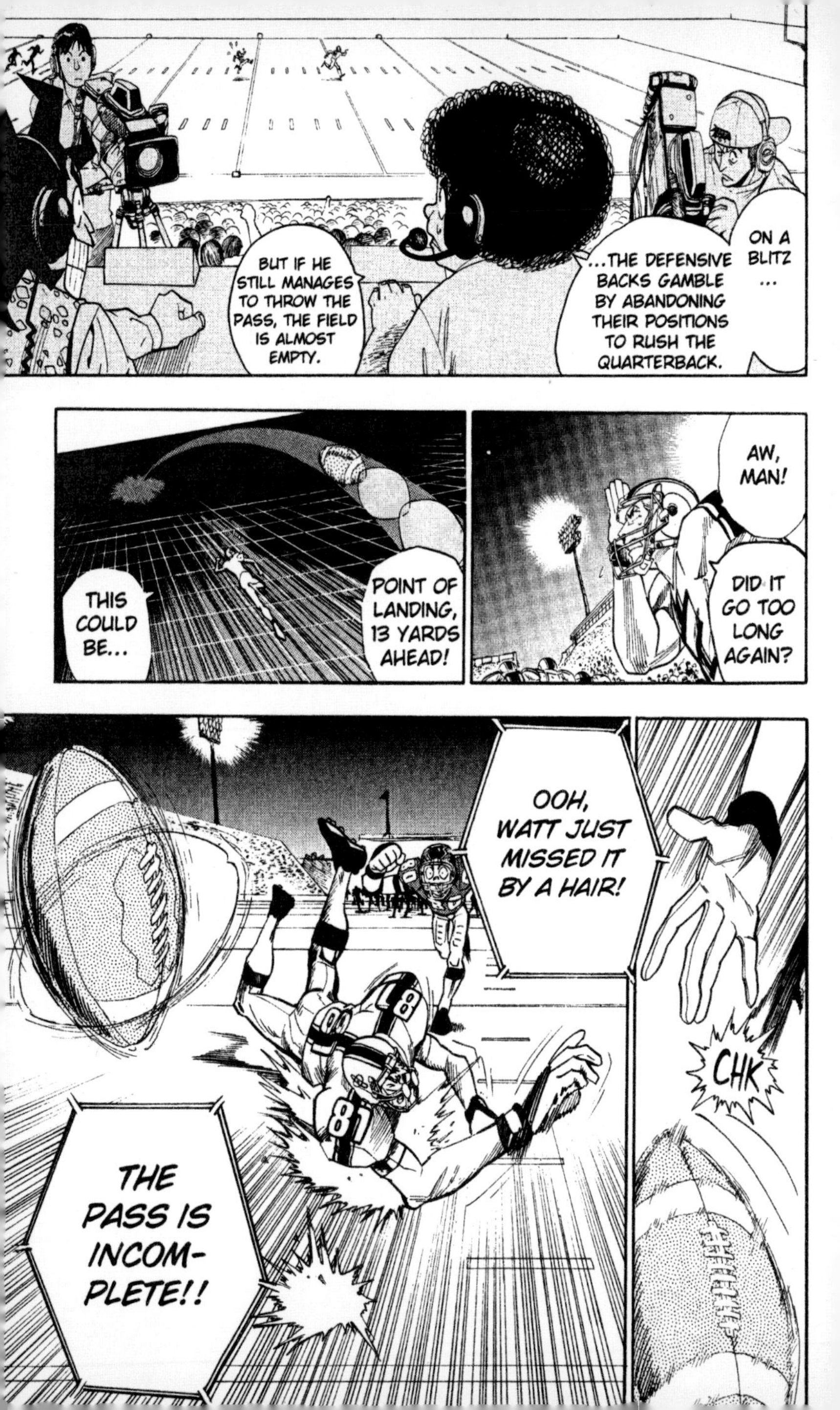
ON A BLITZ ...
...THE DEFENSIVE BACKS GAMBLE BY ABANDONING THEIR POSITIONS TO RUSH THE QUARTERBACK.
BUT IF HE STILL MANAGES TO THROW THE PASS, THE FIELD IS ALMOST EMPTY.
AW, MAN!
DID IT GO TOO LONG AGAIN?
POINT OF LANDING, 13 YARDS AHEAD!
THIS COULD BE...
CHK
OOH, WATT JUST MISSED IT BY A HAIR!
THE PASS IS INCOMPLETE!!

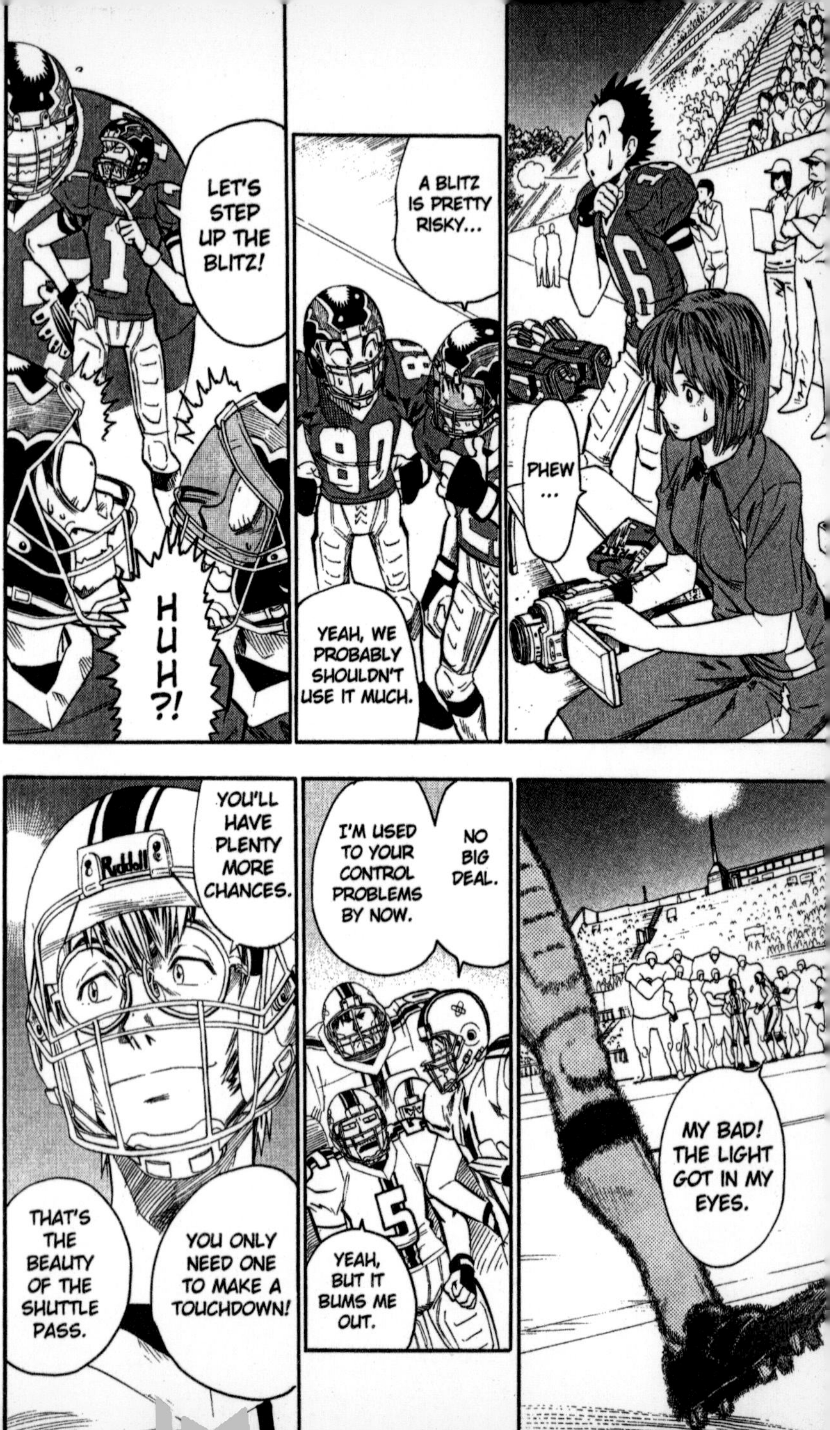
PHEW ...
A BLITZ IS PRETTY RISKY...
YEAH, WE PROBABLY SHOULDN'T USE IT MUCH.
LET'S STEP UP THE BLITZ!
HUH?!
MY BAD! THE LIGHT GOT IN MY EYES.
NO BIG DEAL.
I'M USED TO YOUR CONTROL PROBLEMS BY NOW.
YEAH, BUT IT BUMS ME OUT.
YOU'LL HAVE PLENTY MORE CHANCES.
YOU ONLY NEED ONE TO MAKE A TOUCHDOWN!
THAT'S THE BEAUTY OF THE SHUTTLE PASS.

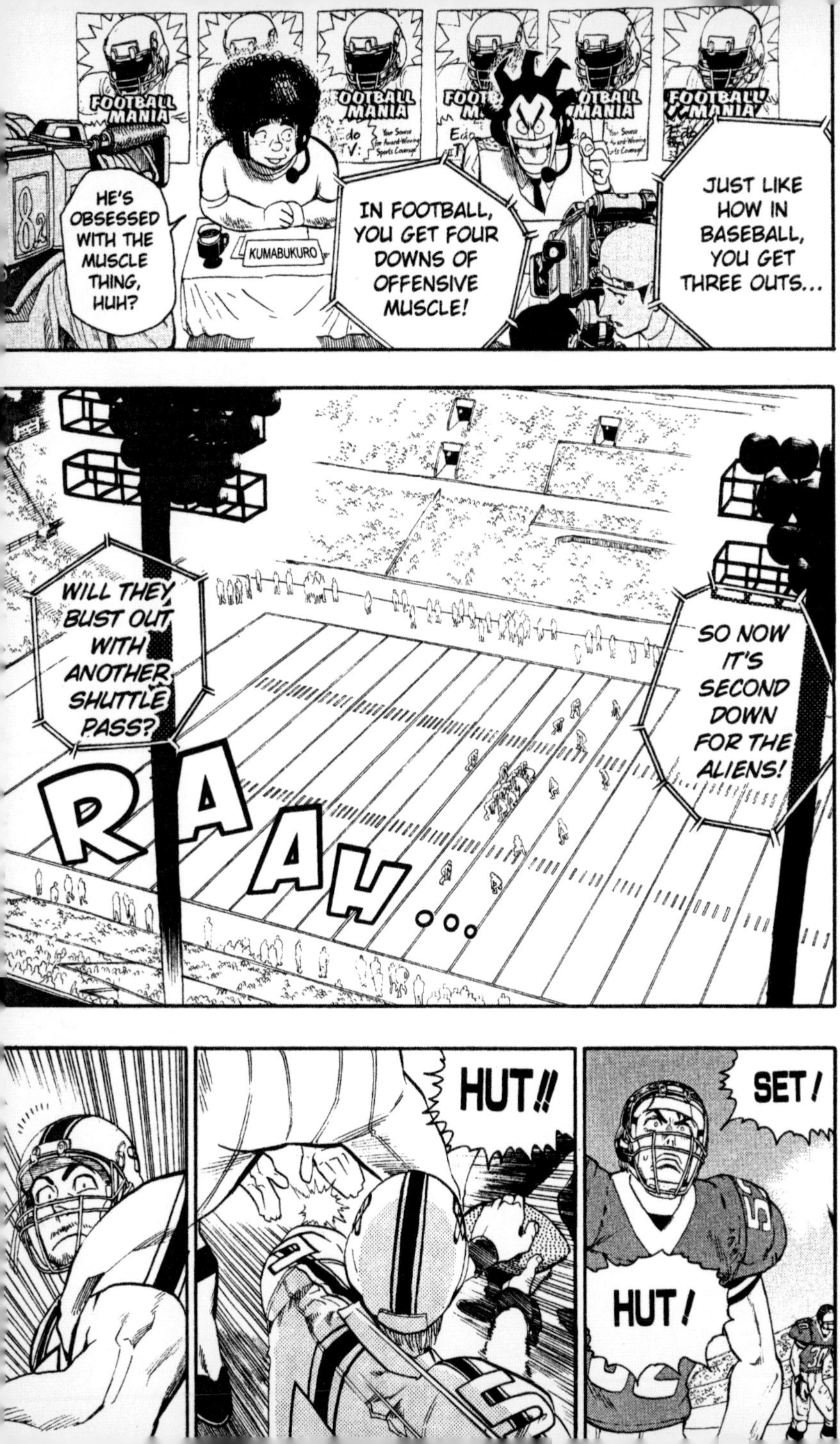
FOOTBALL MANIA
KUMABUKURO
JUST LIKE HOW IN BASEBALL, YOU GET THREE OUTS...
IN FOOTBALL, YOU GET FOUR DOWNS OF OFFENSIVE MUSCLE!
HE'S OBSESSED WITH THE MUSCLE THING, HUH?
SO NOW IT'S SECOND DOWN FOR THE ALIENS!
WILL THEY BUST OUT WITH ANOTHER SHUTTLE PASS?
RAAH...
SET!
HUT!
HUT!!

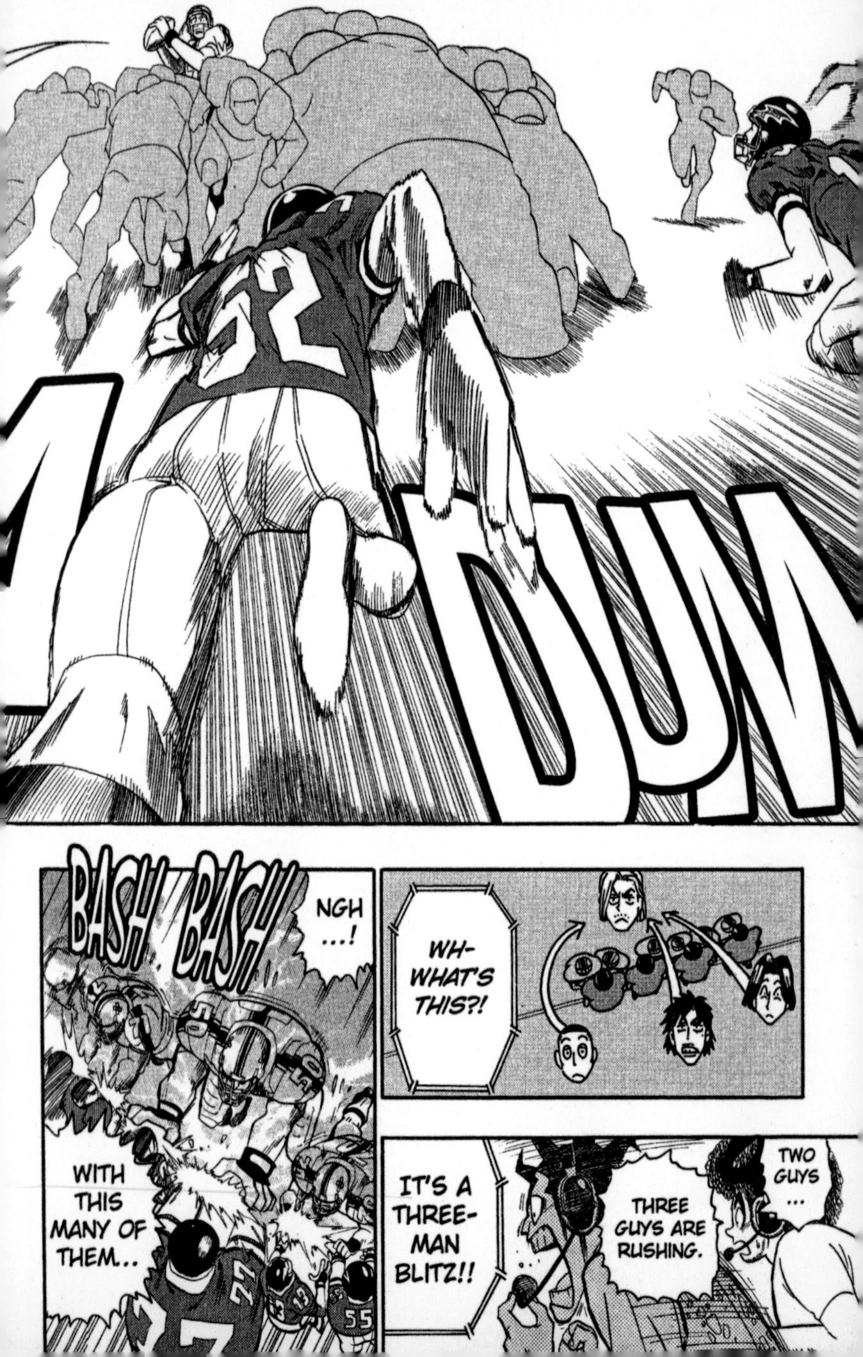
DUM
WH- WHAT'S THIS?!
TWO GUYS...
THREE GUYS ARE RUSHING.
IT'S A THREE-MAN BLITZ!!
BASH BASH
NGH...!
WITH THIS MANY OF THEM...

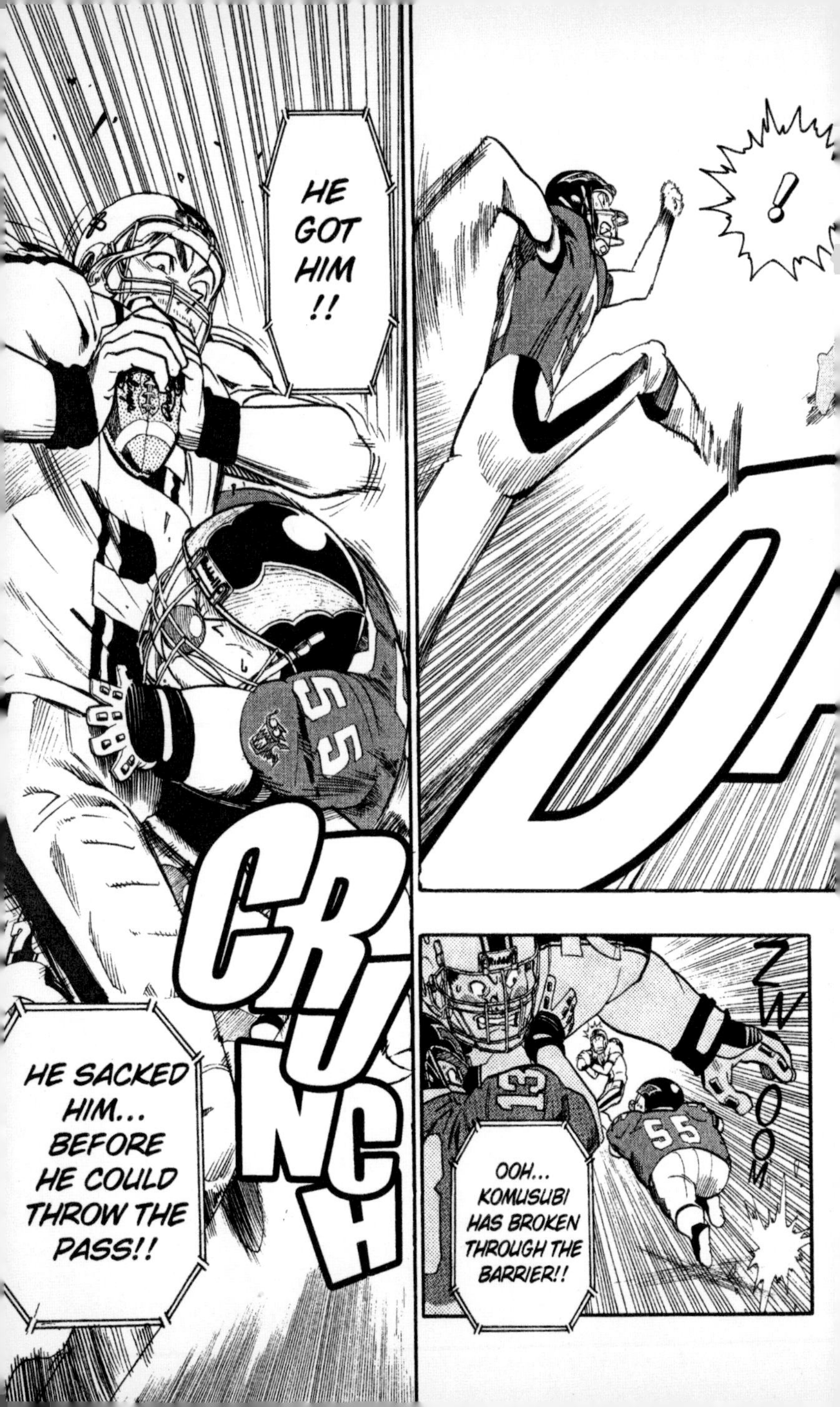
!
NWOOOM
OOH... KOMUSUBI HAS BROKEN THROUGH THE BARRIER!!
HE GOT HIM!!
CRUNCH
HE SACKED HIM... BEFORE HE COULD THROW THE PASS!!

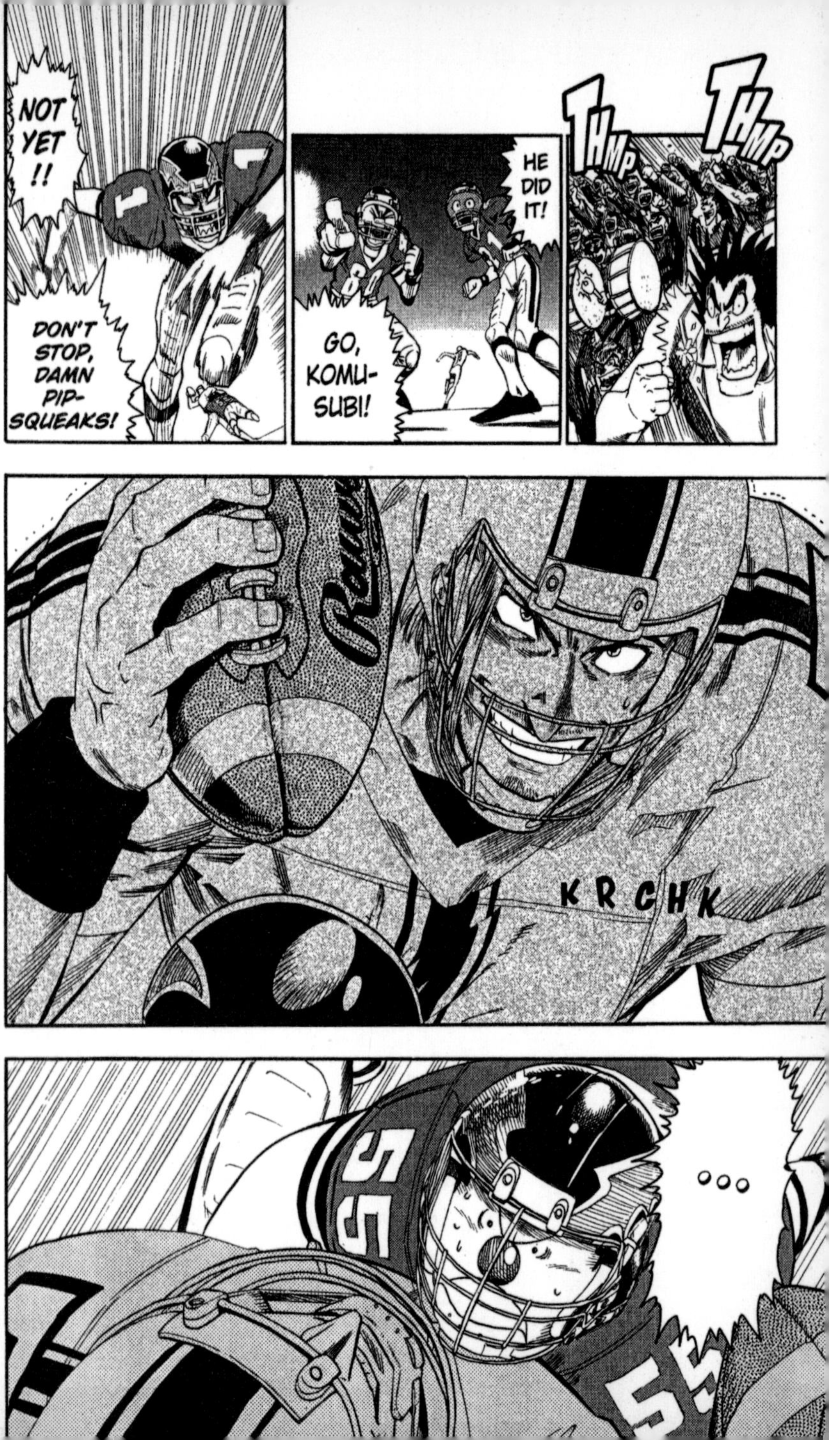
THMP
THMP
HE DID IT!
GO, KOMUSUBI!
NOT YET!!
DON'T STOP, DAMN PIPSQUEAKS!
KRCHK
...

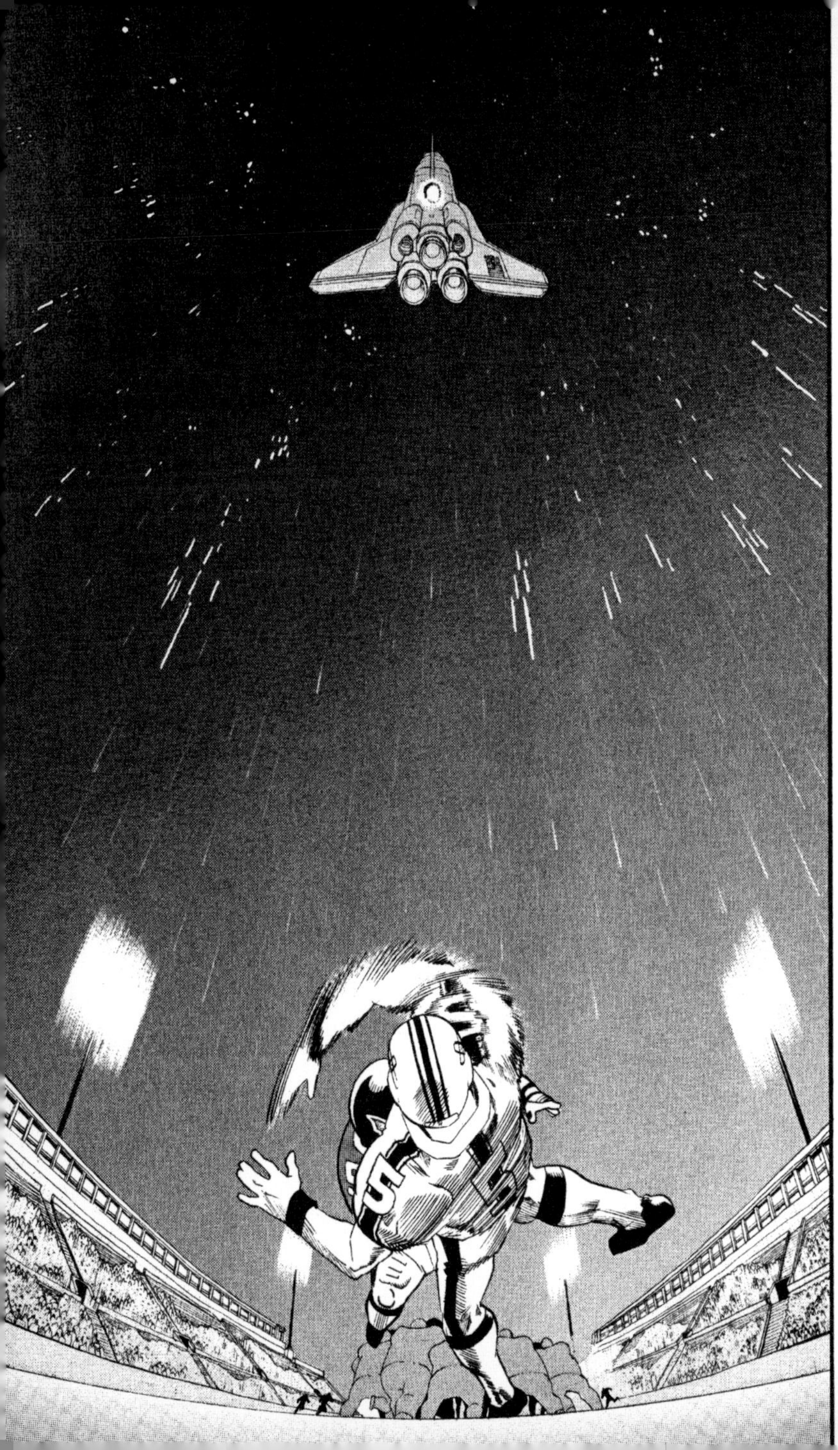

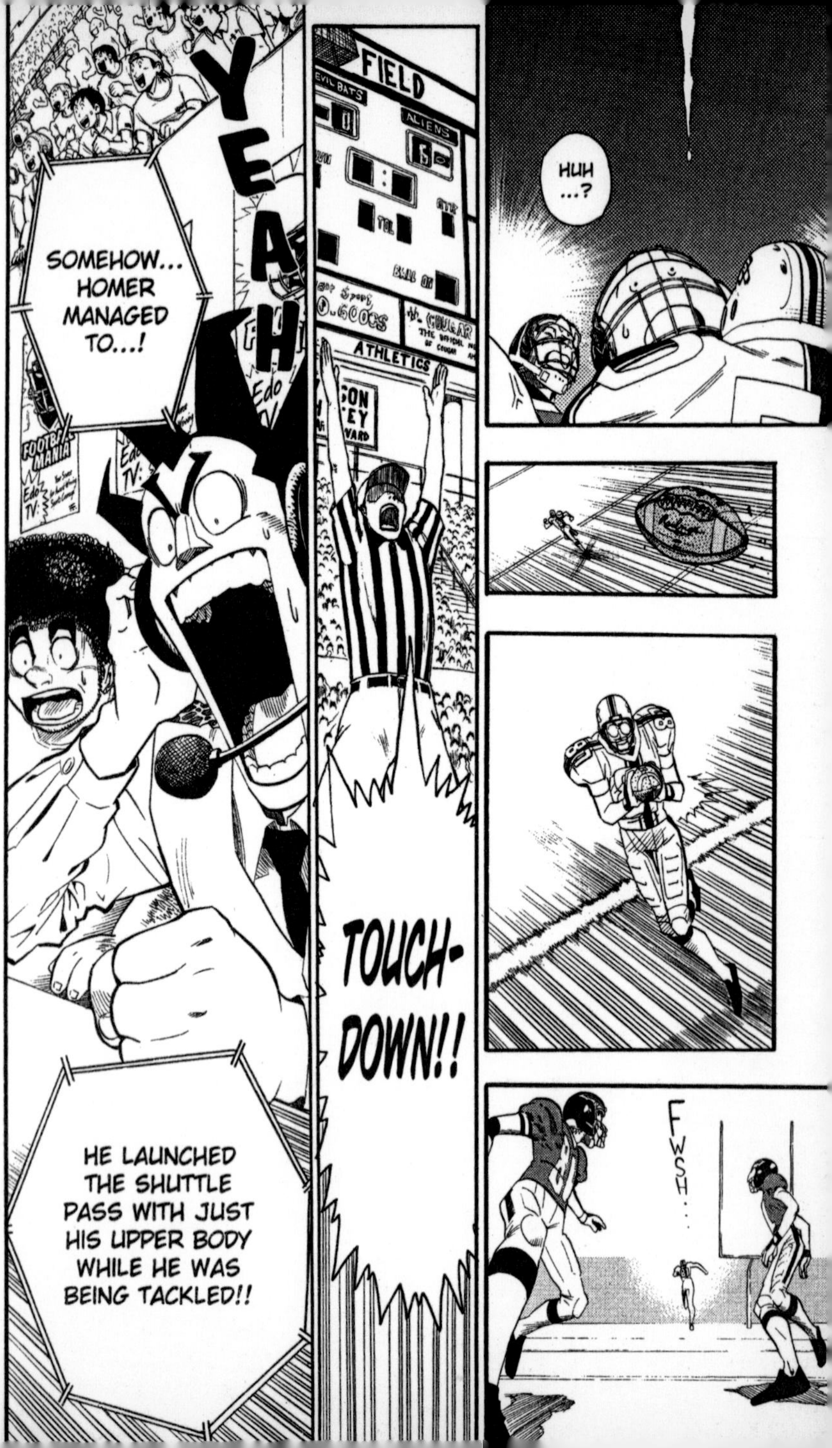
HUH ...?
FWSH..
FIELD
ALIENS
ATHLETICS
TOUCH-DOWN!!
YEAH
SOMEHOW... HOMER MANAGED TO...!
HE LAUNCHED THE SHUTTLE PASS WITH JUST HIS UPPER BODY WHILE HE WAS BEING TACKLED!!

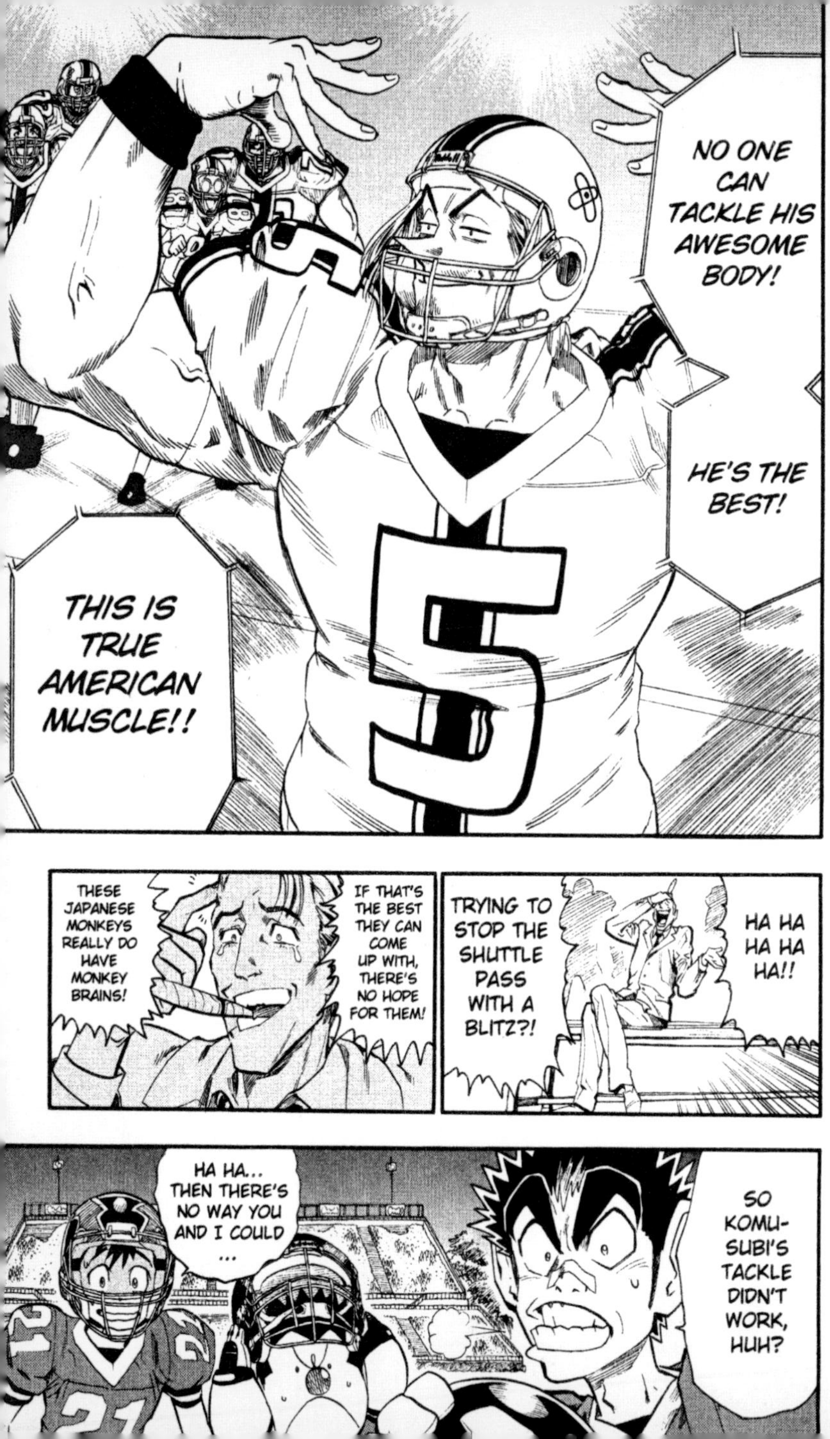
NO ONE CAN TACKLE HIS AWESOME BODY!
HE'S THE BEST!
THIS IS TRUE AMERICAN MUSCLE!!
HA HA HA HA HA!!
TRYING TO STOP THE SHUTTLE PASS WITH A BLITZ?!
IF THAT'S THE BEST THEY CAN COME UP WITH, THERE'S NO HOPE FOR THEM!
THESE JAPANESE MONKEYS REALLY DO HAVE MONKEY BRAINS!
SO KOMUSUBI'S TACKLE DIDN'T WORK, HUH?
HA HA... THEN THERE'S NO WAY YOU AND I COULD ...

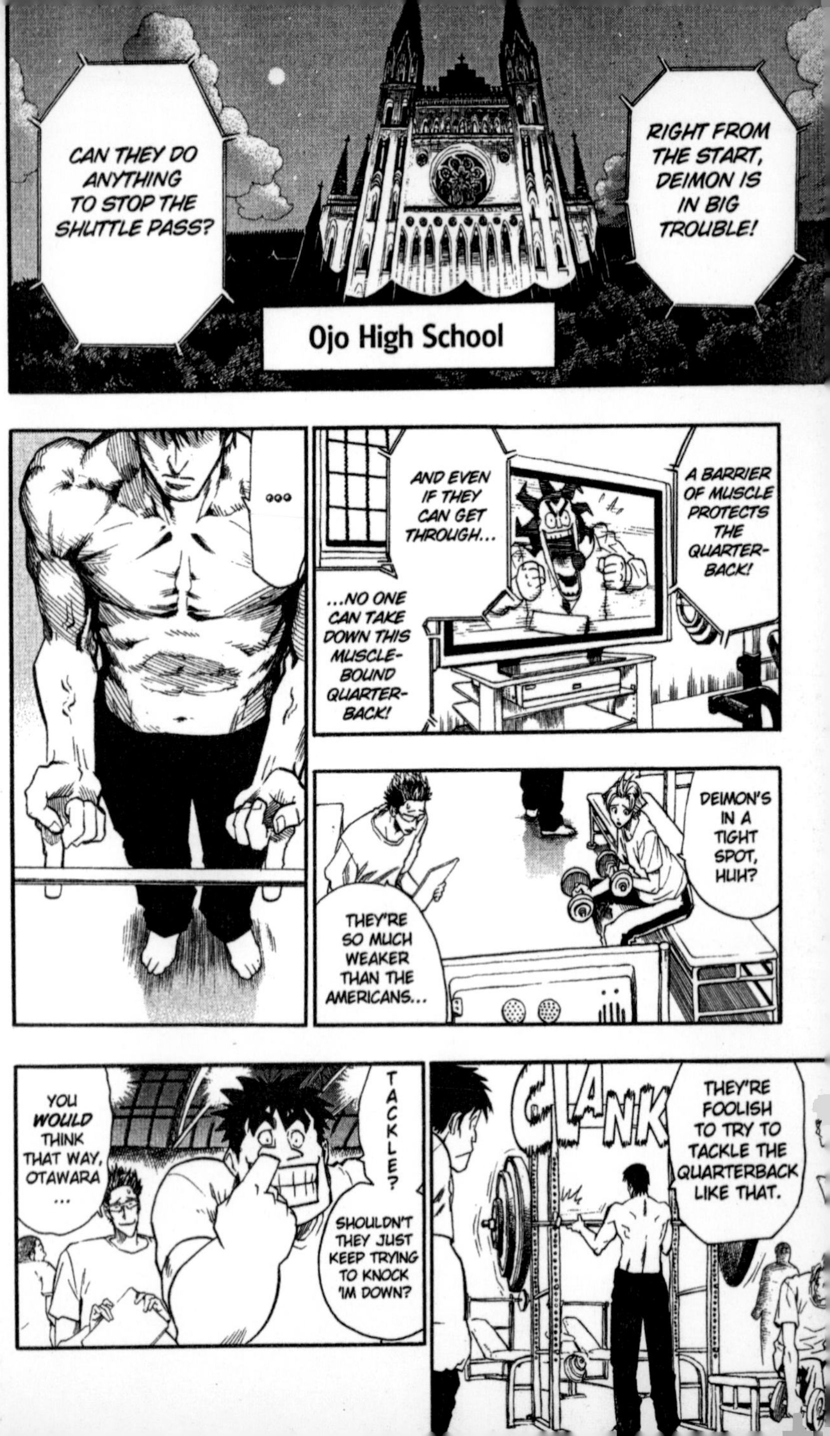
RIGHT FROM THE START, DEIMON IS IN BIG TROUBLE!
CAN THEY DO ANYTHING TO STOP THE SHUTTLE PASS?
Ojo High School
A BARRIER OF MUSCLE PROTECTS THE QUARTER-BACK!
AND EVEN IF THEY CAN GET THROUGH...
...NO ONE CAN TAKE DOWN THIS MUSCLE-BOUND QUARTER-BACK!
DEIMON'S IN A TIGHT SPOT, HUH?
THEY'RE SO MUCH WEAKER THAN THE AMERICANS...
...
CLANK
THEY'RE FOOLISH TO TRY TO TACKLE THE QUARTERBACK LIKE THAT.
TACKLE?
SHOULDN'T THEY JUST KEEP TRYING TO KNOCK 'IM DOWN?
YOU WOULD THINK THAT WAY, OTAWARA ...

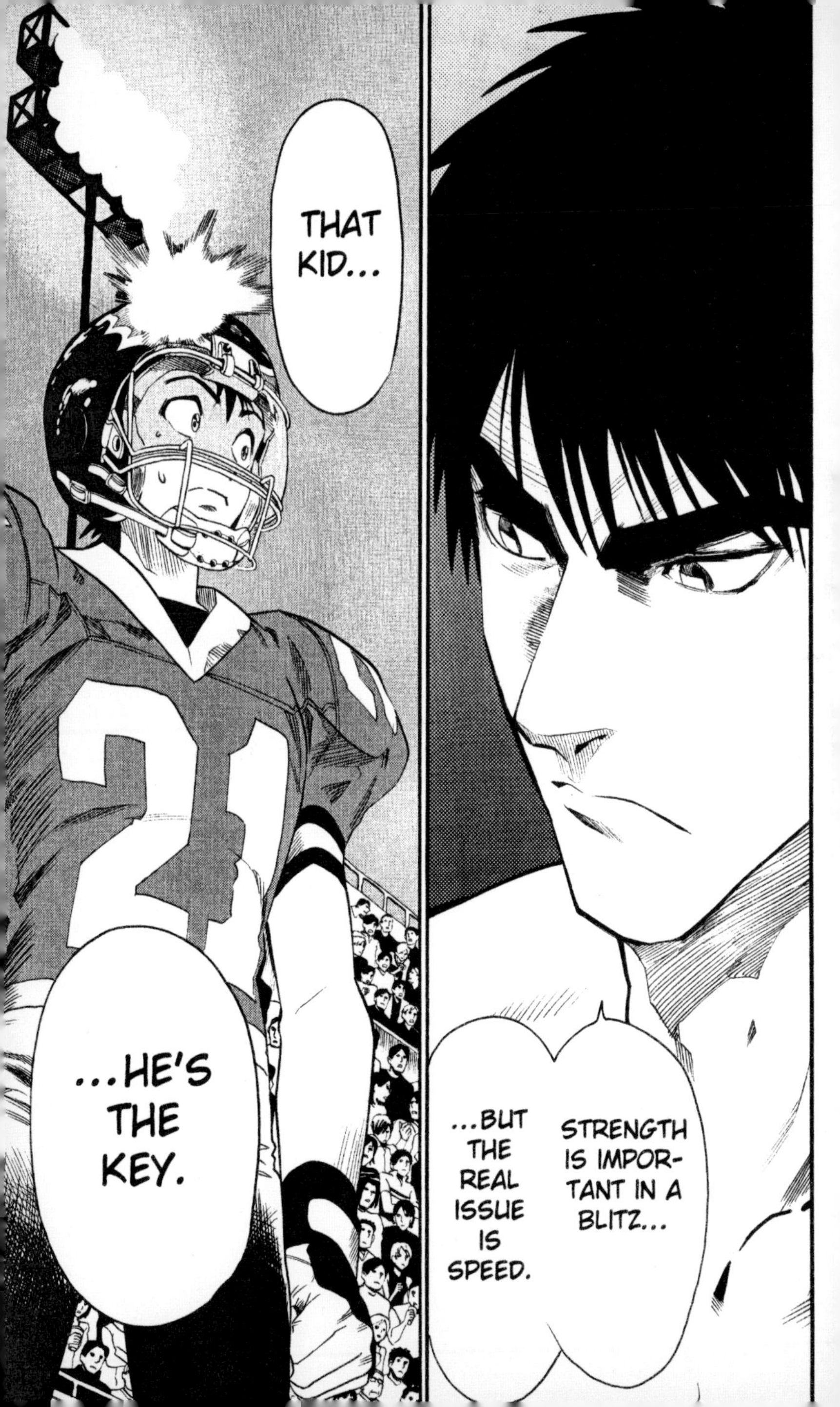
STRENGTH IS IMPORTANT IN A BLITZ...
...BUT THE REAL ISSUE IS SPEED.
THAT KID...
...HE'S THE KEY.

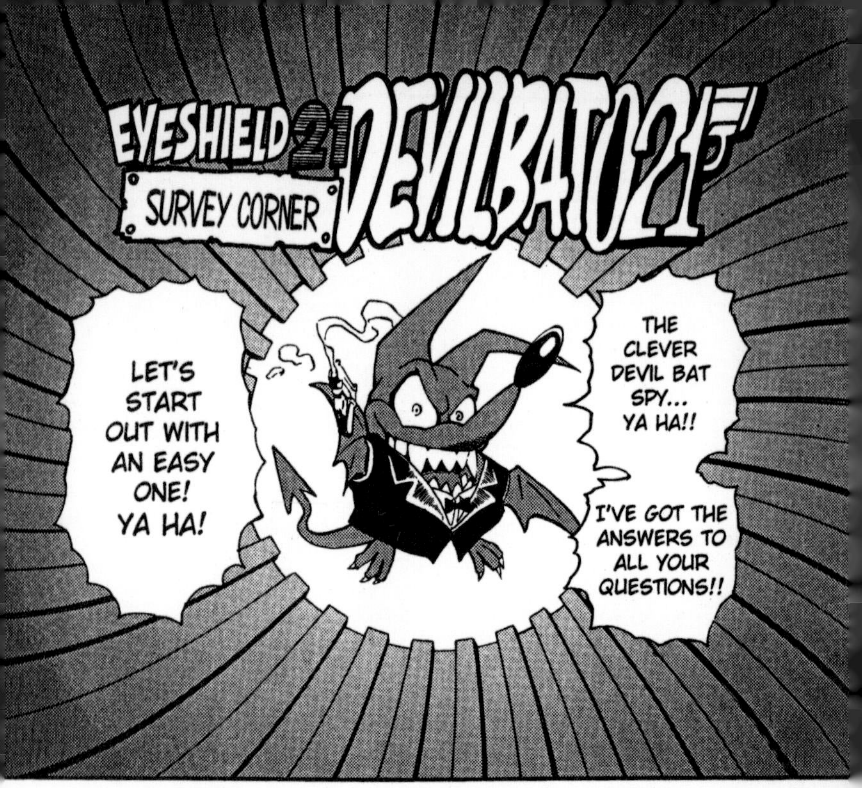
EYESHIELD 21
SURVEY CORNER
DEVILBAT 021
THE CLEVER DEVIL BAT SPY... YA HA!!
I'VE GOT THE ANSWERS TO ALL YOUR QUESTIONS!!
LET'S START OUT WITH AN EASY ONE! YA HA!

Investigation File #001

Solve the mystery of the bandage!!

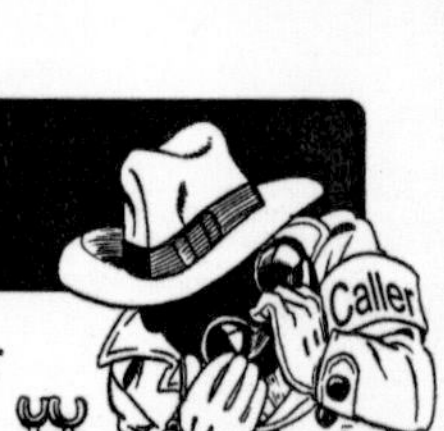
Caller

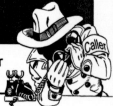

WHAT KIND OF INJURY DOES MONTA HAVE THAT HE ALWAYS WEARS A BANDAGE ON HIS NOSE?

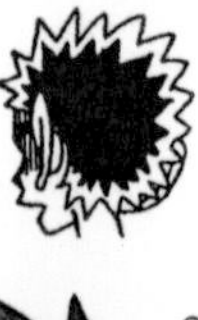

I ONLY WEAR IT AS A FASHION STATEMENT...

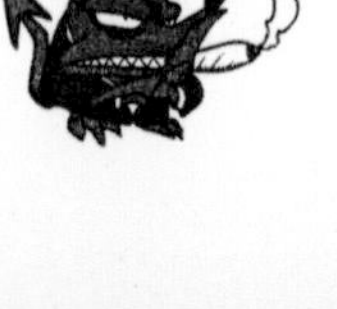

THAT'S IT.
END OF INVESTIGATION.

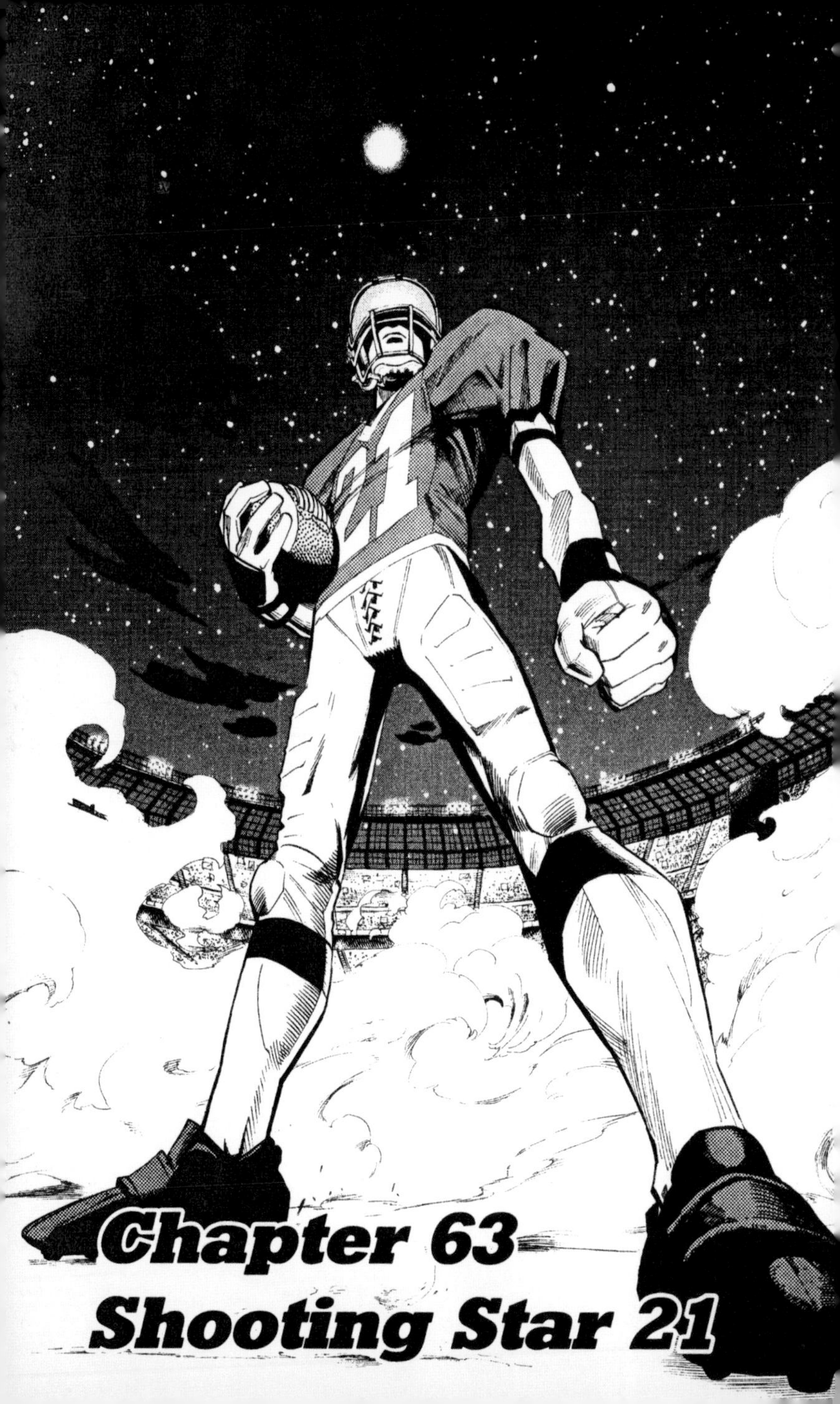
Chapter 63
Shooting Star 21

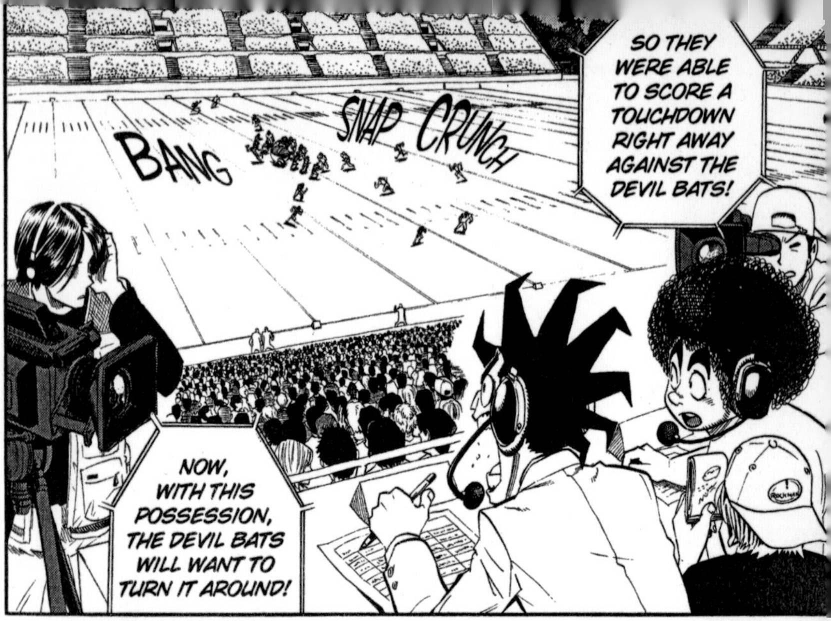
SO THEY WERE ABLE TO SCORE A TOUCHDOWN RIGHT AWAY AGAINST THE DEVIL BATS!
CRUNCH
SNAP
BANG
NOW, WITH THIS POSSESSION, THE DEVIL BATS WILL WANT TO TURN IT AROUND!

↓ GONZALES THINKS HIS KANJI TATTOO MEANS "BIG HELP," BUT IT REALLY SAYS "POOP."

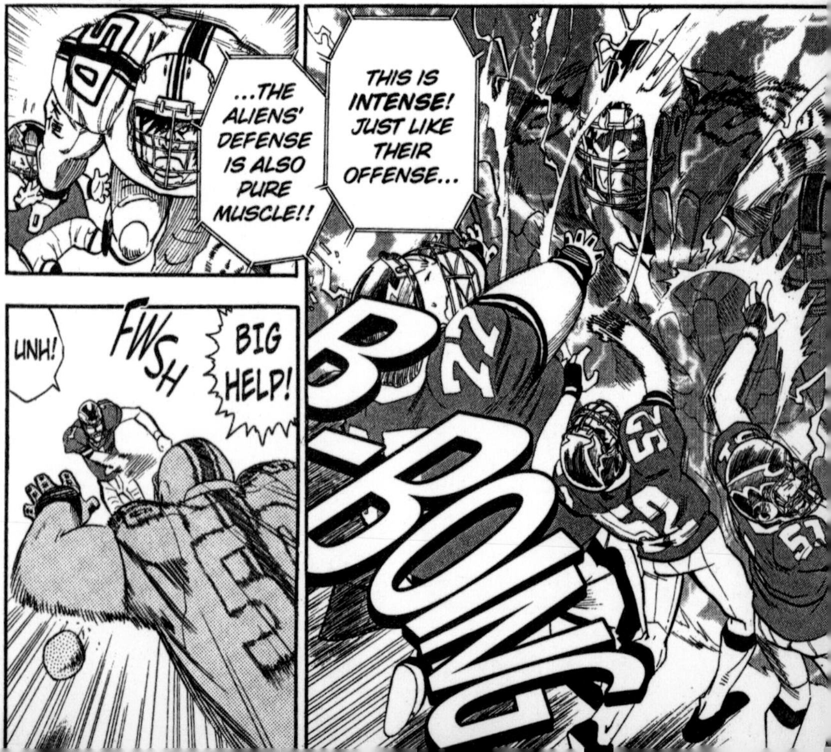
THIS IS INTENSE! JUST LIKE THEIR OFFENSE...
BOING
...THE ALIENS' DEFENSE IS ALSO PURE MUSCLE!!
BIG HELP!
FWSH
UNH!

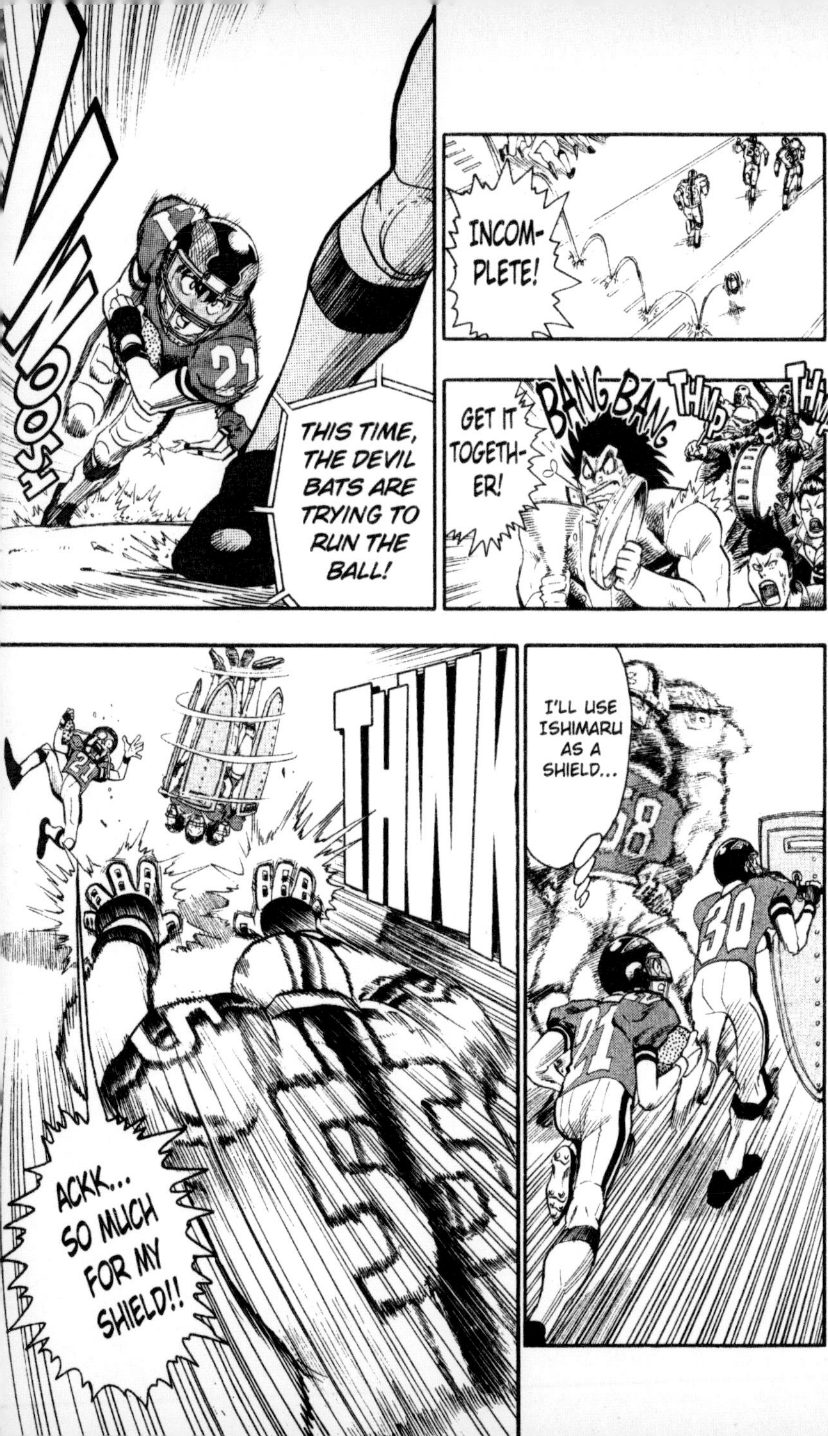
INCOMPLETE!
GET IT TOGETHER!
BANG BANG
THMP THMP
WHOOSH
THIS TIME, THE DEVIL BATS ARE TRYING TO RUN THE BALL!
I'LL USE ISHIMARU AS A SHIELD...
THWK
ACKK... SO MUCH FOR MY SHIELD!!

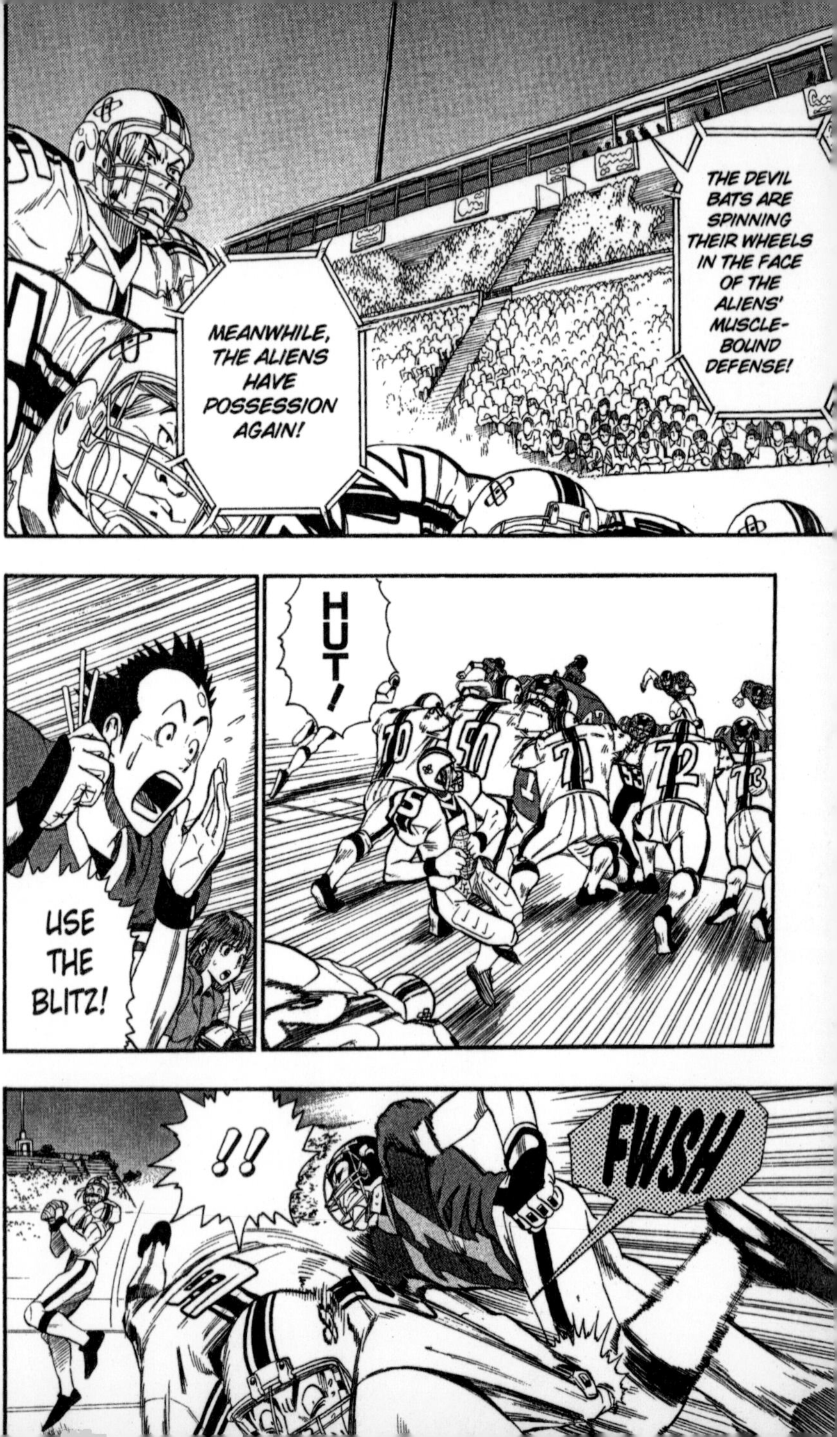
THE DEVIL BATS ARE SPINNING THEIR WHEELS IN THE FACE OF THE ALIENS' MUSCLE-BOUND DEFENSE!
MEANWHILE, THE ALIENS HAVE POSSESSION AGAIN!
HUT!
USE THE BLITZ!
FWSH
!!

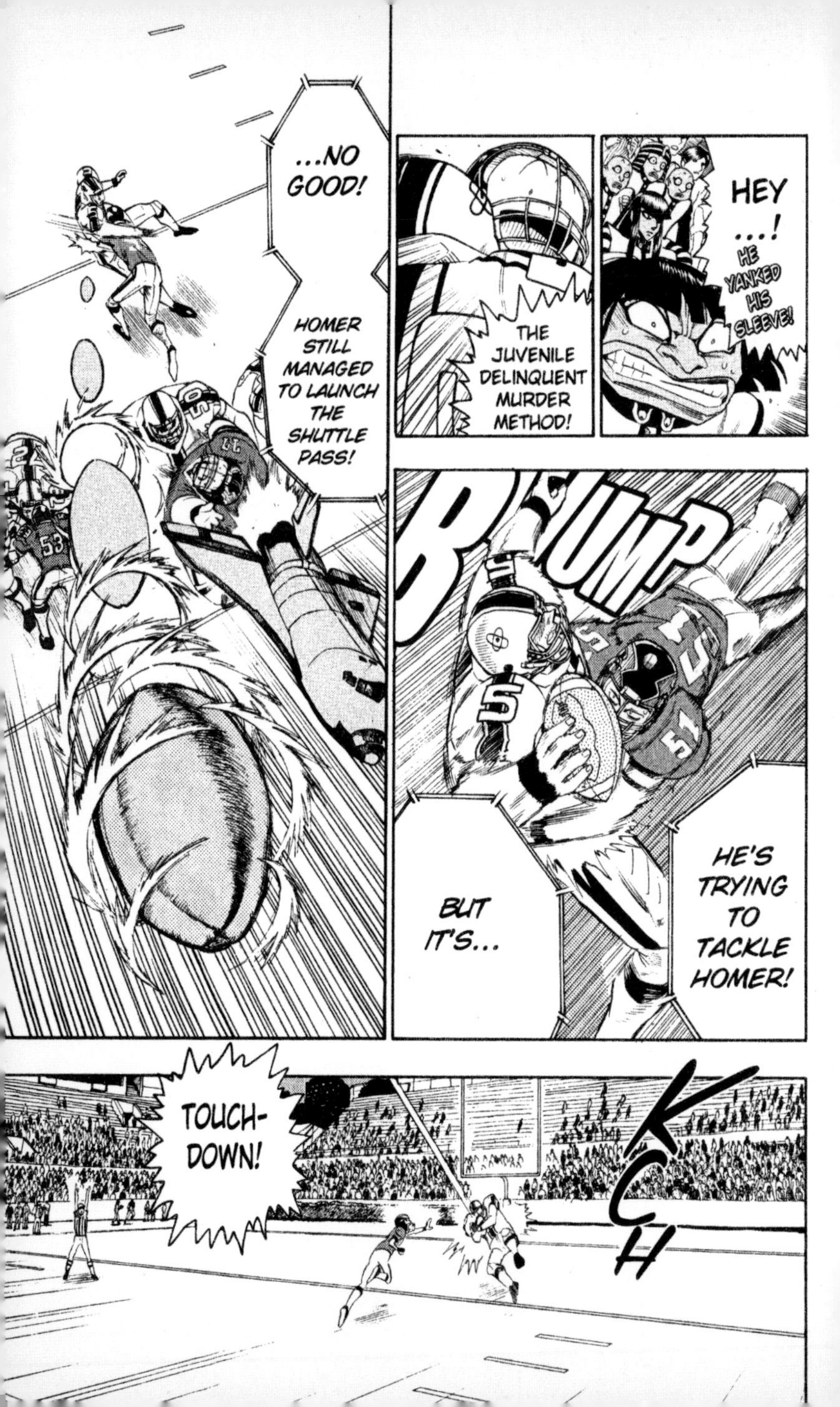
HEY ...!
HE YANKED HIS SLEEVE!
THE JUVENILE DELINQUENT MURDER METHOD!
BUMP
HE'S TRYING TO TACKLE HOMER!
BUT IT'S...
...NO GOOD!
HOMER STILL MANAGED TO LAUNCH THE SHUTTLE PASS!
KCH
TOUCH-DOWN!

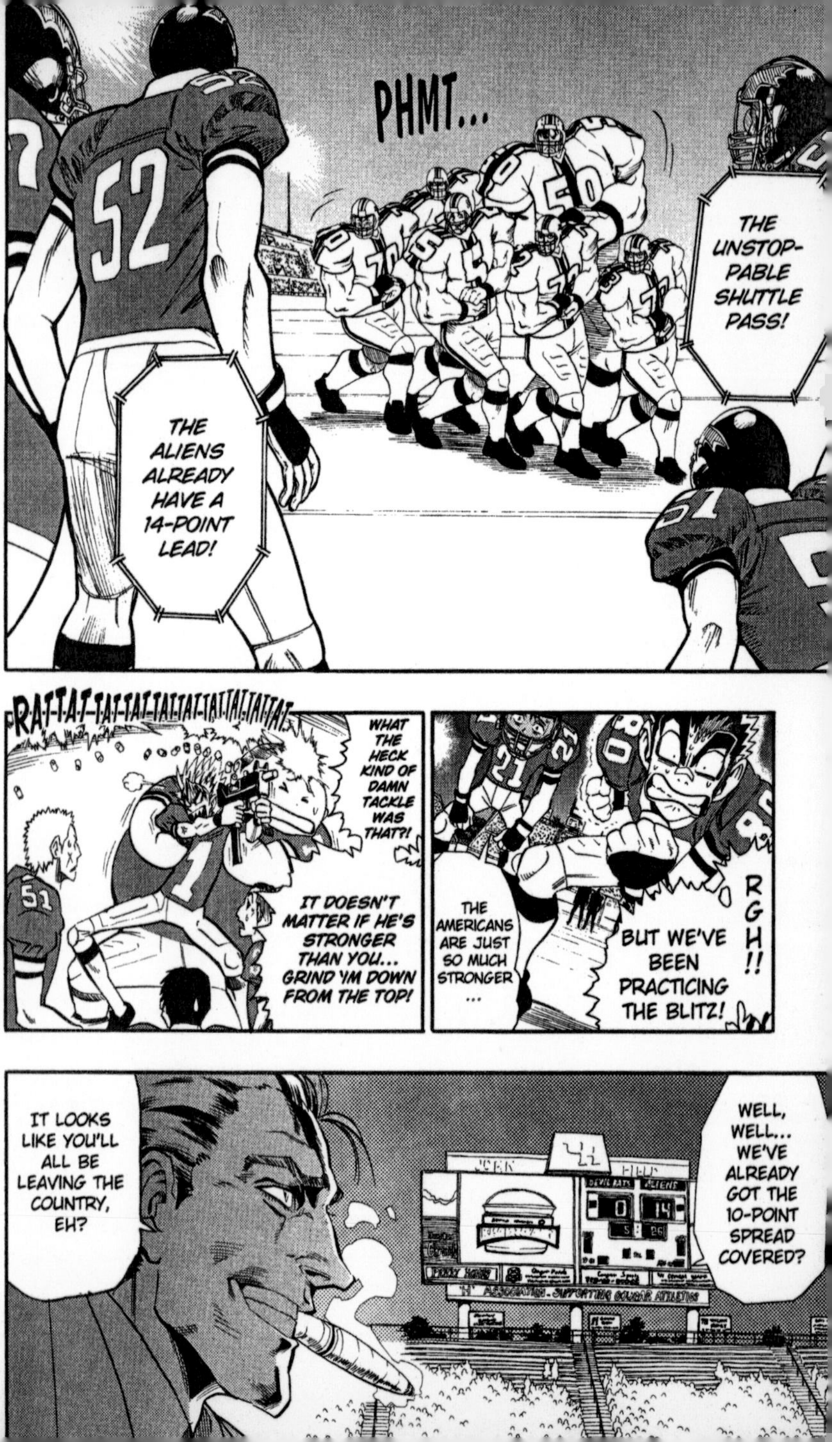
PHMT...
THE UNSTOPPABLE SHUTTLE PASS!
THE ALIENS ALREADY HAVE A 14-POINT LEAD!
RGH!!
BUT WE'VE BEEN PRACTICING THE BLITZ!
THE AMERICANS ARE JUST SO MUCH STRONGER...
RATTAT-TAT-TAT-TATTAT-TATTAT-TATTAT
WHAT THE HECK KIND OF DAMN TACKLE WAS THAT?!
IT DOESN'T MATTER IF HE'S STRONGER THAN YOU... GRIND 'YM DOWN FROM THE TOP!
WELL, WELL... WE'VE ALREADY GOT THE 10-POINT SPREAD COVERED?
IT LOOKS LIKE YOU'LL ALL BE LEAVING THE COUNTRY, EH?

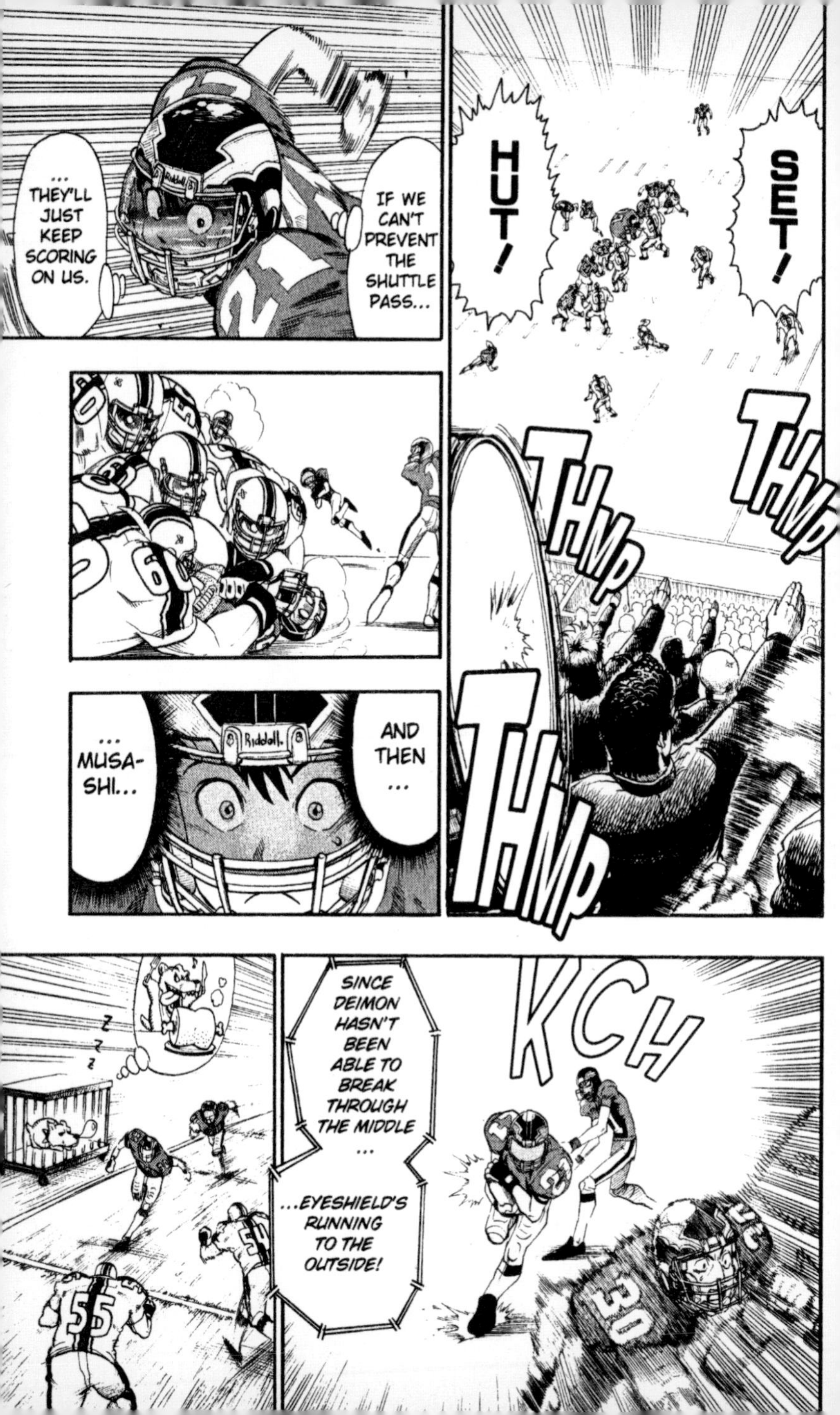
SET!
HUT!
THMP
THMP
THMP
IF WE CAN'T PREVENT THE SHUTTLE PASS...
... THEY'LL JUST KEEP SCORING ON US.
AND THEN ...
... MUSA-SHI...
KCH
SINCE DEIMON HASN'T BEEN ABLE TO BREAK THROUGH THE MIDDLE ...
...EYESHIELD'S RUNNING TO THE OUTSIDE!
Z Z Z

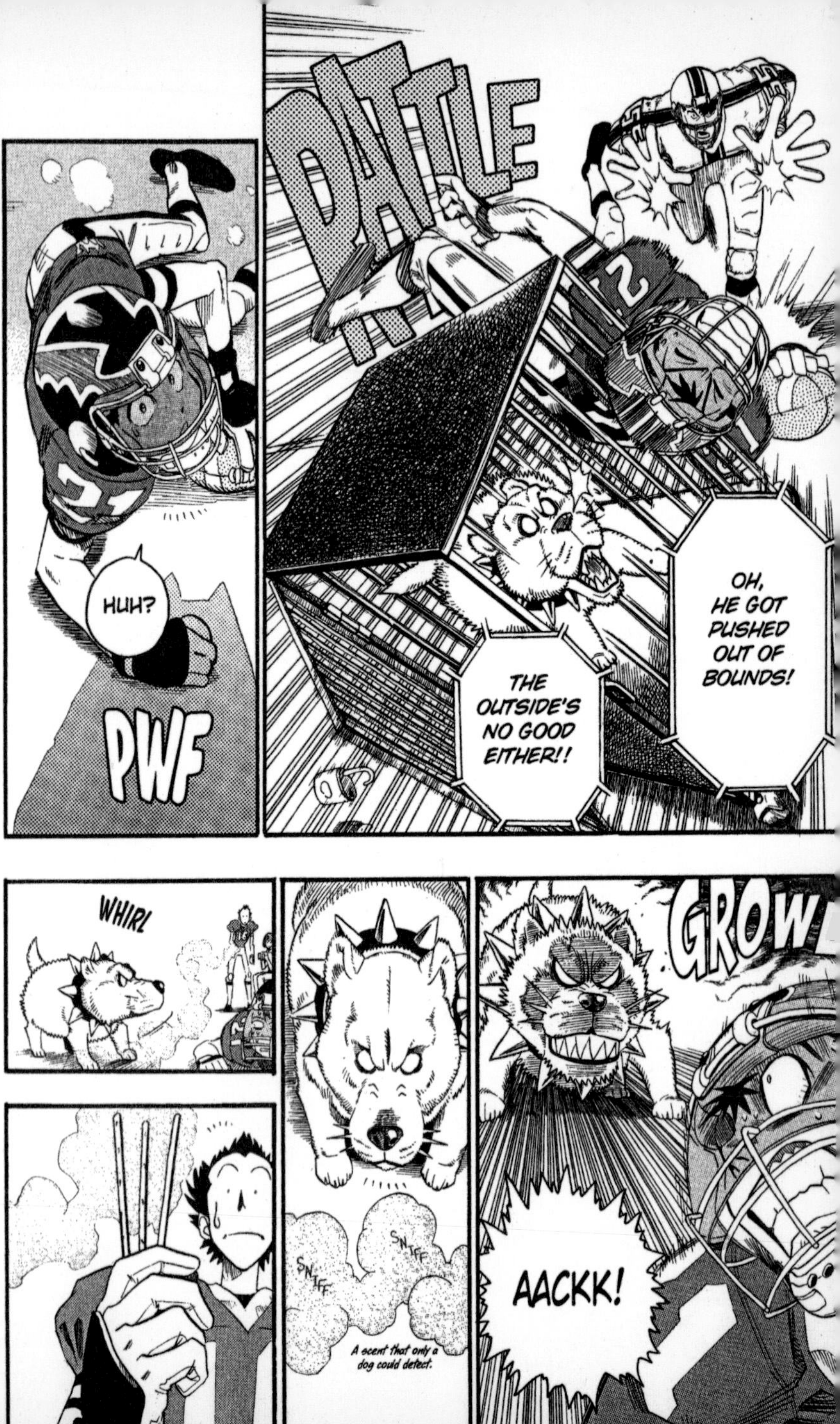
DATTLE
OH, HE GOT PUSHED OUT OF BOUNDS!
THE OUTSIDE'S NO GOOD EITHER!!
HUH?
PWF
GROW
AACKK!
SNIFF
SNIFF
A scent that only a dog could detect.
WHIRL

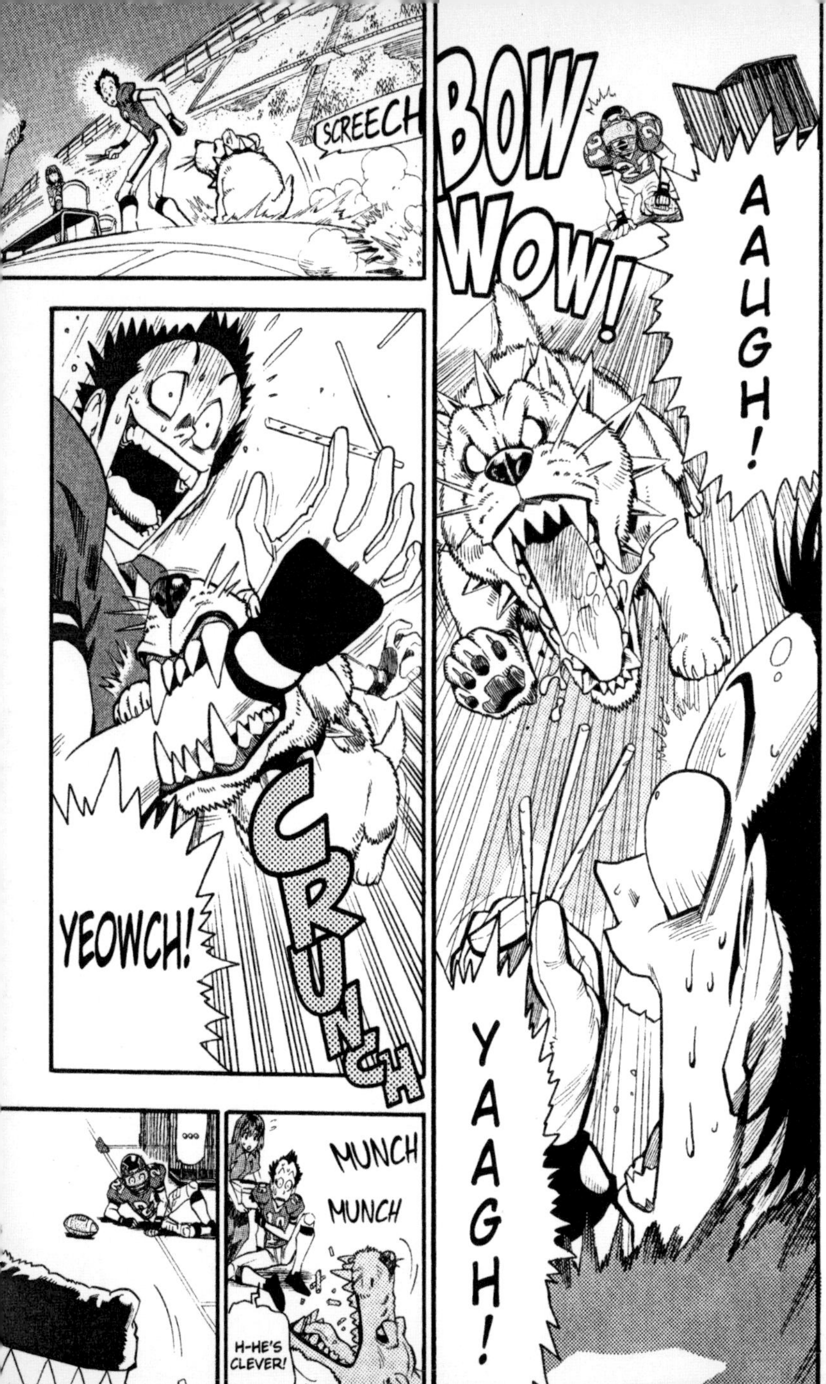
BOW WOW!
AAUGH!
YAAGH!
SCREECH
YEOWCH!
CRUNCH
MUNCH
MUNCH
H-HE'S CLEVER!

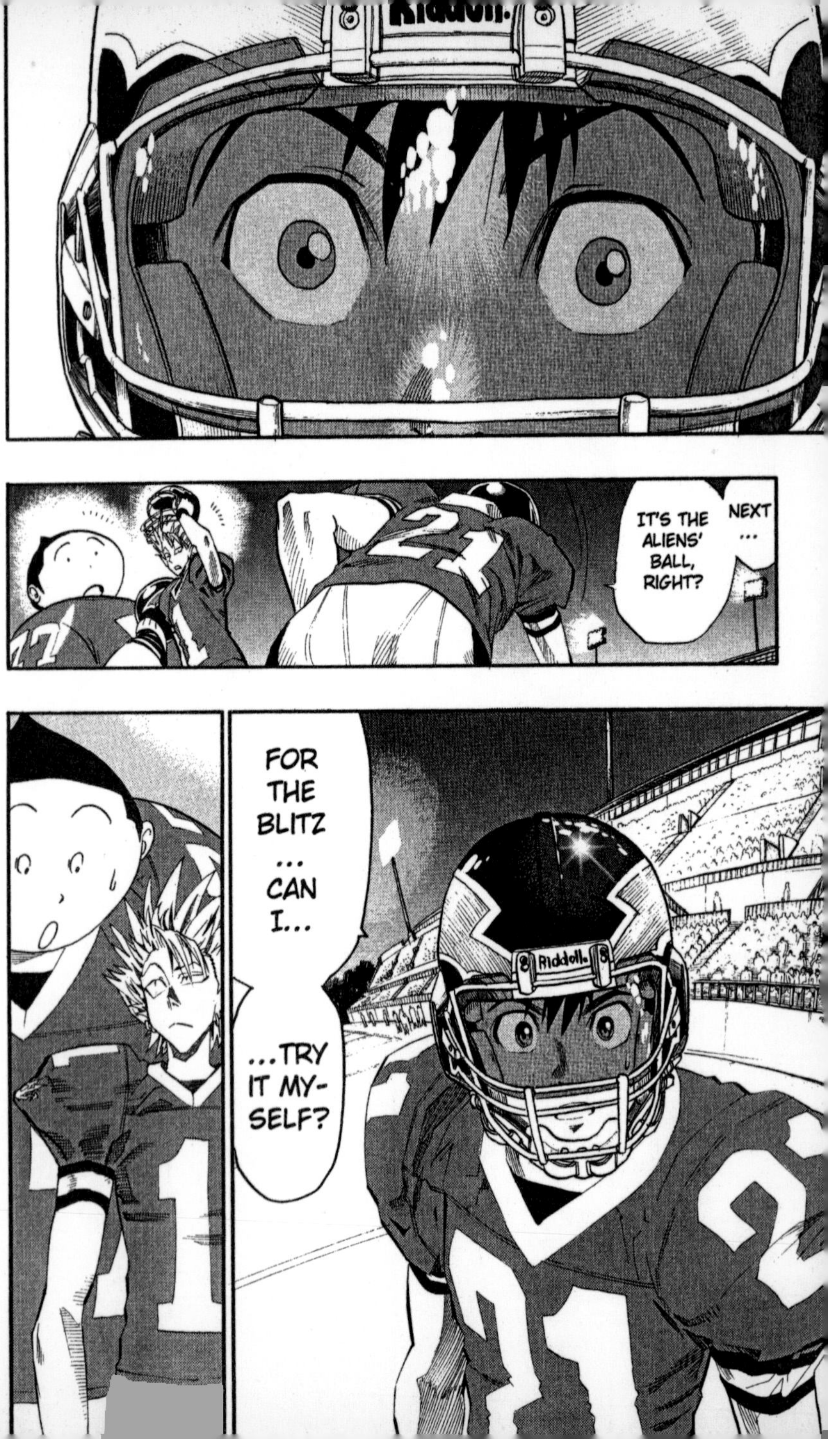

NEXT...
IT'S THE ALIENS' BALL, RIGHT?
FOR THE BLITZ... CAN I...
...TRY IT MY-SELF?

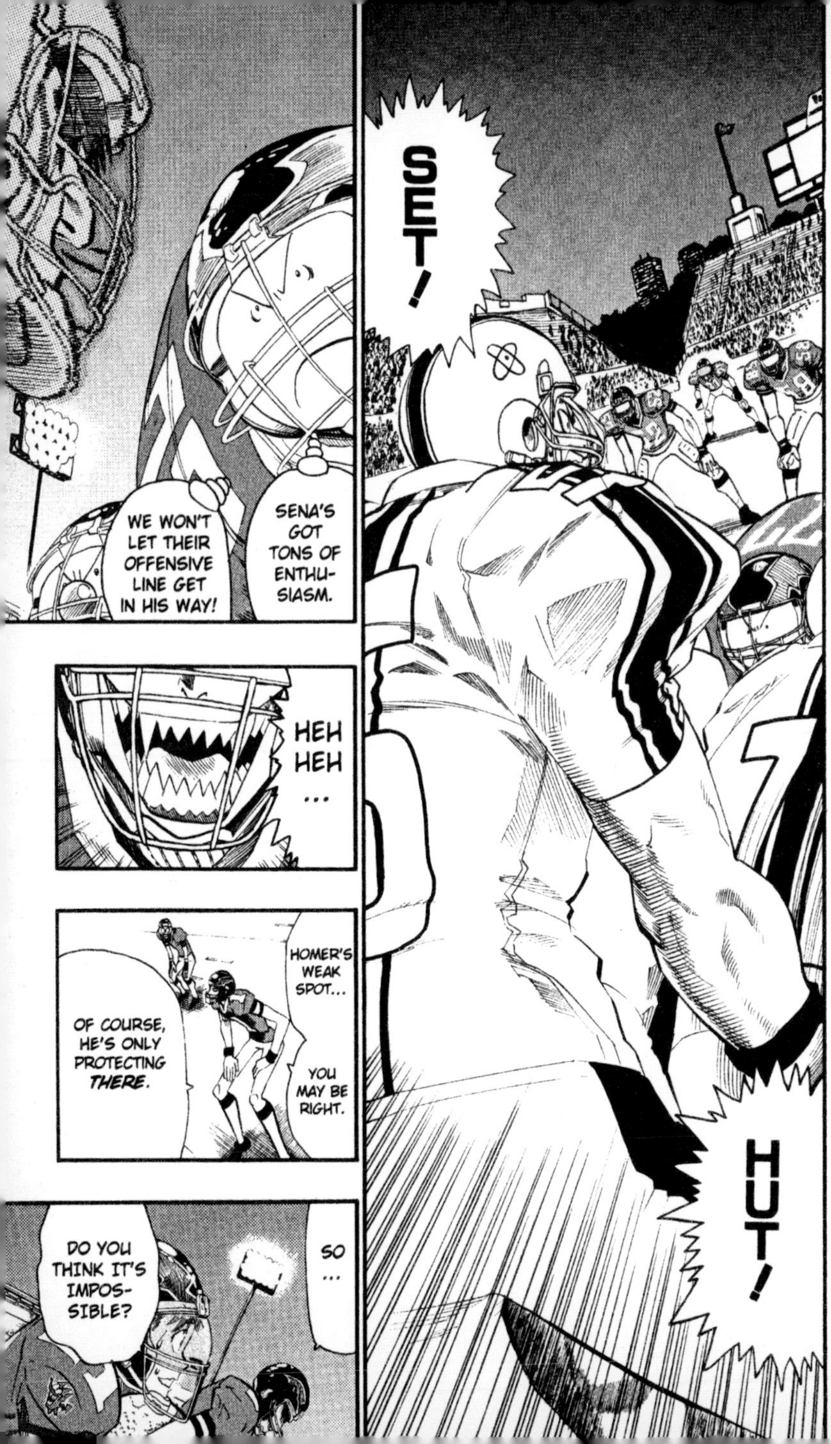
SET!
HUT!
SENA'S GOT TONS OF ENTHUSIASM.
WE WON'T LET THEIR OFFENSIVE LINE GET IN HIS WAY!
HEH HEH ...
HOMER'S WEAK SPOT...
YOU MAY BE RIGHT.
OF COURSE, HE'S ONLY PROTECTING *THERE*.
SO ...
DO YOU THINK IT'S IMPOSSIBLE?

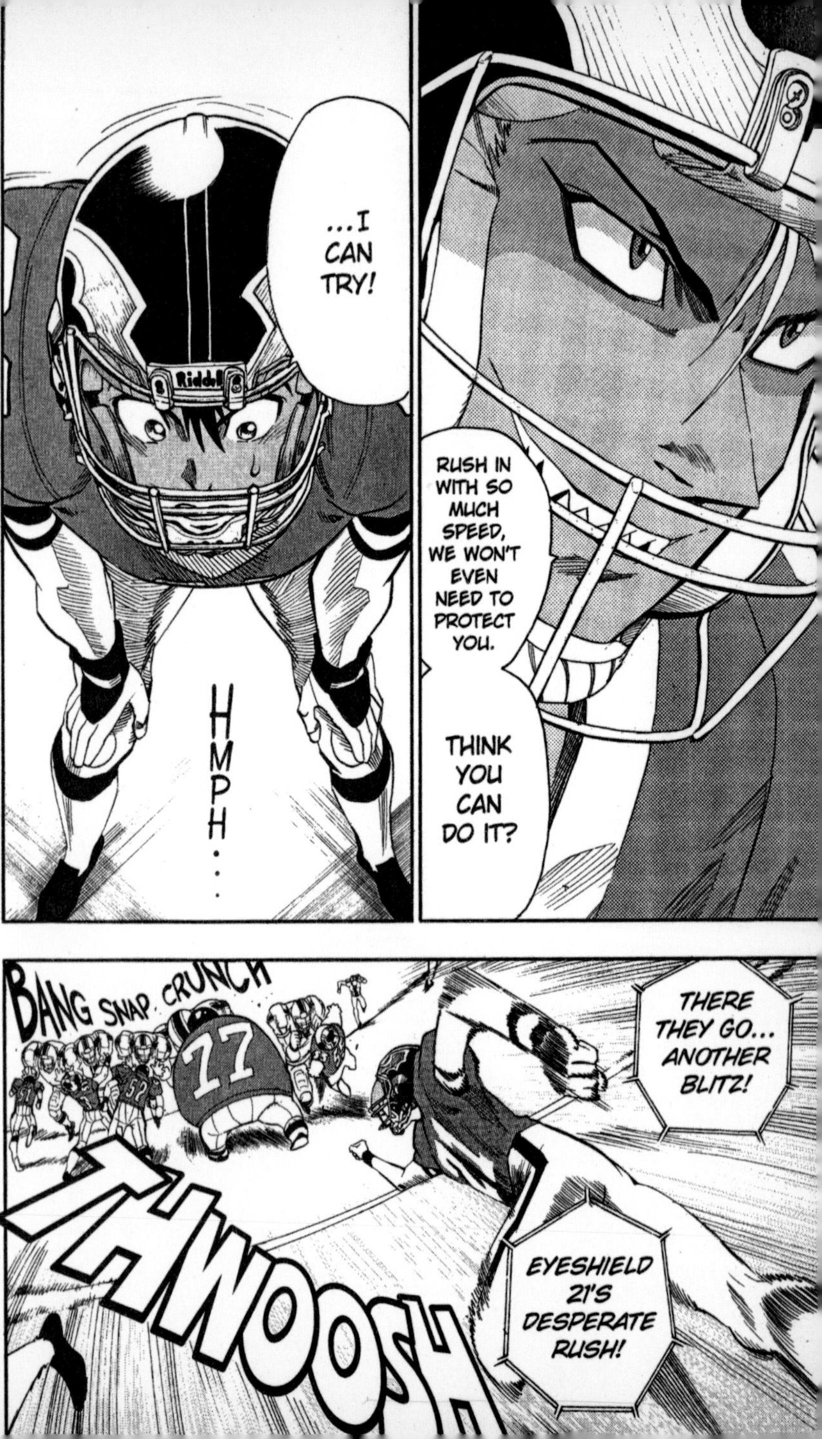

RUSH IN WITH SO MUCH SPEED, WE WON'T EVEN NEED TO PROTECT YOU.
THINK YOU CAN DO IT?
...I CAN TRY!
HMPH...
THERE THEY GO... ANOTHER BLITZ!
BANG SNAP CRUNCH
EYESHIELD 21'S DESPERATE RUSH!
THWOOSH

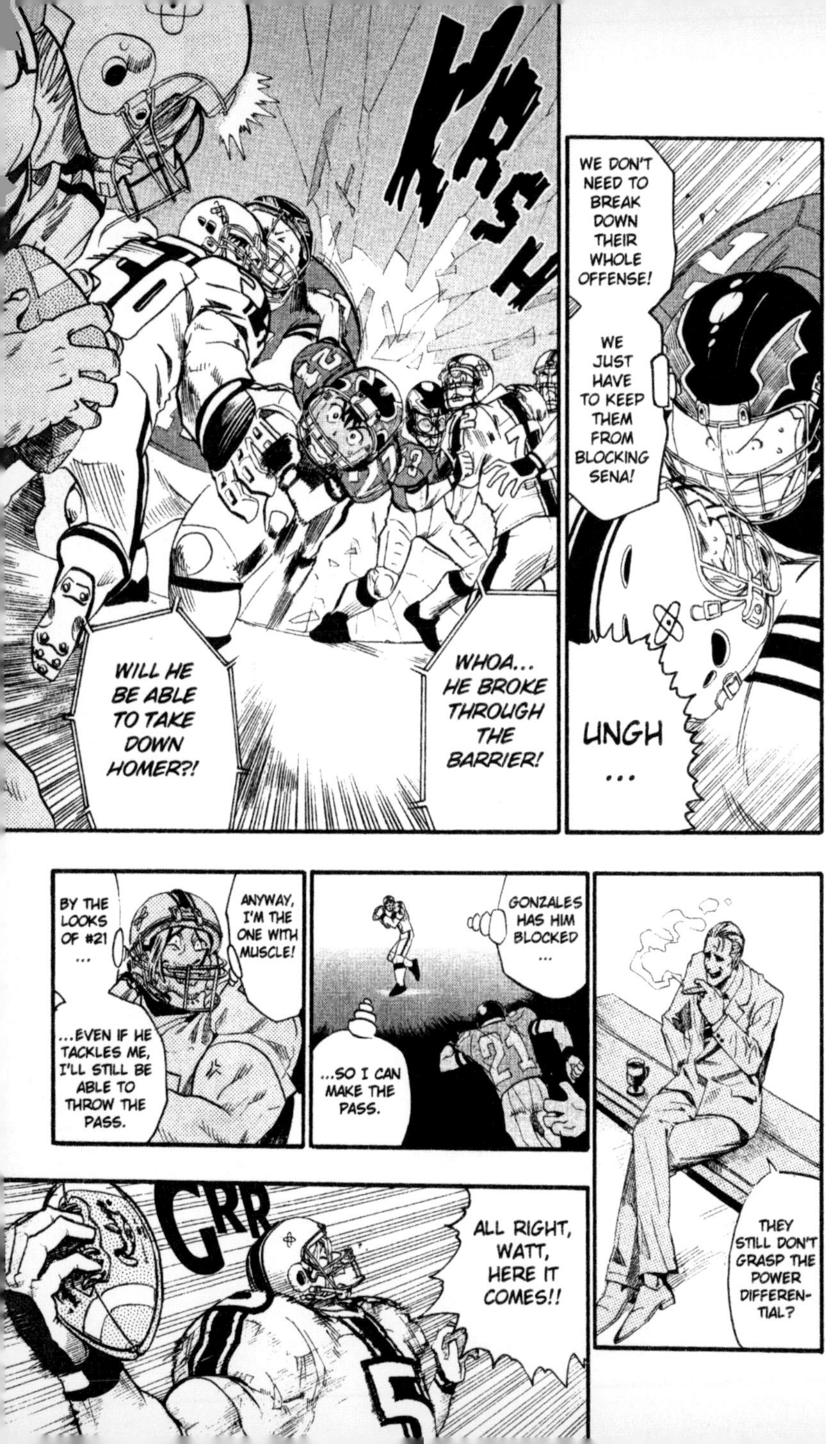
WE DON'T NEED TO BREAK DOWN THEIR WHOLE OFFENSE!
WE JUST HAVE TO KEEP THEM FROM BLOCKING SENA!
UNGH ...
KRSSH
WHOA... HE BROKE THROUGH THE BARRIER!
WILL HE BE ABLE TO TAKE DOWN HOMER?!
THEY STILL DON'T GRASP THE POWER DIFFEREN-TIAL?
GONZALES HAS HIM BLOCKED ...
...SO I CAN MAKE THE PASS.
ANYWAY, I'M THE ONE WITH MUSCLE!
BY THE LOOKS OF #21 ...
...EVEN IF HE TACKLES ME, I'LL STILL BE ABLE TO THROW THE PASS.
ALL RIGHT, WATT, HERE IT COMES!!
GRR

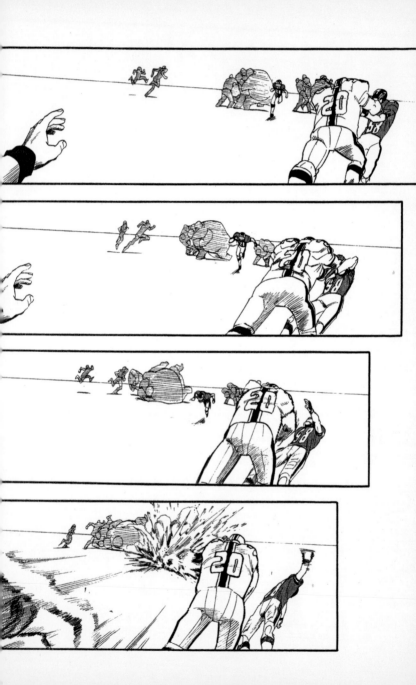

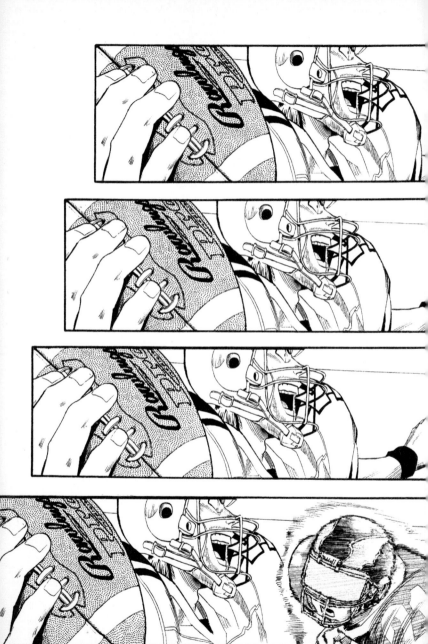

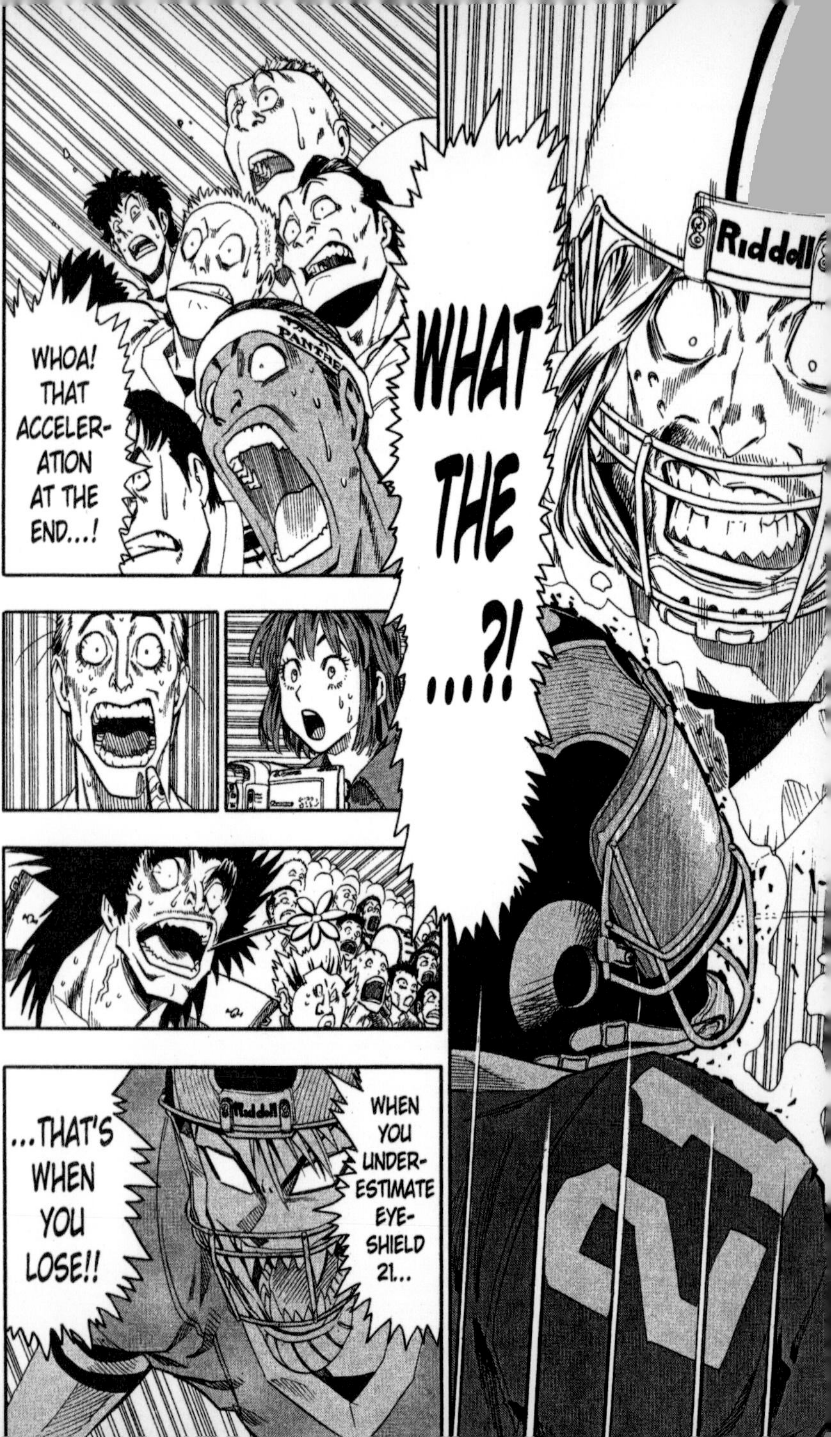
WHAT THE ...?!
WHOA! THAT ACCELER-ATION AT THE END...!
WHEN YOU UNDER-ESTIMATE EYE-SHIELD 21...
...THAT'S WHEN YOU LOSE!!

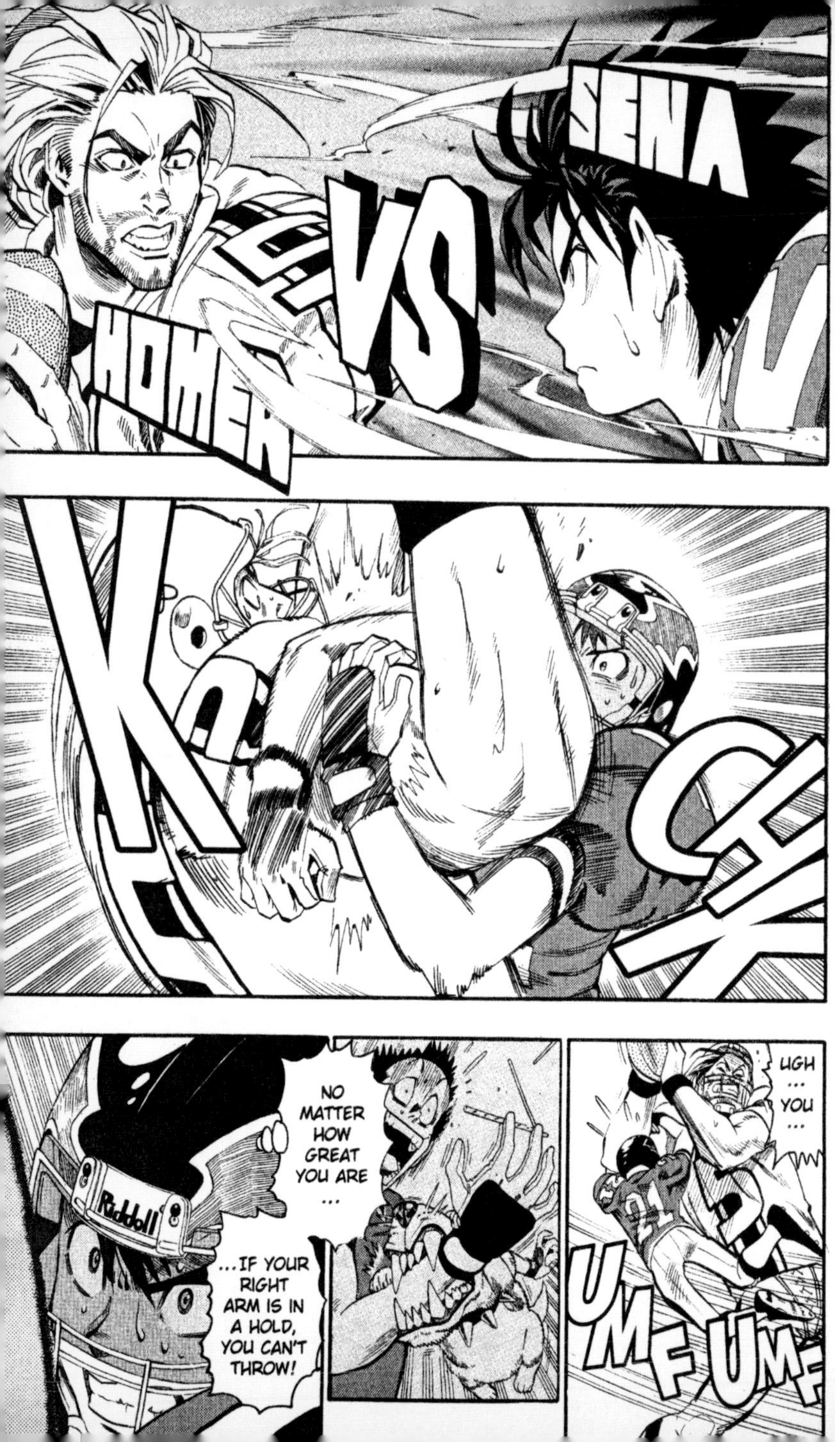
SENA
VS
HOMER
UGH ... YOU ...
UMF UMF
NO MATTER HOW GREAT YOU ARE ...
...IF YOUR RIGHT ARM IS IN A HOLD, YOU CAN'T THROW!
Riddoll

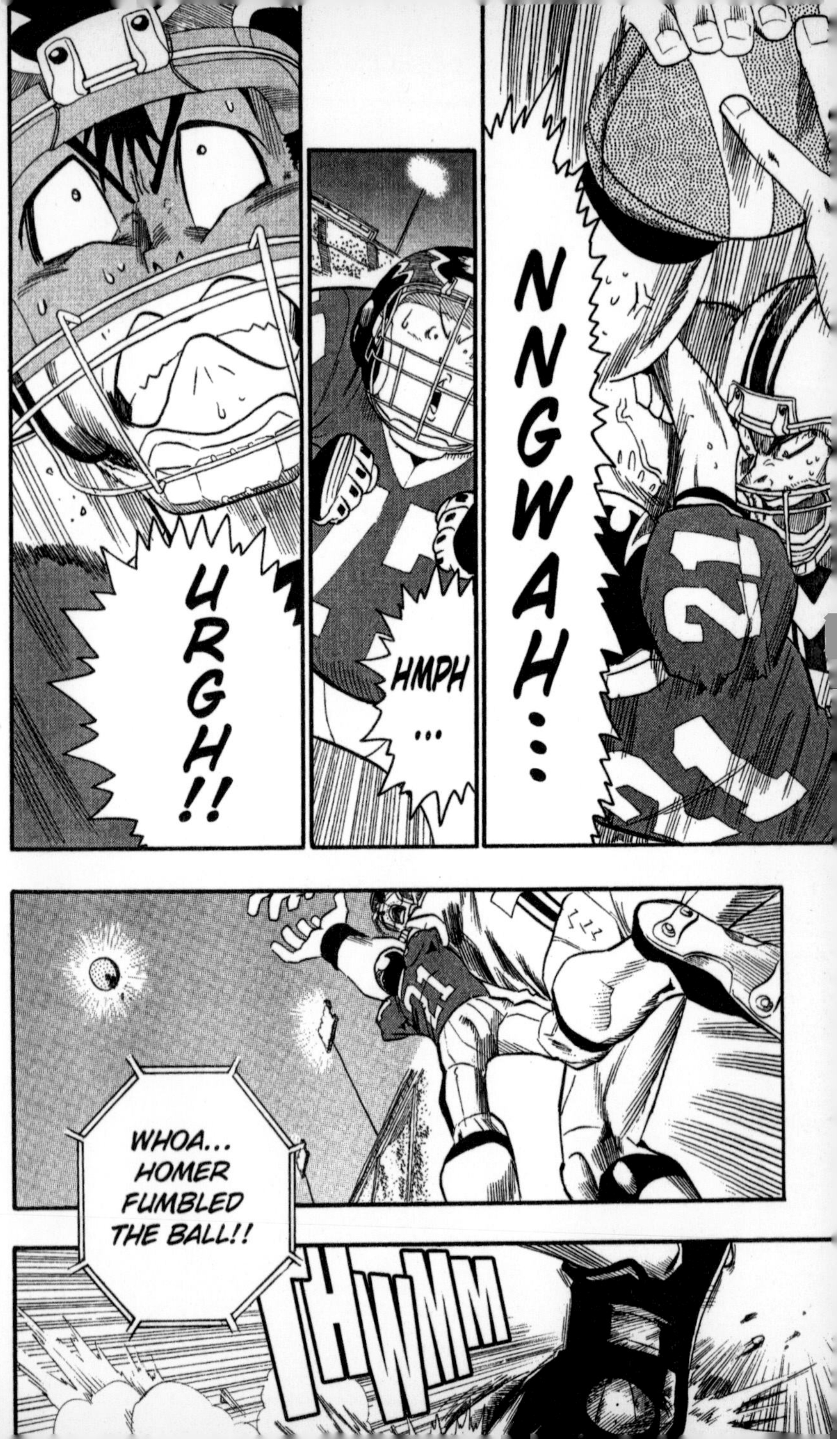
NNGWAH...
HMPH...
URGH!!
WHOA... HOMER FUMBLED THE BALL!!
THWMM

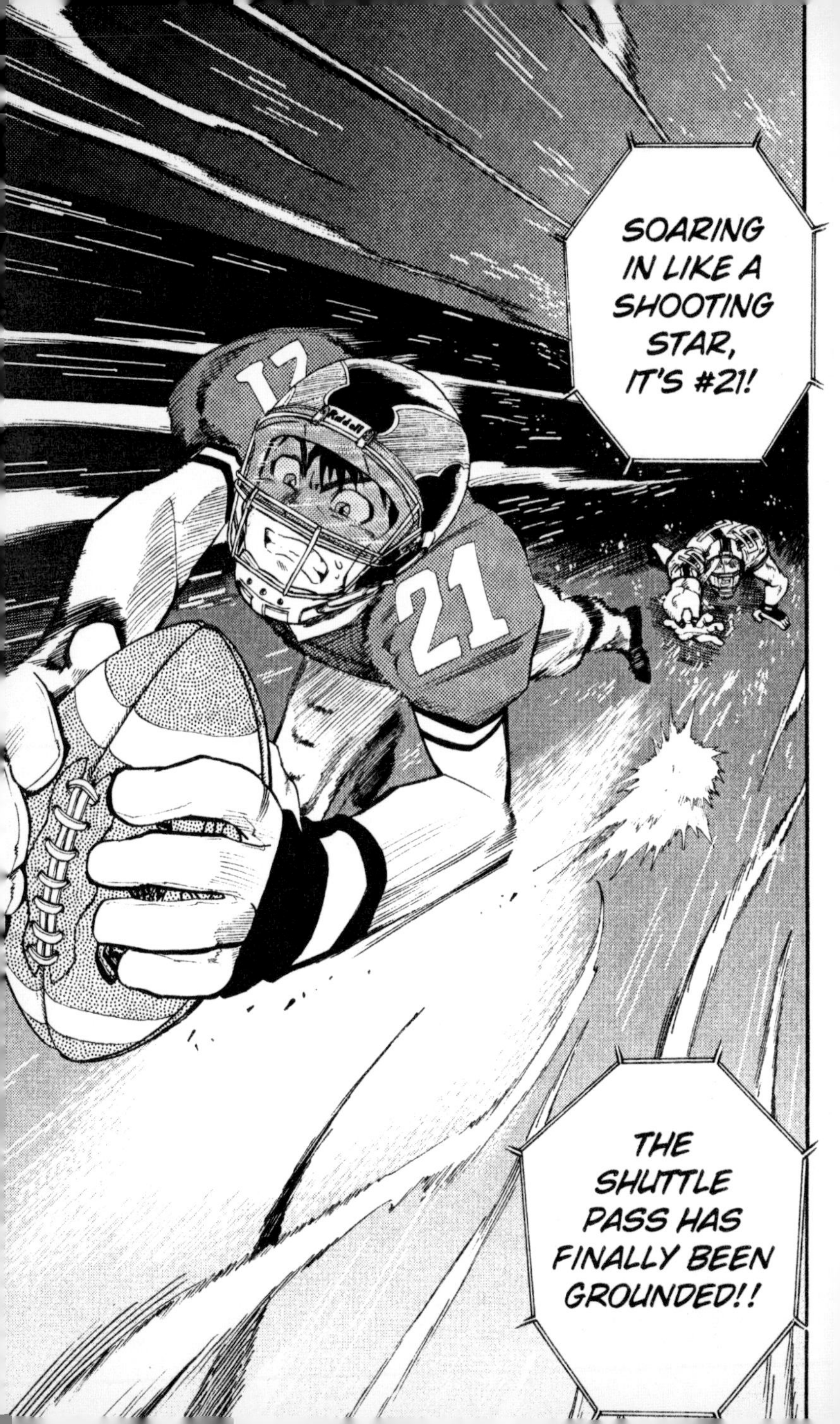
SOARING IN LIKE A SHOOTING STAR, IT'S #21!
THE SHUTTLE PASS HAS FINALLY BEEN GROUNDED!!

Eyeshield 21 Survey Corner **Devil Bat 021**

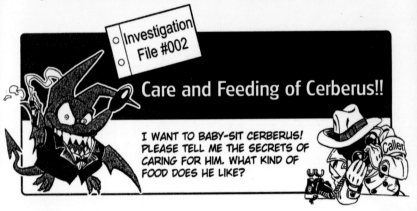

Investigation File #002

Care and Feeding of Cerberus!!

Caller

I WANT TO BABY-SIT CERBERUS! PLEASE TELL ME THE SECRETS OF CARING FOR HIM. WHAT KIND OF FOOD DOES HE LIKE?

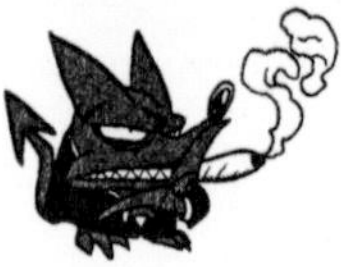

I THINK YOU'VE GOT THE WRONG IDEA. CERBERUS ISN'T HIRUMA'S PET. BASICALLY, HE'S A STRAY DOG.

The spike collar that Hiruma gave him doesn't mean that he's a housepet... it's simply a weapon.

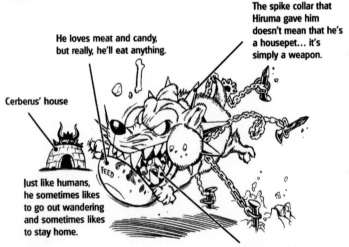

He loves meat and candy, but really, he'll eat anything.

Cerberus' house

FEED

Just like humans, he sometimes likes to go out wandering and sometimes likes to stay home.

His fangs could even chomp down on diamonds.

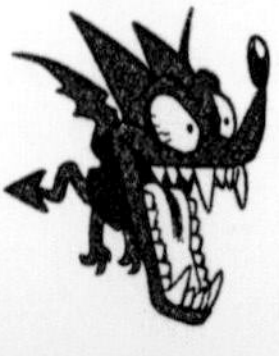

CERBERUS ONLY STICKS AROUND WITH HIRUMA BECAUSE HE KNOWS HIRUMA WILL FEED HIM!

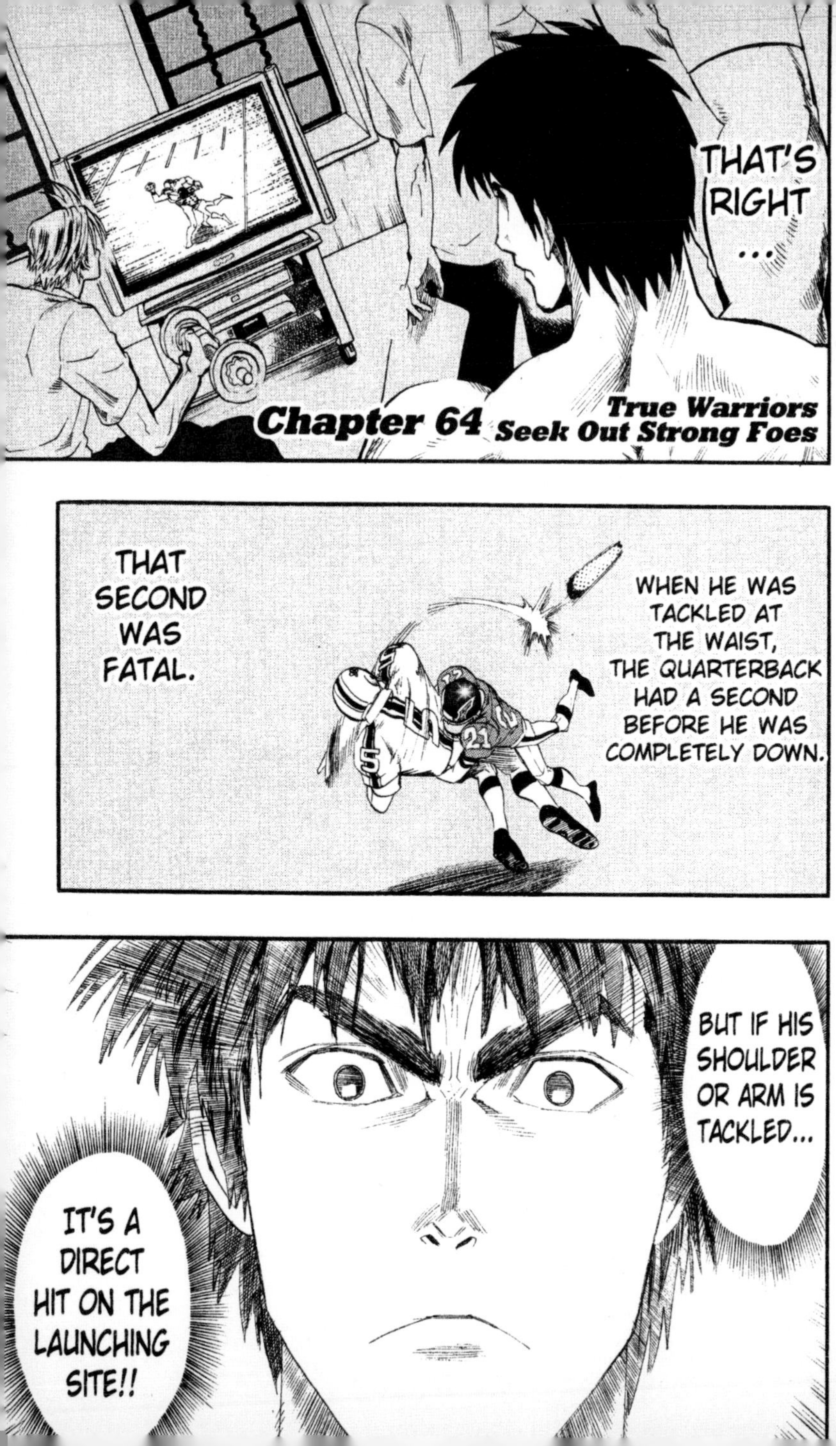
THAT'S RIGHT ...
Chapter 64 True Warriors Seek Out Strong Foes
WHEN HE WAS TACKLED AT THE WAIST, THE QUARTERBACK HAD A SECOND BEFORE HE WAS COMPLETELY DOWN.
THAT SECOND WAS FATAL.
BUT IF HIS SHOULDER OR ARM IS TACKLED...
IT'S A DIRECT HIT ON THE LAUNCHING SITE!!

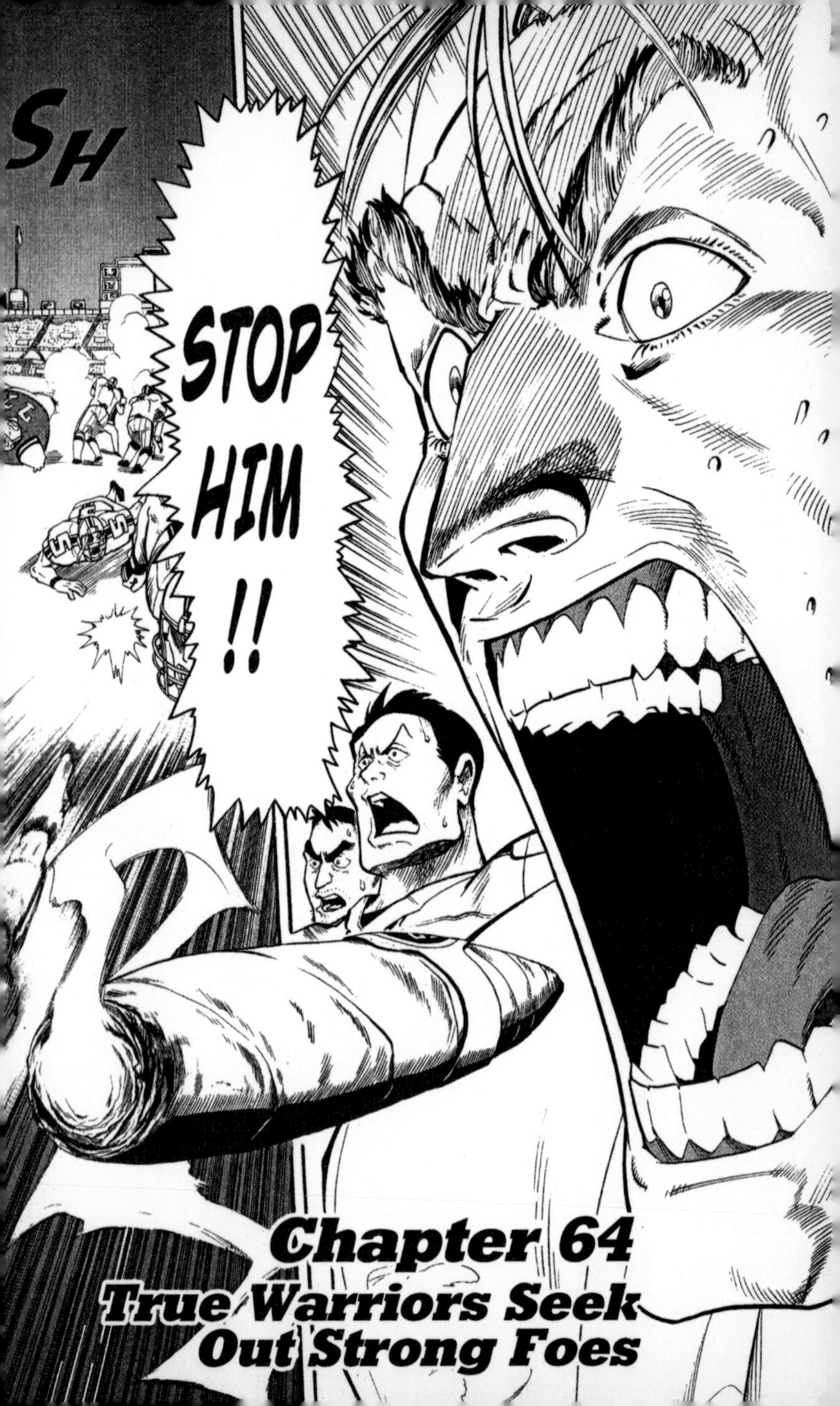
SH
STOP HIM !!
Chapter 64
True Warriors Seek Out Strong Foes

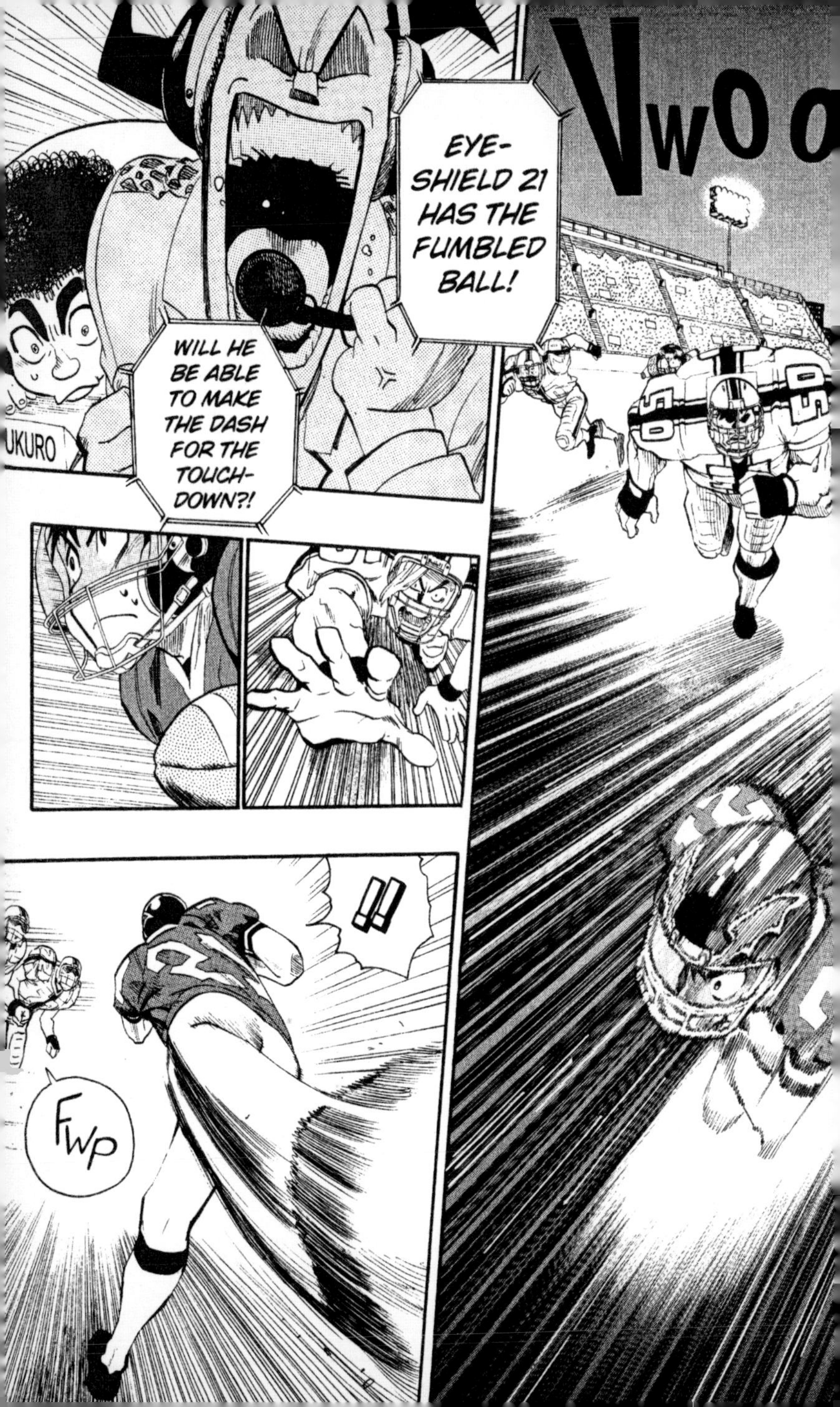

VWOOO
EYE-SHIELD 21 HAS THE FUMBLED BALL!
WILL HE BE ABLE TO MAKE THE DASH FOR THE TOUCH-DOWN?!
UKURO
!!
FWP

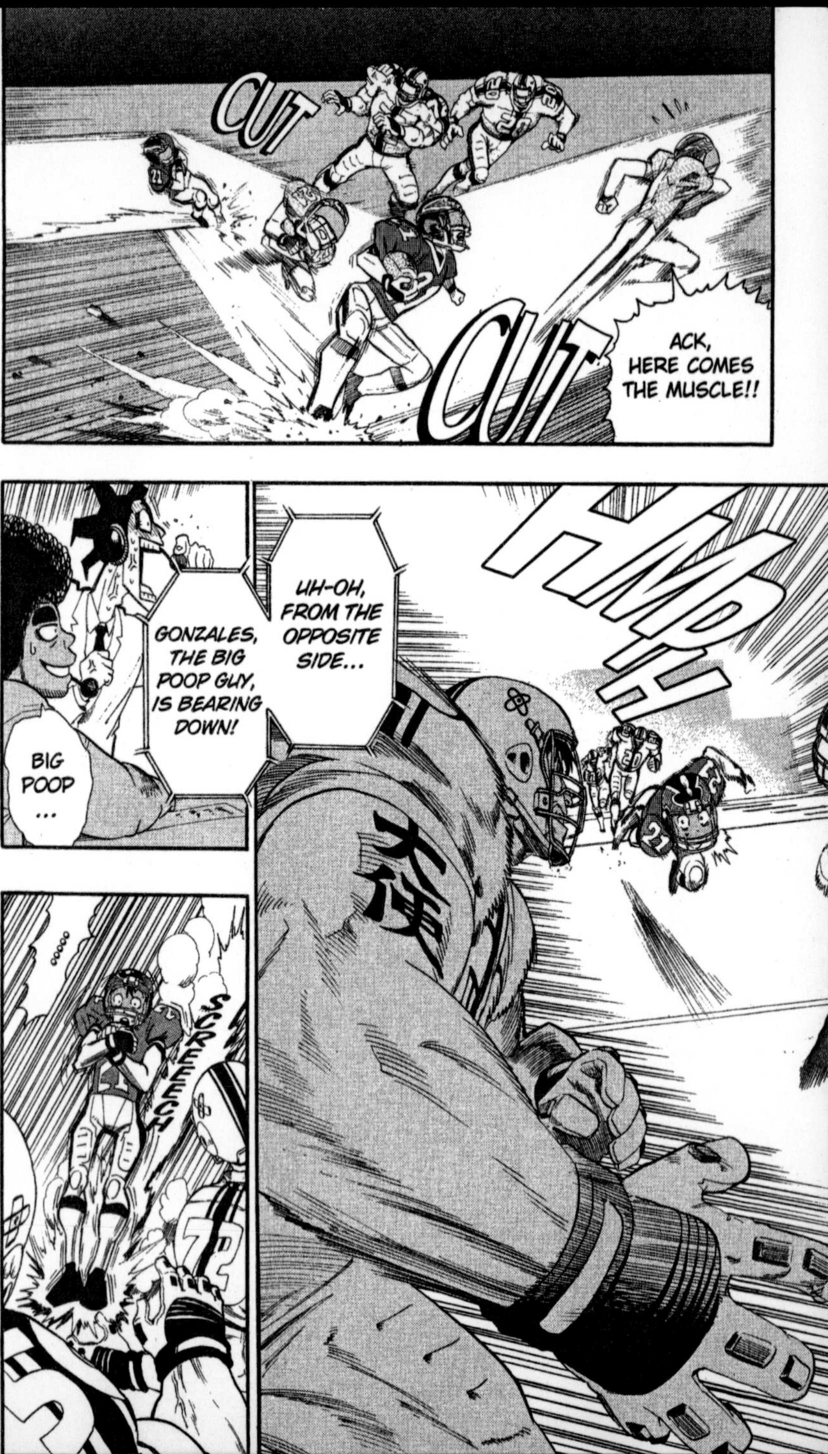
CUT
CUT
ACK, HERE COMES THE MUSCLE!!
HMPH!!
大便
UH-OH, FROM THE OPPOSITE SIDE...
GONZALES, THE BIG POOP GUY, IS BEARING DOWN!
BIG POOP...
ooooo
SCREEEECH

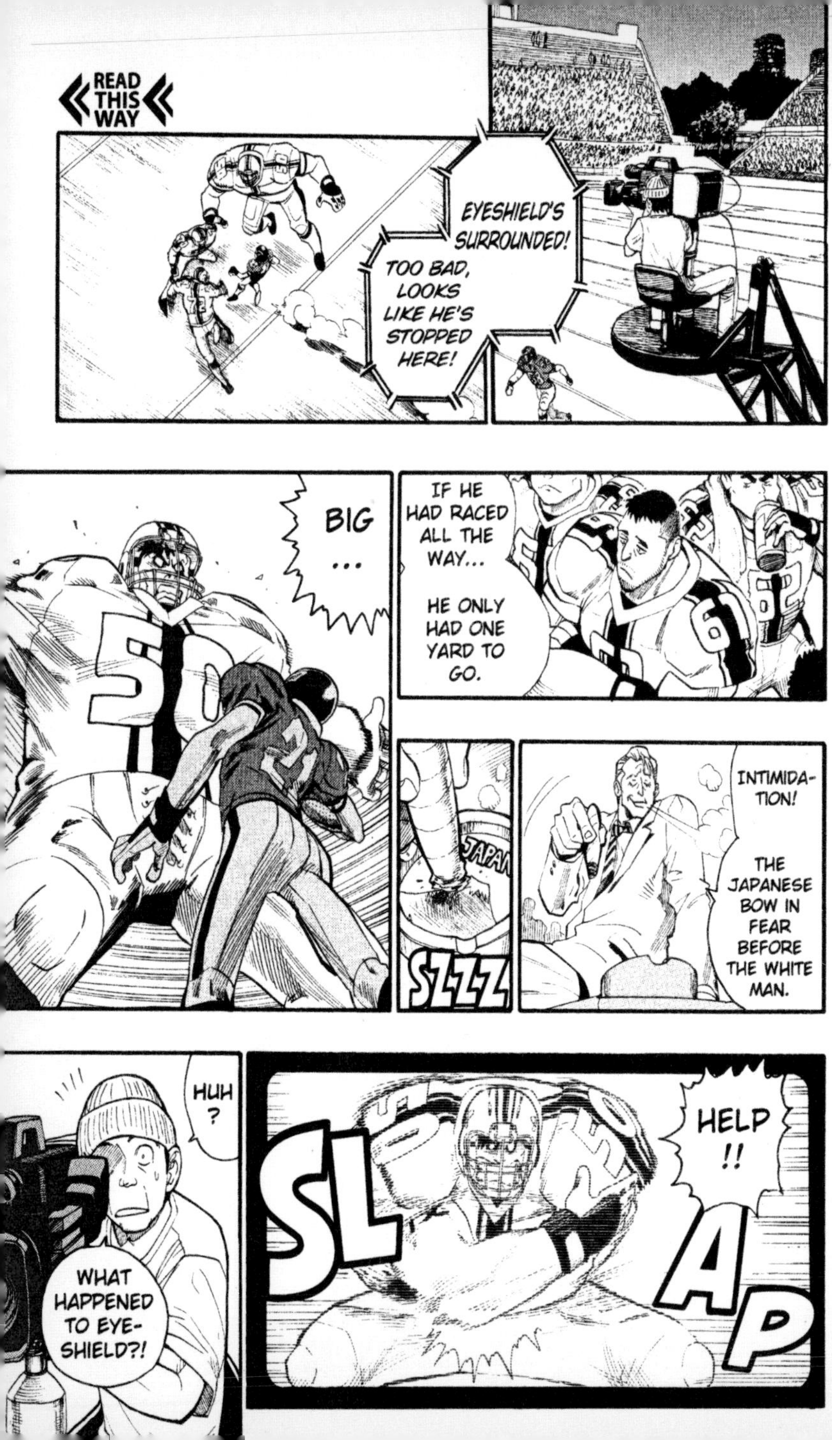
READ THIS WAY
EYESHIELD'S SURROUNDED!
TOO BAD, LOOKS LIKE HE'S STOPPED HERE!
IF HE HAD RACED ALL THE WAY...
HE ONLY HAD ONE YARD TO GO.
INTIMIDATION!
THE JAPANESE BOW IN FEAR BEFORE THE WHITE MAN.
JAPAN
SZZZ
BIG ...
HELP !!
SLAP
HUH ?
WHAT HAPPENED TO EYE-SHIELD?!

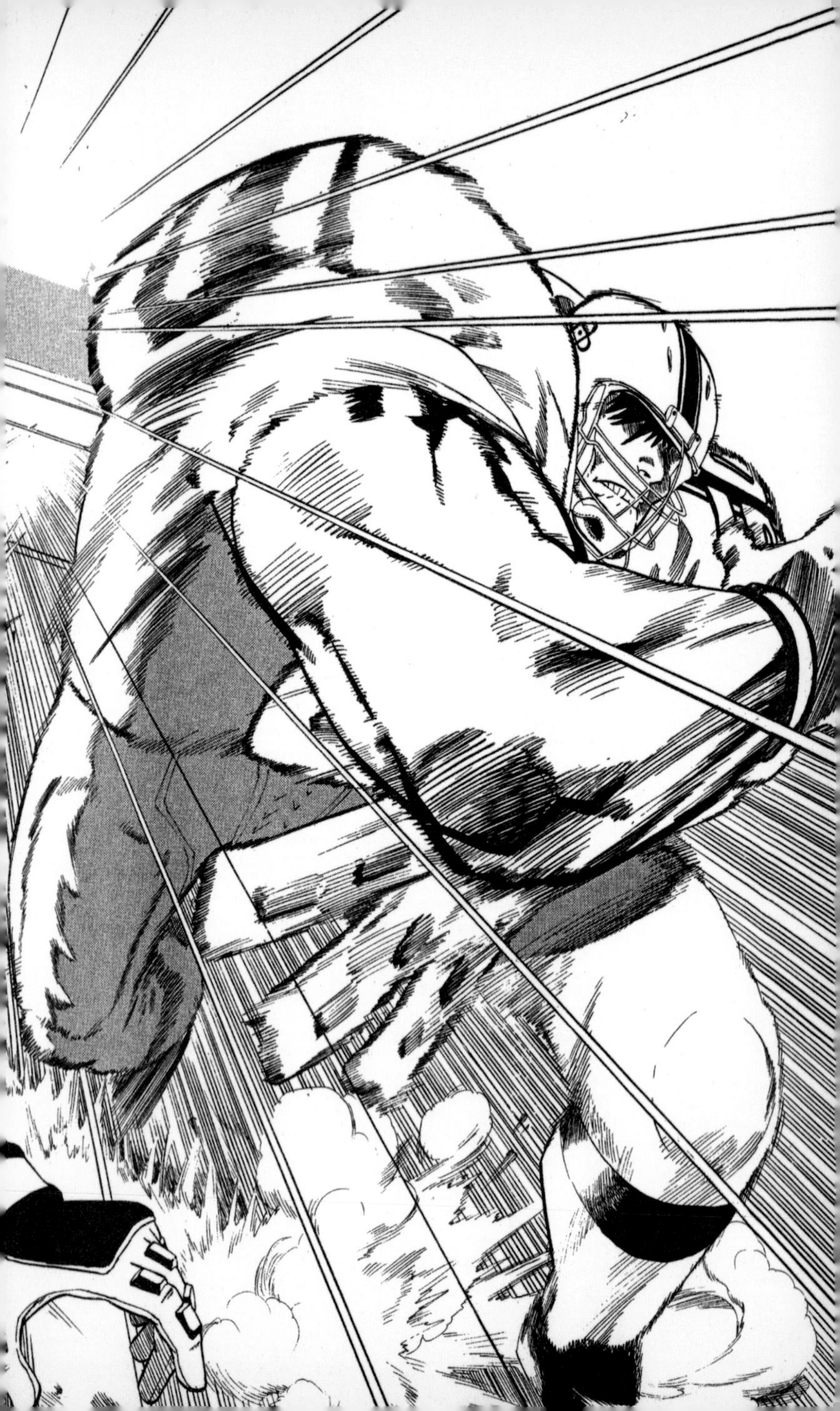

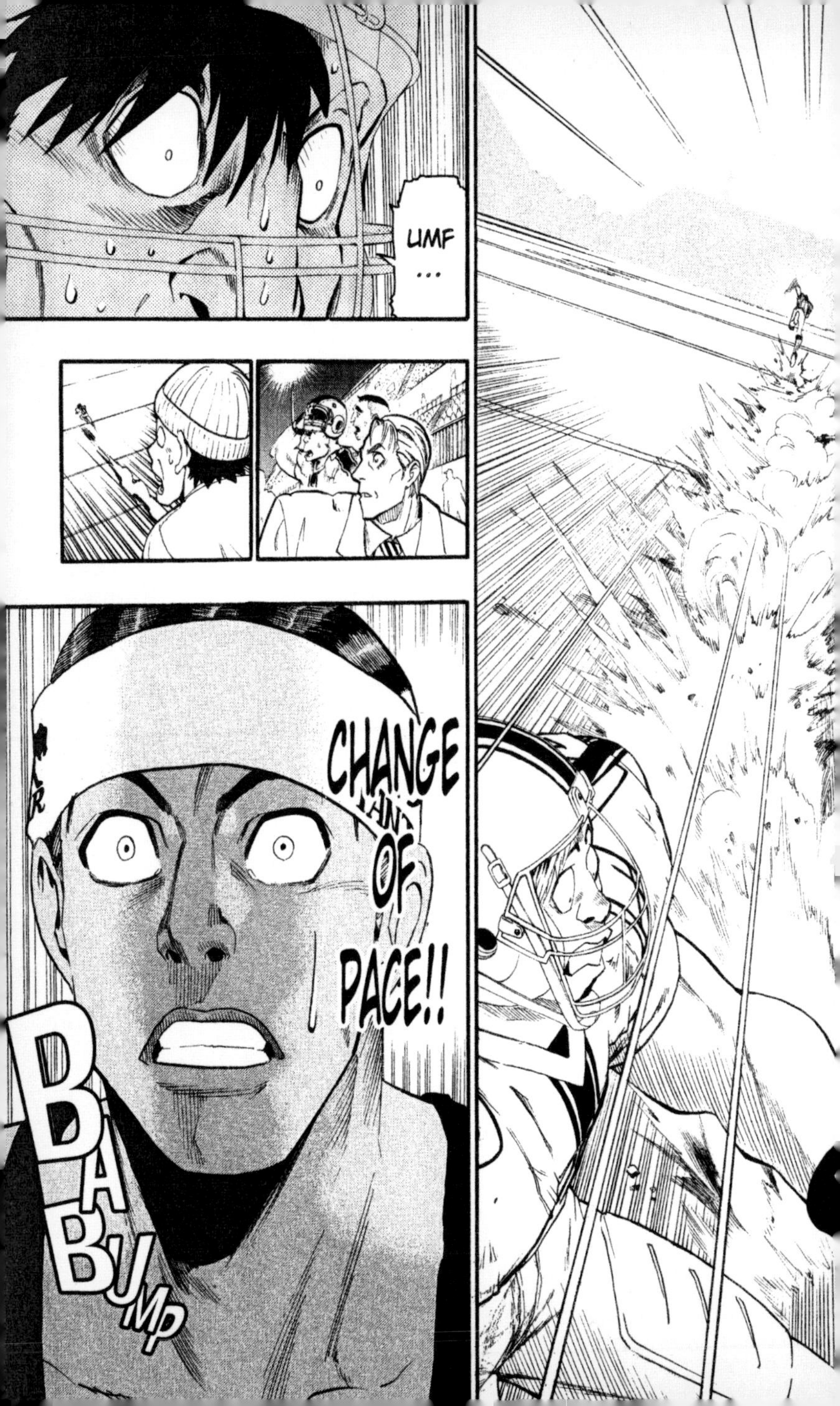
UMF ...
CHANGE OF PACE!!
BABUMP

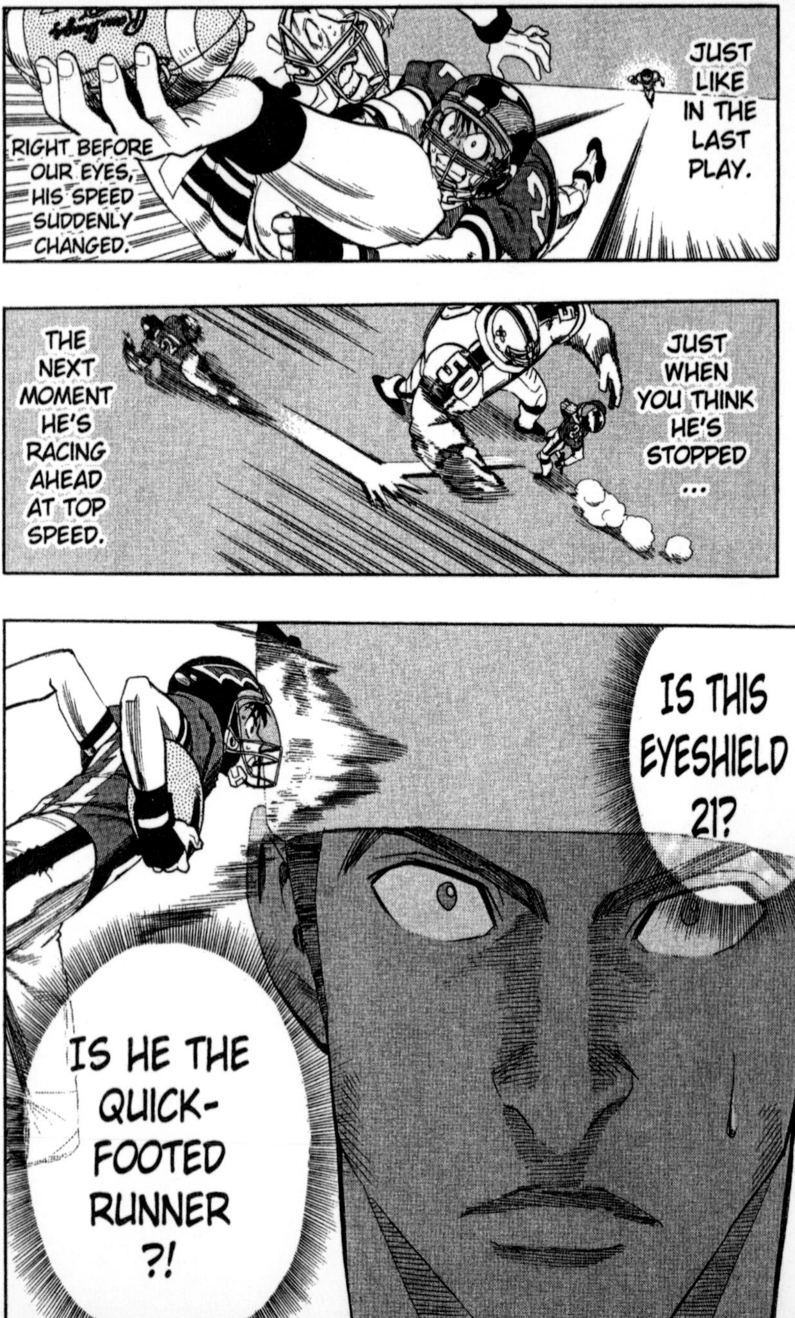
JUST LIKE IN THE LAST PLAY.
RIGHT BEFORE OUR EYES, HIS SPEED SUDDENLY CHANGED.
JUST WHEN YOU THINK HE'S STOPPED ...
THE NEXT MOMENT HE'S RACING AHEAD AT TOP SPEED.
IS THIS EYESHIELD 21?
IS HE THE QUICK-FOOTED RUNNER ?!

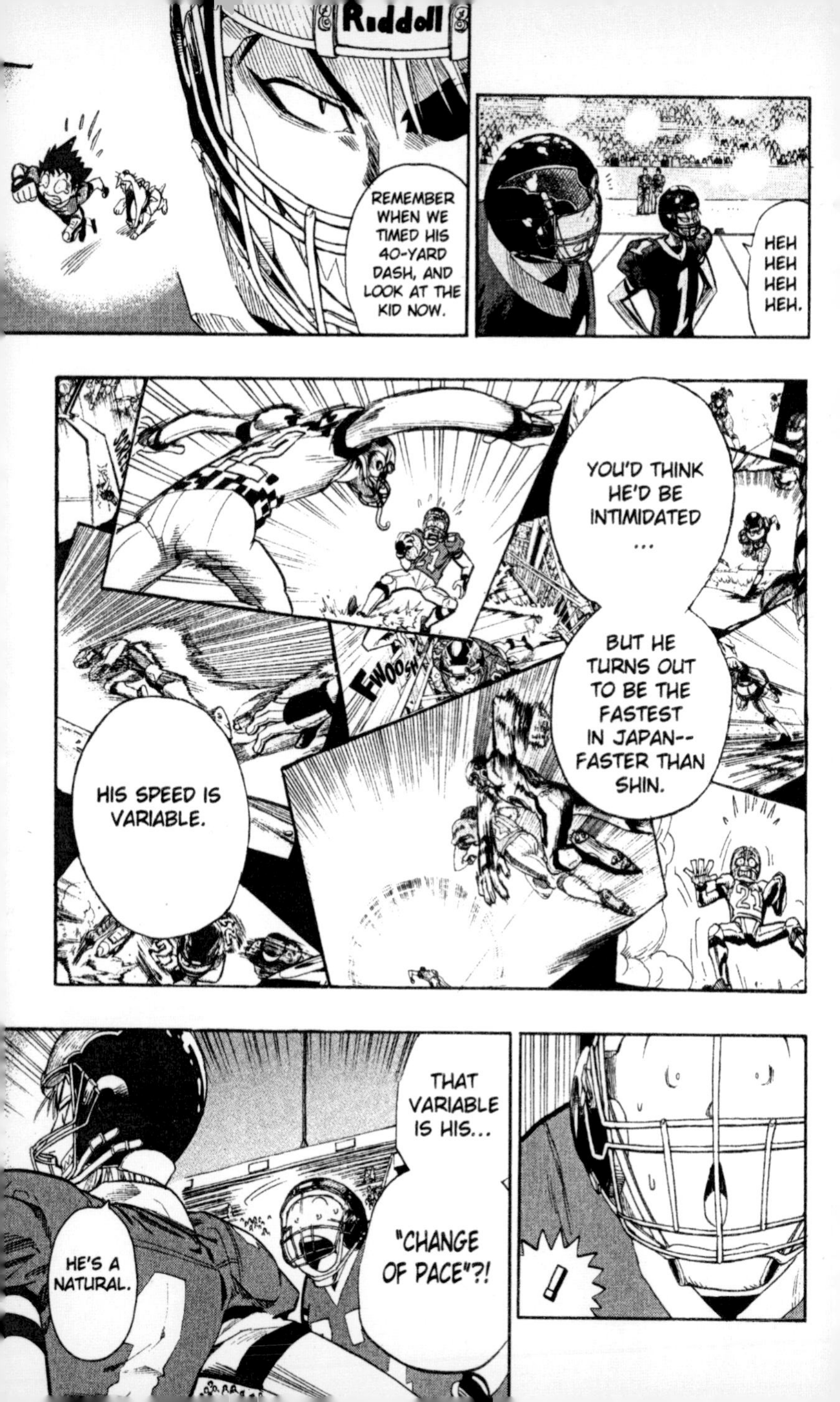
HEH HEH HEH HEH.
Riddell
REMEMBER WHEN WE TIMED HIS 40-YARD DASH, AND LOOK AT THE KID NOW.
YOU'D THINK HE'D BE INTIMIDATED ...
BUT HE TURNS OUT TO BE THE FASTEST IN JAPAN-- FASTER THAN SHIN.
FWOOSH
HIS SPEED IS VARIABLE.
!
THAT VARIABLE IS HIS...
"CHANGE OF PACE"?!
HE'S A NATURAL.

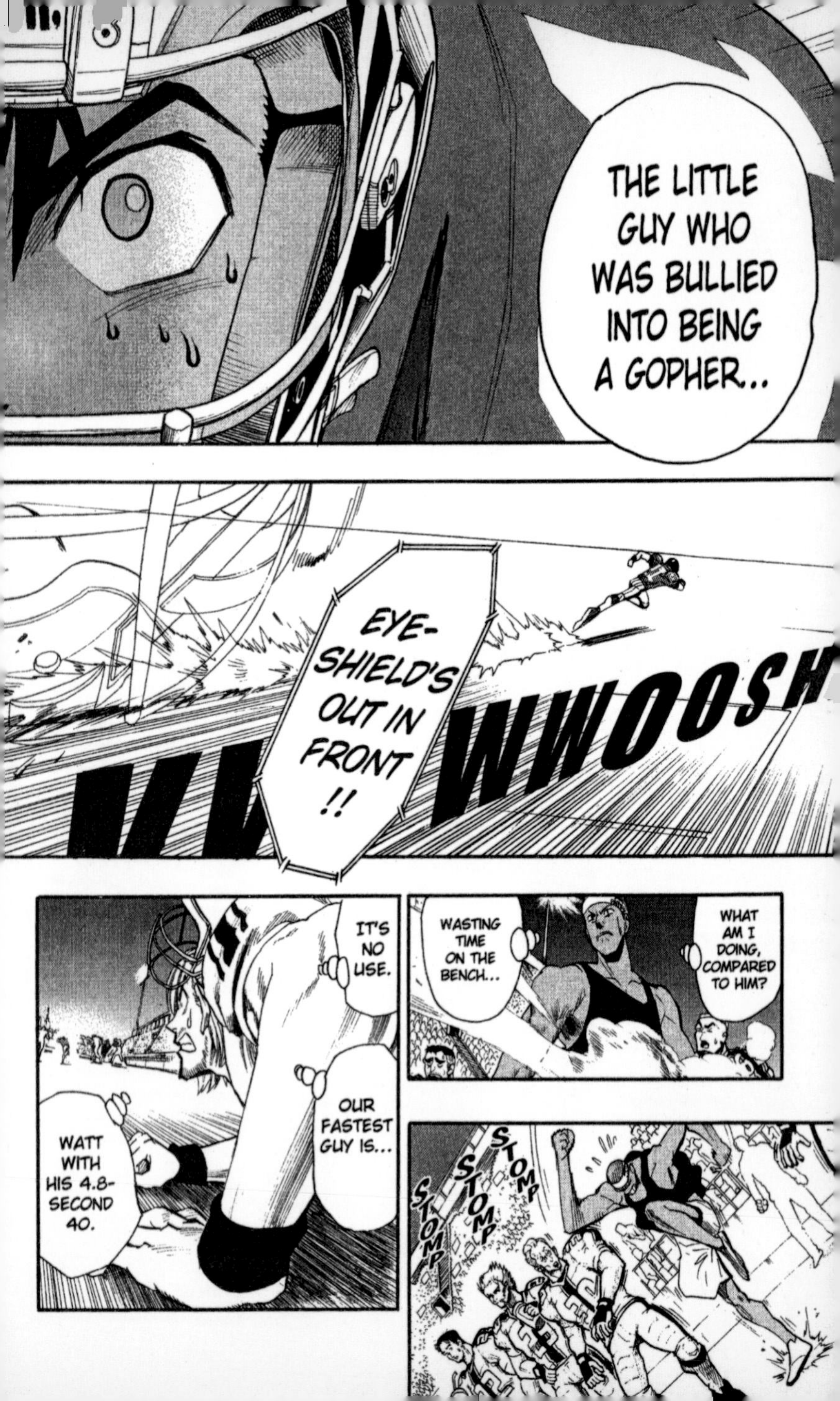
THE LITTLE GUY WHO WAS BULLIED INTO BEING A GOPHER...
EYE-SHIELD'S OUT IN FRONT!!
WWOOSH
WHAT AM I DOING, COMPARED TO HIM?
WASTING TIME ON THE BENCH...
STOMP
STOMP
STOMP
IT'S NO USE.
OUR FASTEST GUY IS...
WATT WITH HIS 4.8-SECOND 40.

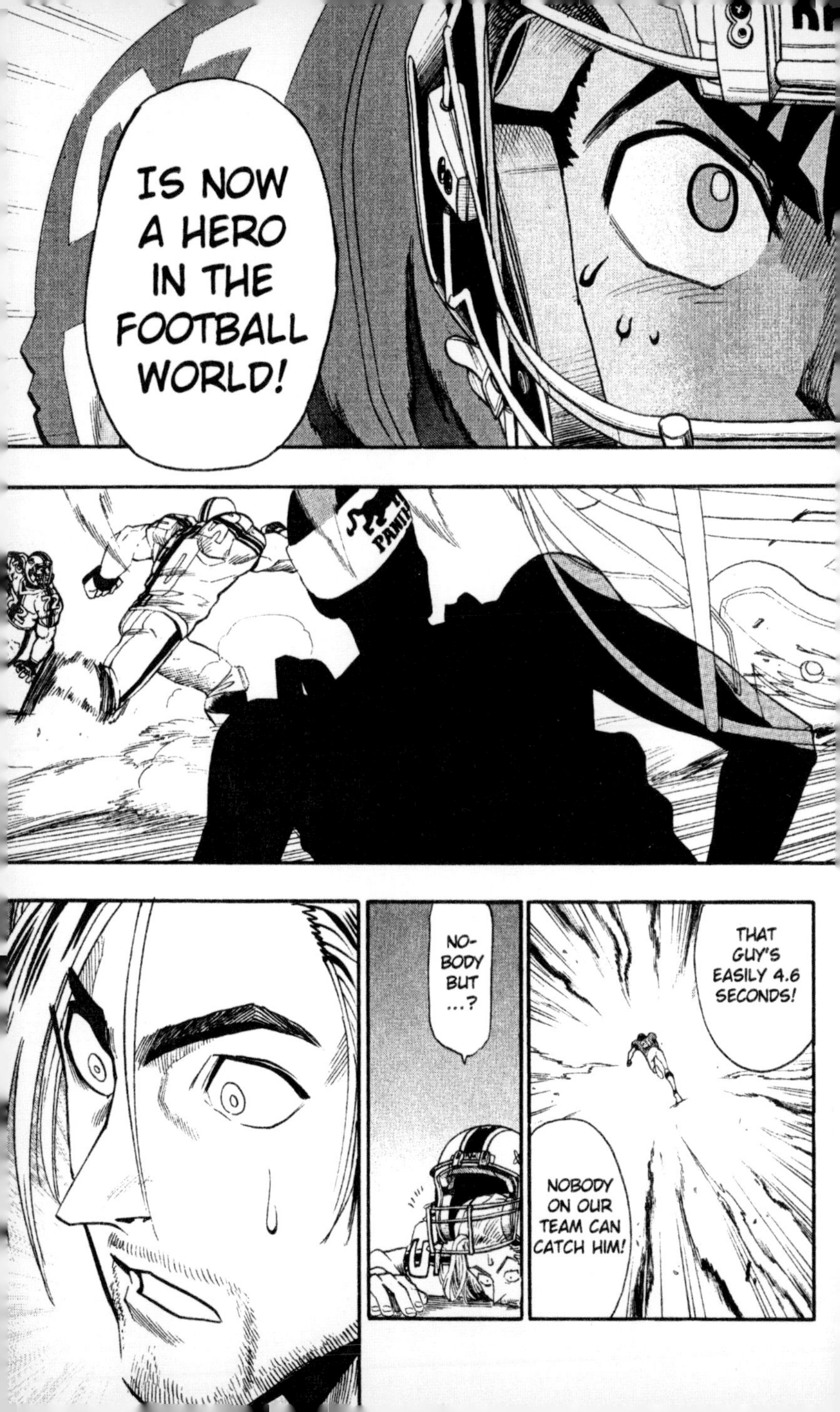
IS NOW A HERO IN THE FOOTBALL WORLD!
THAT GUY'S EASILY 4.6 SECONDS!
NOBODY ON OUR TEAM CAN CATCH HIM!
NO-BODY BUT ...?

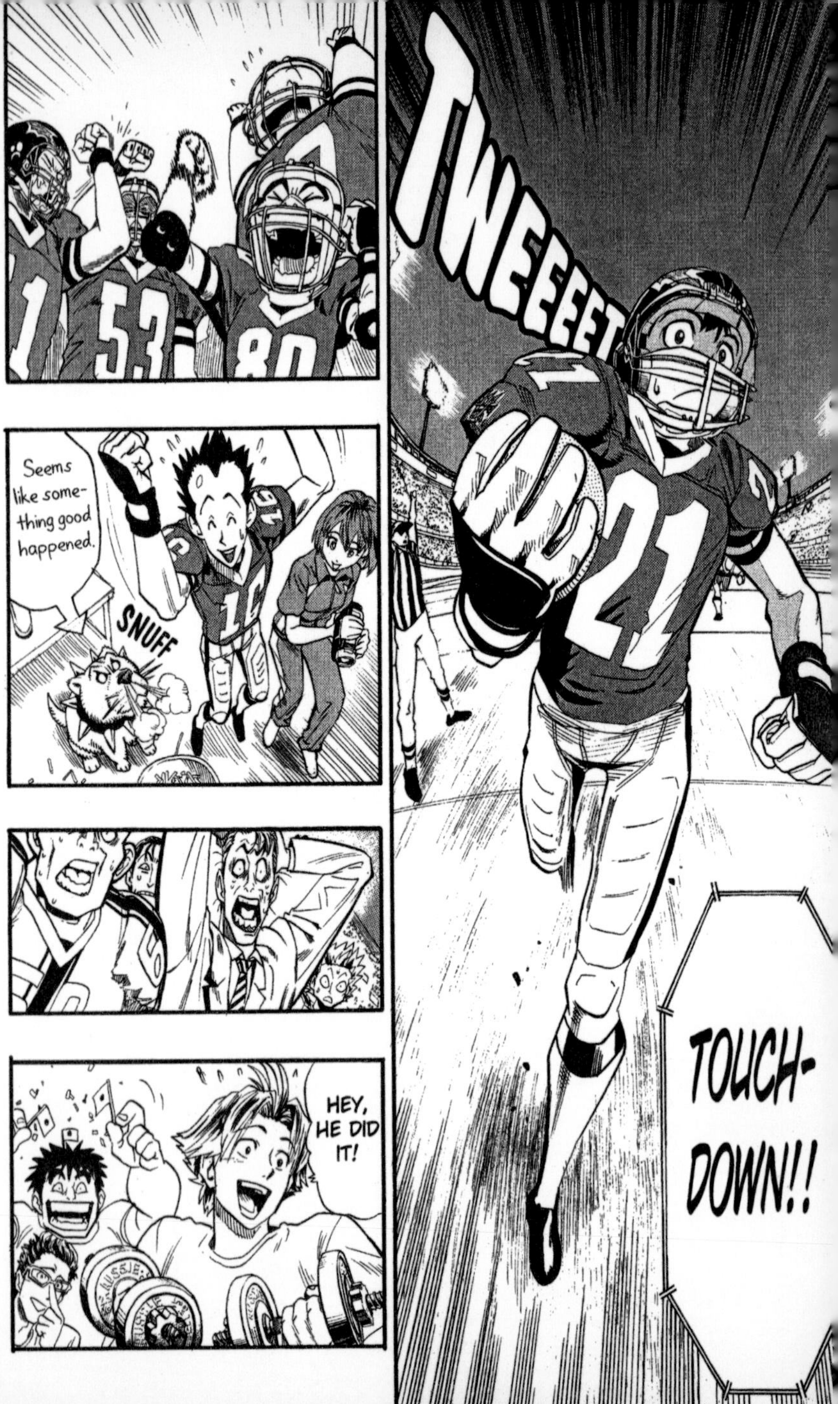
TWEEEET
TOUCH-DOWN!!
Seems like some-thing good happened.
SNUFF
HEY, HE DID IT!

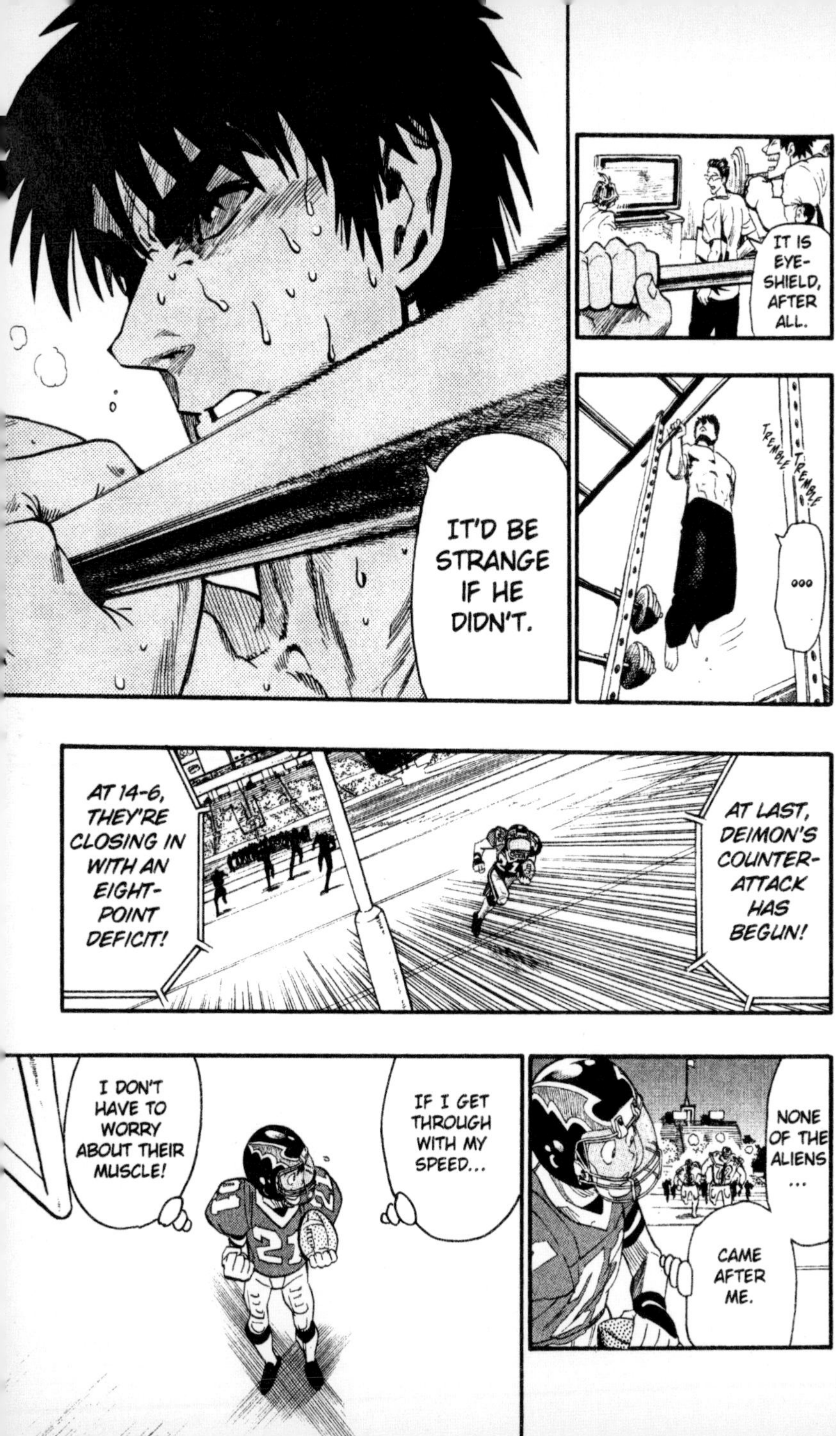
IT IS EYE-SHIELD, AFTER ALL.
TREMBLE TREMBLE
...
IT'D BE STRANGE IF HE DIDN'T.
AT LAST, DEIMON'S COUNTER-ATTACK HAS BEGUN!
AT 14-6, THEY'RE CLOSING IN WITH AN EIGHT-POINT DEFICIT!
NONE OF THE ALIENS...
CAME AFTER ME.
IF I GET THROUGH WITH MY SPEED...
I DON'T HAVE TO WORRY ABOUT THEIR MUSCLE!

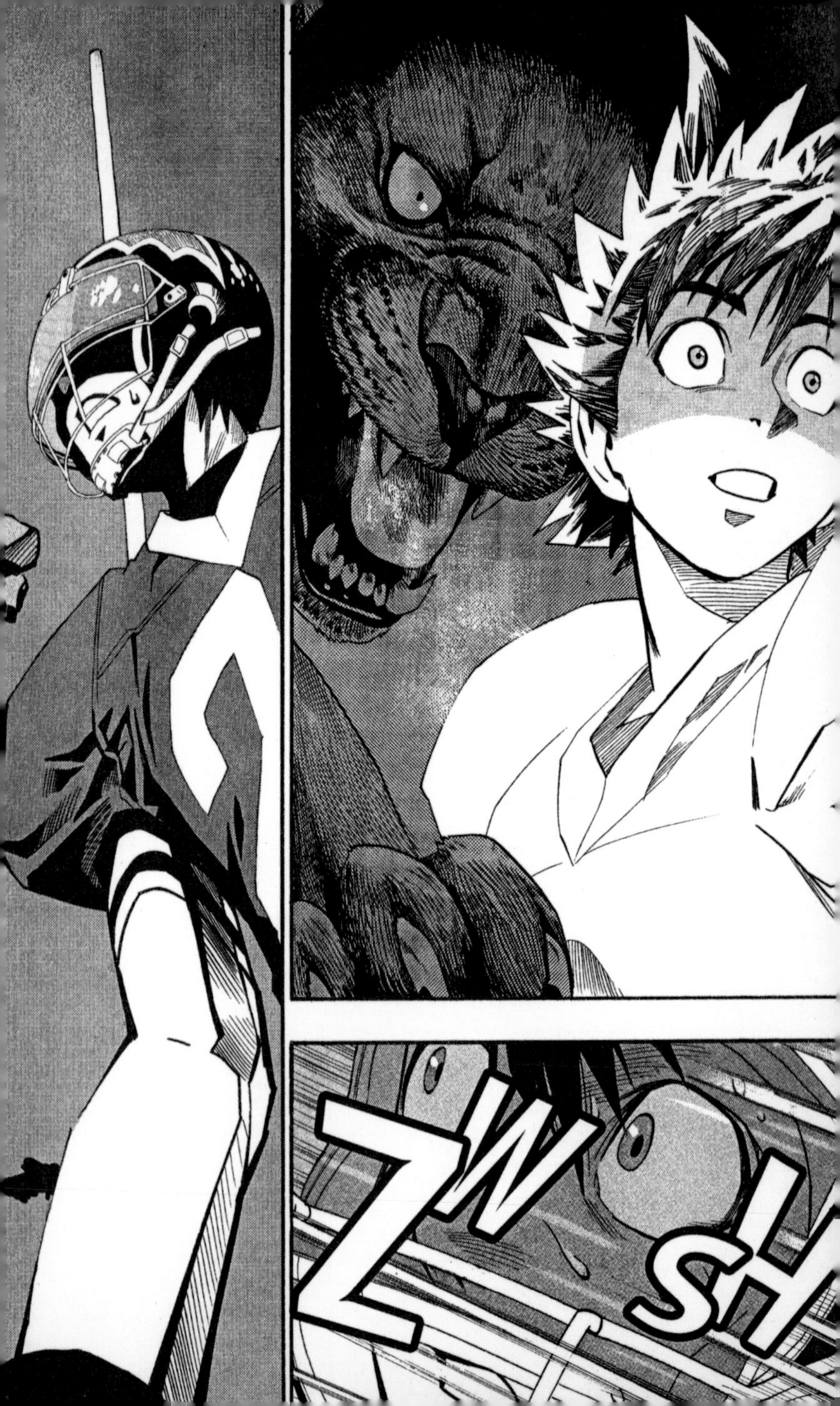
ZW
SH

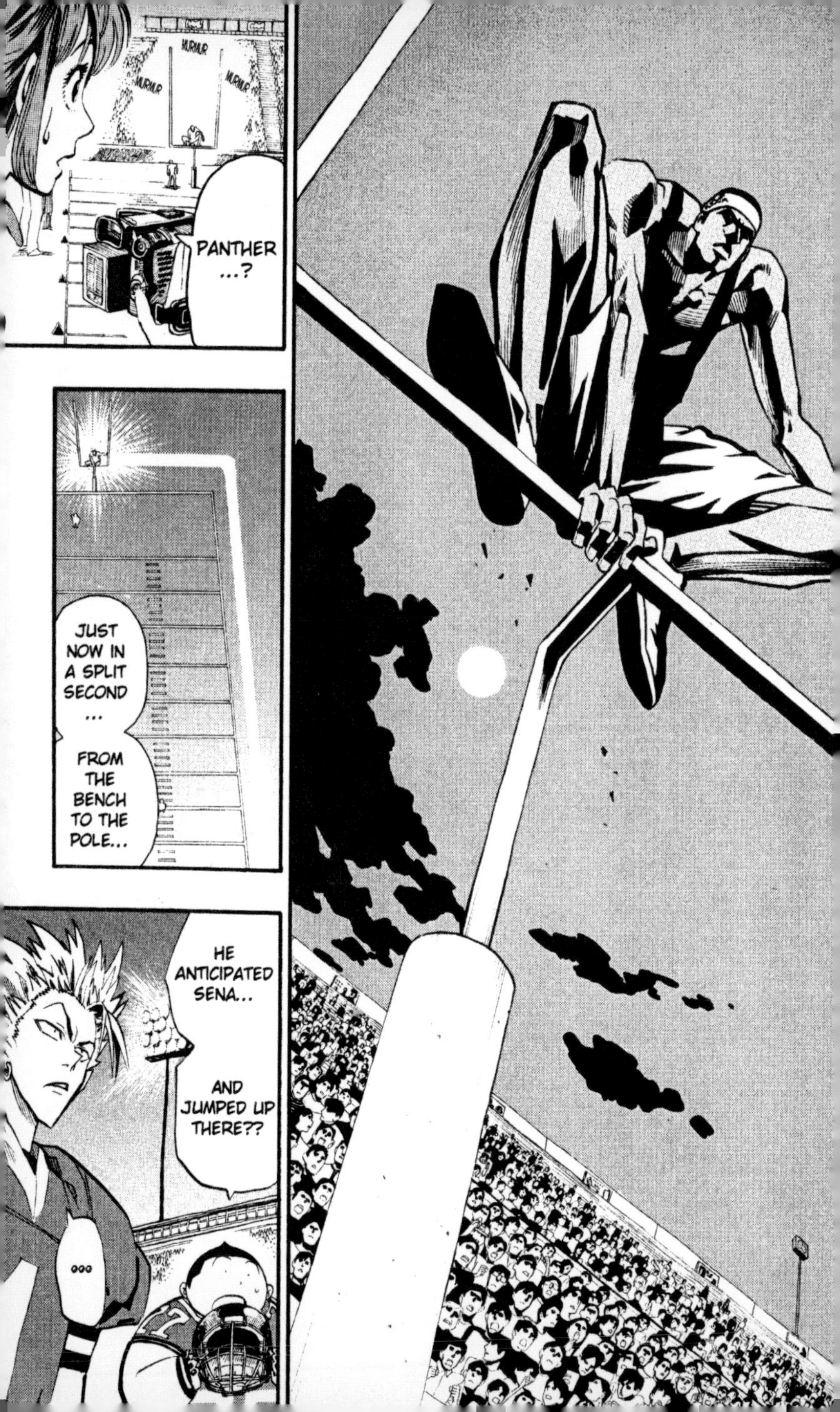

MURMUR
MURMUR
MURMUR
PANTHER ...?
JUST NOW IN A SPLIT SECOND ...
FROM THE BENCH TO THE POLE...
HE ANTICIPATED SENA...
AND JUMPED UP THERE??
...

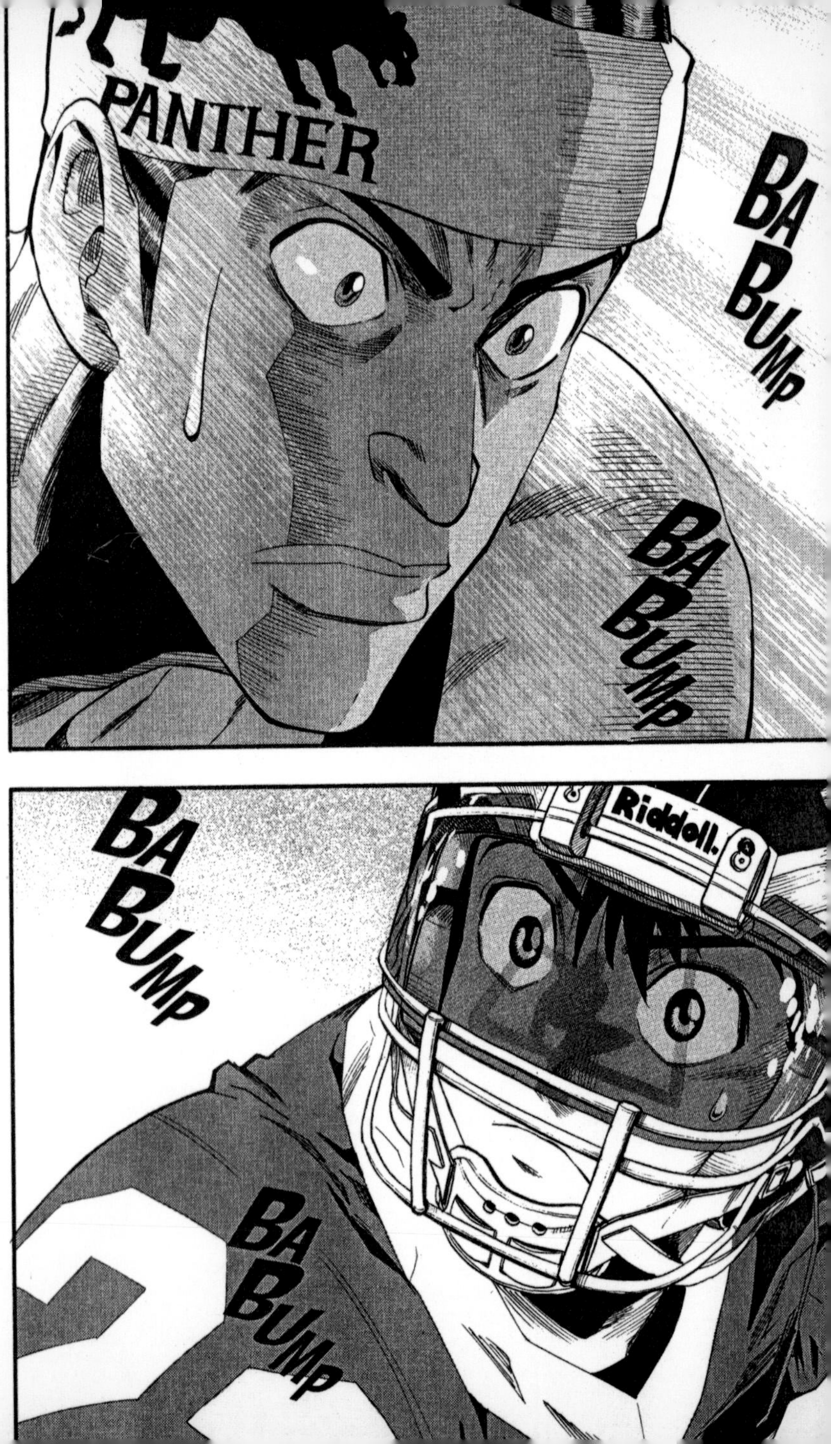
PANTHER
BABUMP
BABUMP
Riddell 8
BABUMP
BABUMP

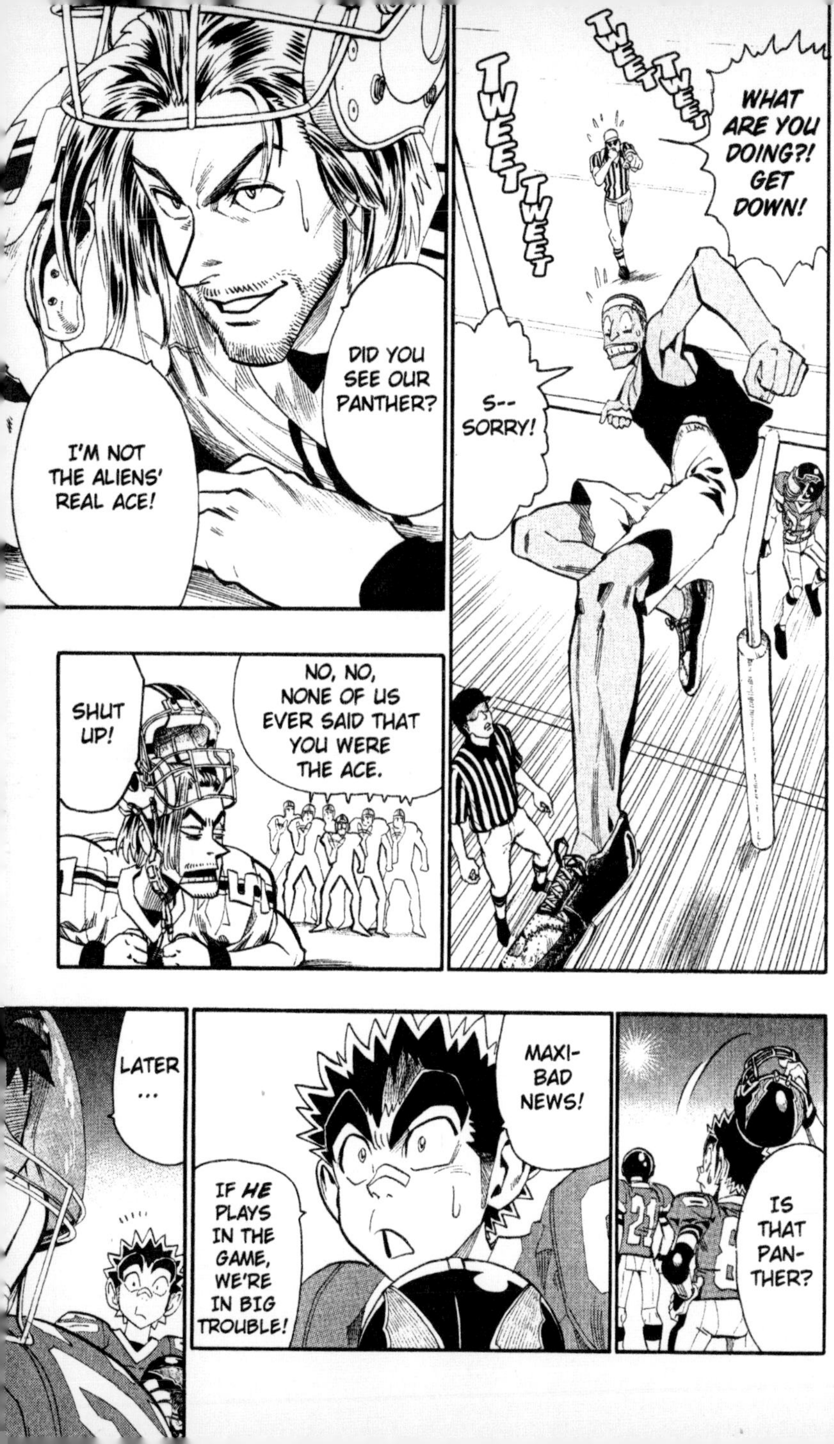
TWEET TWEET
TWEET TWEET
WHAT ARE YOU DOING?! GET DOWN!
S-- SORRY!
DID YOU SEE OUR PANTHER?
I'M NOT THE ALIENS' REAL ACE!
NO, NO, NONE OF US EVER SAID THAT YOU WERE THE ACE.
SHUT UP!
IS THAT PANTHER?
MAXI-BAD NEWS!
IF *HE* PLAYS IN THE GAME, WE'RE IN BIG TROUBLE!
LATER ...

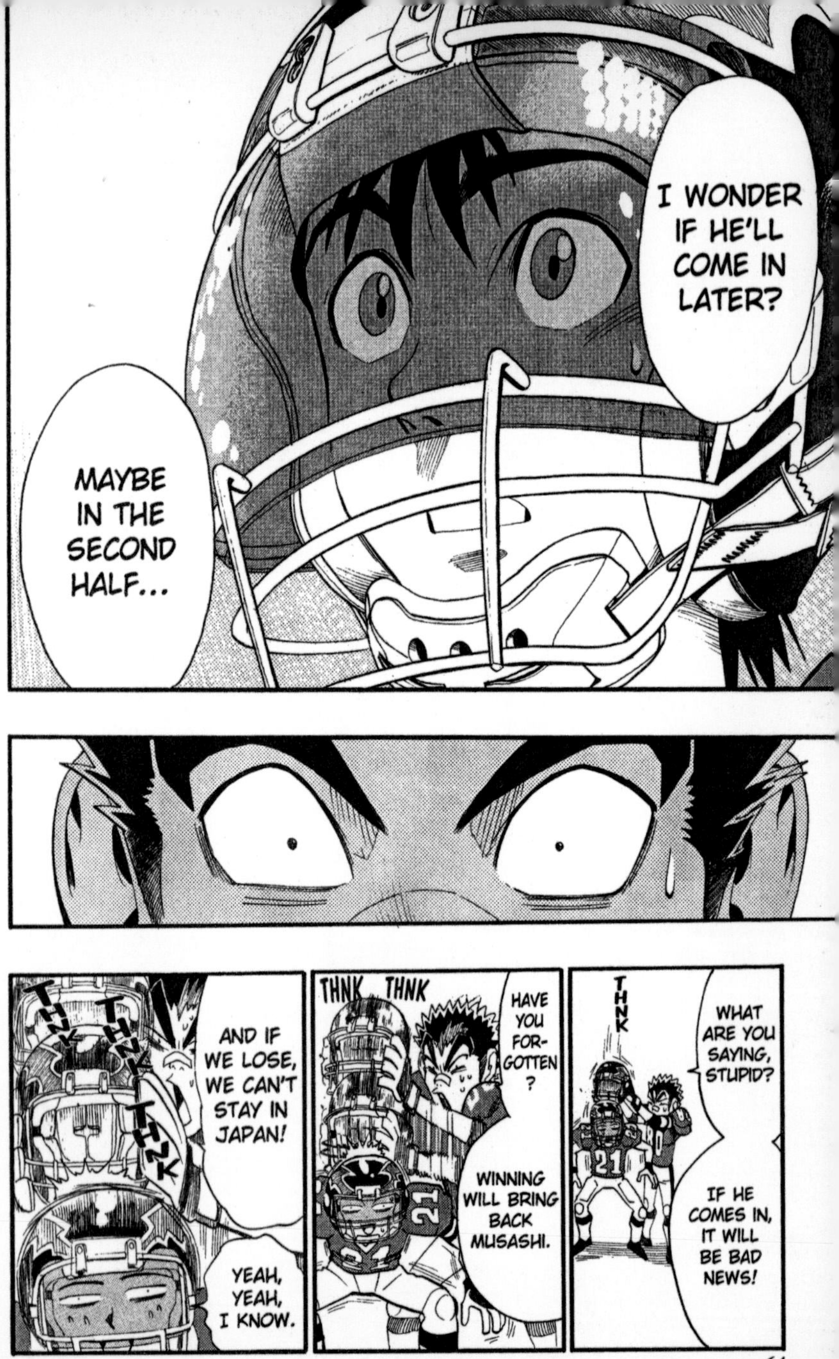
I WONDER IF HE'LL COME IN LATER?
MAYBE IN THE SECOND HALF...
THNK
WHAT ARE YOU SAYING, STUPID?
IF HE COMES IN, IT WILL BE BAD NEWS!
THNK THNK
HAVE YOU FOR-GOTTEN?
WINNING WILL BRING BACK MUSASHI.
THNK THNK THNK
AND IF WE LOSE, WE CAN'T STAY IN JAPAN!
YEAH, YEAH, I KNOW.

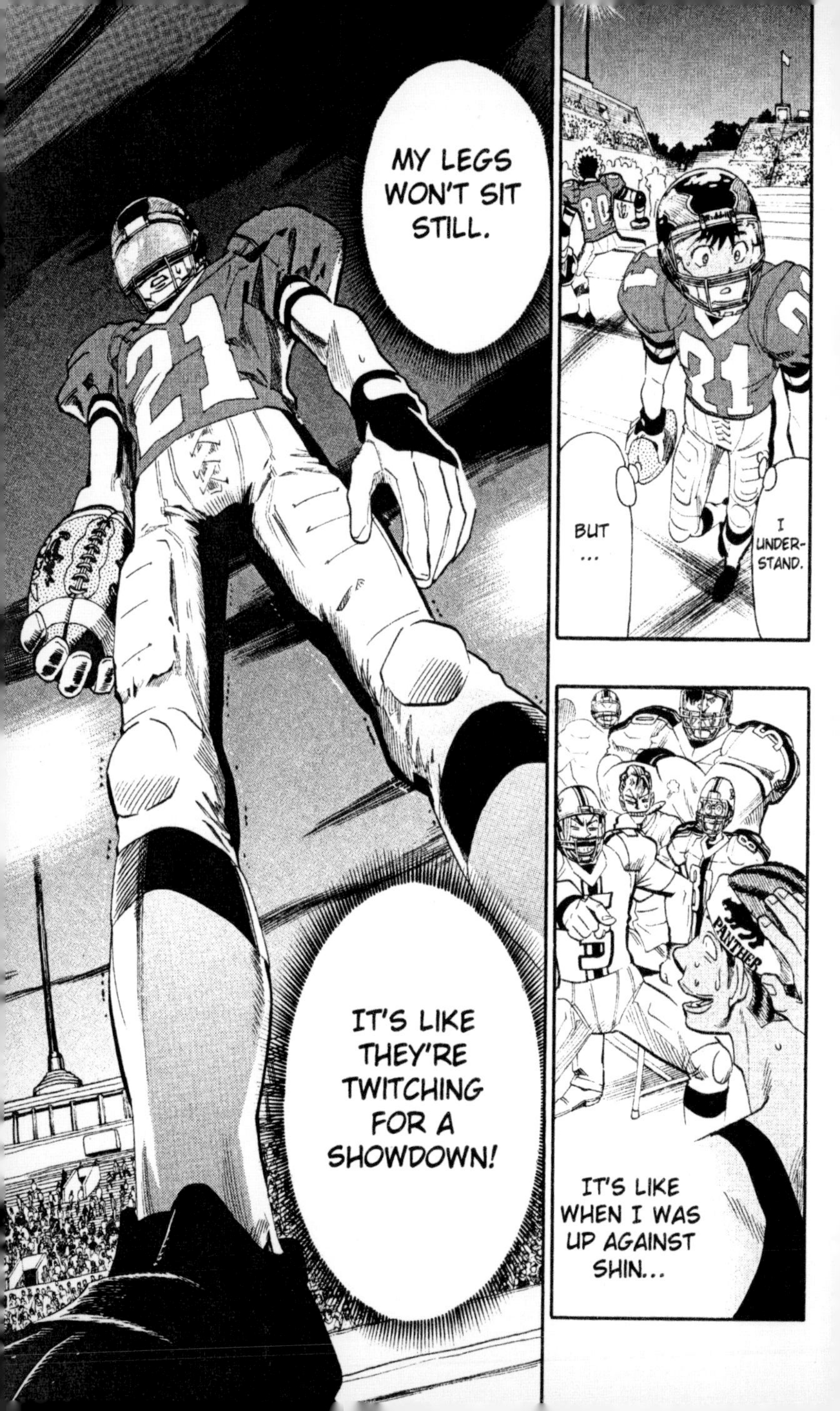
I UNDER-STAND.
BUT...
IT'S LIKE WHEN I WAS UP AGAINST SHIN...
MY LEGS WON'T SIT STILL.
IT'S LIKE THEY'RE TWITCHING FOR A SHOWDOWN!
PANTHER

Eyeshield 21 Survey Corner **Devil Bat 021**

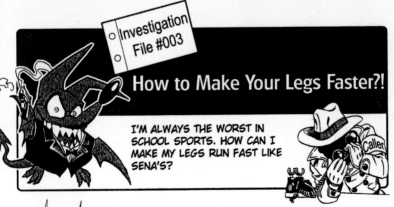

Investigation File #003

How to Make Your Legs Faster?!

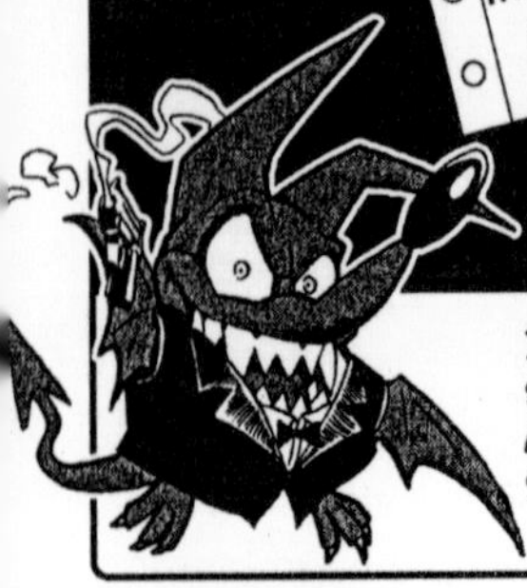

I'M ALWAYS THE WORST IN SCHOOL SPORTS. HOW CAN I MAKE MY LEGS RUN FAST LIKE SENA'S?

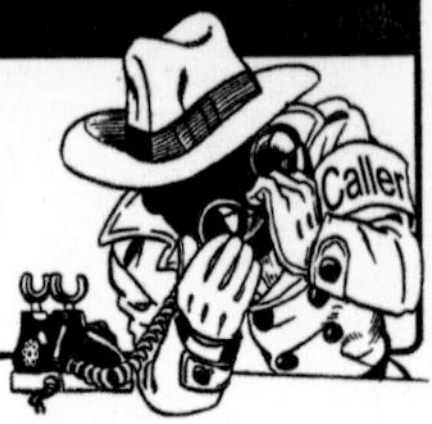
Caller

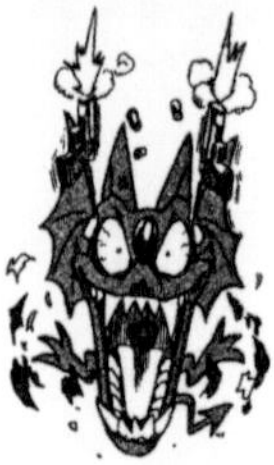

LIKE SENA WHEN HE WAS A GOPHER, YOU'VE GOT TO RUN! JUMPING ROPE AND DOING SQUATS ARE ALSO GOOD WAYS TO TRAIN YOUR LEGS!

AND YOU CAN USE A LADDER LIKE THE DEVIL BATS DO IN PRACTICE!

Ladder training

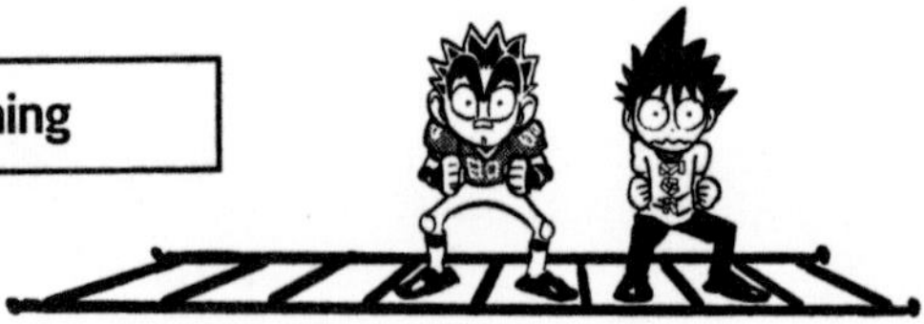

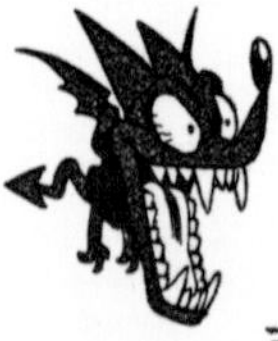

YOU'LL PROBABLY SAY YOU DON'T HAVE A ROPE LADDER, RIGHT? YOU CAN DRAW ONE ON THE PAVEMENT!

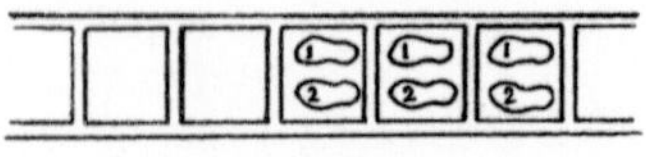
1
2
1
2
1
2

MARK TWO FEET FOR EACH STEP...

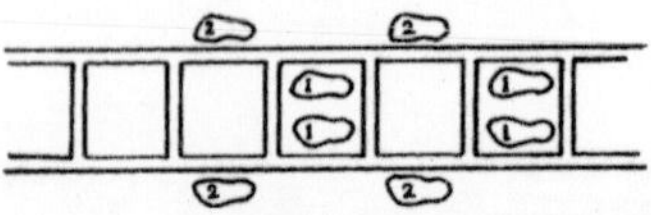
2
2
1
1
1
1
2
2

THEN ALTERNATE INSIDE AND OUTSIDE.

AND RUN LIKE HELL!

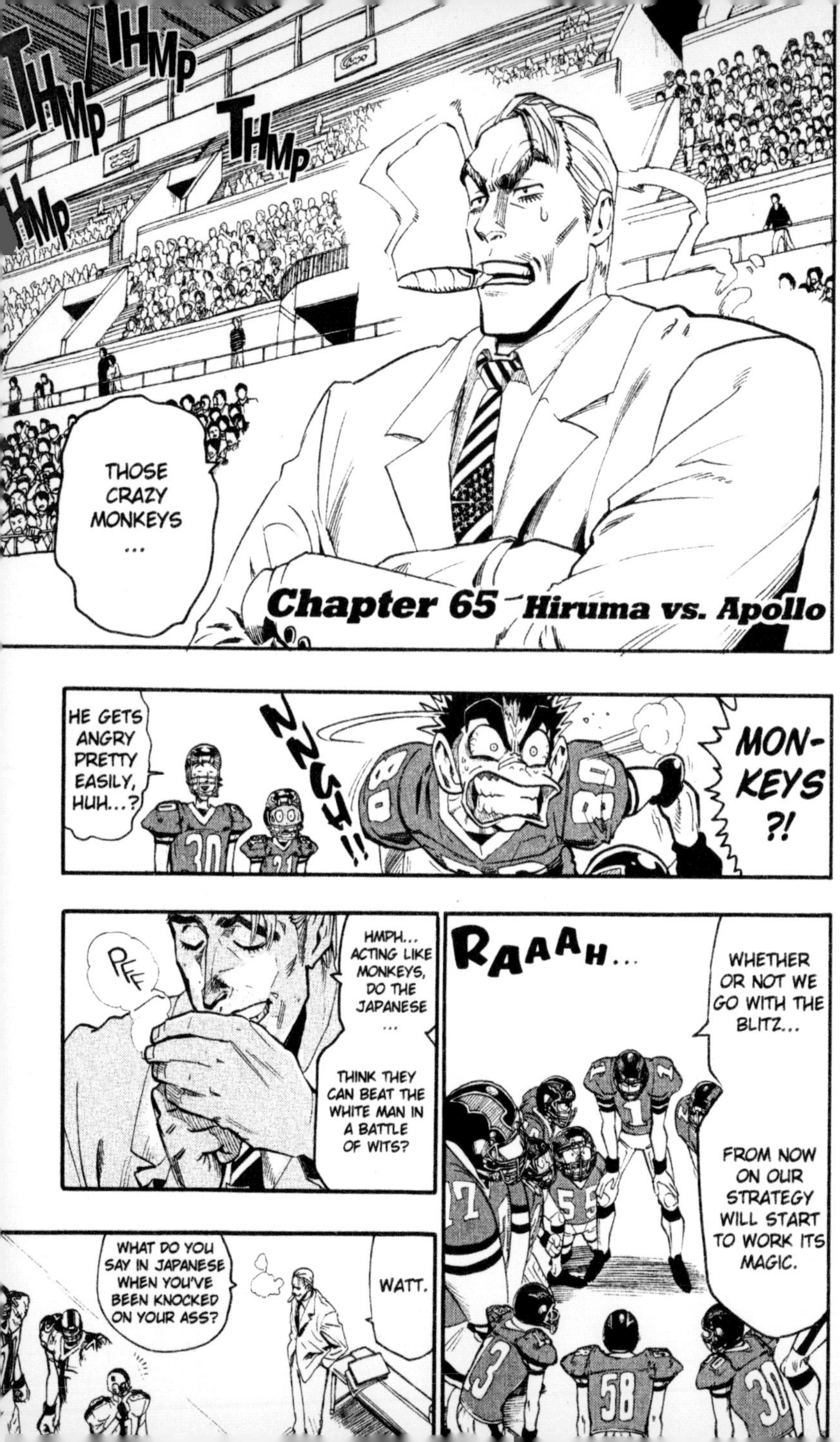
THMP
THMP
THMP
THMP
THOSE CRAZY MONKEYS...
Chapter 65 Hiruma vs. Apollo
MON-KEYS?!
NNSH!!
HE GETS ANGRY PRETTY EASILY, HUH...?
RAAAH...
WHETHER OR NOT WE GO WITH THE BLITZ...
FROM NOW ON OUR STRATEGY WILL START TO WORK ITS MAGIC.
HMPH... ACTING LIKE MONKEYS, DO THE JAPANESE...
THINK THEY CAN BEAT THE WHITE MAN IN A BATTLE OF WITS?
PFFF
WATT.
WHAT DO YOU SAY IN JAPANESE WHEN YOU'VE BEEN KNOCKED ON YOUR ASS?

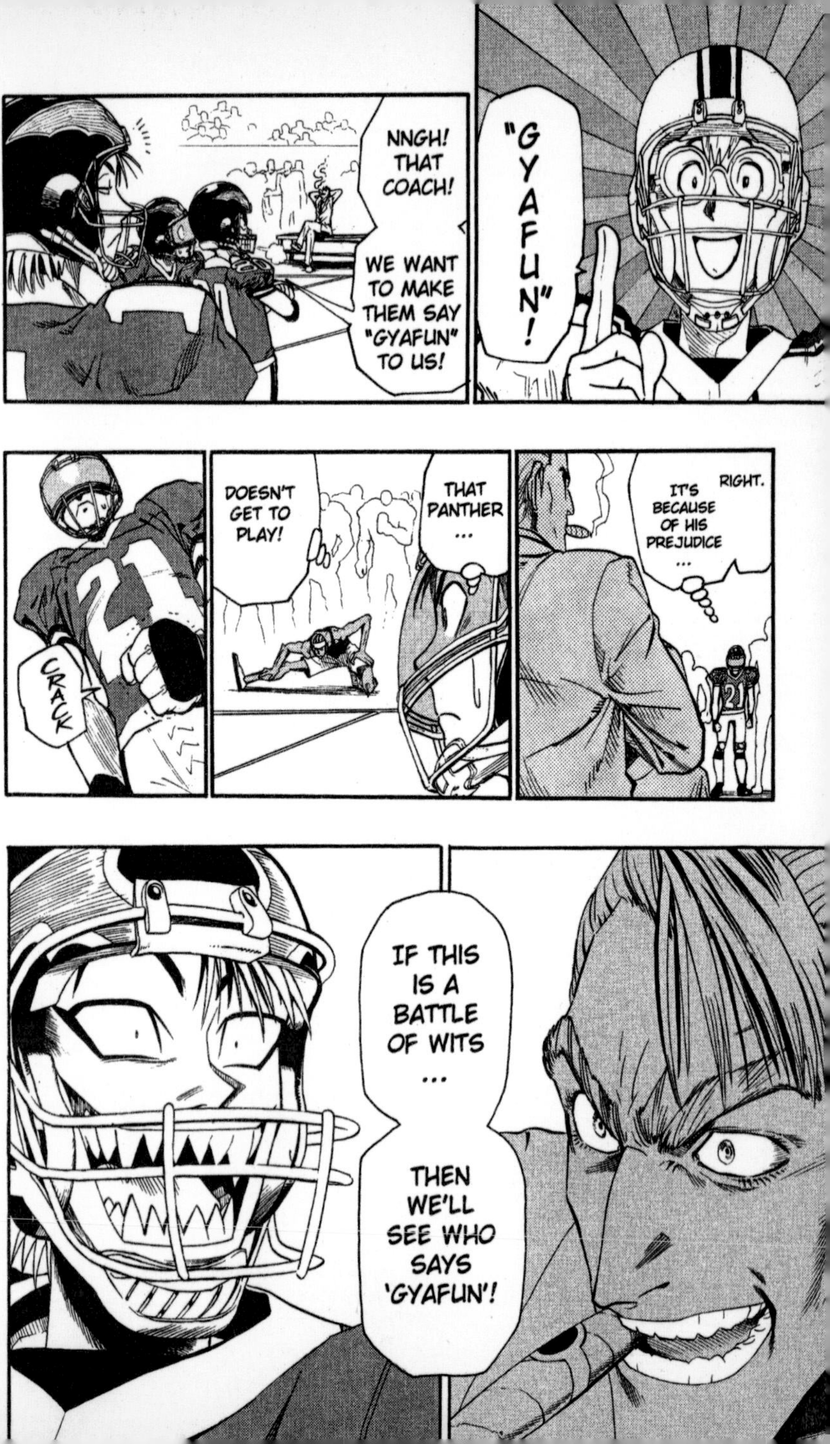
"GYAFUN"!
NNGH! THAT COACH!
WE WANT TO MAKE THEM SAY "GYAFUN" TO US!
RIGHT.
IT'S BECAUSE OF HIS PREJUDICE ...
THAT PANTHER ...
DOESN'T GET TO PLAY!
CRACK
IF THIS IS A BATTLE OF WITS ...
THEN WE'LL SEE WHO SAYS 'GYAFUN'!

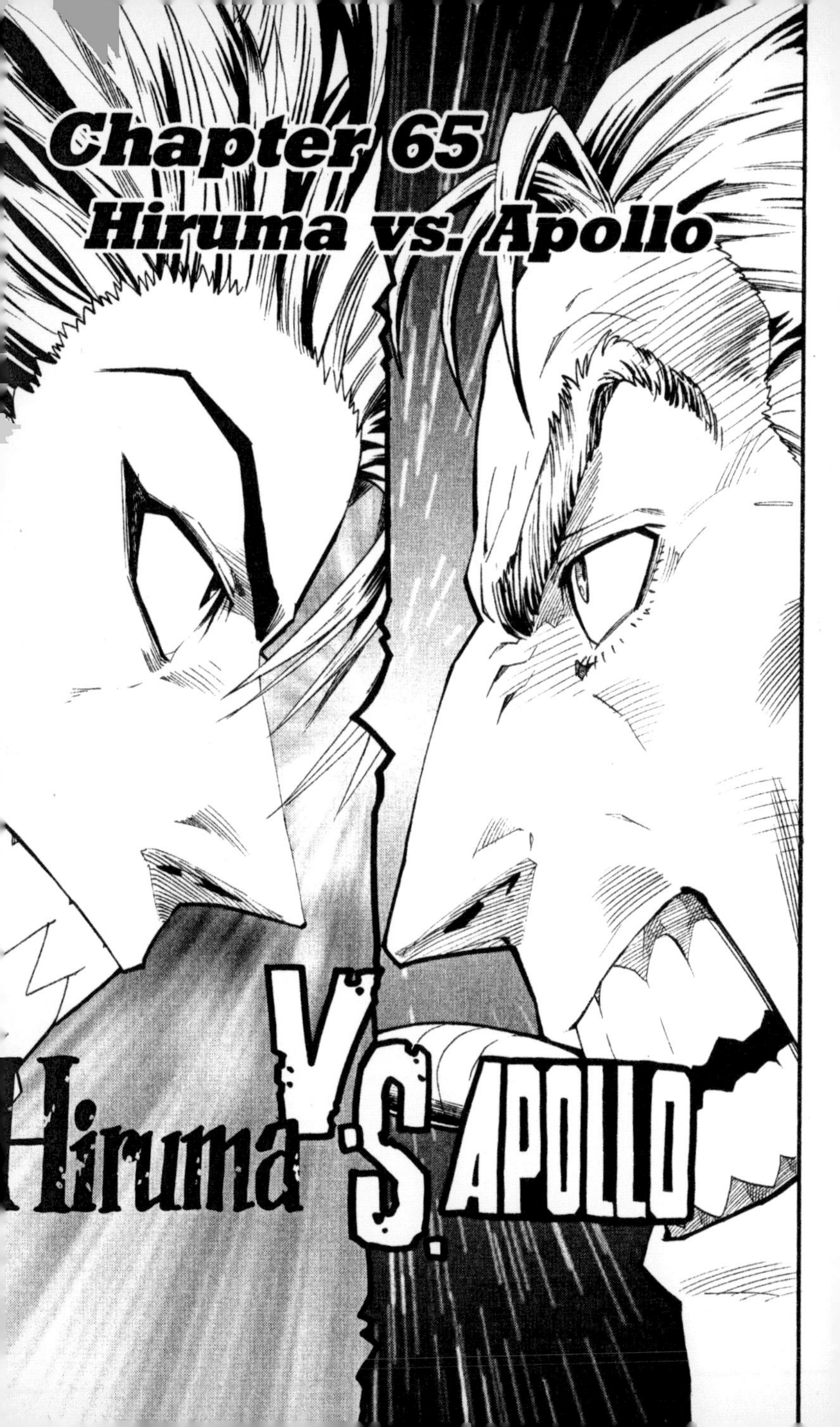
Chapter 65
Hiruma vs. Apollo
Hiruma V.S. APOLLO

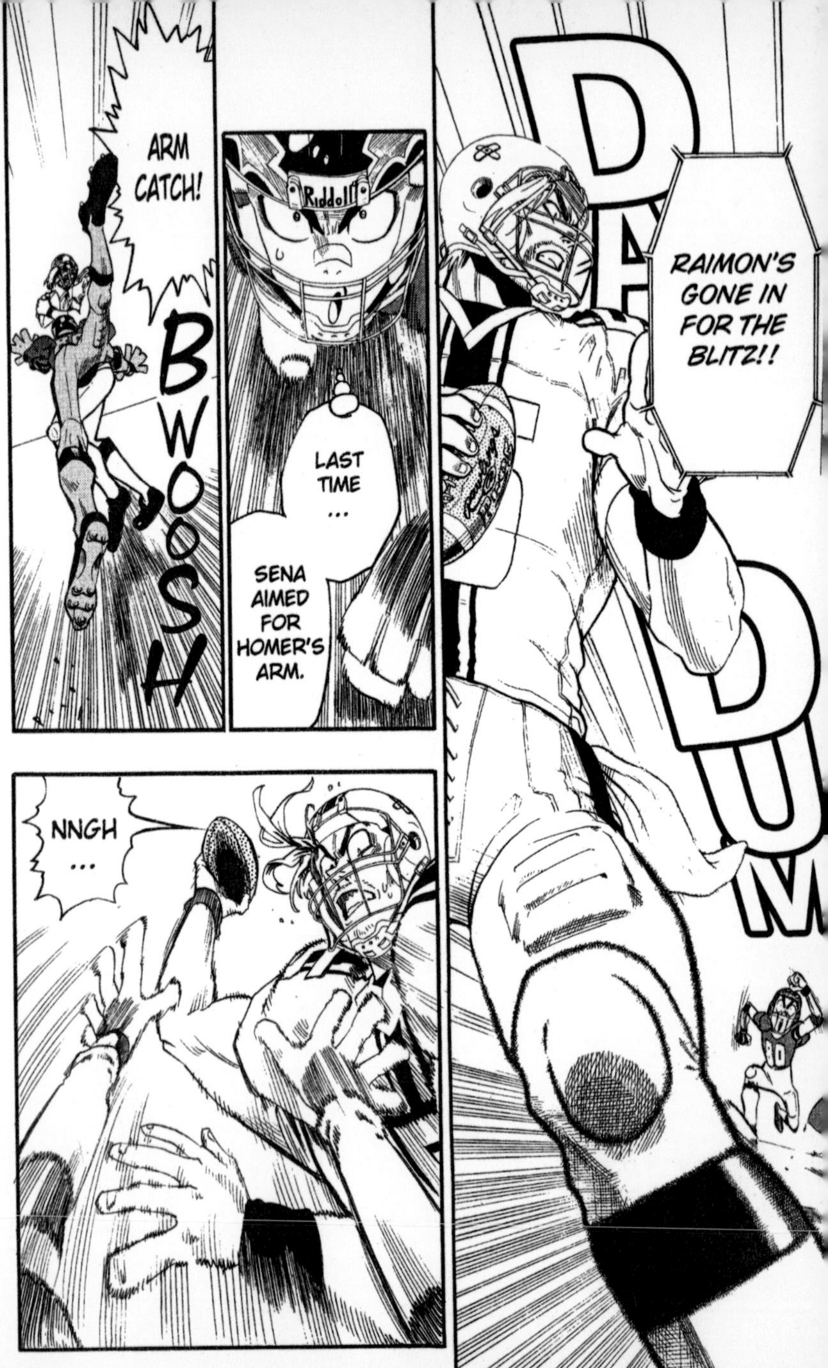
RAIMON'S GONE IN FOR THE BLITZ!!
LAST TIME...
SENA AIMED FOR HOMER'S ARM.
ARM CATCH!
BWOOSH
NNGH...

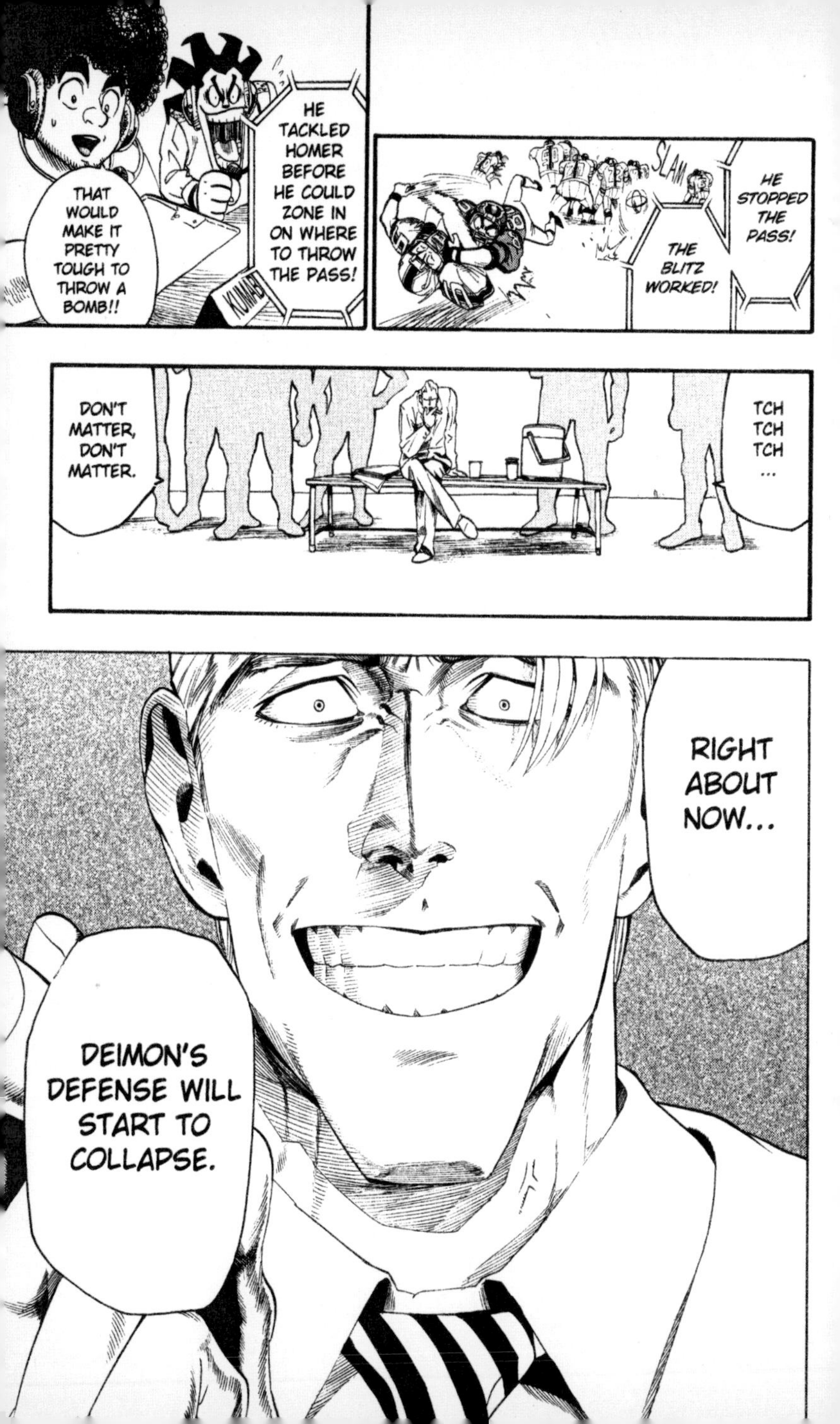
SLAM
HE STOPPED THE PASS!
THE BLITZ WORKED!
HE TACKLED HOMER BEFORE HE COULD ZONE IN ON WHERE TO THROW THE PASS!
THAT WOULD MAKE IT PRETTY TOUGH TO THROW A BOMB!!
TCH TCH TCH ...
DON'T MATTER, DON'T MATTER.
RIGHT ABOUT NOW...
DEIMON'S DEFENSE WILL START TO COLLAPSE.

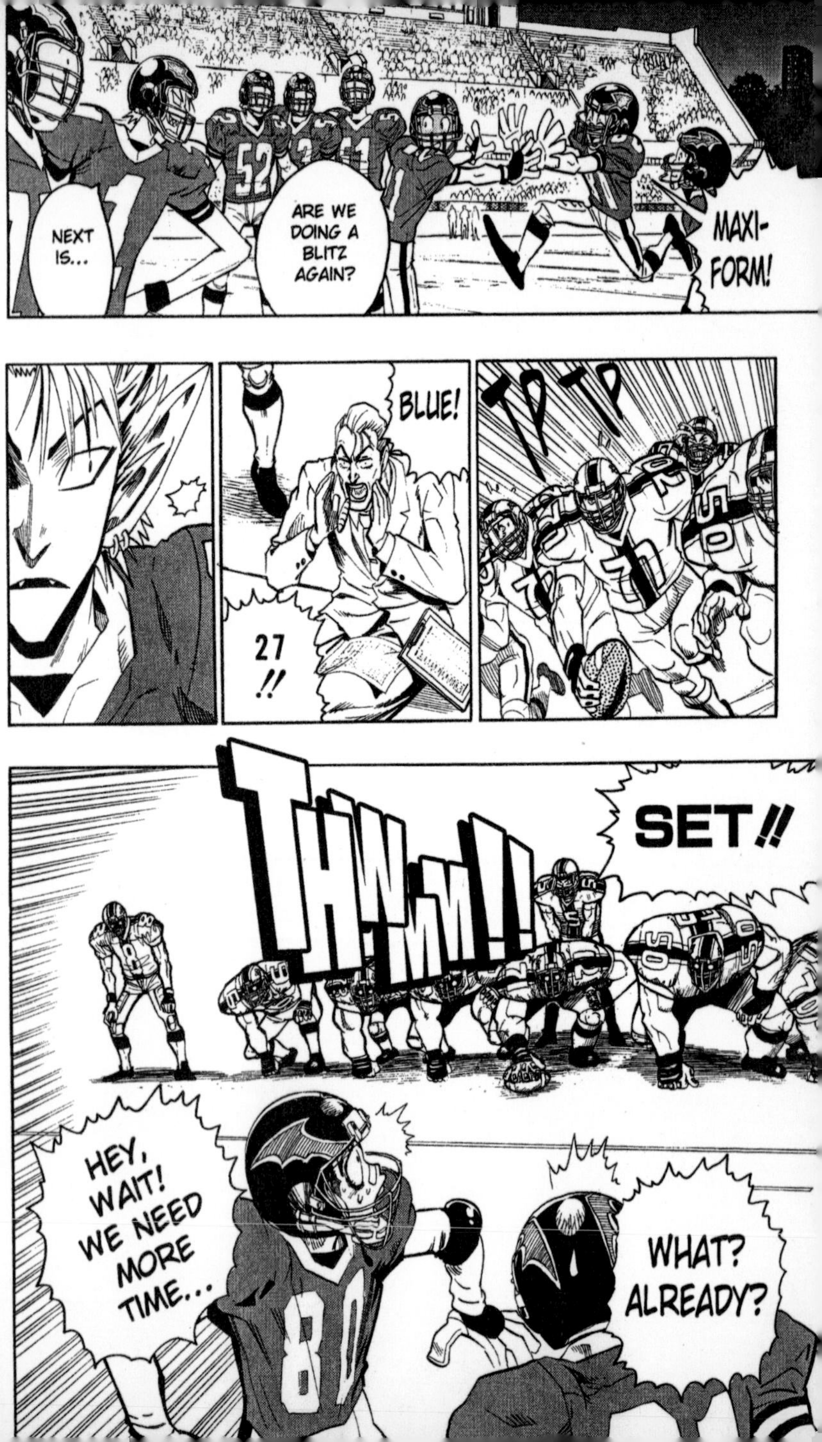
MAXI-FORM!
ARE WE DOING A BLITZ AGAIN?
NEXT IS...
TP TP
BLUE!
27!!
SET!!
THMMM!!
WHAT? ALREADY?
HEY, WAIT! WE NEED MORE TIME...

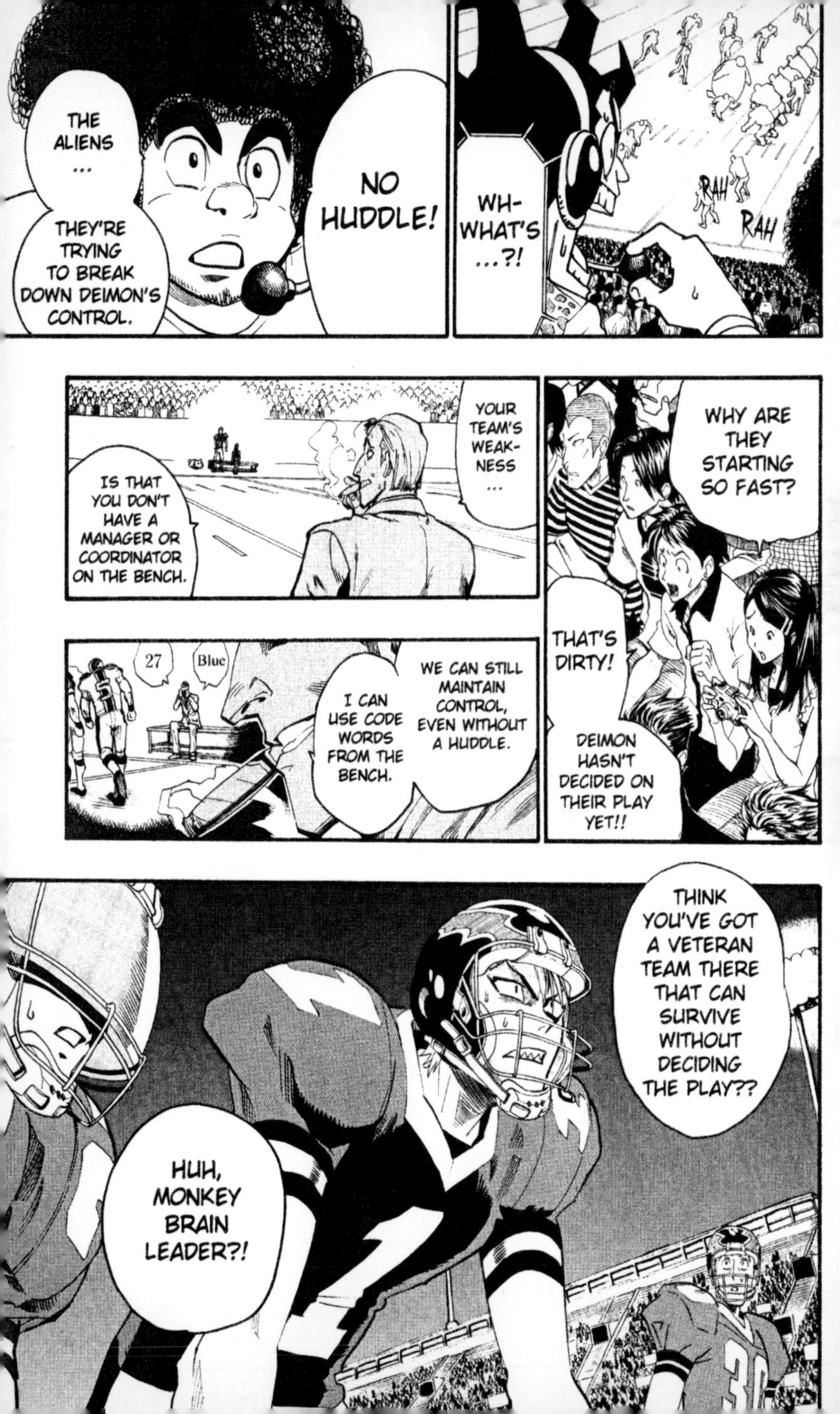
RAH
RAH
WH-WHAT'S ...?!
NO HUDDLE!
THE ALIENS ...
THEY'RE TRYING TO BREAK DOWN DEIMON'S CONTROL.
WHY ARE THEY STARTING SO FAST?
THAT'S DIRTY!
DEIMON HASN'T DECIDED ON THEIR PLAY YET!!
YOUR TEAM'S WEAK-NESS ...
IS THAT YOU DON'T HAVE A MANAGER OR COORDINATOR ON THE BENCH.
WE CAN STILL MAINTAIN CONTROL, EVEN WITHOUT A HUDDLE.
I CAN USE CODE WORDS FROM THE BENCH.
Blue
27
THINK YOU'VE GOT A VETERAN TEAM THERE THAT CAN SURVIVE WITHOUT DECIDING THE PLAY??
HUH, MONKEY BRAIN LEADER?!

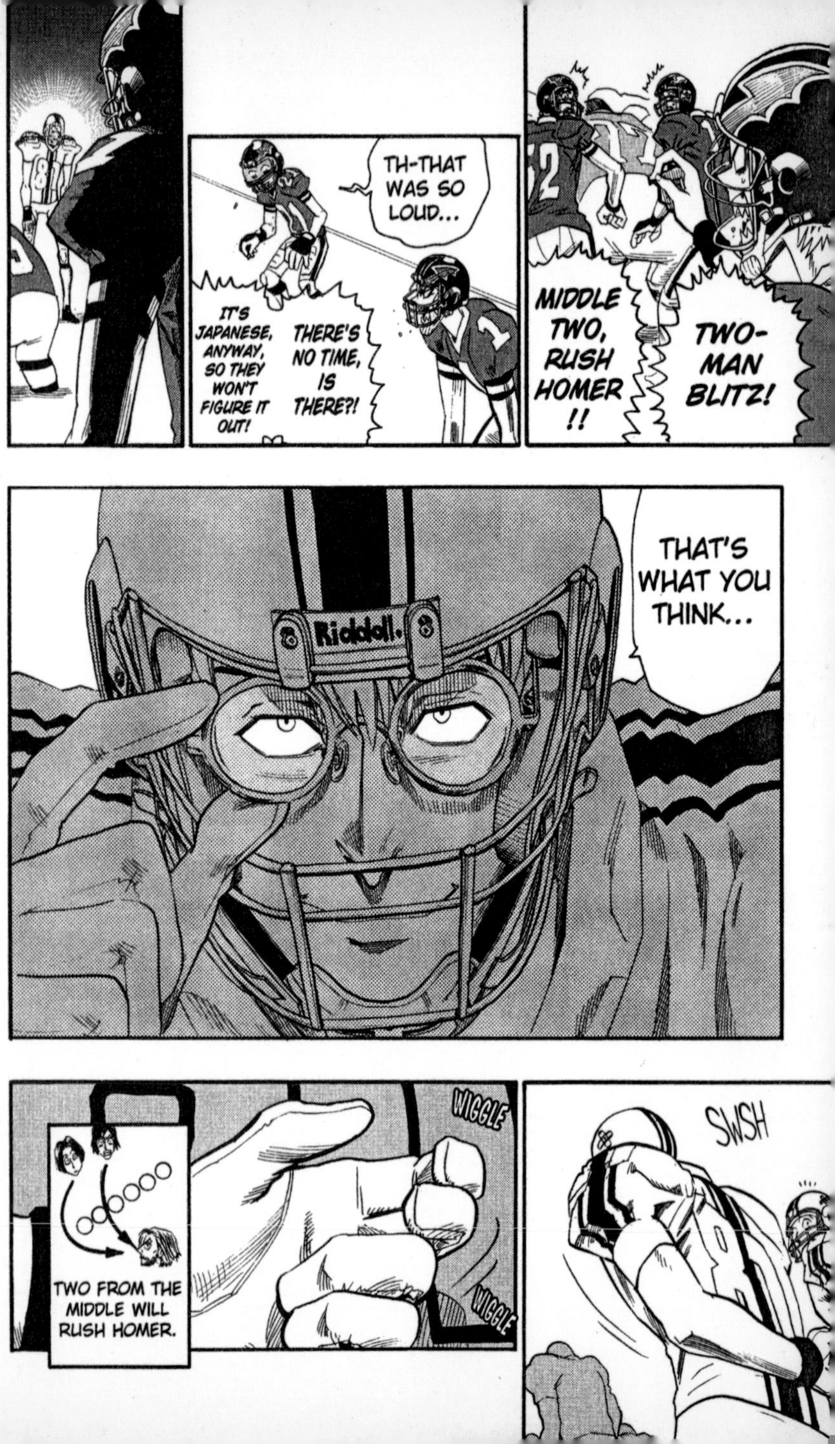
TWO-MAN BLITZ!
MIDDLE TWO, RUSH HOMER!!
TH-THAT WAS SO LOUD...
THERE'S NO TIME, IS THERE?!
IT'S JAPANESE, ANYWAY, SO THEY WON'T FIGURE IT OUT!
THAT'S WHAT YOU THINK...
Riddell
SWSH
WIGGLE
WIGGLE
TWO FROM THE MIDDLE WILL RUSH HOMER.

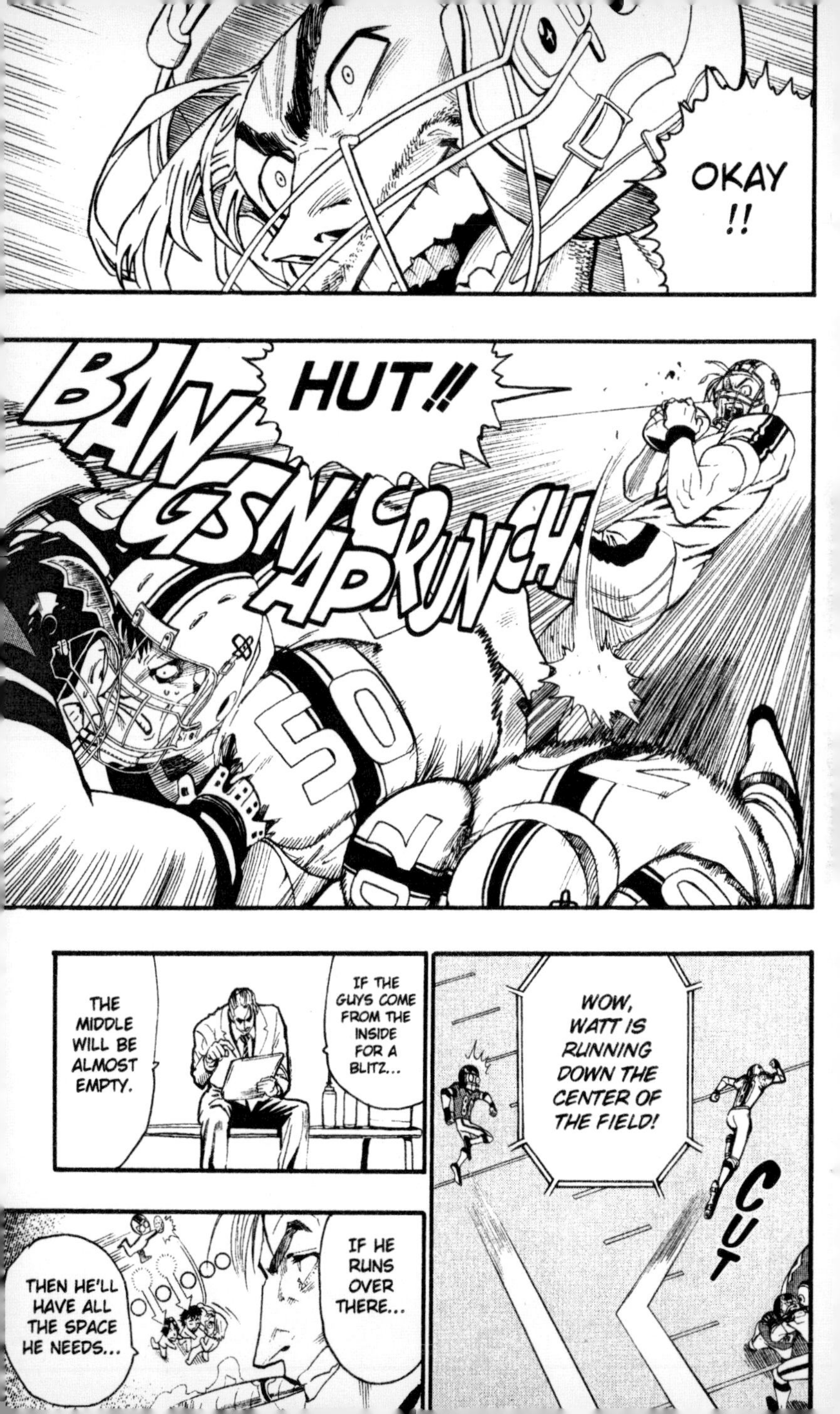
OKAY !!
HUT!!
BANG
SNAP
CRUNCH
WOW, WATT IS RUNNING DOWN THE CENTER OF THE FIELD!
CUT
IF THE GUYS COME FROM THE INSIDE FOR A BLITZ...
THE MIDDLE WILL BE ALMOST EMPTY.
IF HE RUNS OVER THERE...
THEN HE'LL HAVE ALL THE SPACE HE NEEDS...

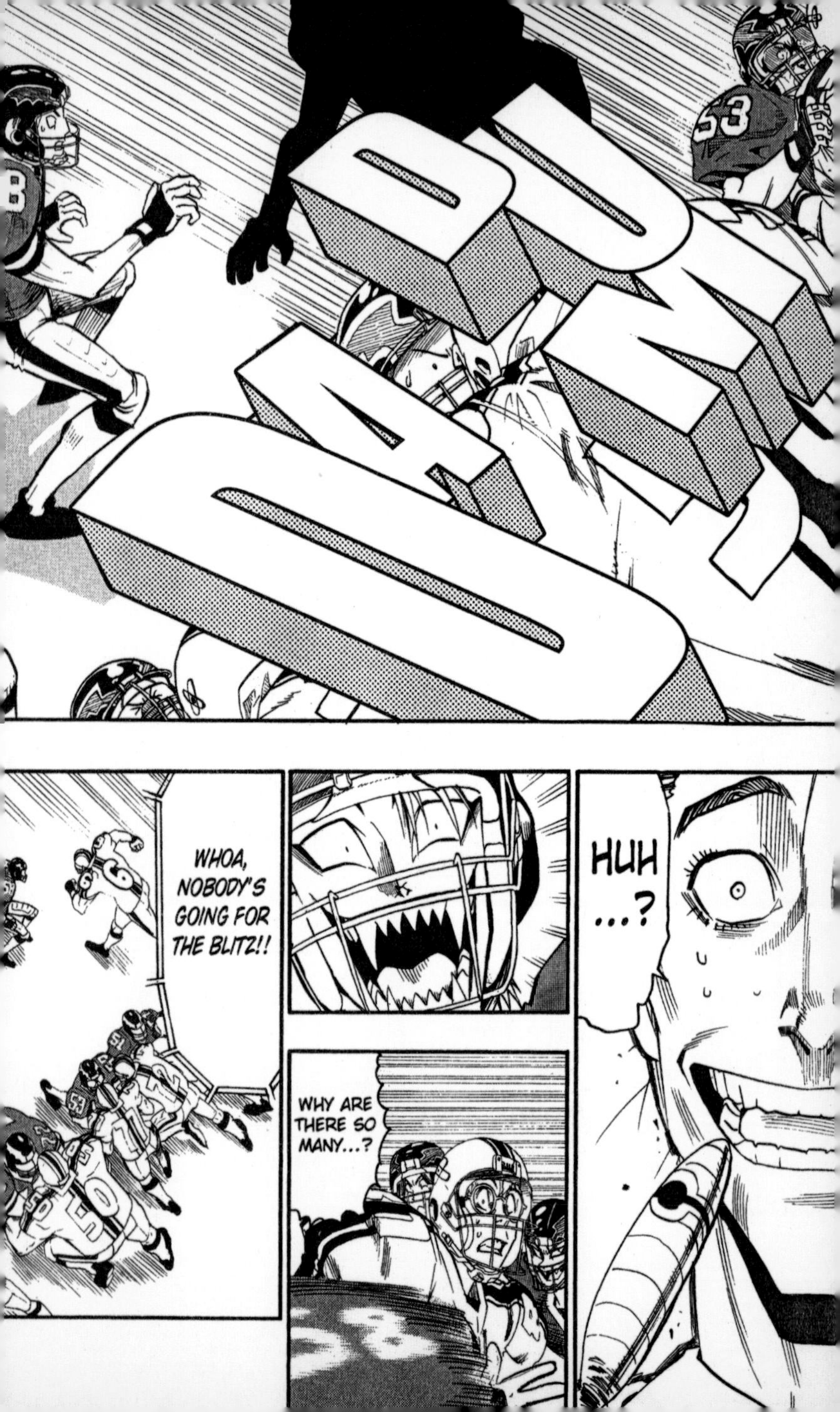
HUH ...?
WHY ARE THERE SO MANY...?
WHOA, NOBODY'S GOING FOR THE BLITZ!!

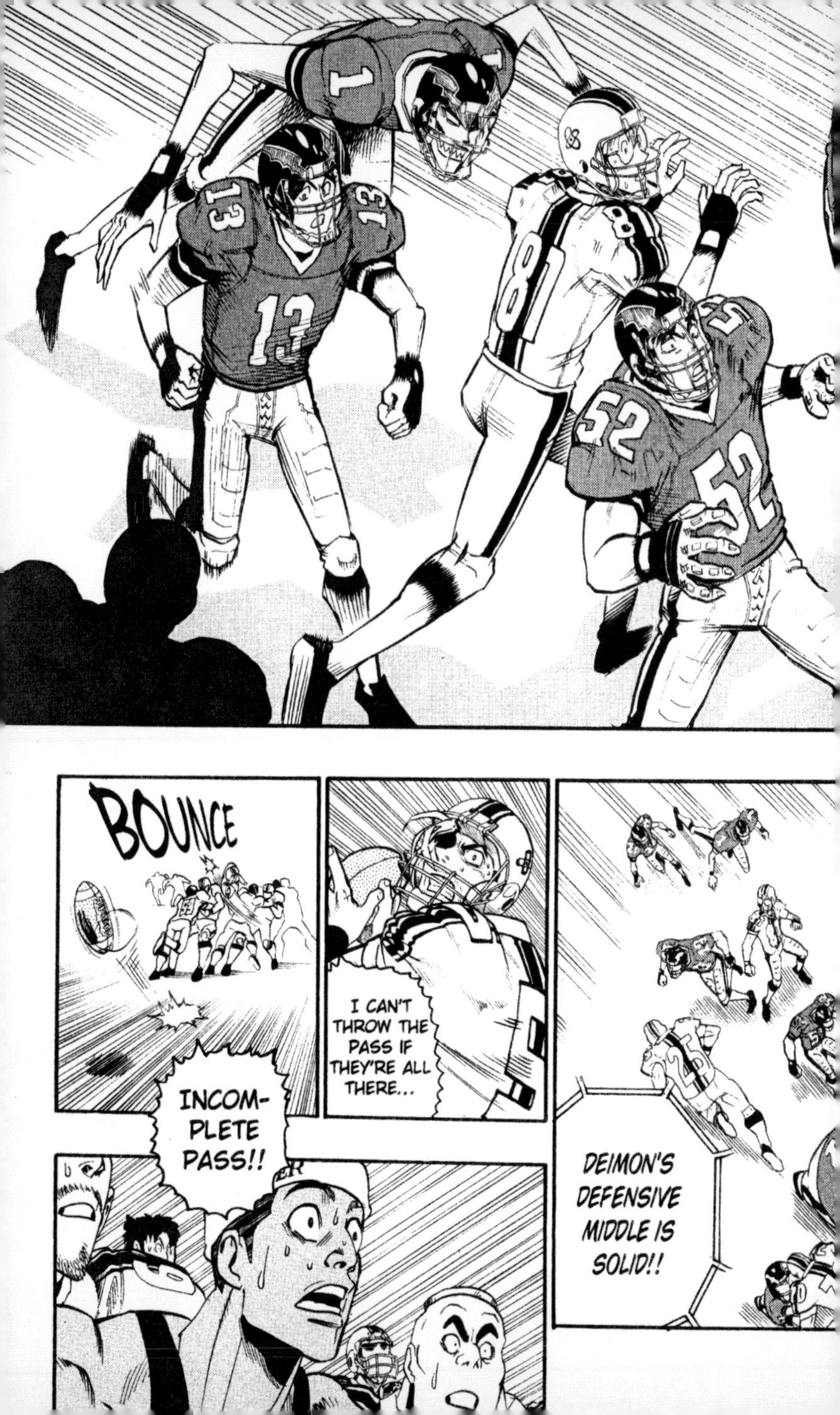
DEIMON'S DEFENSIVE MIDDLE IS SOLID!!
I CAN'T THROW THE PASS IF THEY'RE ALL THERE...
BOUNCE
INCOMPLETE PASS!!

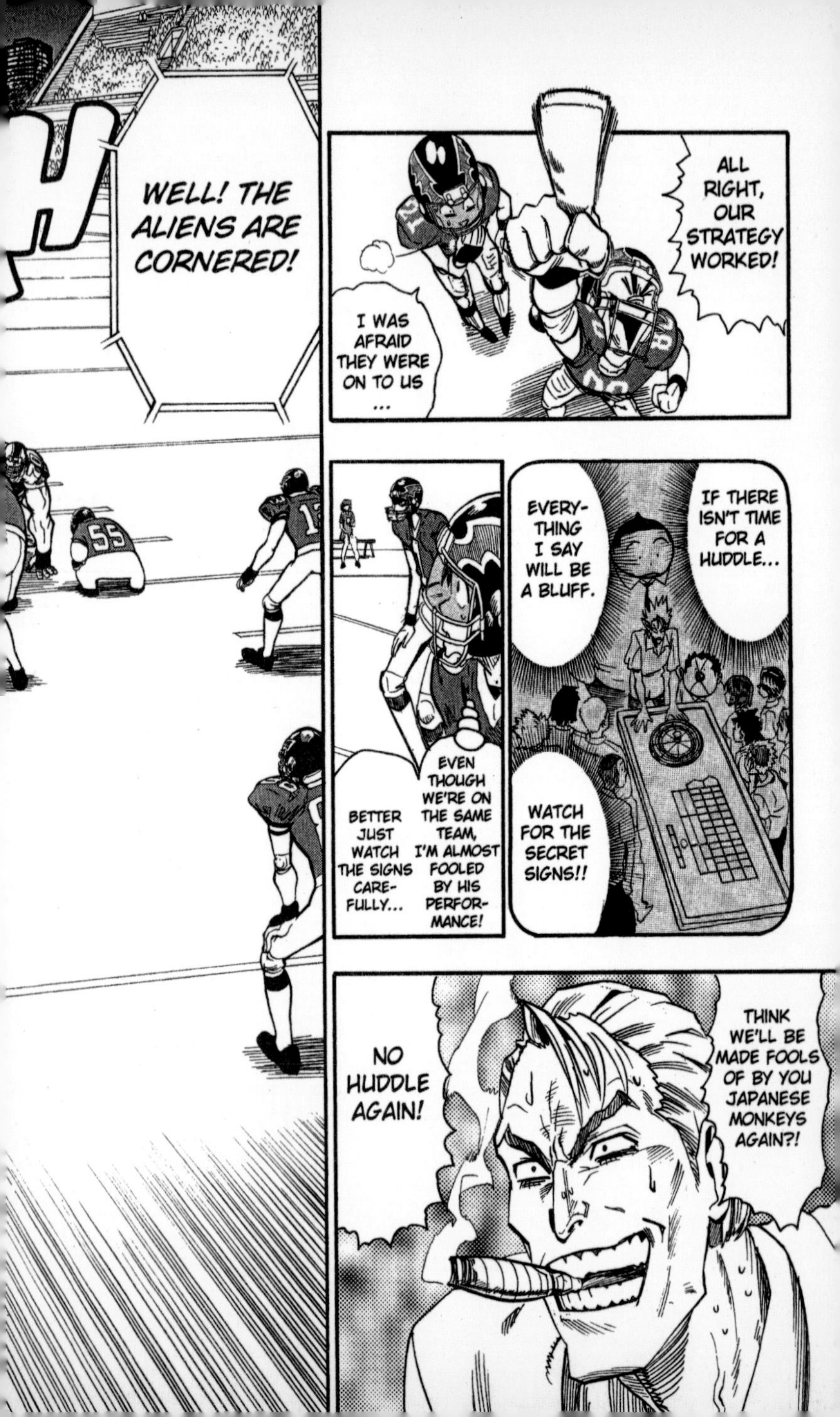
ALL RIGHT, OUR STRATEGY WORKED!
I WAS AFRAID THEY WERE ON TO US ...
IF THERE ISN'T TIME FOR A HUDDLE...
EVERY-THING I SAY WILL BE A BLUFF.
WATCH FOR THE SECRET SIGNS!!
EVEN THOUGH WE'RE ON THE SAME TEAM, I'M ALMOST FOOLED BY HIS PERFOR-MANCE!
BETTER JUST WATCH THE SIGNS CARE-FULLY...
THINK WE'LL BE MADE FOOLS OF BY YOU JAPANESE MONKEYS AGAIN?!
NO HUDDLE AGAIN!
WELL! THE ALIENS ARE CORNERED!

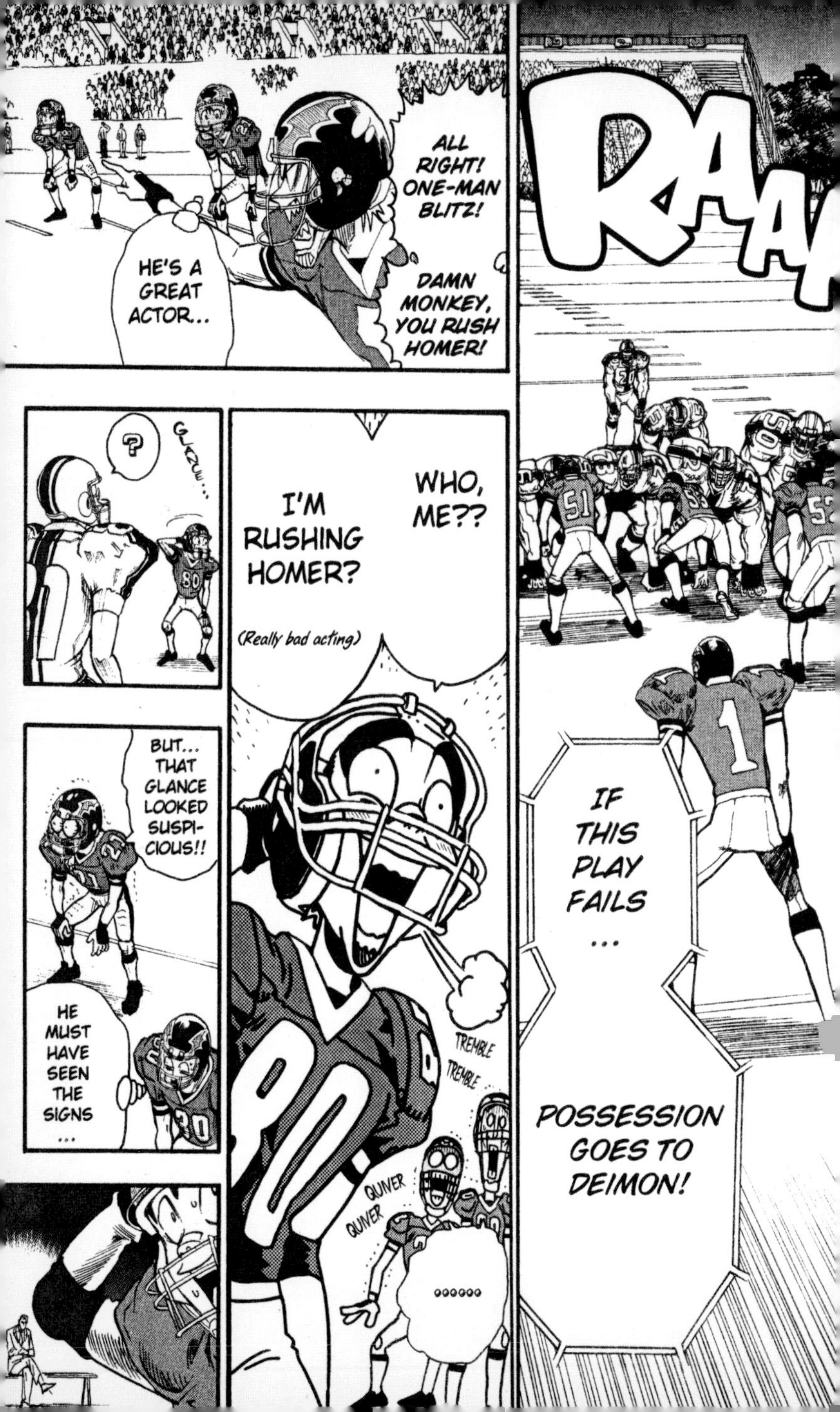

RAAA
IF THIS PLAY FAILS...
POSSESSION GOES TO DEIMON!
ALL RIGHT! ONE-MAN BLITZ!
DAMN MONKEY, YOU RUSH HOMER!
HE'S A GREAT ACTOR...
WHO, ME??
I'M RUSHING HOMER?
(Really bad acting)
TREMBLE
TREMBLE
QUIVER
QUIVER
......
?
GLANCE...
BUT... THAT GLANCE LOOKED SUSPICIOUS!!
HE MUST HAVE SEEN THE SIGNS...

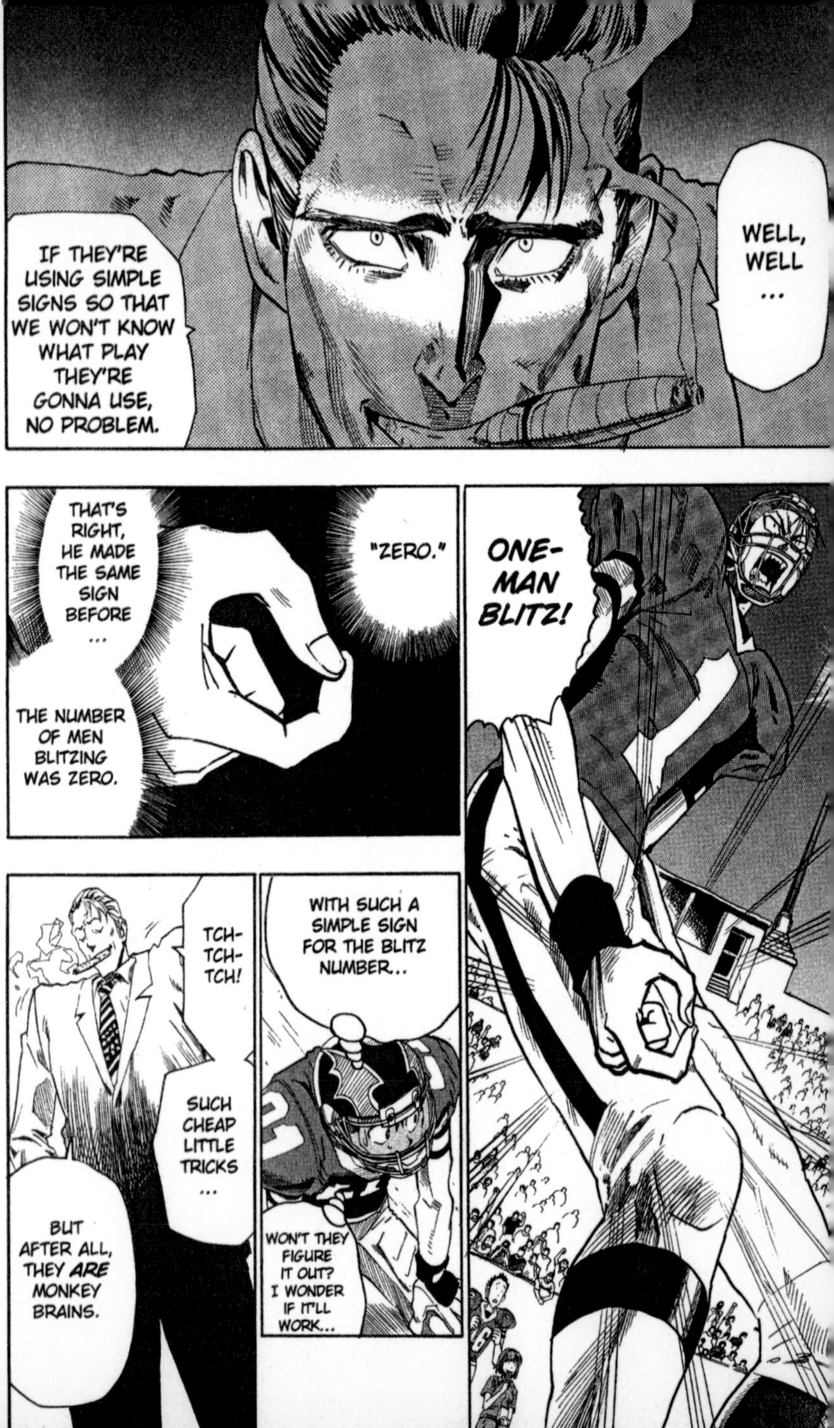
WELL, WELL ...
IF THEY'RE USING SIMPLE SIGNS SO THAT WE WON'T KNOW WHAT PLAY THEY'RE GONNA USE, NO PROBLEM.
ONE-MAN BLITZ!
"ZERO."
THAT'S RIGHT, HE MADE THE SAME SIGN BEFORE ...
THE NUMBER OF MEN BLITZING WAS ZERO.
WITH SUCH A SIMPLE SIGN FOR THE BLITZ NUMBER...
WON'T THEY FIGURE IT OUT? I WONDER IF IT'LL WORK...
TCH-TCH-TCH!
SUCH CHEAP LITTLE TRICKS ...
BUT AFTER ALL, THEY *ARE* MONKEY BRAINS.

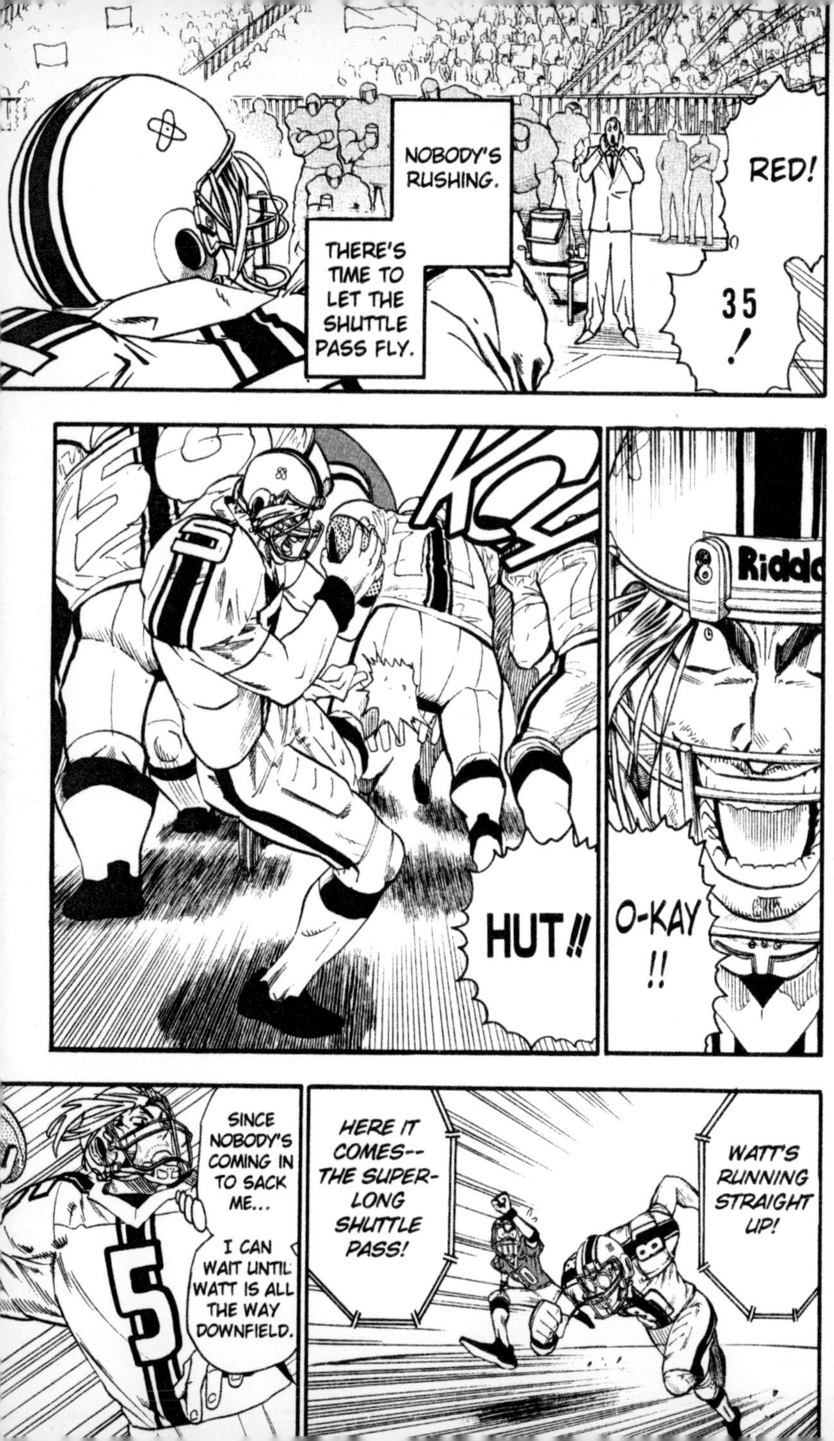
RED!
35!
NOBODY'S RUSHING.
THERE'S TIME TO LET THE SHUTTLE PASS FLY.
O-KAY!!
HUT!!
WATT'S RUNNING STRAIGHT UP!
HERE IT COMES-- THE SUPER-LONG SHUTTLE PASS!
SINCE NOBODY'S COMING IN TO SACK ME...
I CAN WAIT UNTIL WATT IS ALL THE WAY DOWNFIELD.

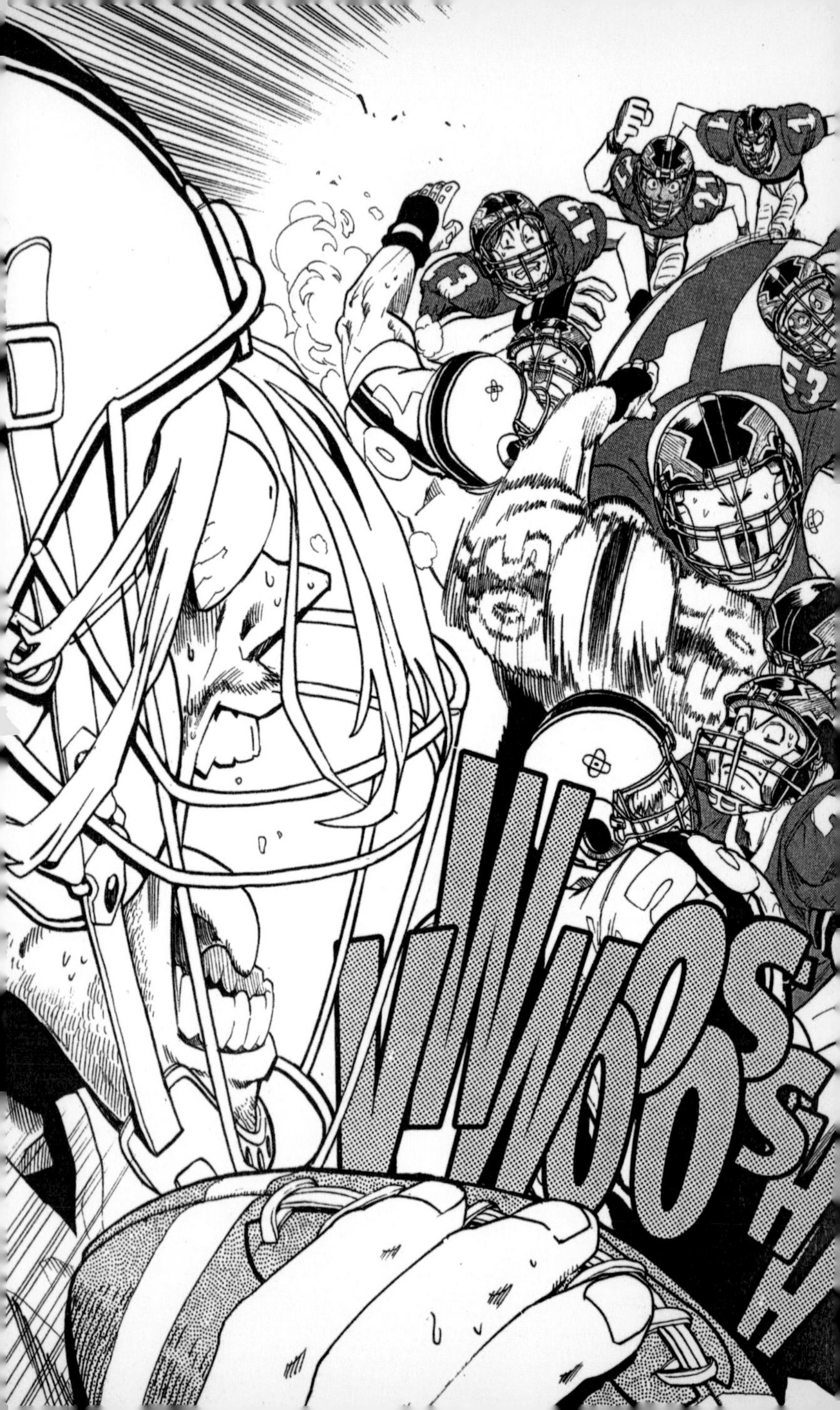
WHOOSH

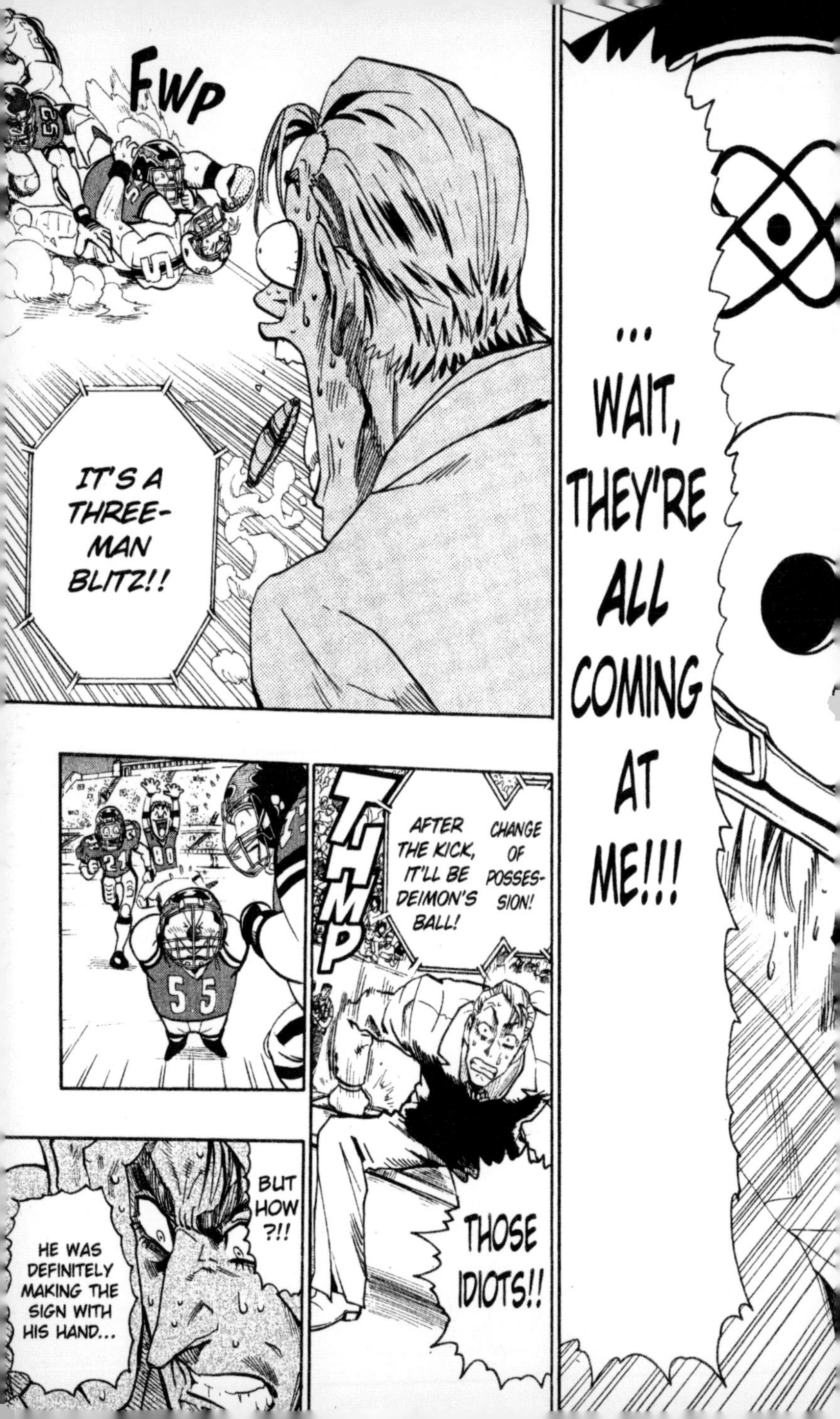
... WAIT, THEY'RE ALL COMING AT ME!!!
FWP
IT'S A THREE-MAN BLITZ!!
THMP
CHANGE OF POSSESSION!
AFTER THE KICK, IT'LL BE DEIMON'S BALL!
THOSE IDIOTS!!
BUT HOW?!!
HE WAS DEFINITELY MAKING THE SIGN WITH HIS HAND...

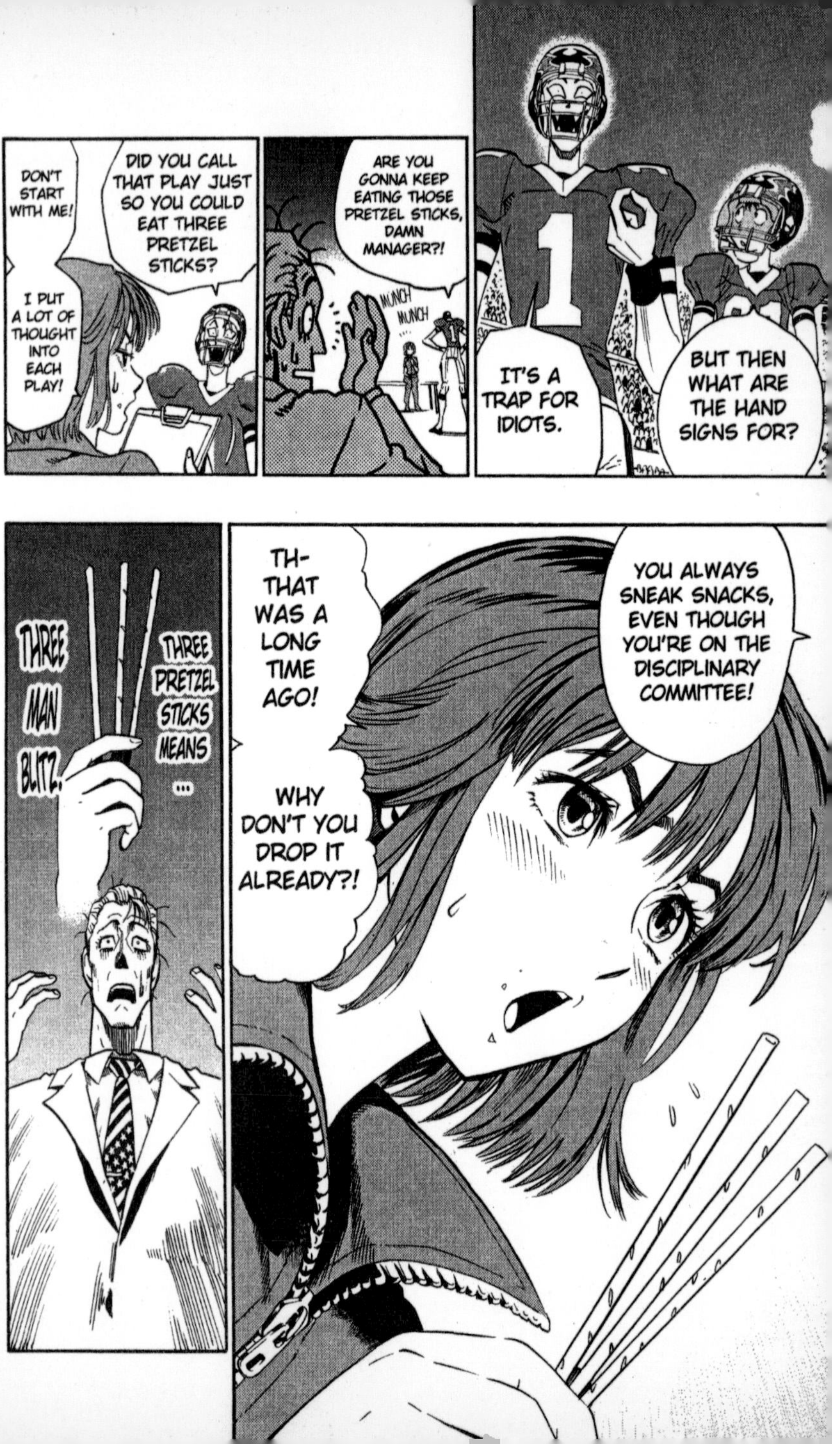
BUT THEN WHAT ARE THE HAND SIGNS FOR?
IT'S A TRAP FOR IDIOTS.
ARE YOU GONNA KEEP EATING THOSE PRETZEL STICKS, DAMN MANAGER?!
MUNCH MUNCH
DID YOU CALL THAT PLAY JUST SO YOU COULD EAT THREE PRETZEL STICKS?
DON'T START WITH ME!
I PUT A LOT OF THOUGHT INTO EACH PLAY!
YOU ALWAYS SNEAK SNACKS, EVEN THOUGH YOU'RE ON THE DISCIPLINARY COMMITTEE!
TH-THAT WAS A LONG TIME AGO!
WHY DON'T YOU DROP IT ALREADY?!
THREE PRETZEL STICKS MEANS...
THREE MAN BLITZ.

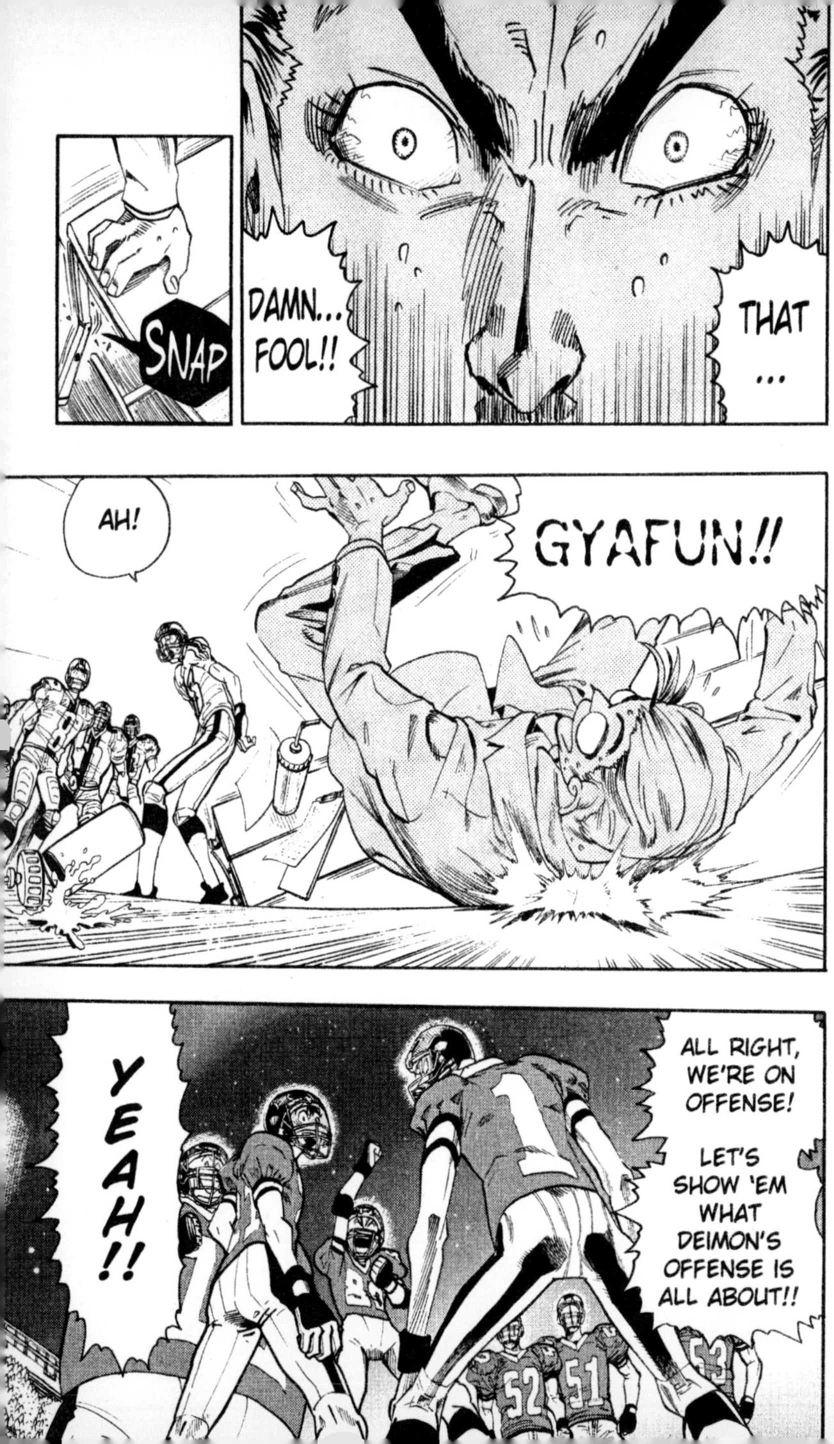
THAT ...
DAMN... FOOL!!
SNAP
GYAFUN!!
AH!
ALL RIGHT, WE'RE ON OFFENSE!
LET'S SHOW 'EM WHAT DEIMON'S OFFENSE IS ALL ABOUT!!
YEAH!!

Eyeshield 21 Survey Corner **Devil Bat 021**

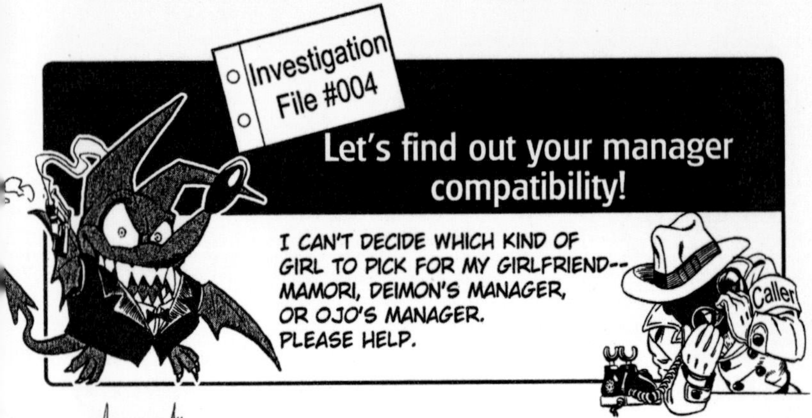
Investigation File #004
Let's find out your manager compatibility!
I CAN'T DECIDE WHICH KIND OF GIRL TO PICK FOR MY GIRLFRIEND--MAMORI, DEIMON'S MANAGER, OR OJO'S MANAGER. PLEASE HELP.
Caller

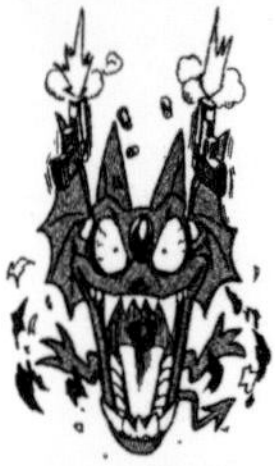

WHAAAT??!!
SEE FOR YOURSELF ON THE DIAGNOSTIC CHART BELOW!!

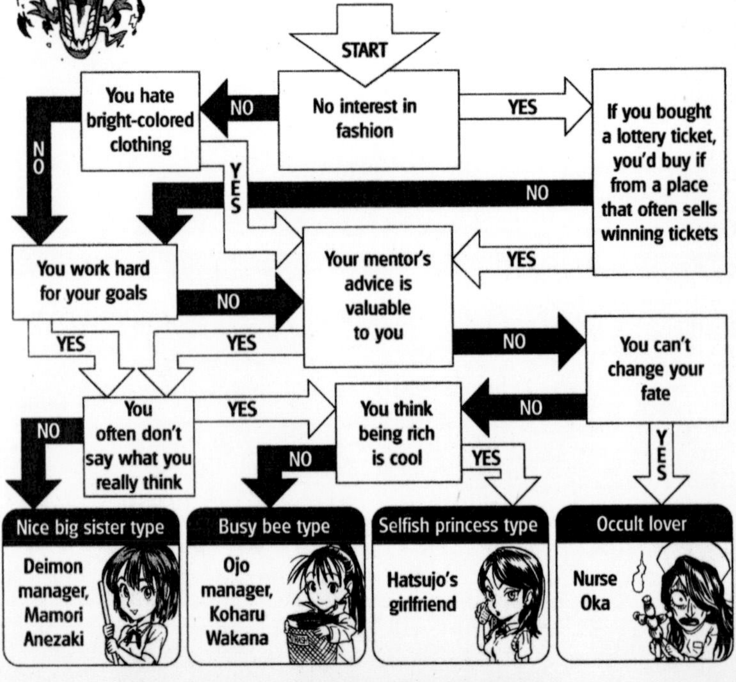
START
No interest in fashion
YES
If you bought a lottery ticket, you'd buy if from a place that often sells winning tickets
NO
You hate bright-colored clothing
NO
YES
NO
YES
You work hard for your goals
NO
YES
Your mentor's advice is valuable to you
YES
NO
You can't change your fate
NO
YES
You often don't say what you really think
YES
NO
You think being rich is cool
NO
YES
Nice big sister type
Deimon manager, Mamori Anezaki
Busy bee type
Ojo manager, Koharu Wakana
TRASH
Selfish princess type
Hatsujo's girlfriend
Occult lover
Nurse Oka

WHAT TYPE ARE YOU COMPATIBLE WITH...?

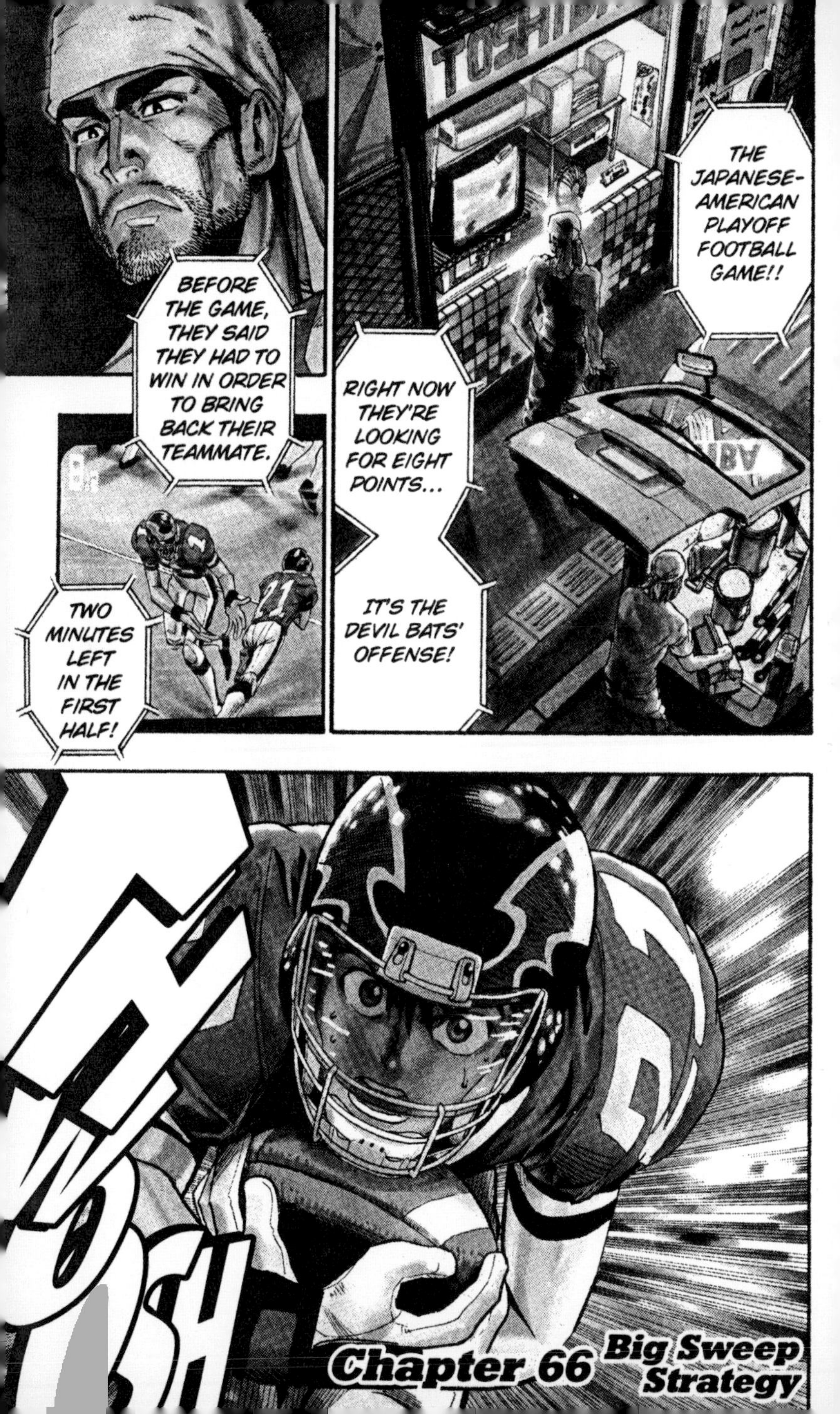
THE JAPANESE-AMERICAN PLAYOFF FOOTBALL GAME!!
RIGHT NOW THEY'RE LOOKING FOR EIGHT POINTS...
IT'S THE DEVIL BATS' OFFENSE!
BEFORE THE GAME, THEY SAID THEY HAD TO WIN IN ORDER TO BRING BACK THEIR TEAMMATE.
TWO MINUTES LEFT IN THE FIRST HALF!

Chapter 66 Big Sweep Strategy

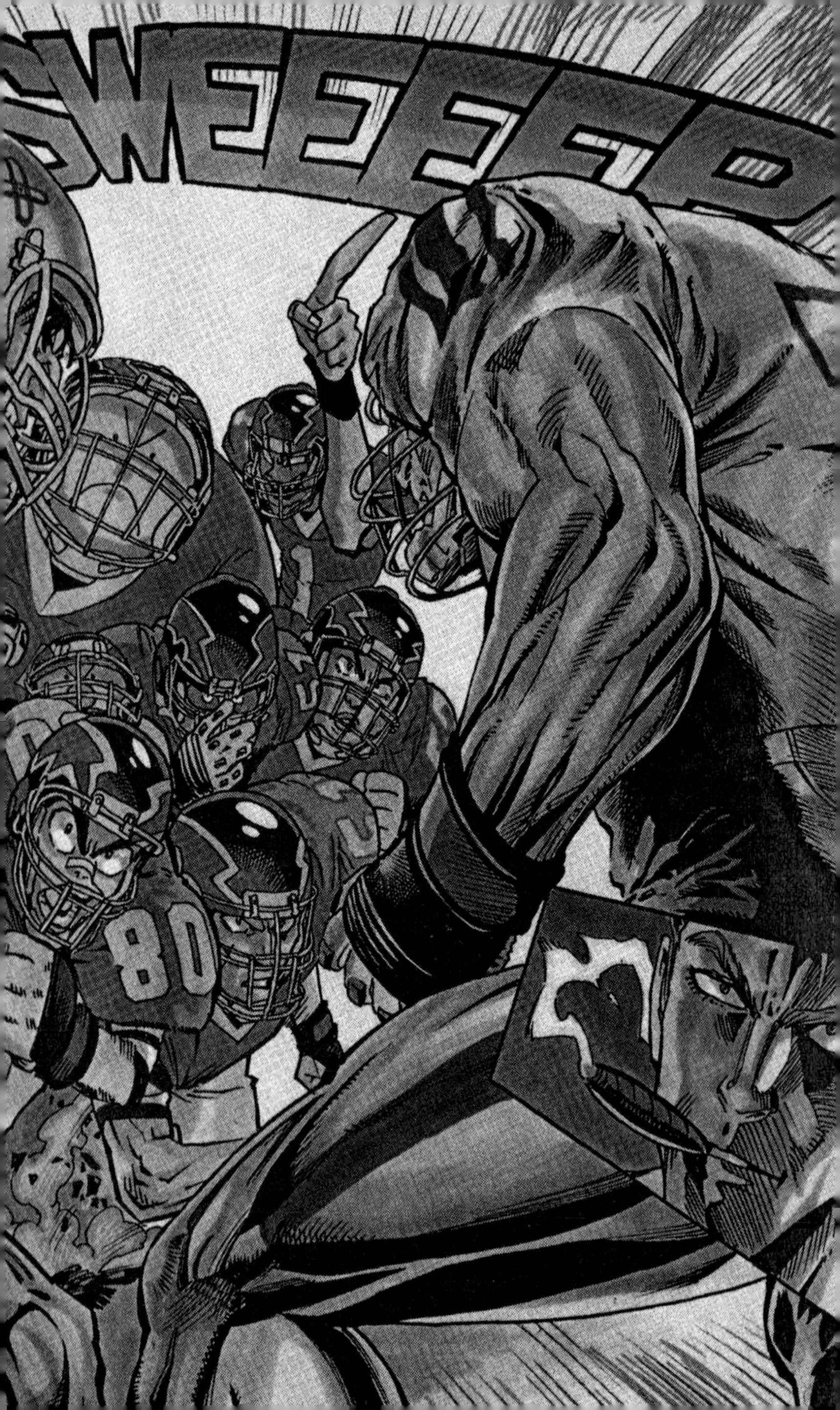
SWEEEEP

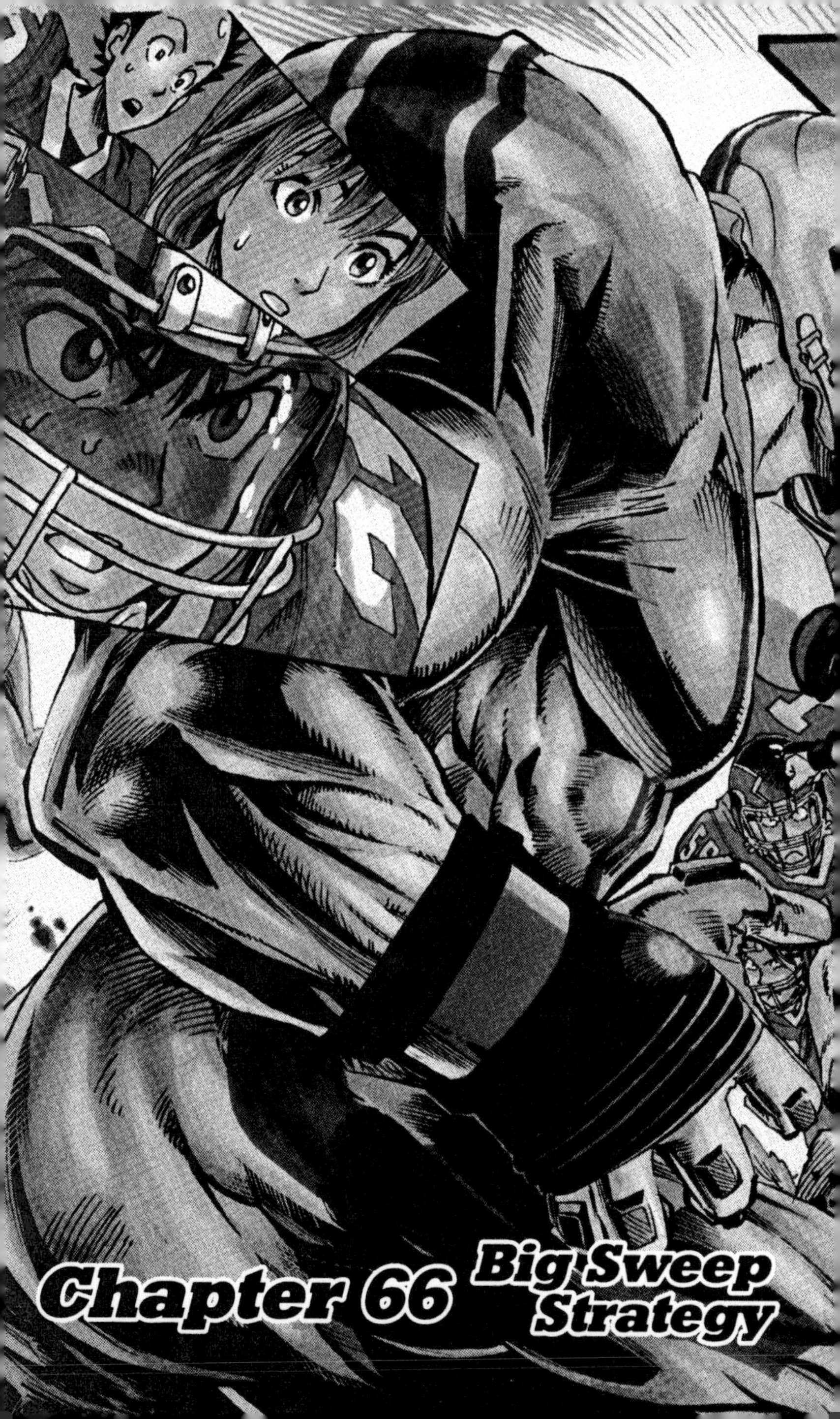

Chapter 66
Big Sweep Strategy

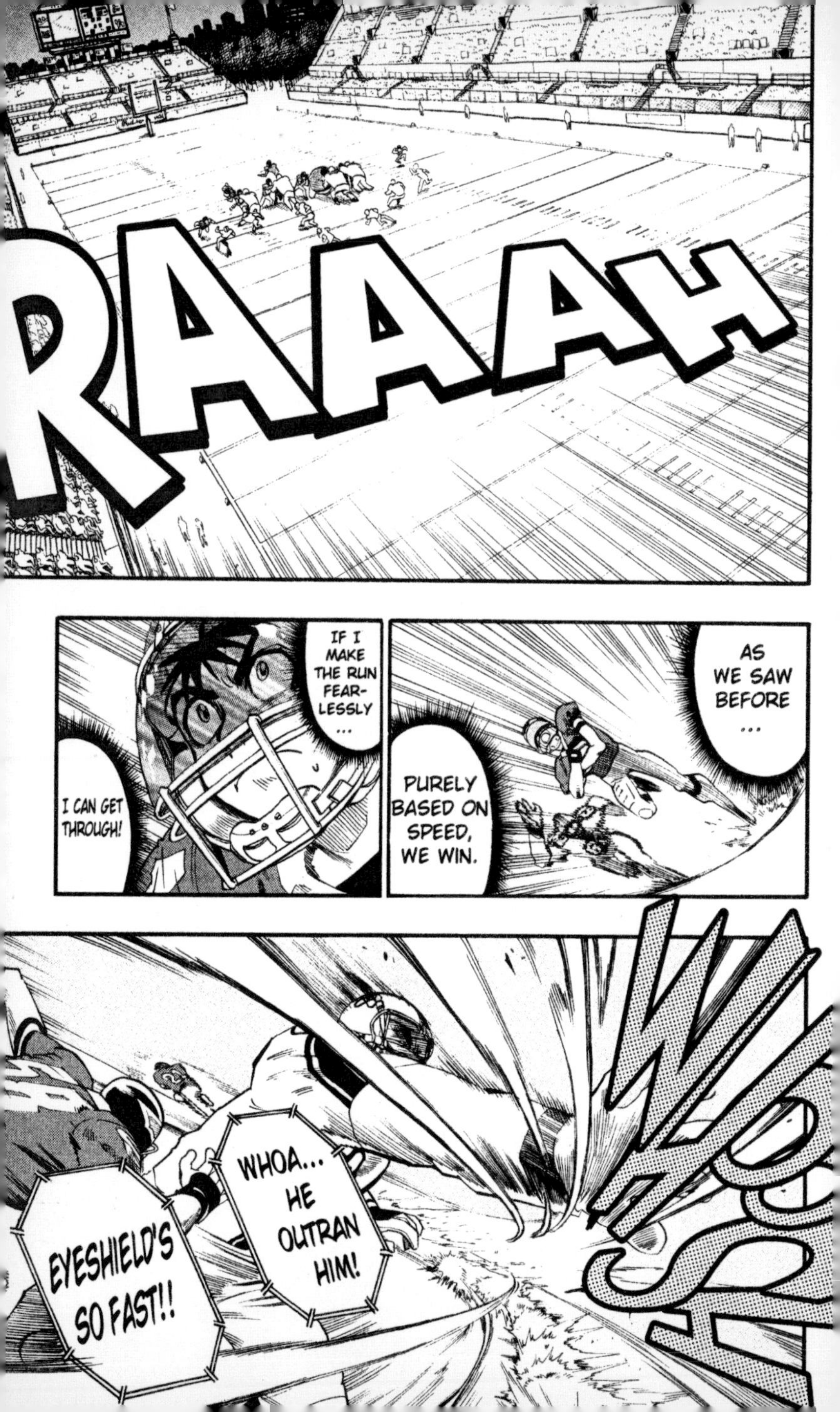
RAAAH
AS WE SAW BEFORE ...
PURELY BASED ON SPEED, WE WIN.
IF I MAKE THE RUN FEARLESSLY ...
I CAN GET THROUGH!
WHOA... HE OUTRAN HIM!
EYESHIELD'S SO FAST!!

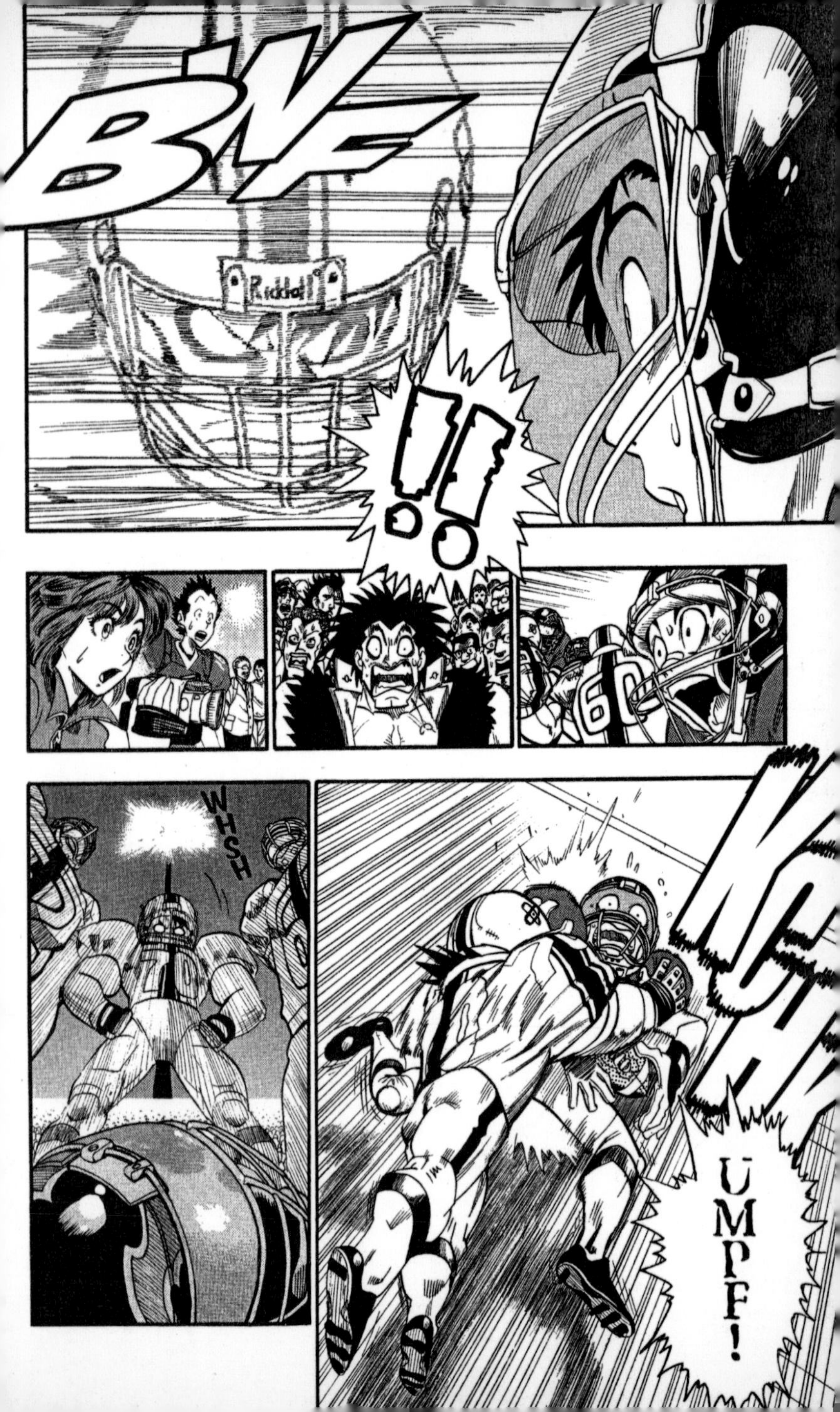
!!
UMPF!
WHSH

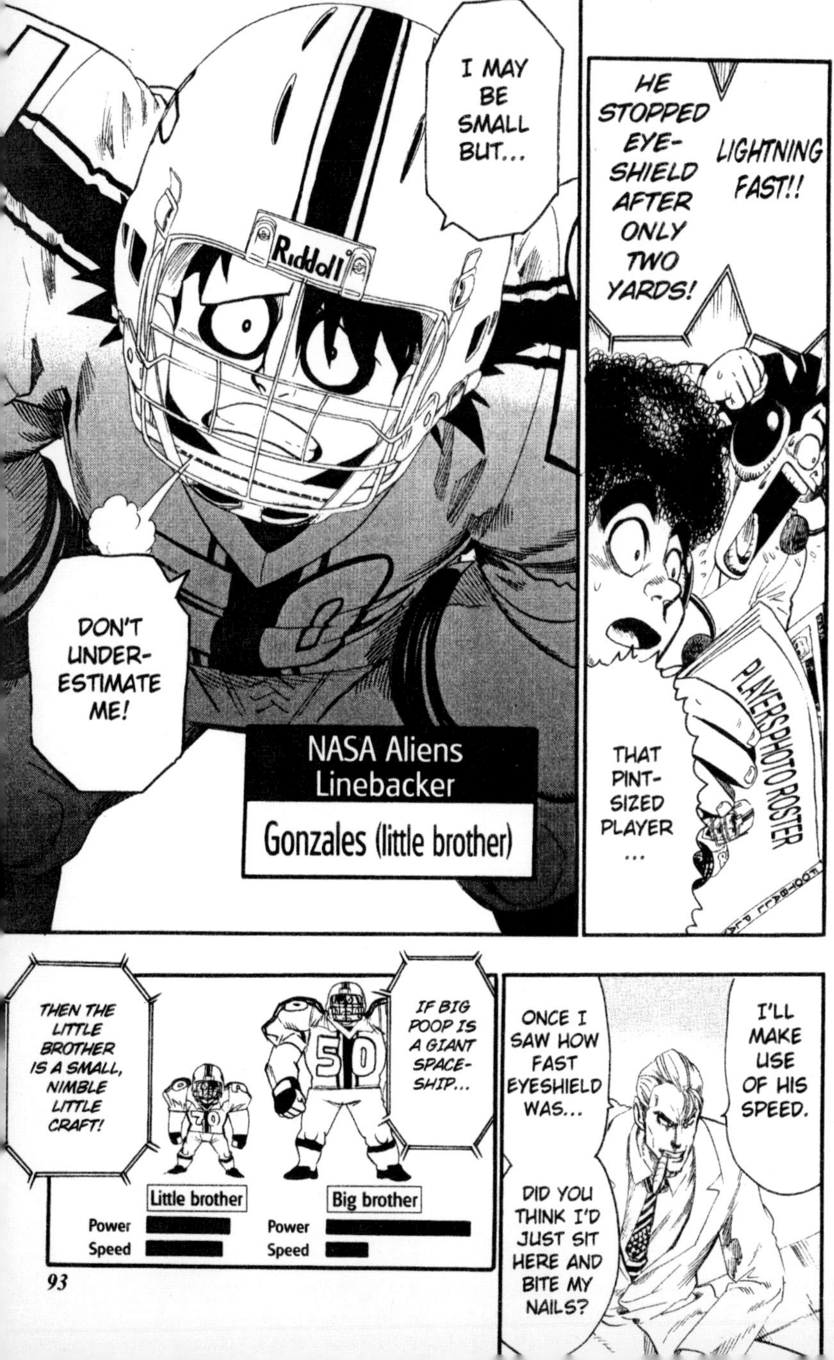
LIGHTNING FAST!!
HE STOPPED EYE-SHIELD AFTER ONLY TWO YARDS!
THAT PINT-SIZED PLAYER ...
PLAYERS PHOTO ROSTER
I MAY BE SMALL BUT...
DON'T UNDER-ESTIMATE ME!
NASA Aliens Linebacker
Gonzales (little brother)
ONCE I SAW HOW FAST EYESHIELD WAS...
I'LL MAKE USE OF HIS SPEED.
DID YOU THINK I'D JUST SIT HERE AND BITE MY NAILS?
IF BIG POOP IS A GIANT SPACE-SHIP...
THEN THE LITTLE BROTHER IS A SMALL, NIMBLE LITTLE CRAFT!
Little brother
Power
Speed
Big brother
Power
Speed

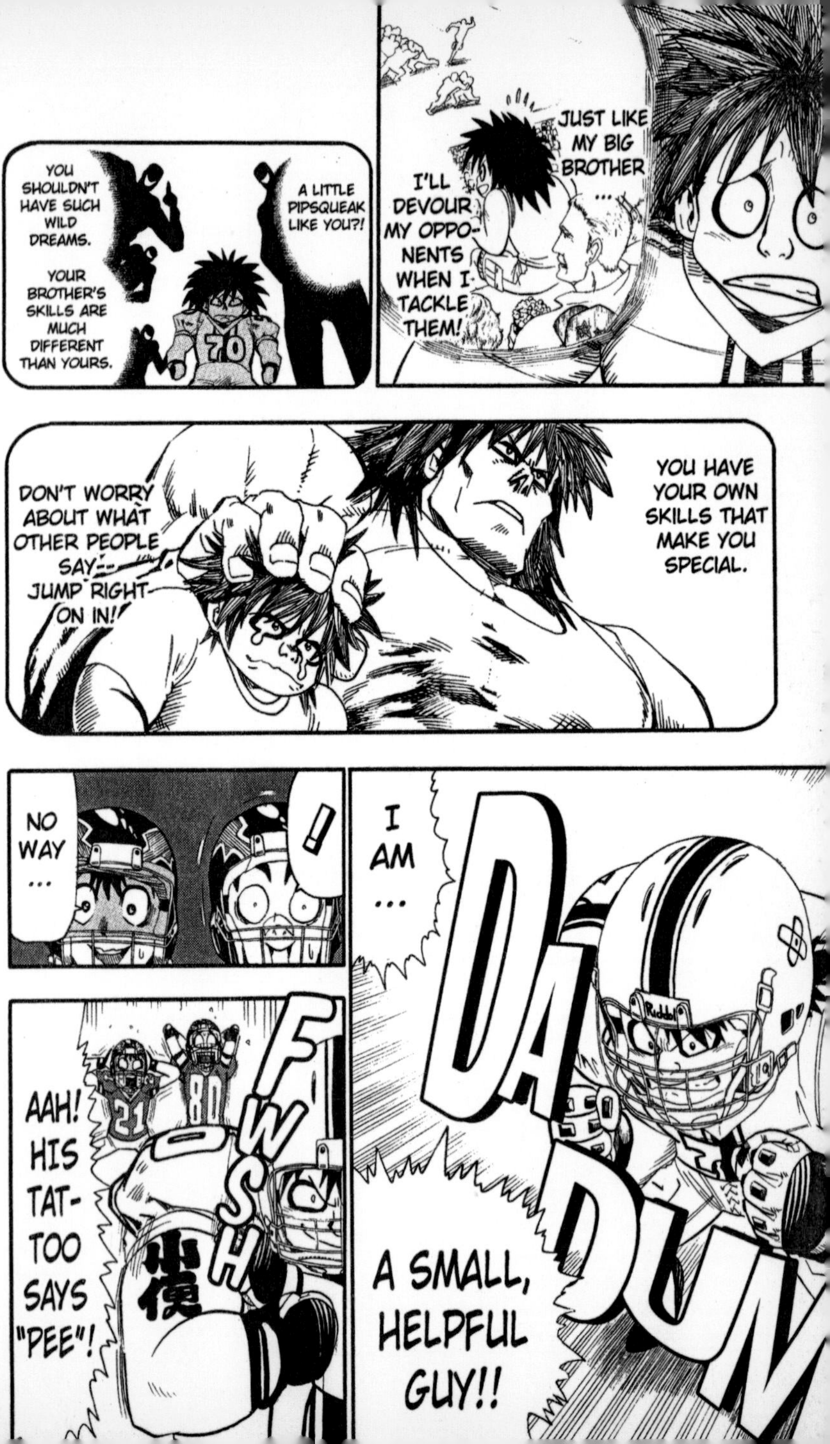

JUST LIKE MY BIG BROTHER...
I'LL DEVOUR MY OPPONENTS WHEN I TACKLE THEM!
A LITTLE PIPSQUEAK LIKE YOU?!
YOU SHOULDN'T HAVE SUCH WILD DREAMS.
YOUR BROTHER'S SKILLS ARE MUCH DIFFERENT THAN YOURS.
YOU HAVE YOUR OWN SKILLS THAT MAKE YOU SPECIAL.
DON'T WORRY ABOUT WHAT OTHER PEOPLE SAY-- JUMP RIGHT ON IN!
I AM...
DA DUN
A SMALL, HELPFUL GUY!!
!
NO WAY...
FWSH
AAH! HIS TAT-TOO SAYS "PEE"!
小便

THE YOUNGER GONZALES BROTHER'S TATTOO COMBINES THE KANJI FOR "SMALL" AND "USEFUL," MAKING THE WORD FOR "PEE"!

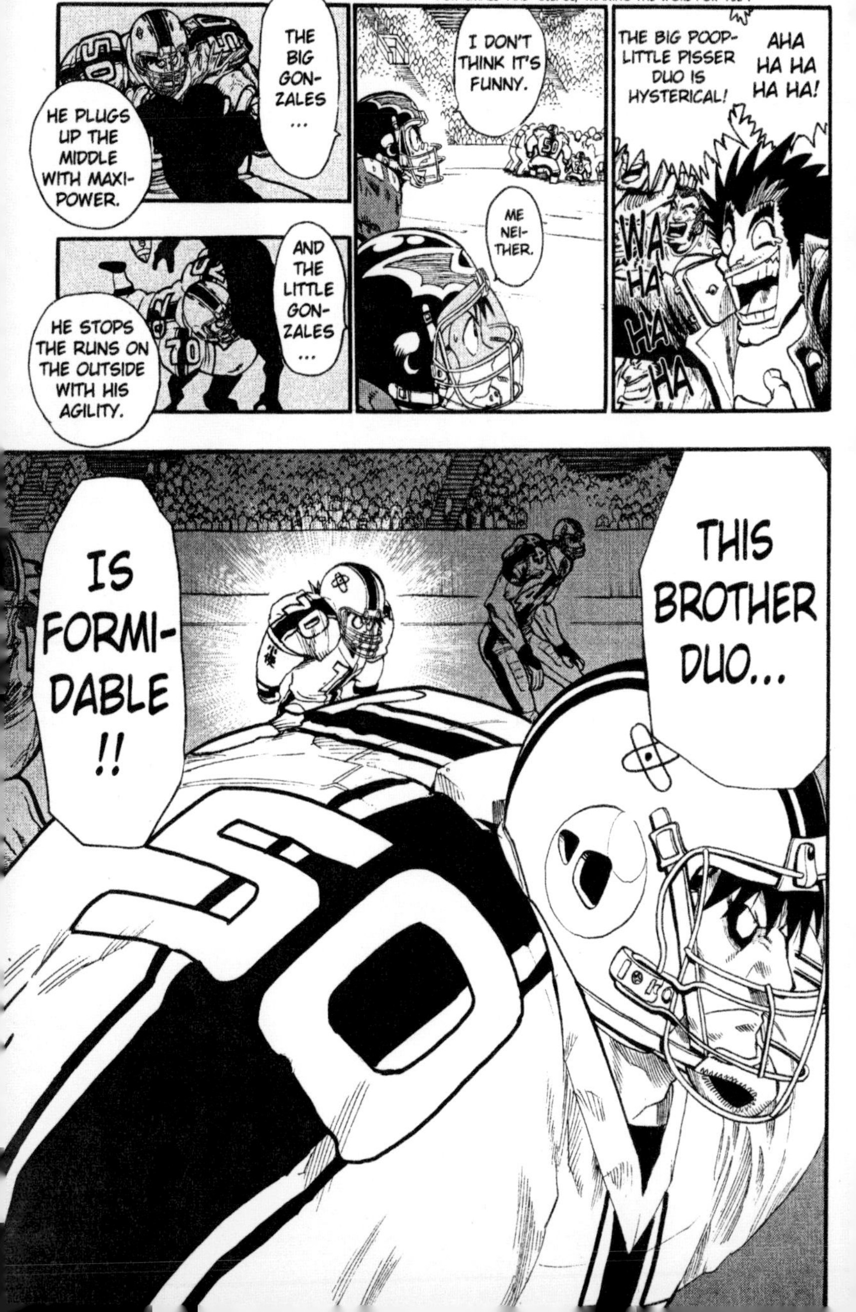
AHA HA HA HA HA!
THE BIG POOP-LITTLE PISSER DUO IS HYSTERICAL!
WA HA HA HA
I DON'T THINK IT'S FUNNY.
ME NEI-THER.
THE BIG GON-ZALES...
HE PLUGS UP THE MIDDLE WITH MAXI-POWER.
AND THE LITTLE GON-ZALES...
HE STOPS THE RUNS ON THE OUTSIDE WITH HIS AGILITY.
THIS BROTHER DUO...
IS FORMI-DABLE!!

BWUMP

NNGH!!

AH, NOT EVEN FIVE SECONDS LEFT...

ACK!

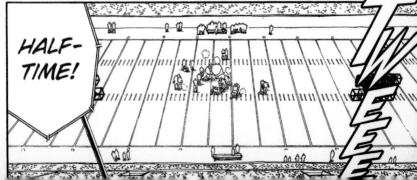

HALF-TIME!

TWEEE

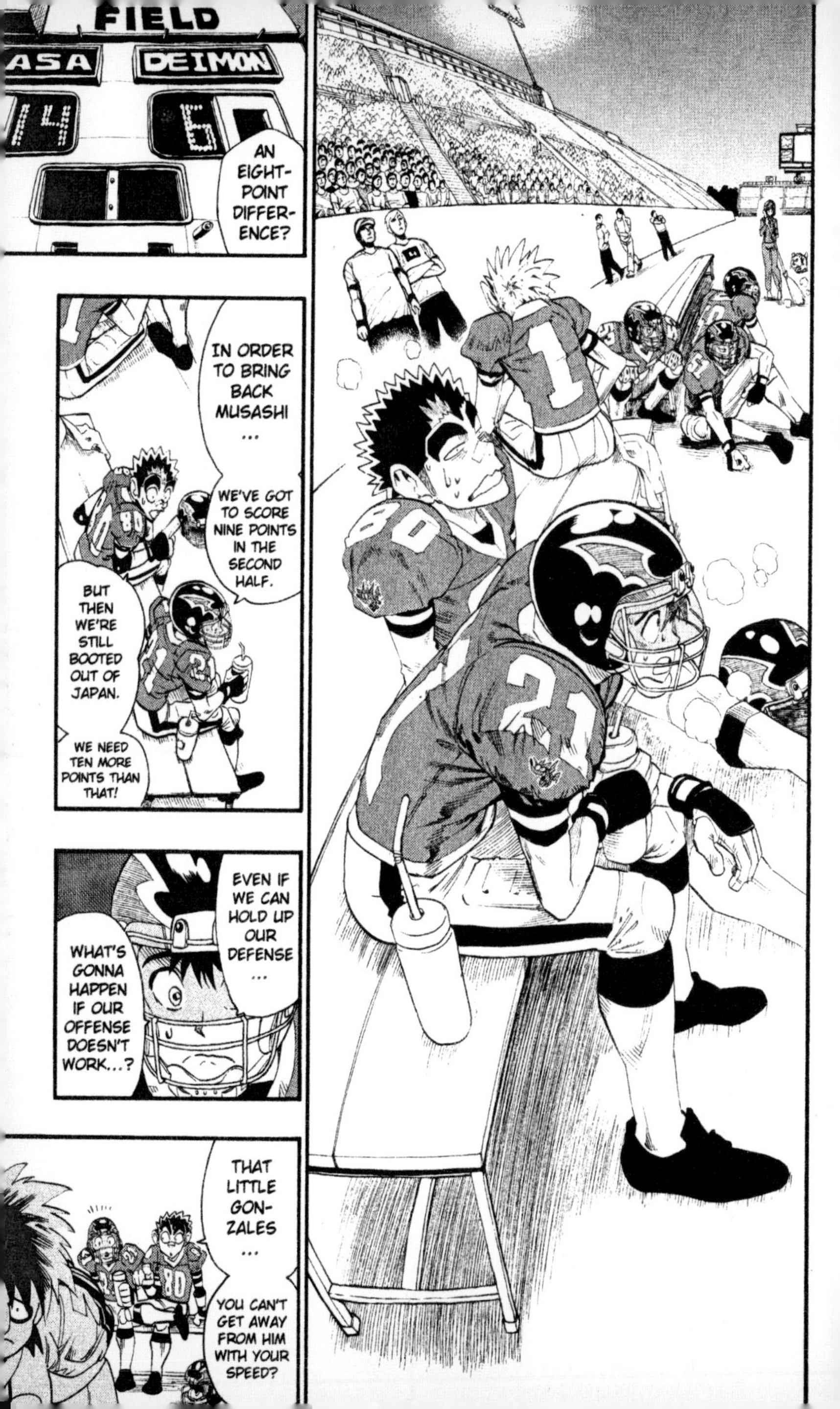

FIELD
ASA
DEIMON
14
6
AN EIGHT-POINT DIFFERENCE?
IN ORDER TO BRING BACK MUSASHI...
WE'VE GOT TO SCORE NINE POINTS IN THE SECOND HALF.
BUT THEN WE'RE STILL BOOTED OUT OF JAPAN.
WE NEED TEN MORE POINTS THAN THAT!
EVEN IF WE CAN HOLD UP OUR DEFENSE...
WHAT'S GONNA HAPPEN IF OUR OFFENSE DOESN'T WORK...?
THAT LITTLE GONZALES...
YOU CAN'T GET AWAY FROM HIM WITH YOUR SPEED?

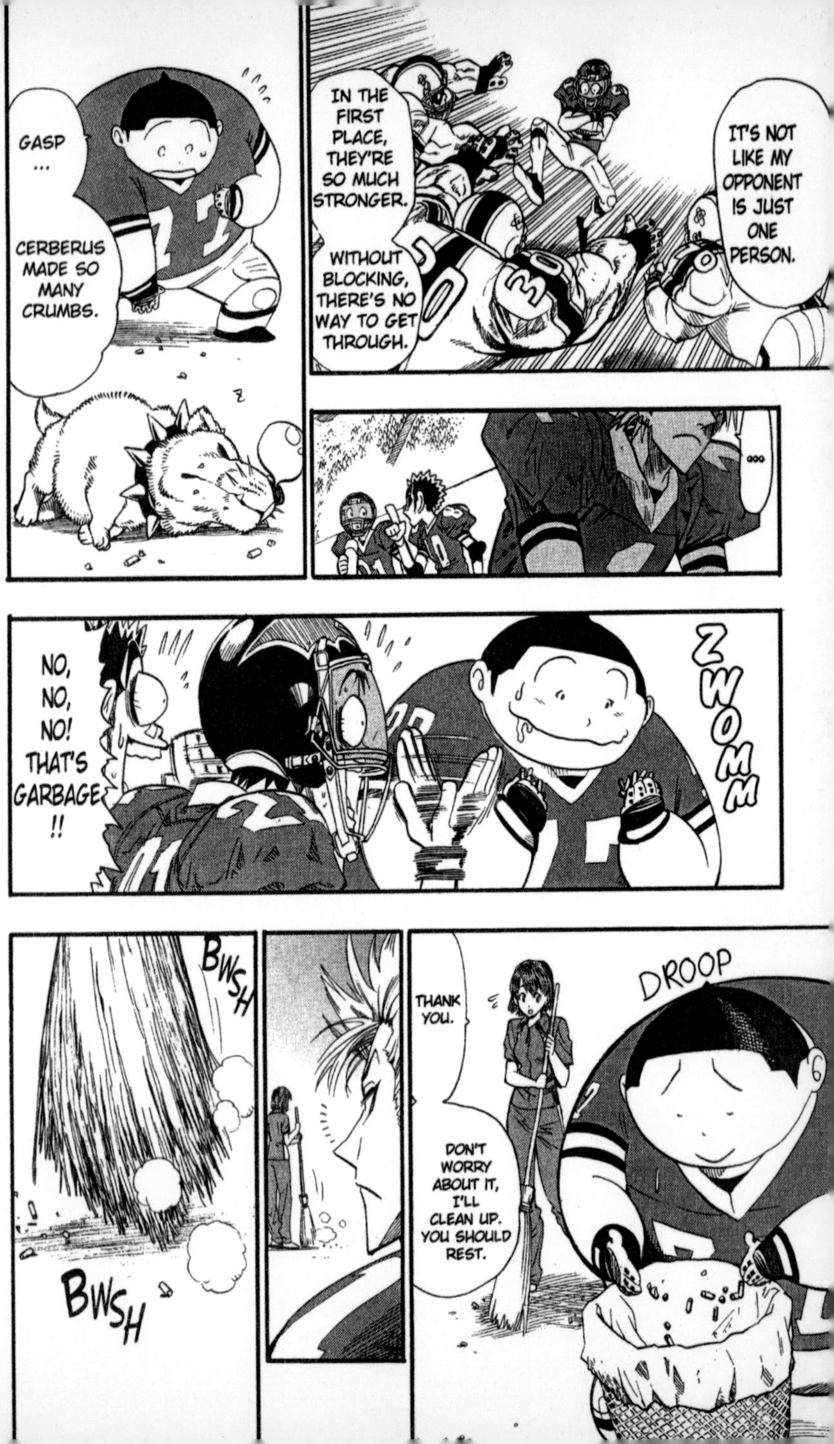
IT'S NOT LIKE MY OPPONENT IS JUST ONE PERSON.
IN THE FIRST PLACE, THEY'RE SO MUCH STRONGER.
WITHOUT BLOCKING, THERE'S NO WAY TO GET THROUGH.
...
GASP ...
CERBERUS MADE SO MANY CRUMBS.
ZWOMM
NO, NO, NO! THAT'S GARBAGE!!
DROOP
THANK YOU.
DON'T WORRY ABOUT IT, I'LL CLEAN UP. YOU SHOULD REST.
BWSH
BWSH

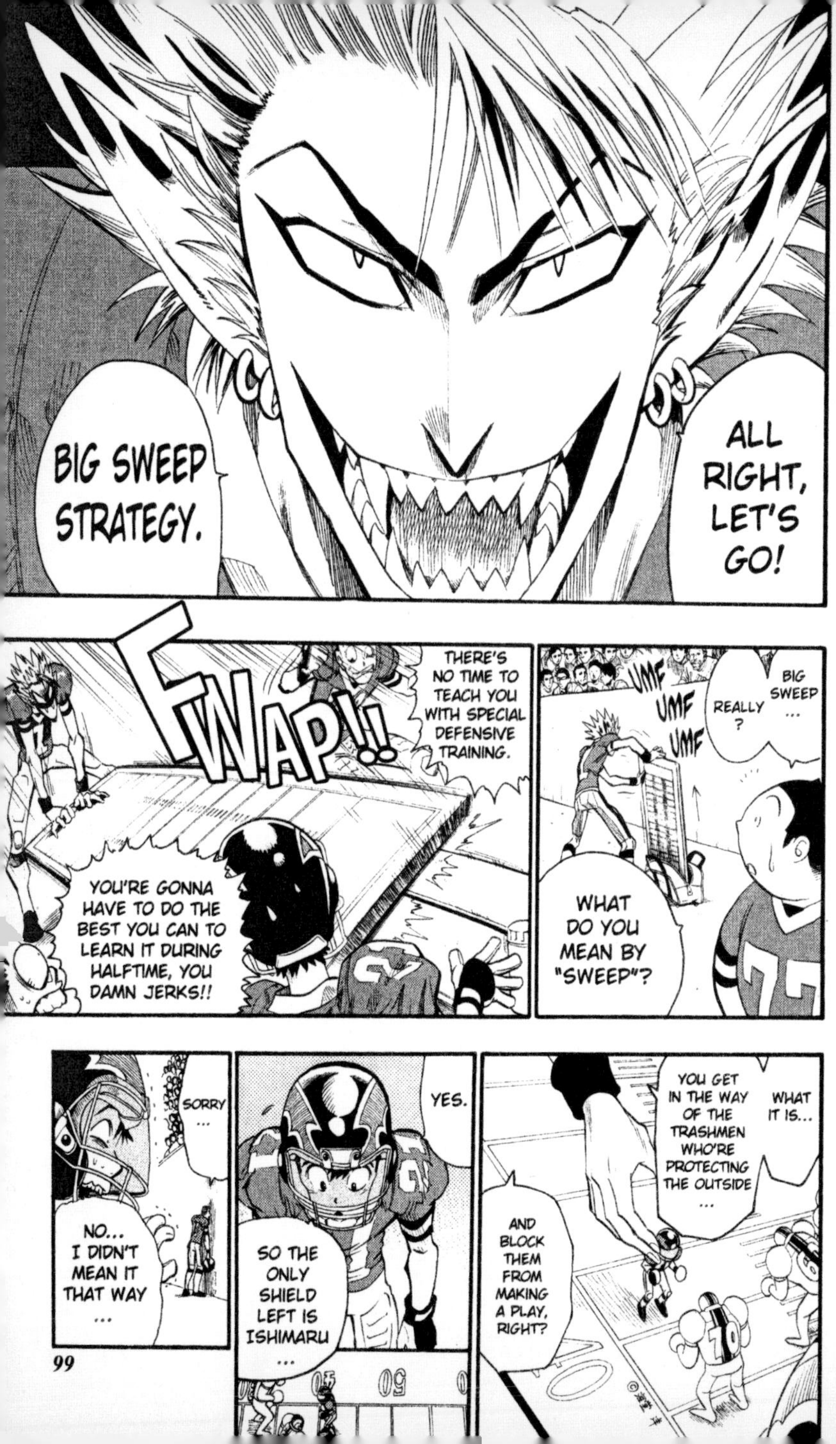
ALL RIGHT, LET'S GO!
BIG SWEEP STRATEGY.
BIG SWEEP ...
REALLY ?
UMF
UMF
UMF
WHAT DO YOU MEAN BY "SWEEP"?
THERE'S NO TIME TO TEACH YOU WITH SPECIAL DEFENSIVE TRAINING.
FWAP!!
YOU'RE GONNA HAVE TO DO THE BEST YOU CAN TO LEARN IT DURING HALFTIME, YOU DAMN JERKS!!
WHAT IT IS...
YOU GET IN THE WAY OF THE TRASHMEN WHO'RE PROTECTING THE OUTSIDE ...
AND BLOCK THEM FROM MAKING A PLAY, RIGHT?
YES.
SO THE ONLY SHIELD LEFT IS ISHIMARU ...
SORRY ...
NO... I DIDN'T MEAN IT THAT WAY ...

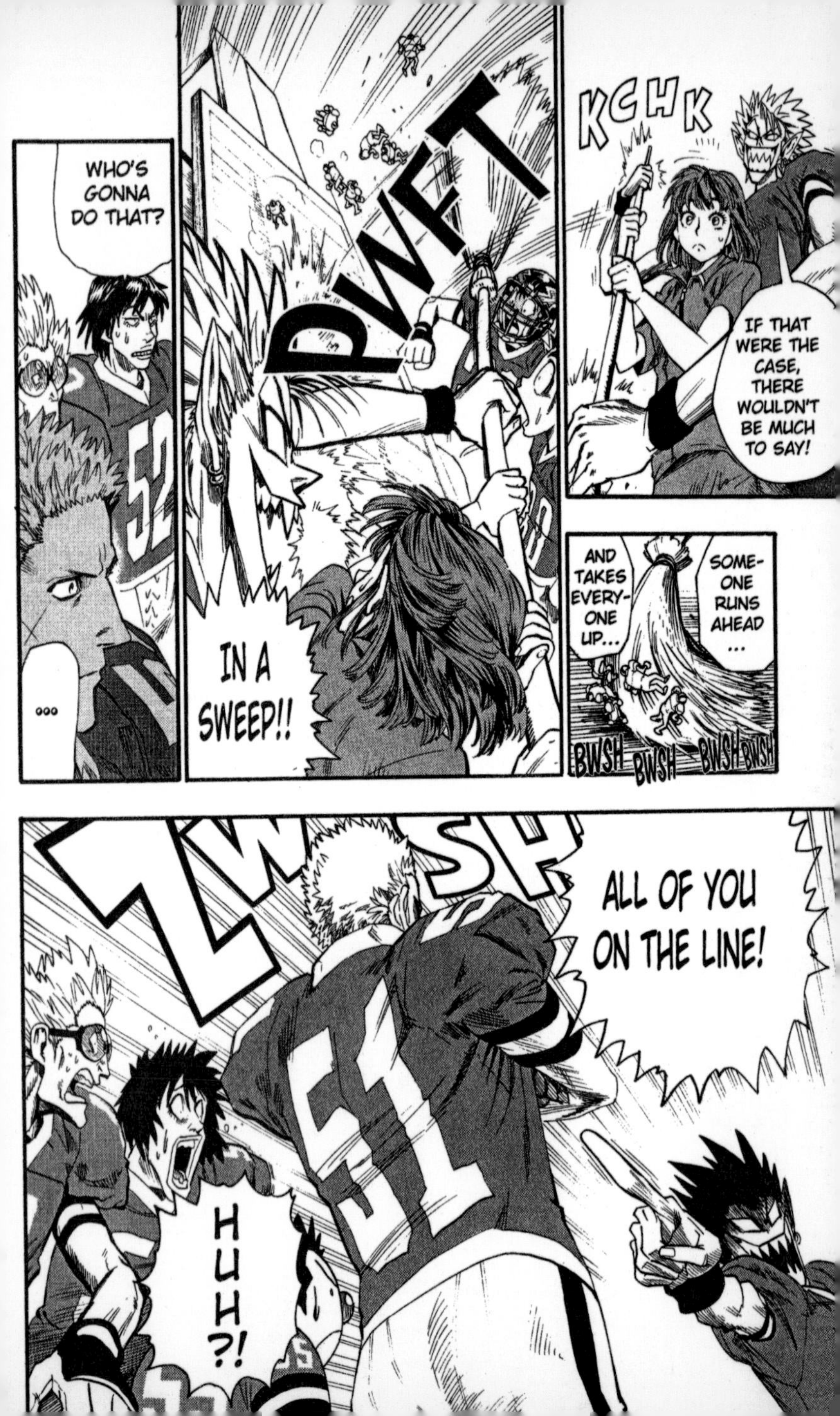
KCHK
IF THAT WERE THE CASE, THERE WOULDN'T BE MUCH TO SAY!
SOME-ONE RUNS AHEAD ...
AND TAKES EVERY-ONE UP...
BWSH BWSH BWSH BWSH
PWFT
IN A SWEEP!!
WHO'S GONNA DO THAT?
...
ALL OF YOU ON THE LINE!
HUH?!

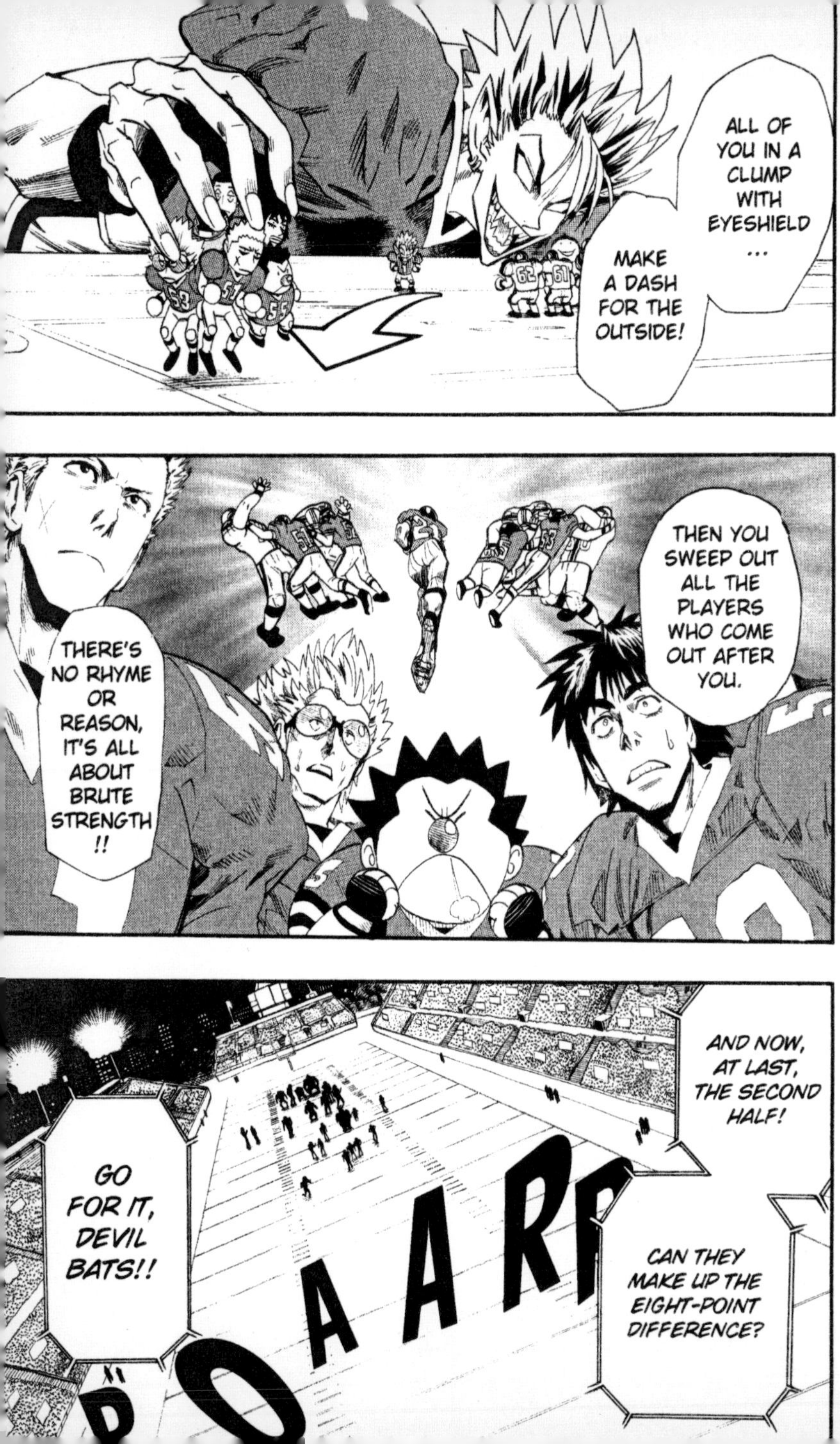
ALL OF YOU IN A CLUMP WITH EYESHIELD ...
MAKE A DASH FOR THE OUTSIDE!
THEN YOU SWEEP OUT ALL THE PLAYERS WHO COME OUT AFTER YOU.
THERE'S NO RHYME OR REASON, IT'S ALL ABOUT BRUTE STRENGTH!!
AND NOW, AT LAST, THE SECOND HALF!
CAN THEY MAKE UP THE EIGHT-POINT DIFFERENCE?
GO FOR IT, DEVIL BATS!!
O A A R

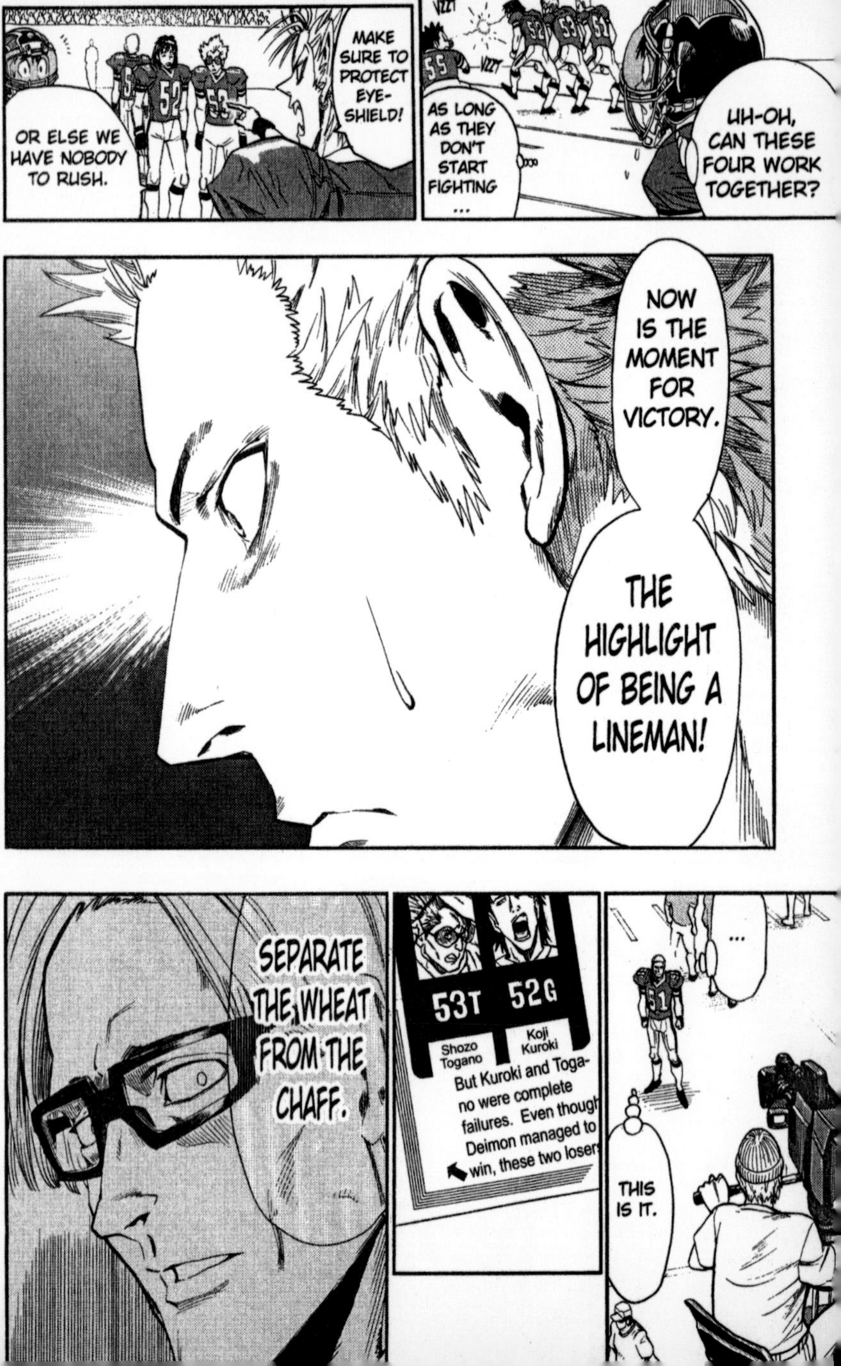
UH-OH, CAN THESE FOUR WORK TOGETHER?
VZZT
VZZT
AS LONG AS THEY DON'T START FIGHTING ...
MAKE SURE TO PROTECT EYE-SHIELD!
OR ELSE WE HAVE NOBODY TO RUSH.
NOW IS THE MOMENT FOR VICTORY.
THE HIGHLIGHT OF BEING A LINEMAN!
...
THIS IS IT.
53T
52G
Shozo Togano
Koji Kuroki
But Kuroki and Togano were complete failures. Even though Deimon managed to win, these two losers
SEPARATE THE WHEAT FROM THE CHAFF.

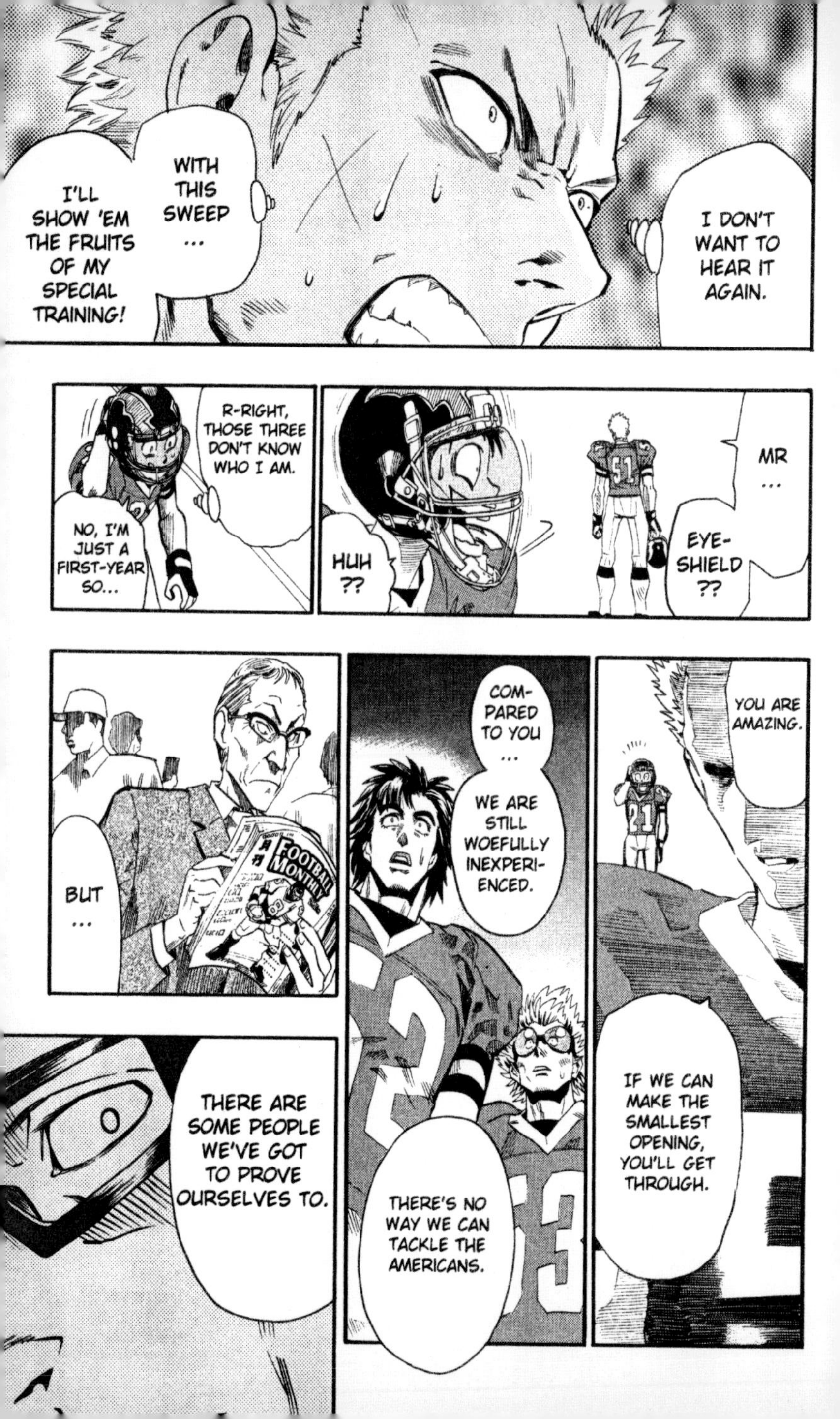
I DON'T WANT TO HEAR IT AGAIN.
WITH THIS SWEEP ...
I'LL SHOW 'EM THE FRUITS OF MY SPECIAL TRAINING!
MR ...
EYE-SHIELD ??
HUH ??
R-RIGHT, THOSE THREE DON'T KNOW WHO I AM.
NO, I'M JUST A FIRST-YEAR SO...
YOU ARE AMAZING.
IF WE CAN MAKE THE SMALLEST OPENING, YOU'LL GET THROUGH.
COMPARED TO YOU ...
WE ARE STILL WOEFULLY INEXPERIENCED.
THERE'S NO WAY WE CAN TACKLE THE AMERICANS.
BUT ...
FOOTBALL MONTHLY
THERE ARE SOME PEOPLE WE'VE GOT TO PROVE OURSELVES TO.

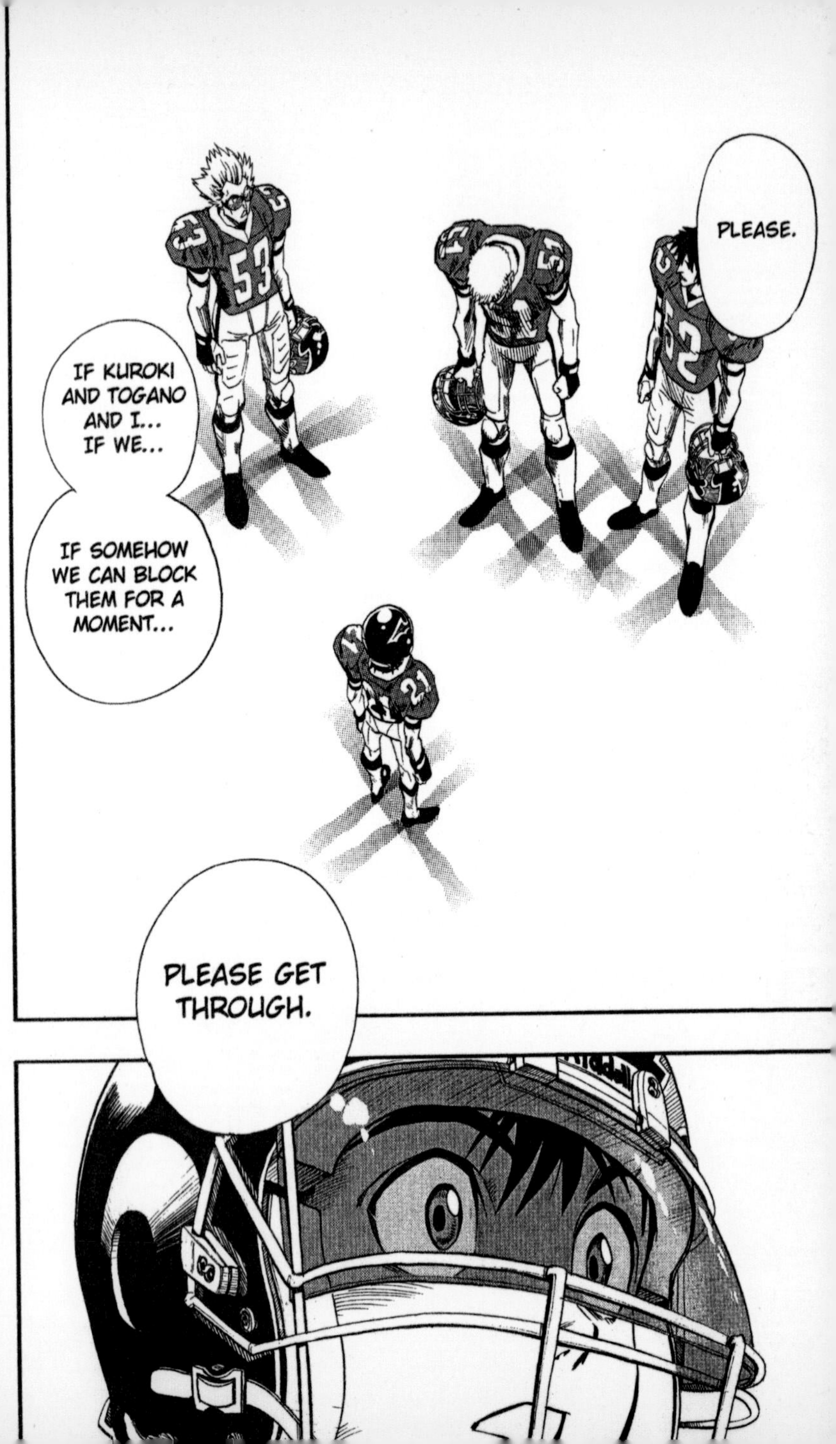
PLEASE.
IF KUROKI AND TOGANO AND I... IF WE...
IF SOMEHOW WE CAN BLOCK THEM FOR A MOMENT...
PLEASE GET THROUGH.

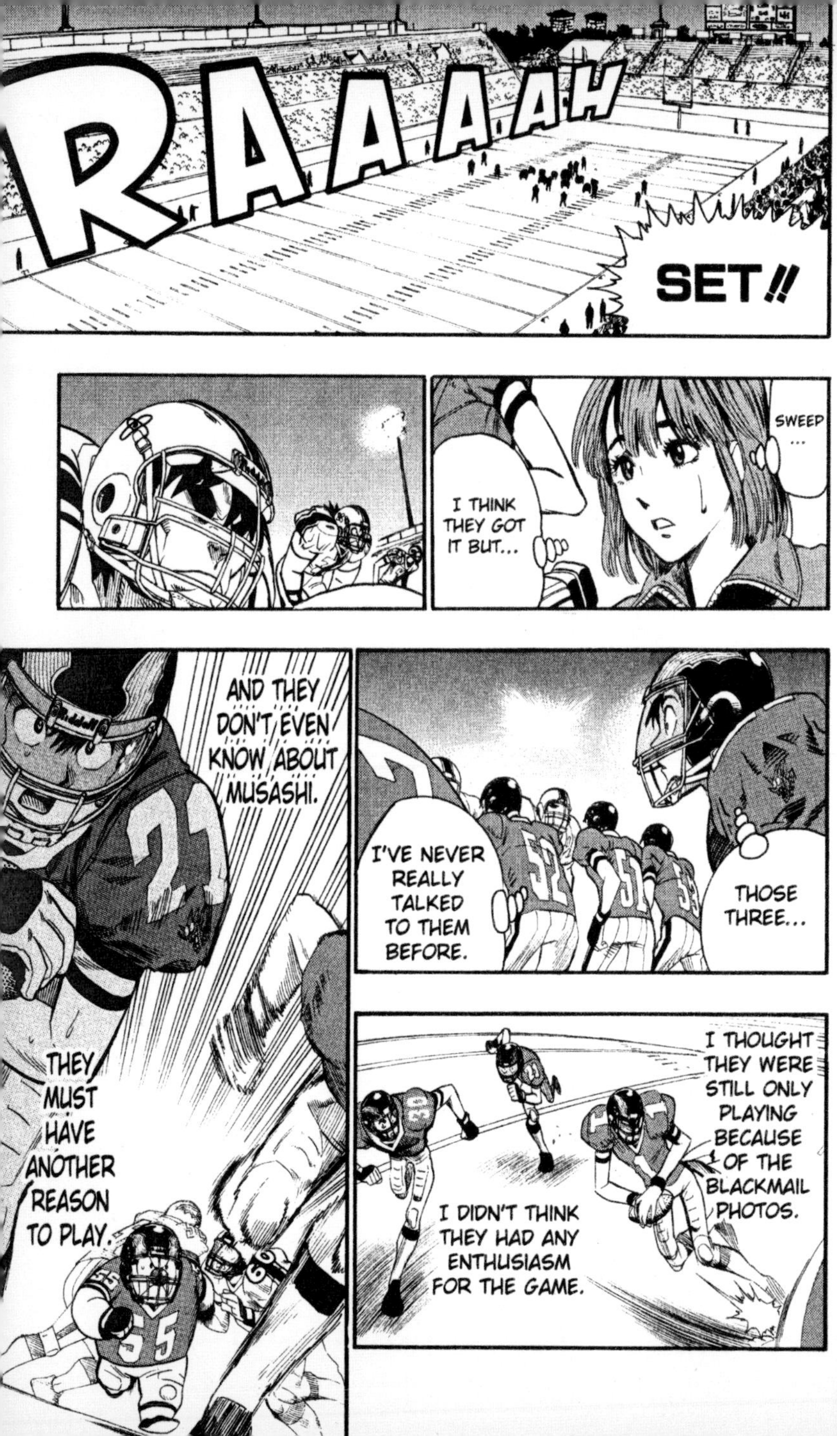
RAAAAH
SET!!
SWEEP...
I THINK THEY GOT IT BUT...
THOSE THREE...
I'VE NEVER REALLY TALKED TO THEM BEFORE.
I THOUGHT THEY WERE STILL ONLY PLAYING BECAUSE OF THE BLACKMAIL PHOTOS.
I DIDN'T THINK THEY HAD ANY ENTHUSIASM FOR THE GAME.
AND THEY DON'T EVEN KNOW ABOUT MUSASHI.
THEY MUST HAVE ANOTHER REASON TO PLAY.

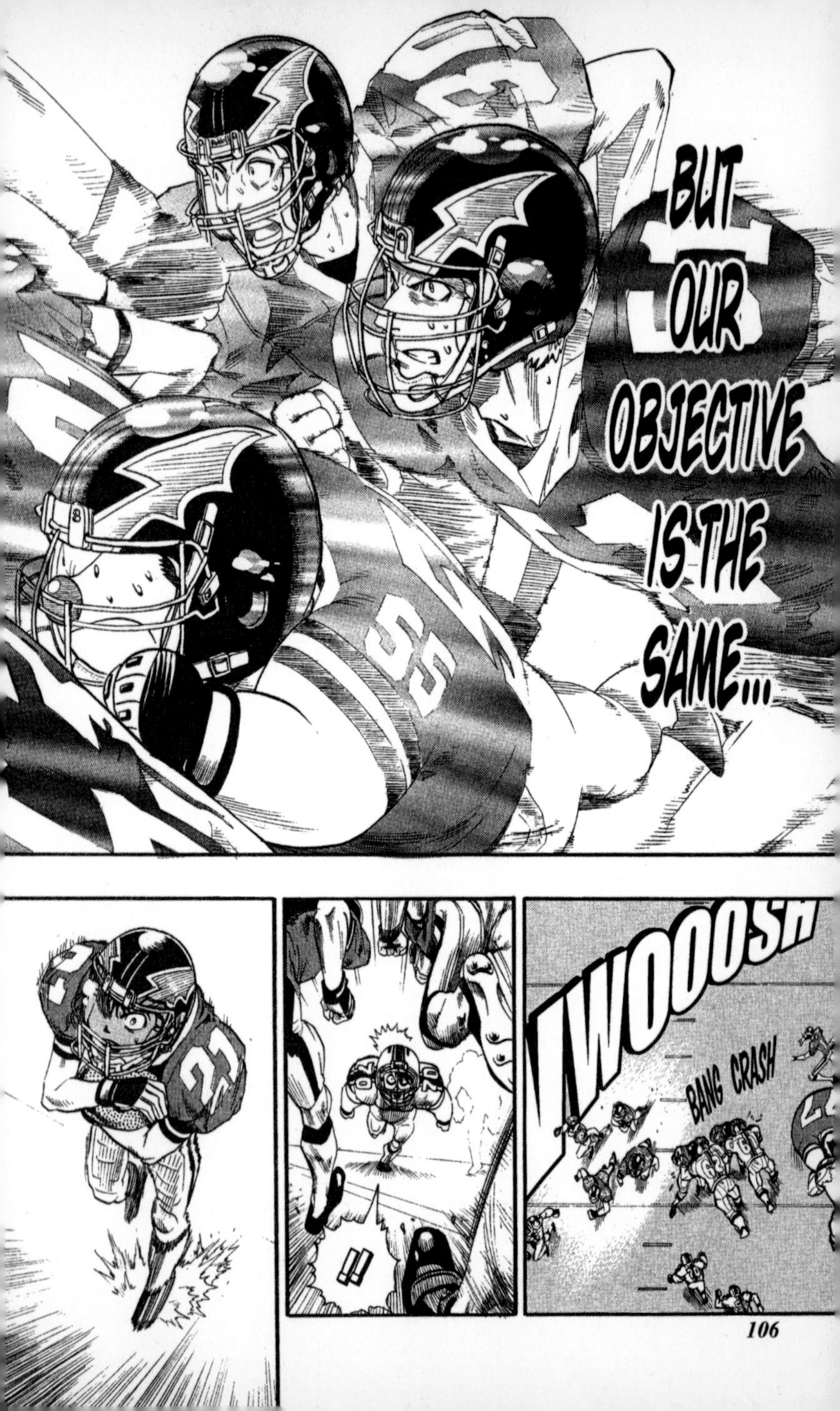
BUT OUR OBJECTIVE IS THE SAME...
WOOOSH
BANG CRASH
!!

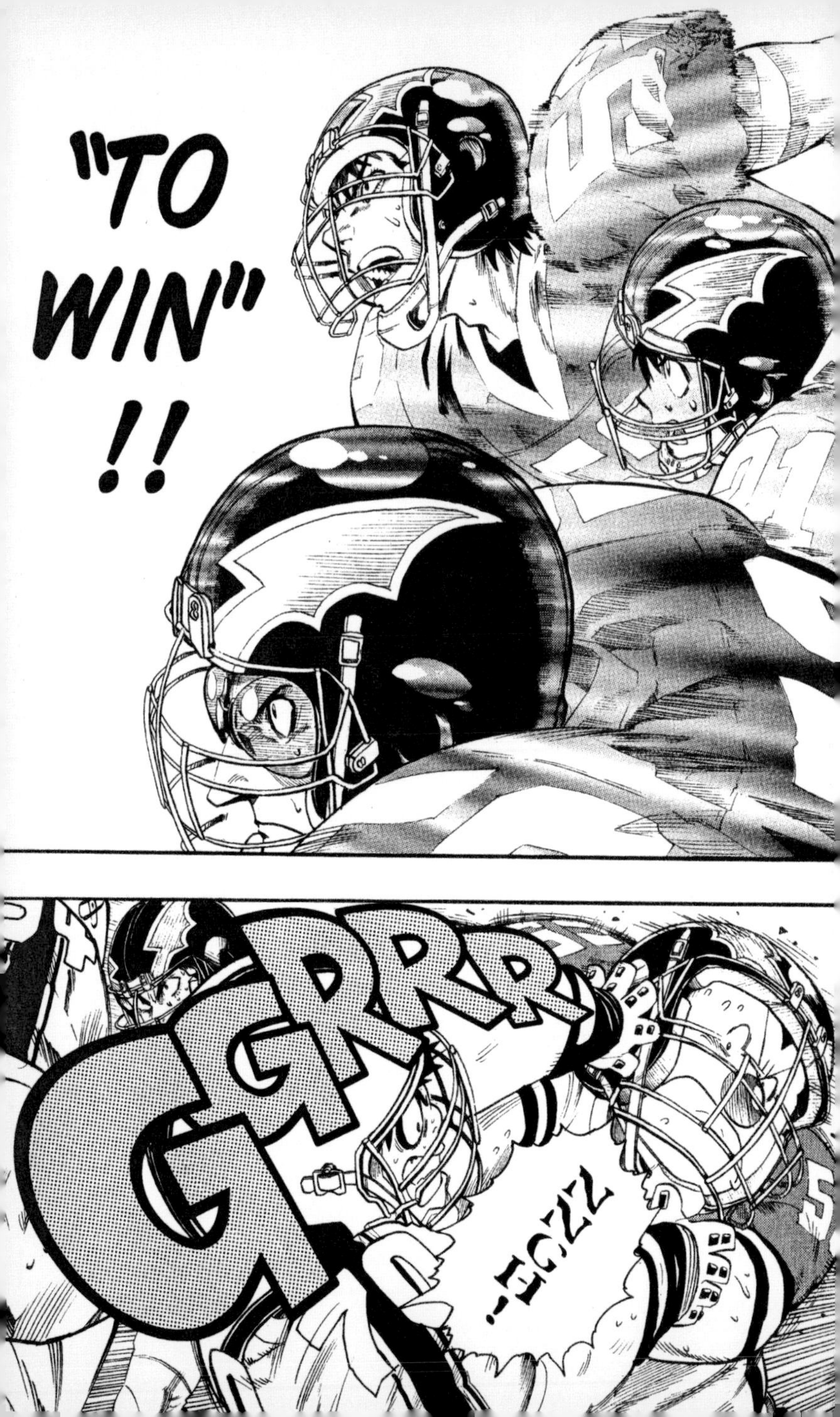
"TO WIN"!!
GRRR
ZZGE!

Japan Scholar WATT'S JAPANESE Culture Class

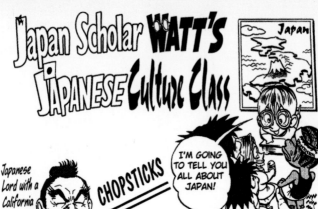

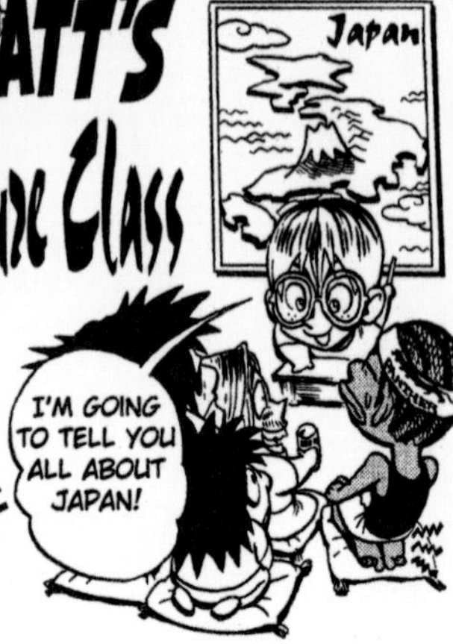
Japan
I'M GOING TO TELL YOU ALL ABOUT JAPAN!

CHOPSTICKS

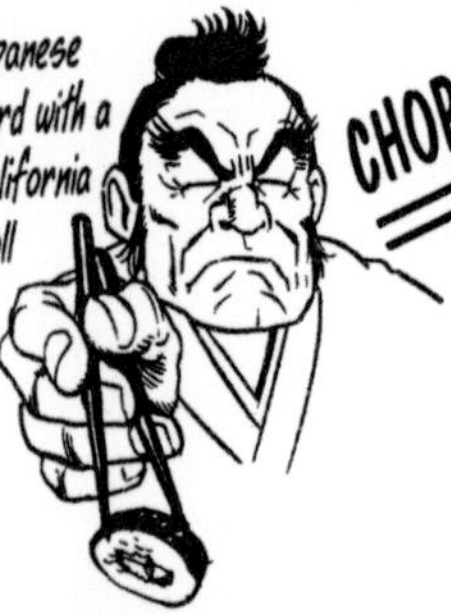
Japanese Lord with a California roll

EVERYBODY KNOWS ABOUT THESE! THEY'RE UTENSILS FOR EATING SUSHI. THEY SAY THIS IS WHAT SAMURAI USED FOR HARA-KIRI.

GO

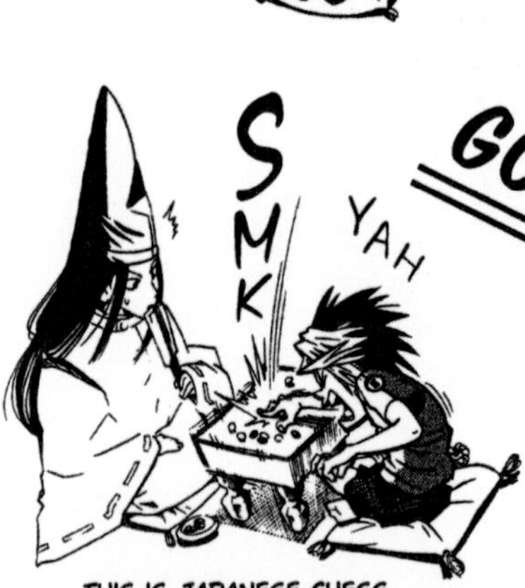
SMK
YAH

THIS IS JAPANESE CHESS. IT SEEMS LIKE ALL THE PLAYERS ARE CALLED "HIKARU."

SUMO

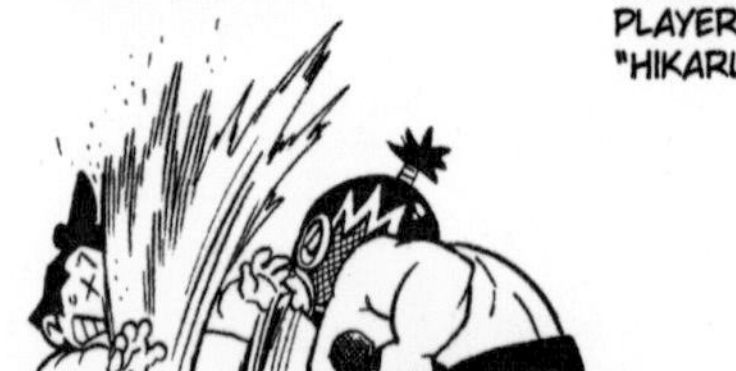

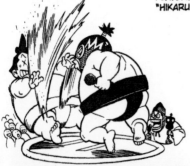

THESE ARE JAPAN'S STRONGEST WRESTLERS. BUT THEY SEEM RATHER COWARDLY WHEN THEY THROW SALT IN EACH OTHER'S EYES BEFORE THE MATCH.

OTOSHIDAMA

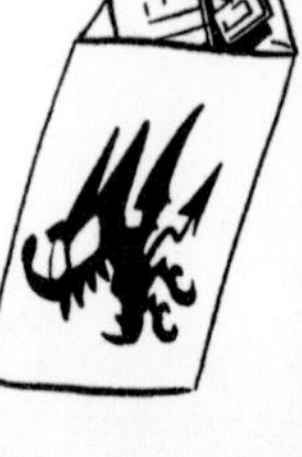

THIS IS A GIFT OF MONEY. ALSO KNOWN AS A BRIBE. WHEN YOU PRESENT THIS, YOU HAVE TO SAY, "IT'S NOTHING, BUT..."

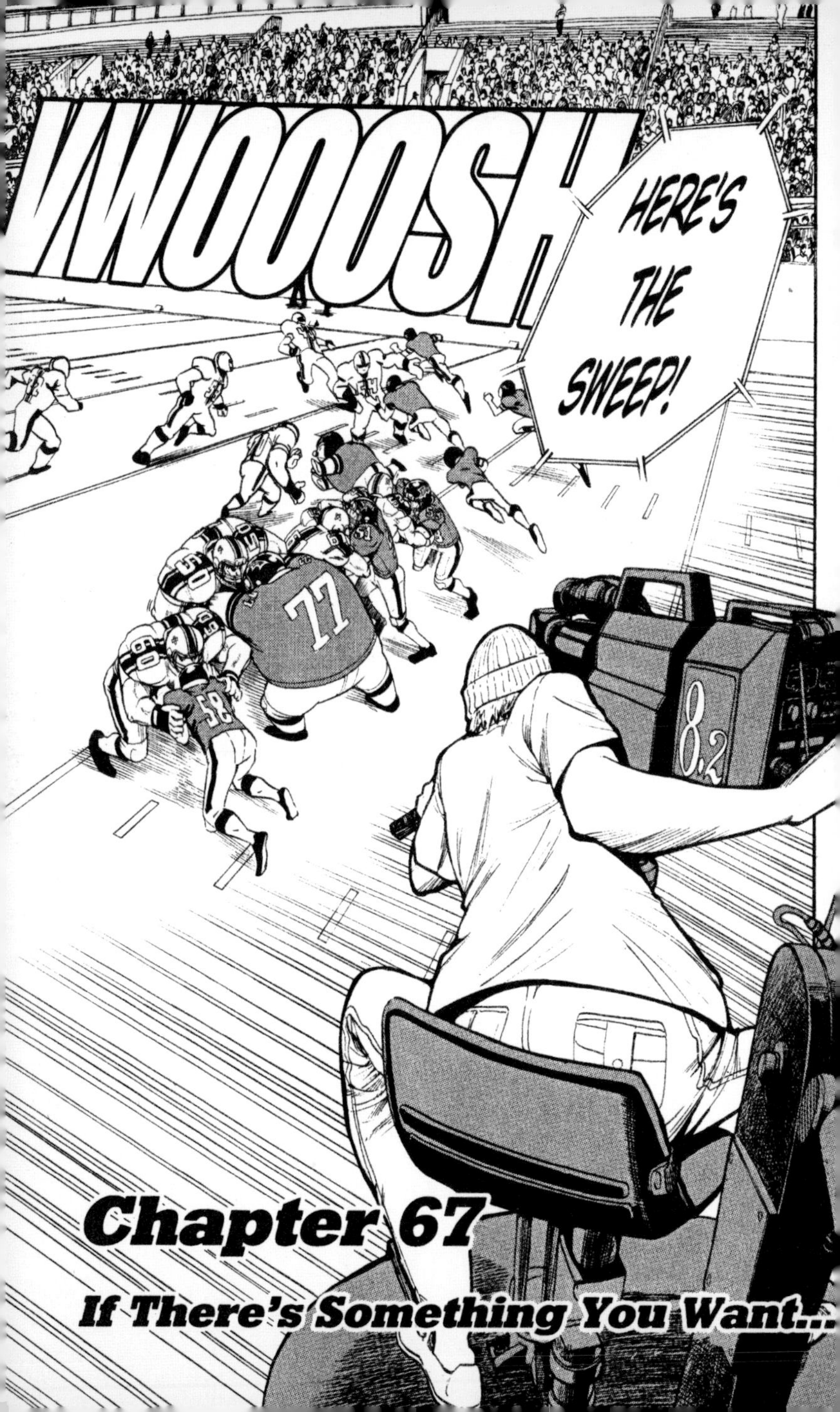
WHOOOSH
HERE'S THE SWEEP!

Chapter 67

If There's Something You Want...

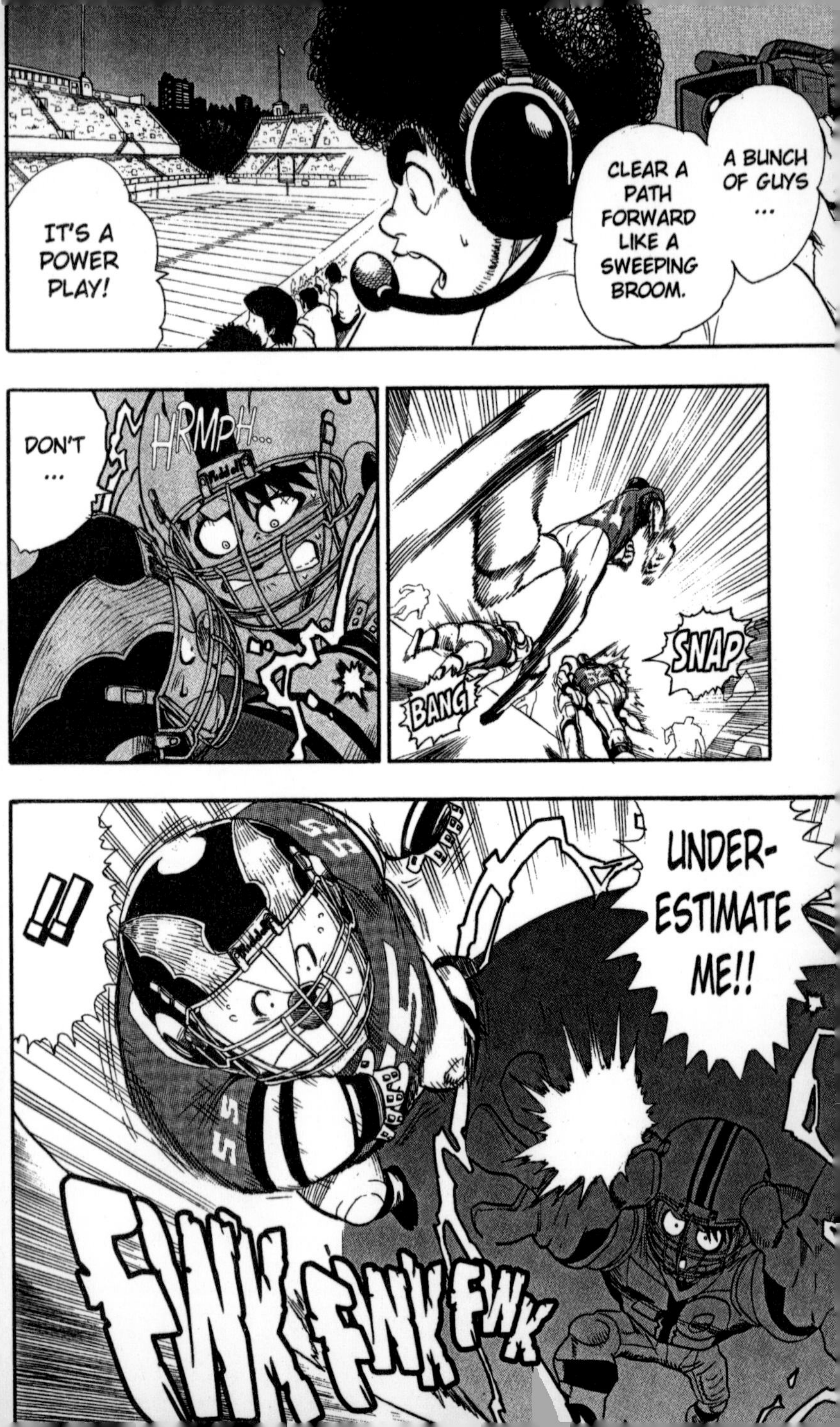

A BUNCH OF GUYS ...
CLEAR A PATH FORWARD LIKE A SWEEPING BROOM.
IT'S A POWER PLAY!
SNAP
BANG
HRMPH...
DON'T ...
UNDER-ESTIMATE ME!!
!!
FWK FWK FWK

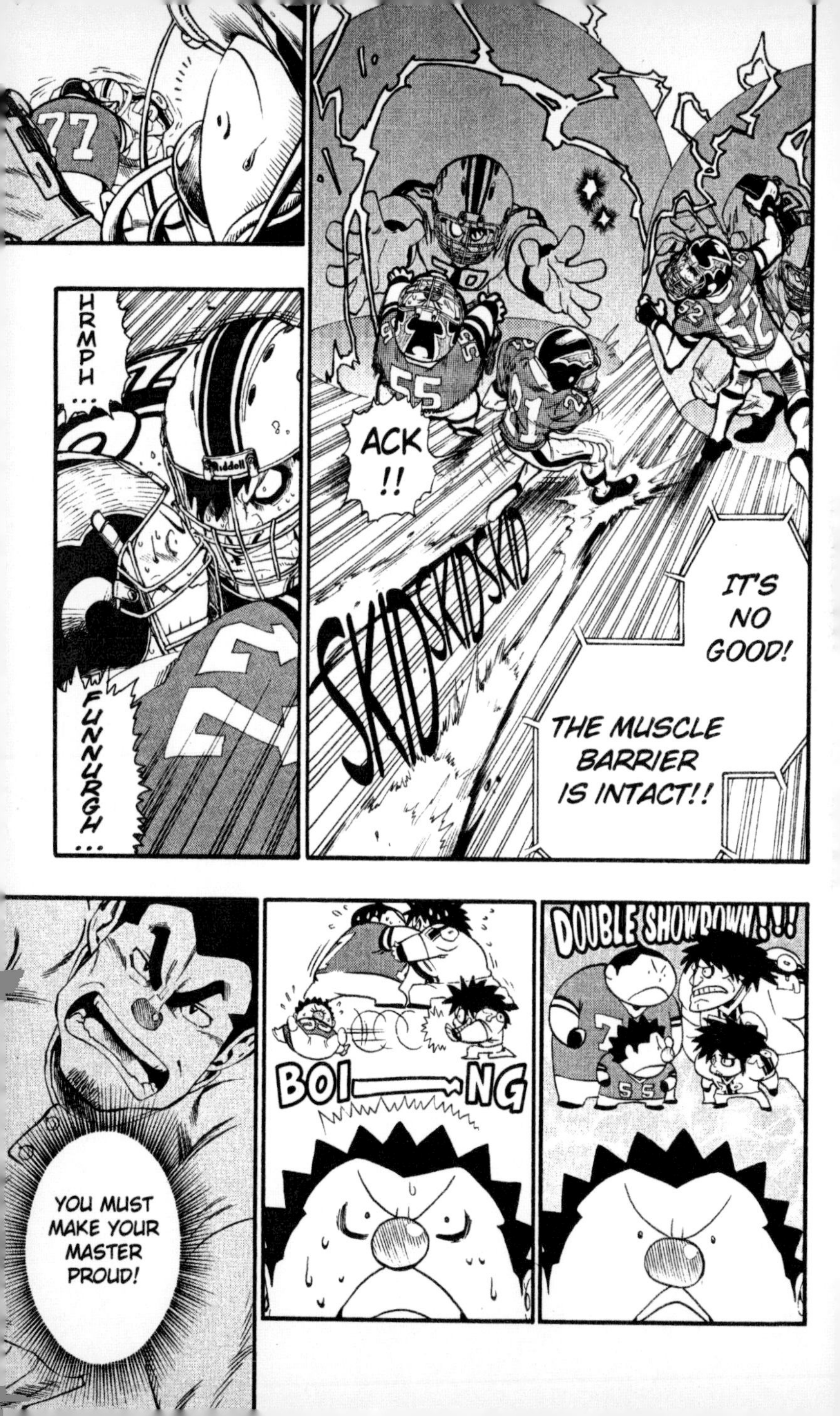
ACK !!
SKIDSKIDSKID
IT'S NO GOOD!
THE MUSCLE BARRIER IS INTACT!!
HRMPH...
FUNNURGH...
DOUBLE SHOWDOWN!!!
BOI——NG
YOU MUST MAKE YOUR MASTER PROUD!

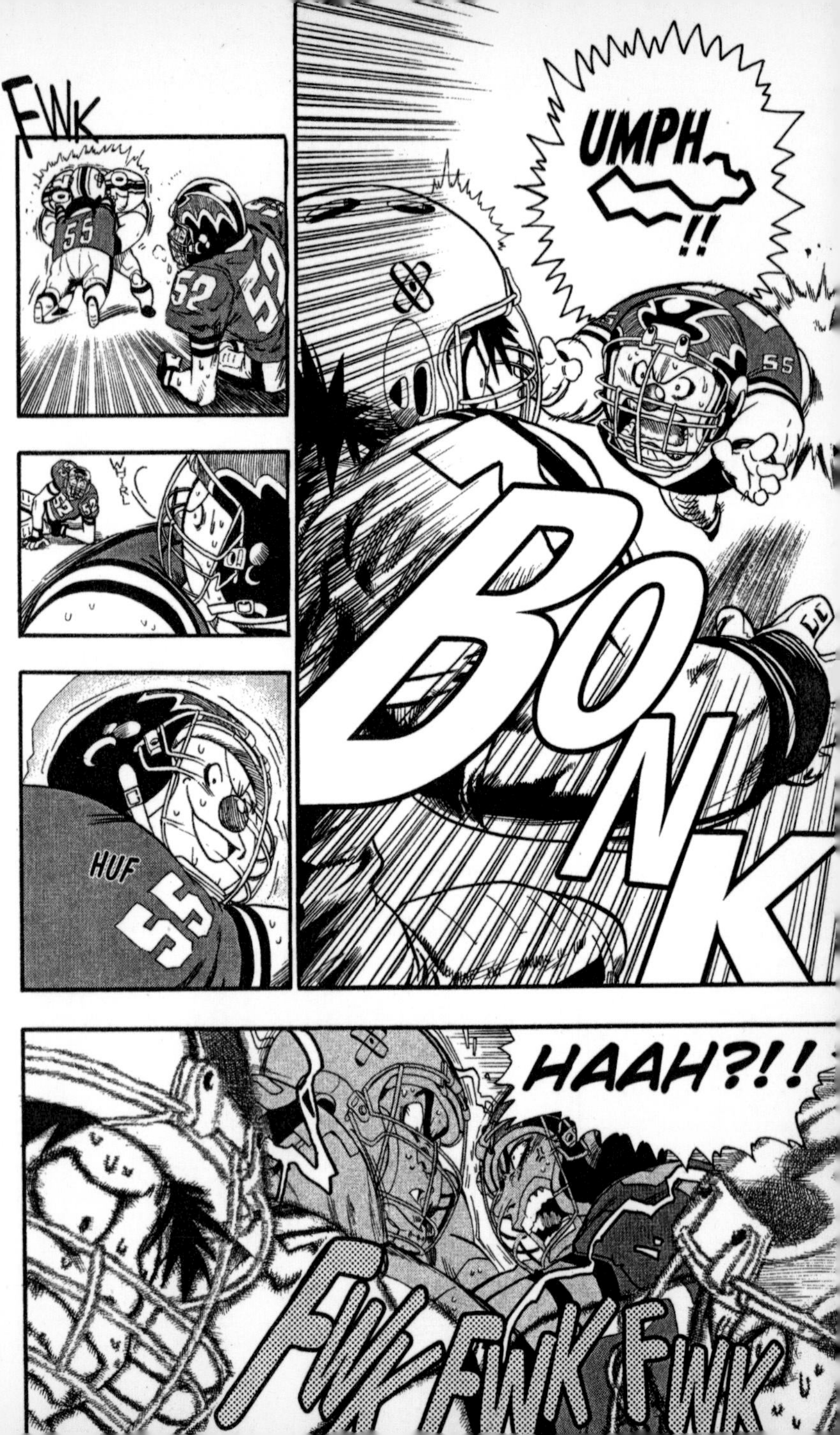
UMPH!!
BONK
FWK
WHIRL
HUF
HAAH?!!
FWK FWK FWK

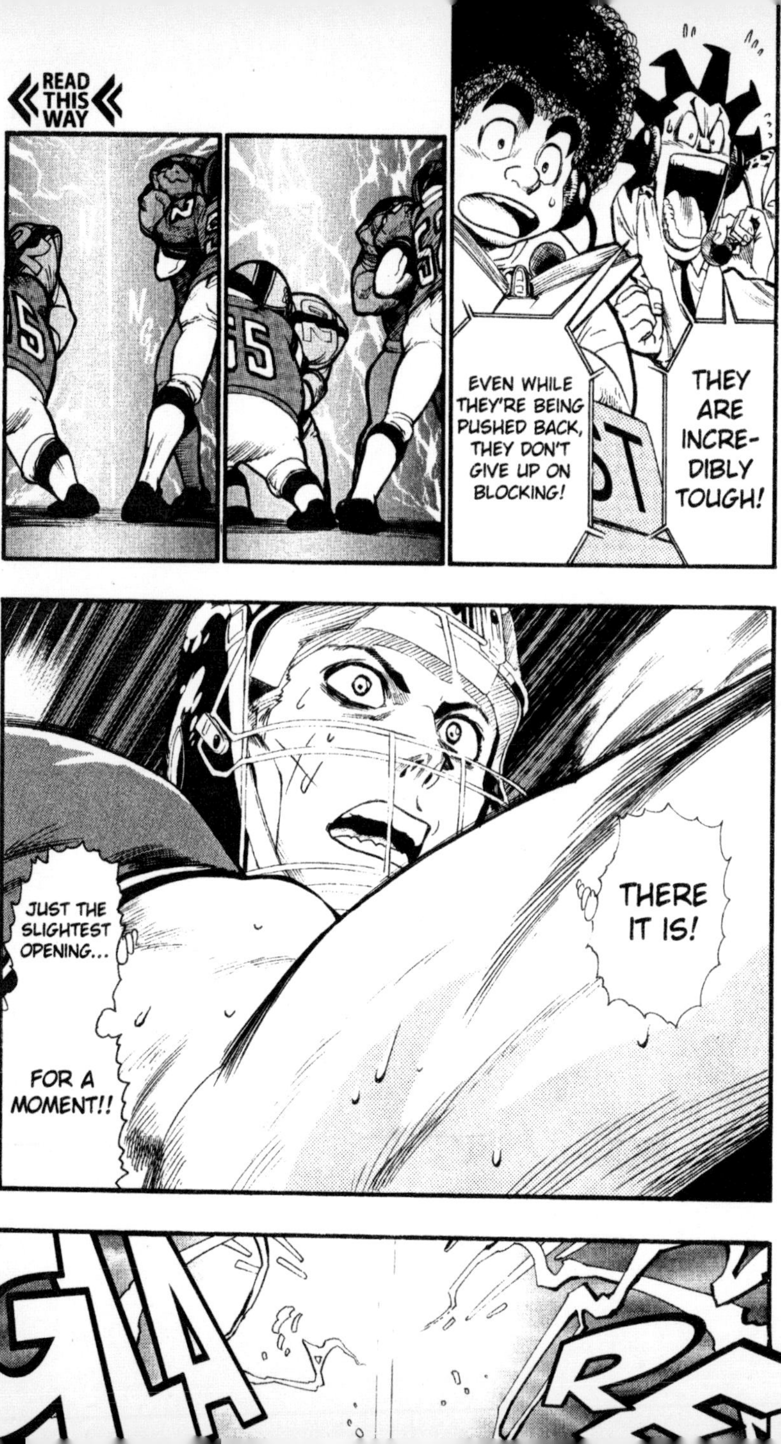
READ THIS WAY
THEY ARE INCREDIBLY TOUGH!
EVEN WHILE THEY'RE BEING PUSHED BACK, THEY DON'T GIVE UP ON BLOCKING!
NGH
THERE IT IS!
JUST THE SLIGHTEST OPENING...
FOR A MOMENT!!

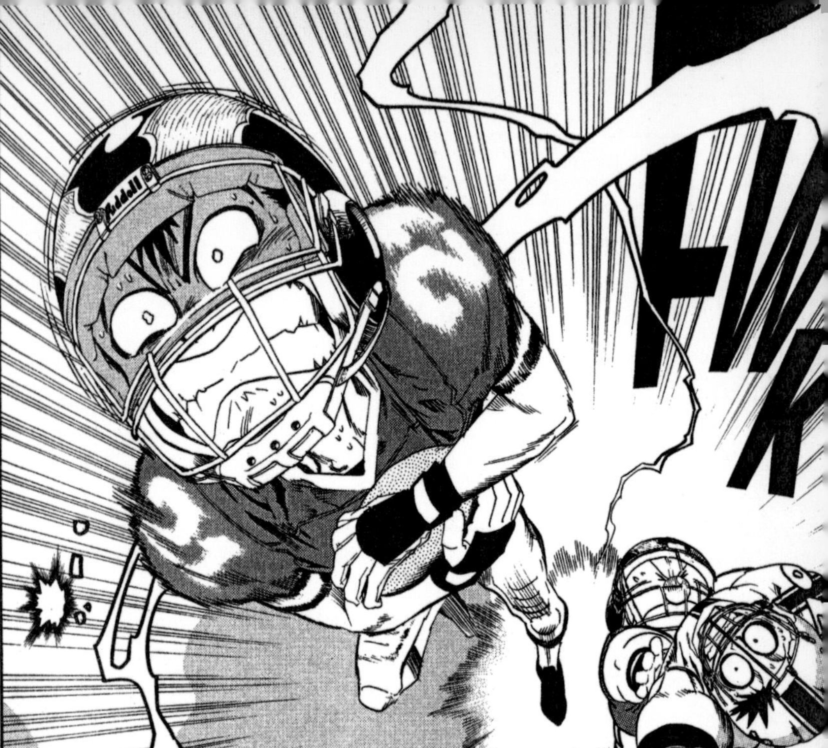
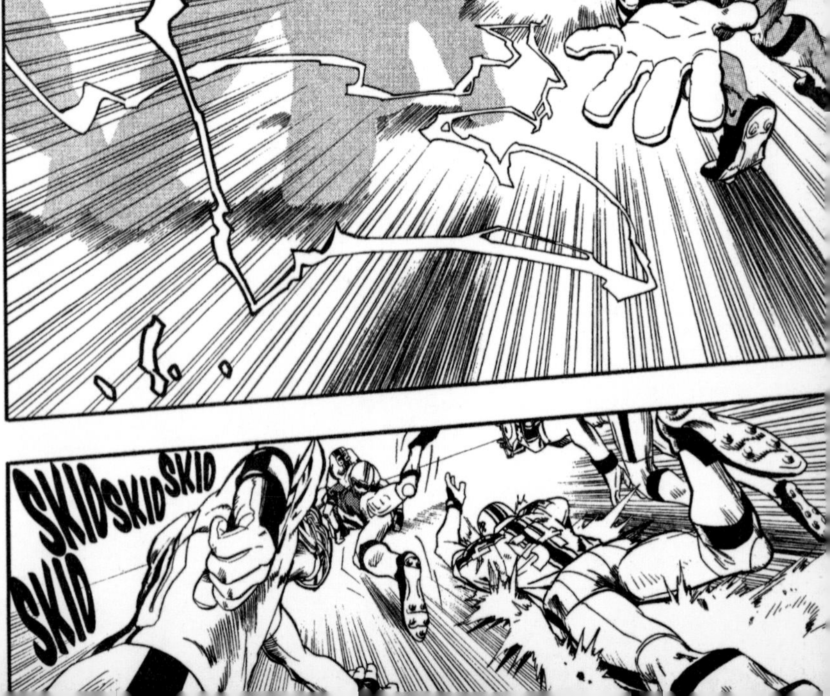
SKID SKID SKID SKID

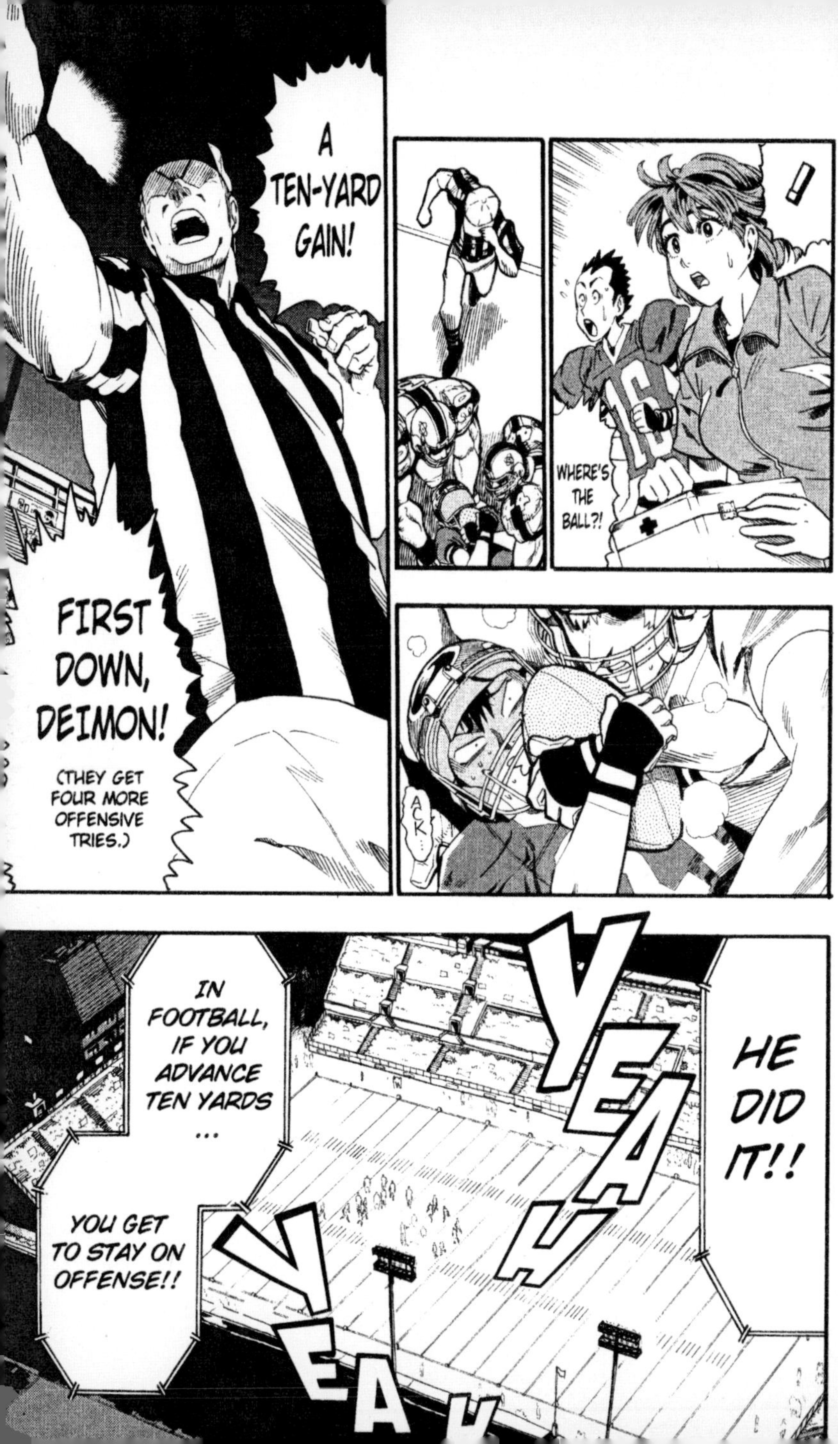
!
WHERE'S THE BALL?!
ACK...
A TEN-YARD GAIN!
FIRST DOWN, DEIMON!
(THEY GET FOUR MORE OFFENSIVE TRIES.)
HE DID IT!!
YEAH
IN FOOTBALL, IF YOU ADVANCE TEN YARDS ...
YOU GET TO STAY ON OFFENSE!!
YEAH

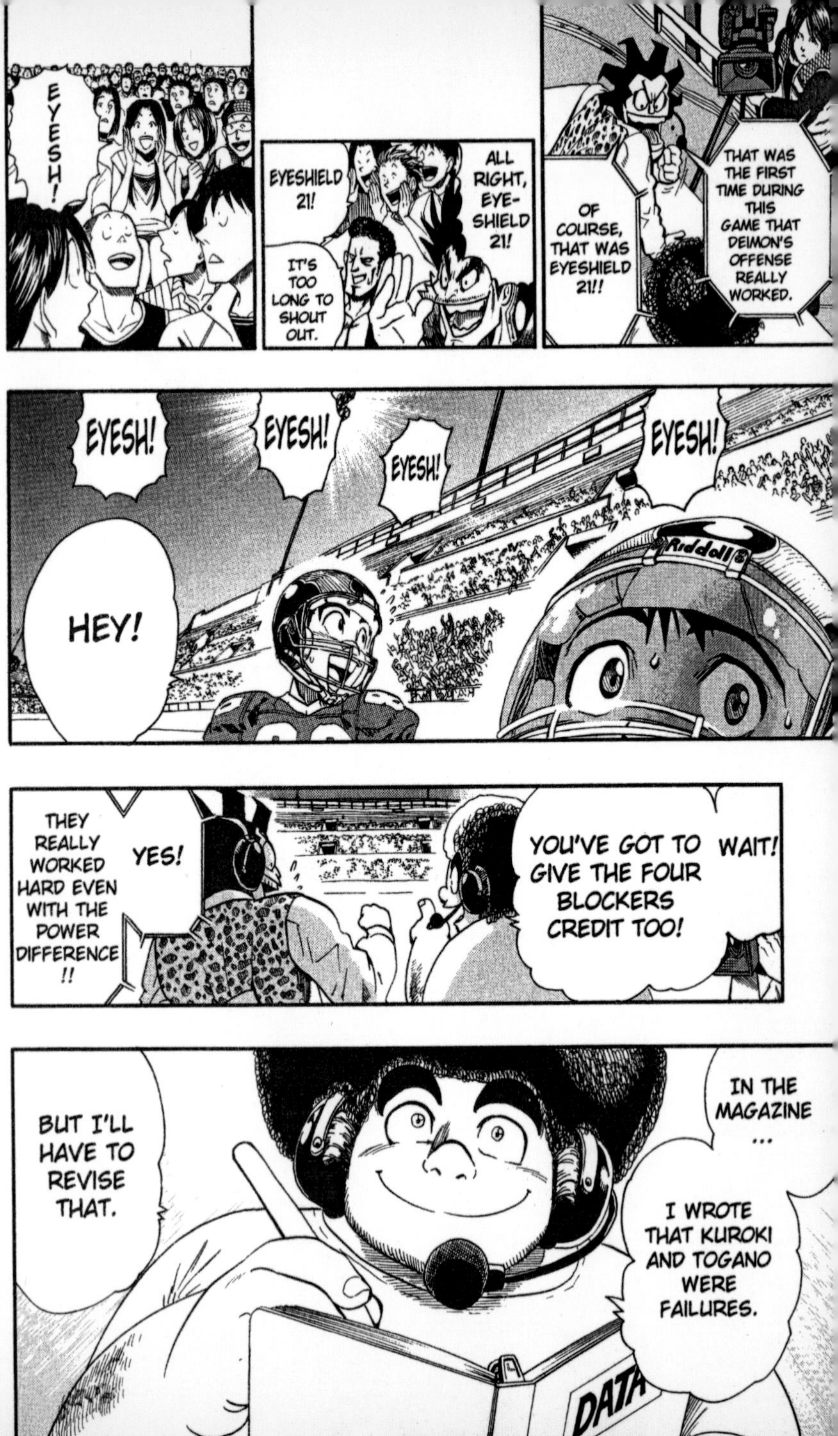
THAT WAS THE FIRST TIME DURING THIS GAME THAT DEIMON'S OFFENSE REALLY WORKED.
OF COURSE, THAT WAS EYESHIELD 21!!
ALL RIGHT, EYE-SHIELD 21!
EYESHIELD 21!
IT'S TOO LONG TO SHOUT OUT.
EYESH!
EYESH!
EYESH!
EYESH!
EYESH!
Riddell
HEY!
WAIT!
YOU'VE GOT TO GIVE THE FOUR BLOCKERS CREDIT TOO!
YES!
THEY REALLY WORKED HARD EVEN WITH THE POWER DIFFERENCE!!
IN THE MAGAZINE...
I WROTE THAT KUROKI AND TOGANO WERE FAILURES.
BUT I'LL HAVE TO REVISE THAT.
DATA

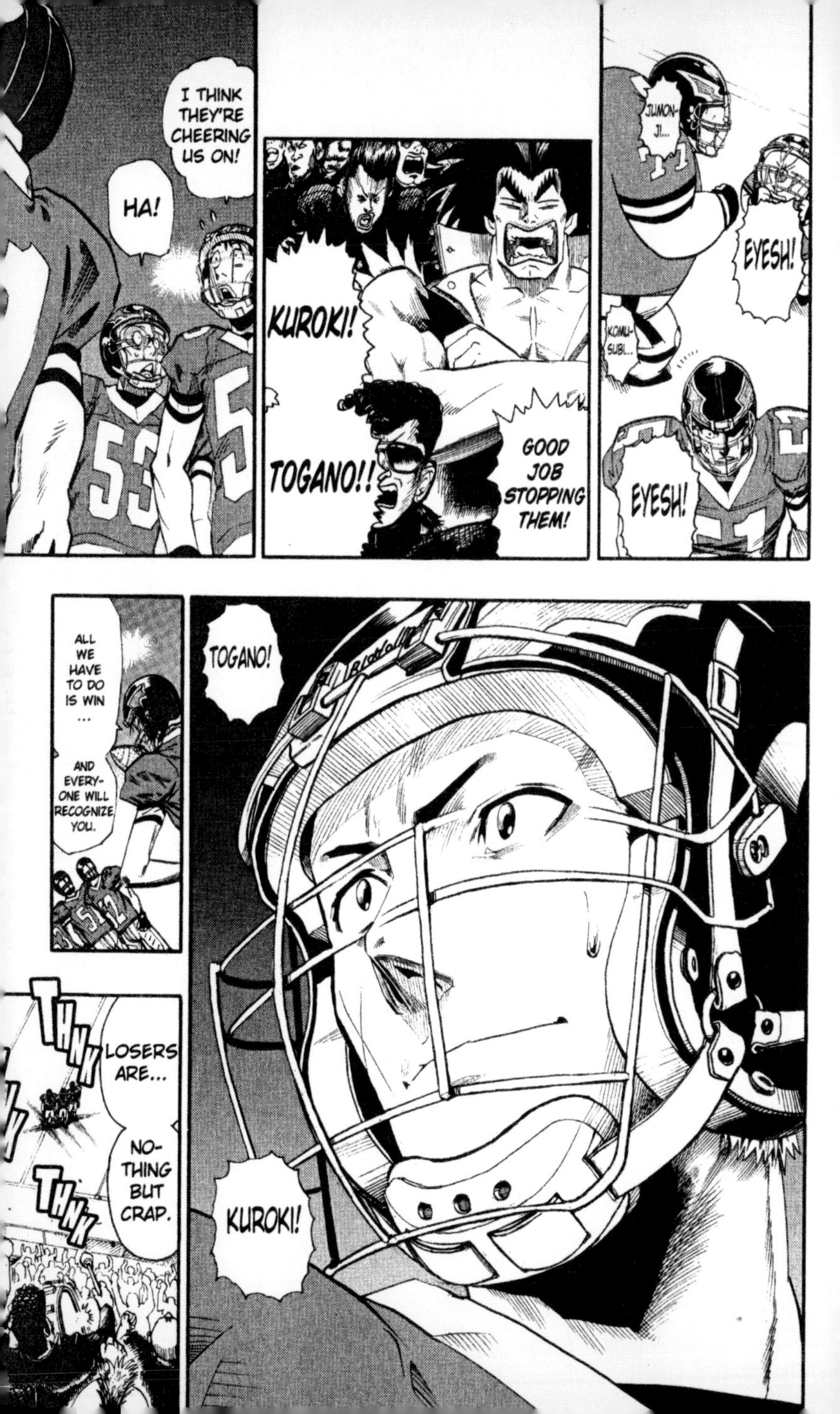
JUMON-JI...
EYESH!
KOMU-SUBI...
EYESH!
KUROKI!
GOOD JOB STOPPING THEM!
TOGANO!!
I THINK THEY'RE CHEERING US ON!
HA!
TOGANO!
KUROKI!
ALL WE HAVE TO DO IS WIN ...
AND EVERY-ONE WILL RECOGNIZE YOU.
LOSERS ARE...
NO-THING BUT CRAP.
THNK
THNK

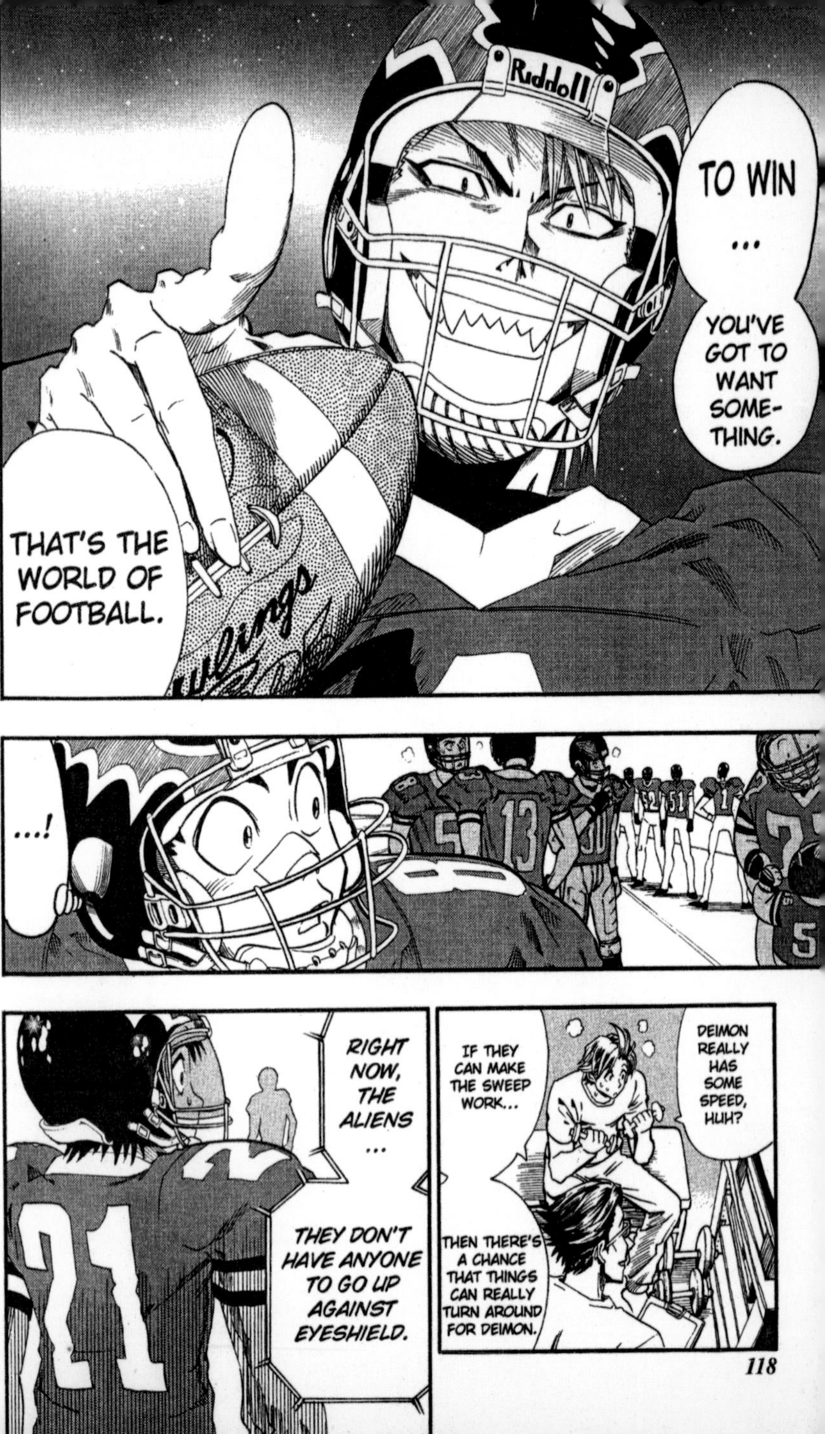

TO WIN ... YOU'VE GOT TO WANT SOME-THING.
THAT'S THE WORLD OF FOOTBALL.
...!
DEIMON REALLY HAS SOME SPEED, HUH?
IF THEY CAN MAKE THE SWEEP WORK...
THEN THERE'S A CHANCE THAT THINGS CAN REALLY TURN AROUND FOR DEIMON.
RIGHT NOW, THE ALIENS ...
THEY DON'T HAVE ANYONE TO GO UP AGAINST EYESHIELD.

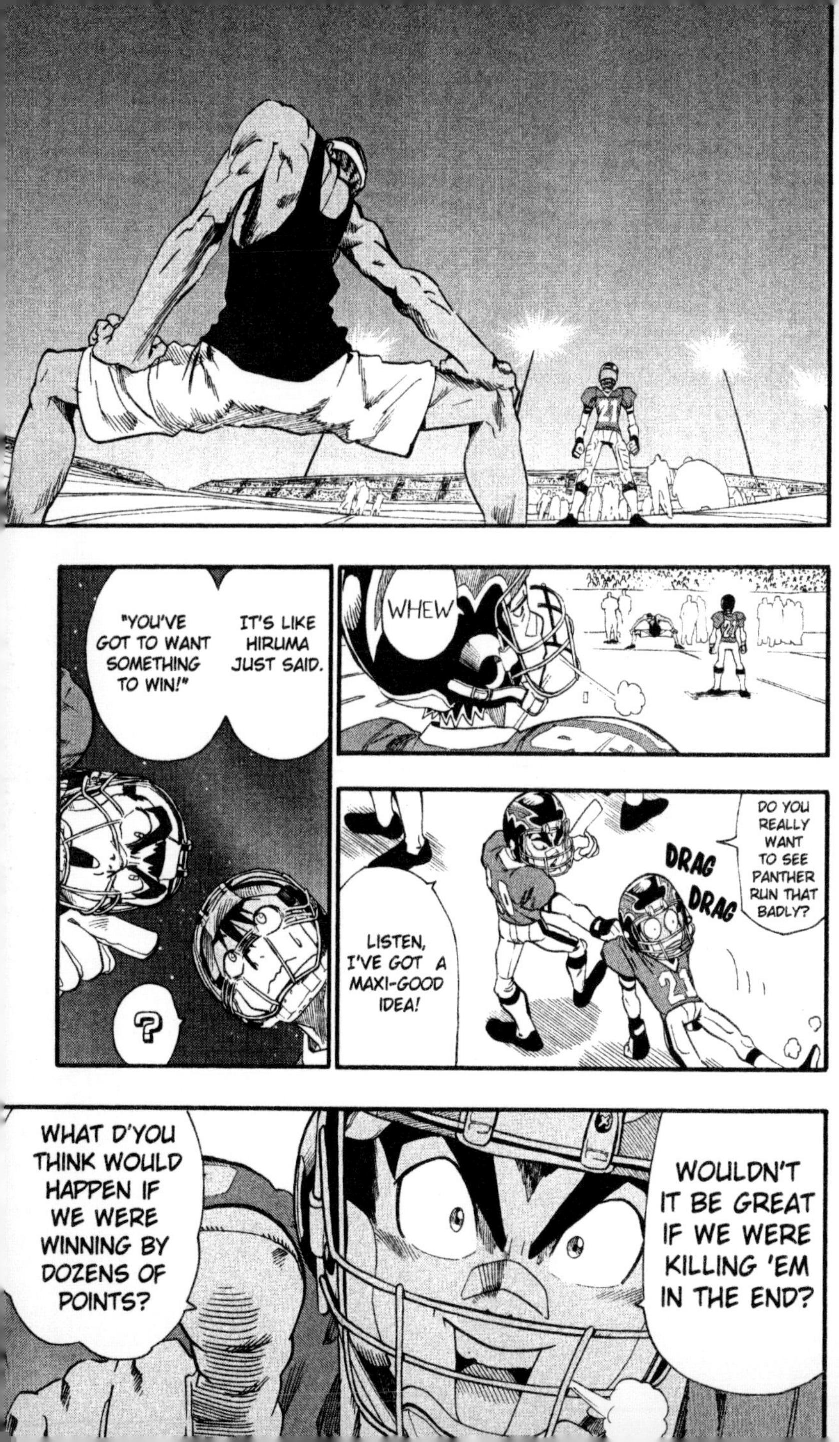
WHEW
DO YOU REALLY WANT TO SEE PANTHER RUN THAT BADLY?
DRAG DRAG
LISTEN, I'VE GOT A MAXI-GOOD IDEA!
IT'S LIKE HIRUMA JUST SAID.
"YOU'VE GOT TO WANT SOMETHING TO WIN!"
?
WOULDN'T IT BE GREAT IF WE WERE KILLING 'EM IN THE END?
WHAT D'YOU THINK WOULD HAPPEN IF WE WERE WINNING BY DOZENS OF POINTS?

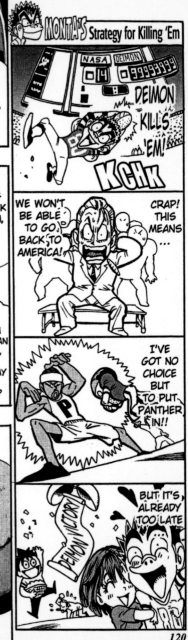

MONTA'S Strategy for Killing 'Em

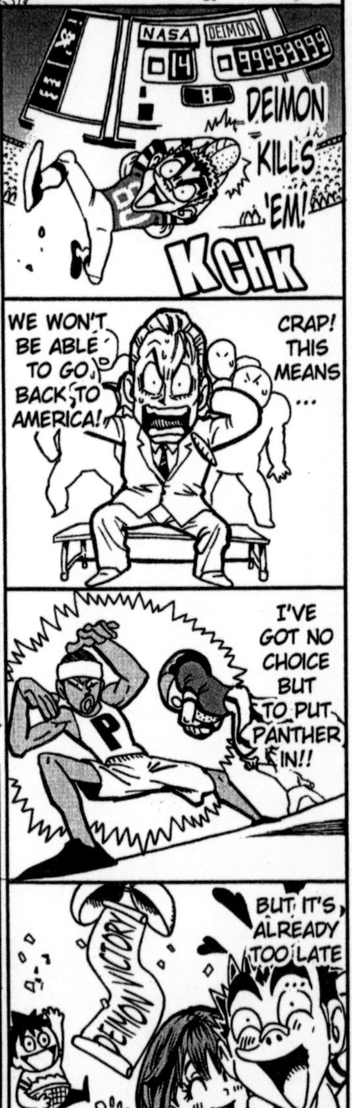
NASA
DEIMON
14
99999999
DEIMON KILLS 'EM!
KCHK
CRAP! THIS MEANS...
WE WON'T BE ABLE TO GO BACK TO AMERICA!
I'VE GOT NO CHOICE BUT TO PUT PANTHER IN!!
BUT IT'S ALREADY TOO LATE
DEIMON VICTORY

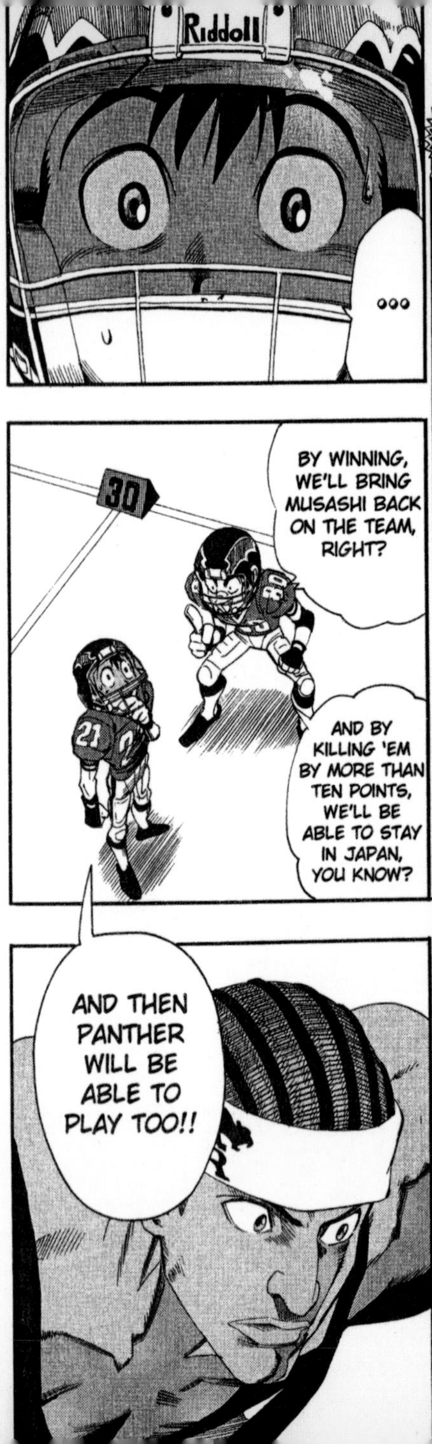
Riddoll
...
BY WINNING, WE'LL BRING MUSASHI BACK ON THE TEAM, RIGHT?
AND BY KILLING 'EM BY MORE THAN TEN POINTS, WE'LL BE ABLE TO STAY IN JAPAN, YOU KNOW?
AND THEN PANTHER WILL BE ABLE TO PLAY TOO!!

READ THIS WAY

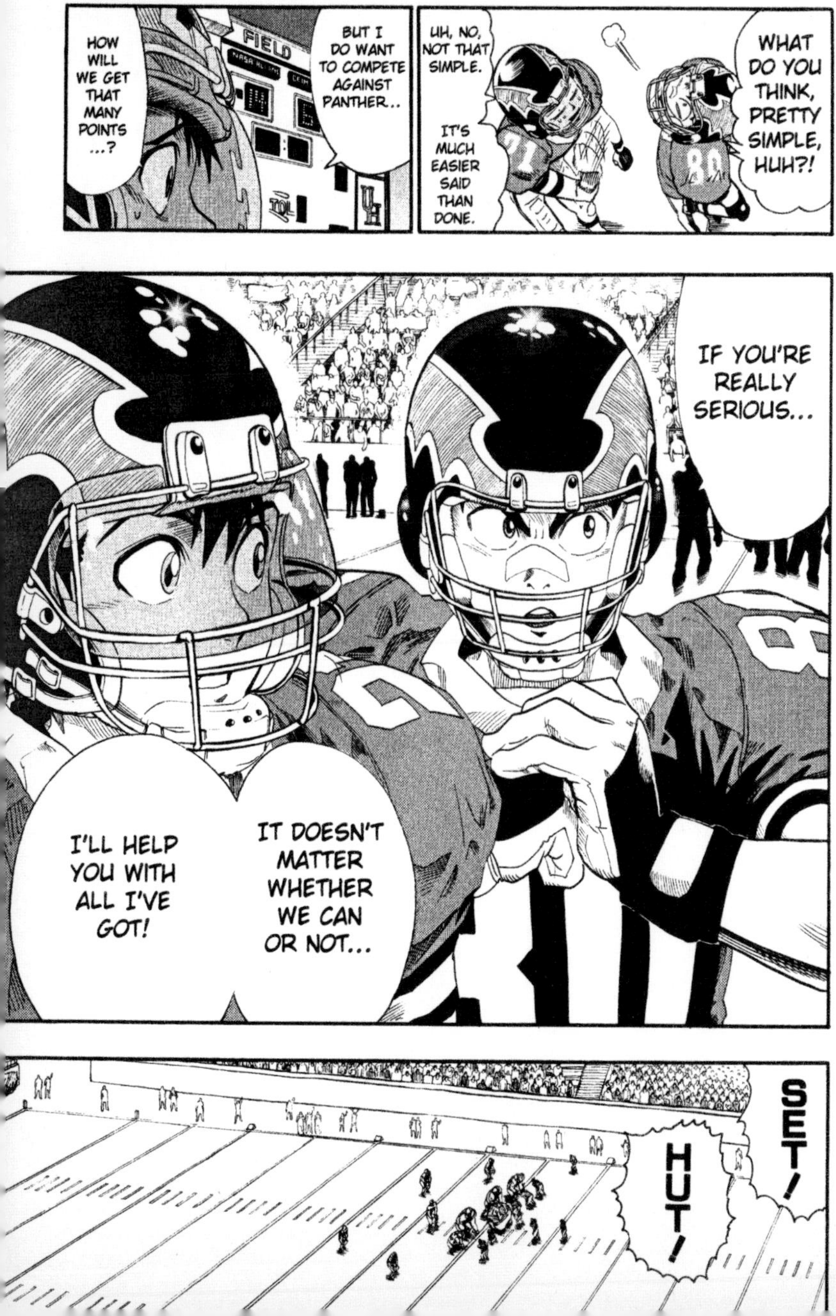
WHAT DO YOU THINK, PRETTY SIMPLE, HUH?!
UH, NO, NOT THAT SIMPLE.
IT'S MUCH EASIER SAID THAN DONE.
BUT I DO WANT TO COMPETE AGAINST PANTHER..
HOW WILL WE GET THAT MANY POINTS ...?
IF YOU'RE REALLY SERIOUS...
IT DOESN'T MATTER WHETHER WE CAN OR NOT...
I'LL HELP YOU WITH ALL I'VE GOT!
SET!
HUT!

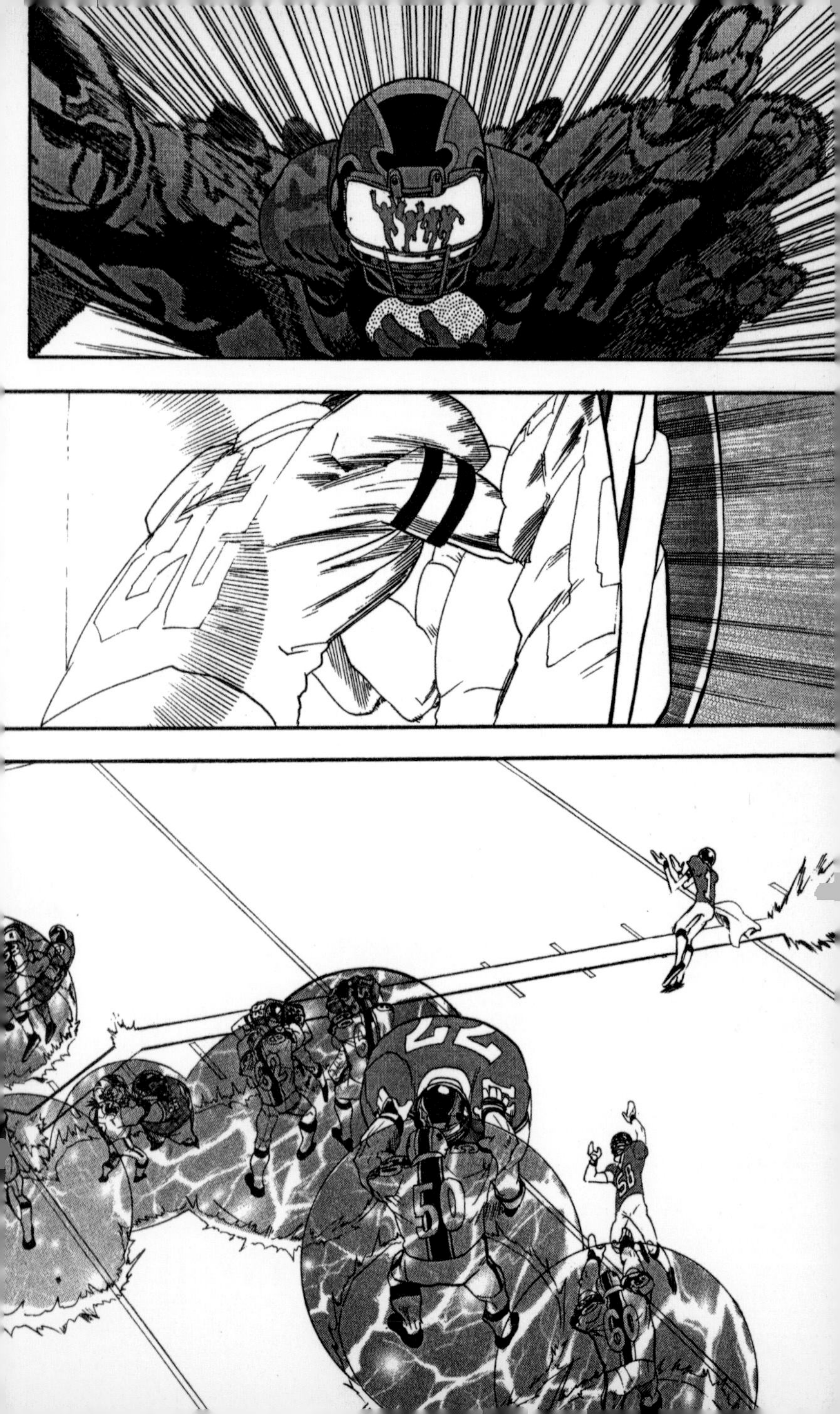

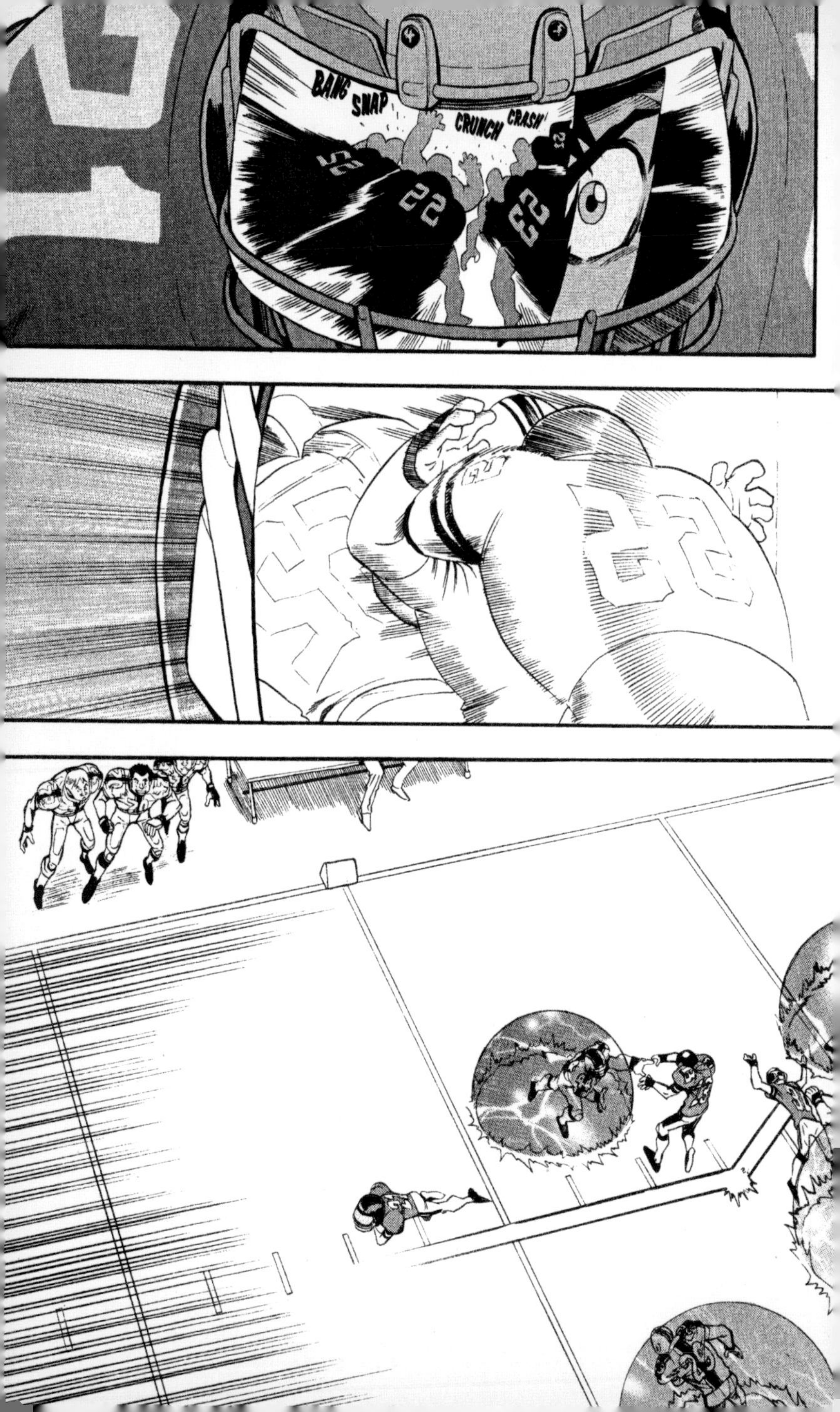
BANG
SNAP
CRUNCH
CRASH

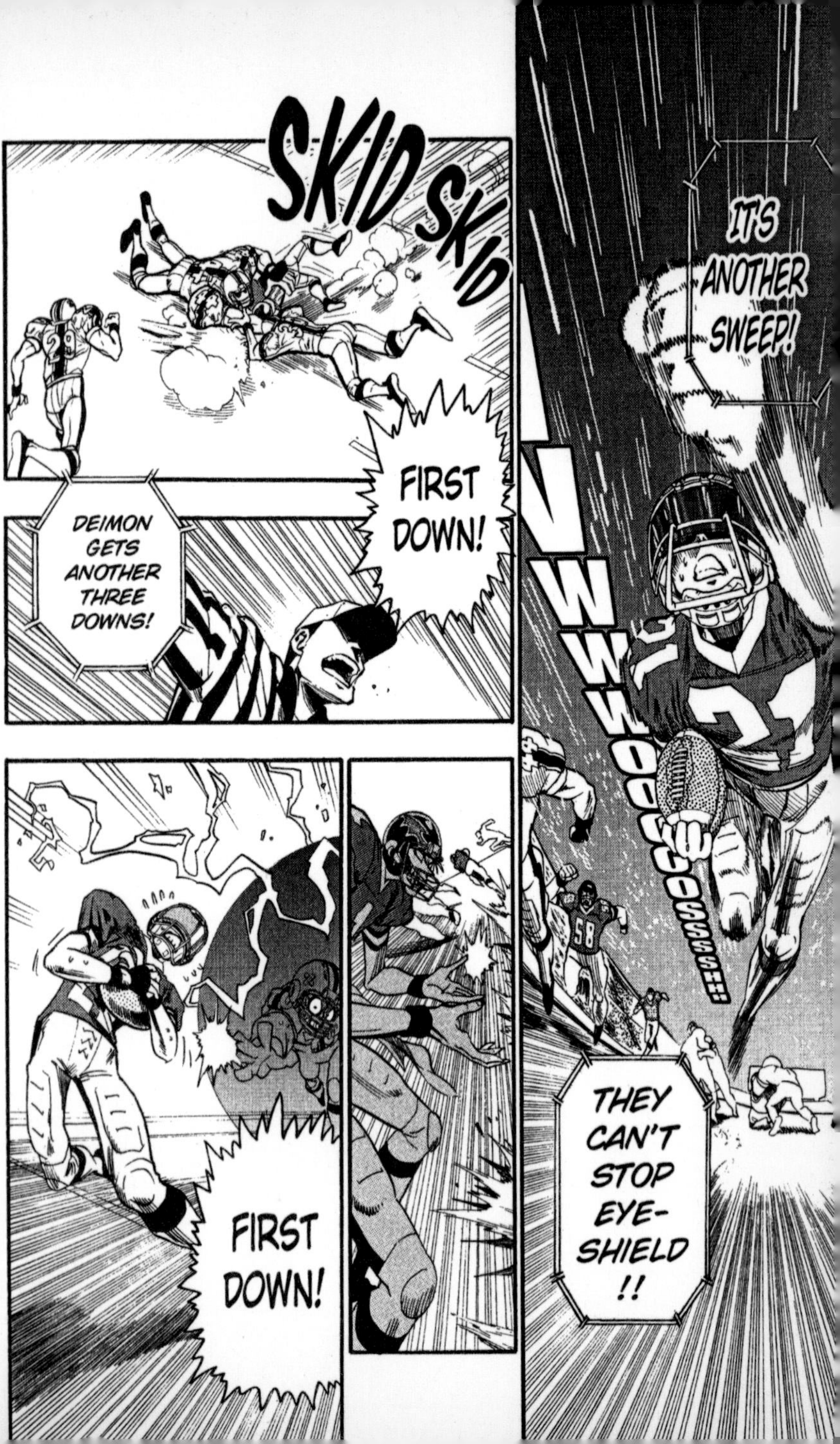
IT'S ANOTHER SWEEP!
WWWWOOOOSSSSH!!
THEY CAN'T STOP EYE-SHIELD!!
SKID SKID
FIRST DOWN!
DEIMON GETS ANOTHER THREE DOWNS!
FIRST DOWN!

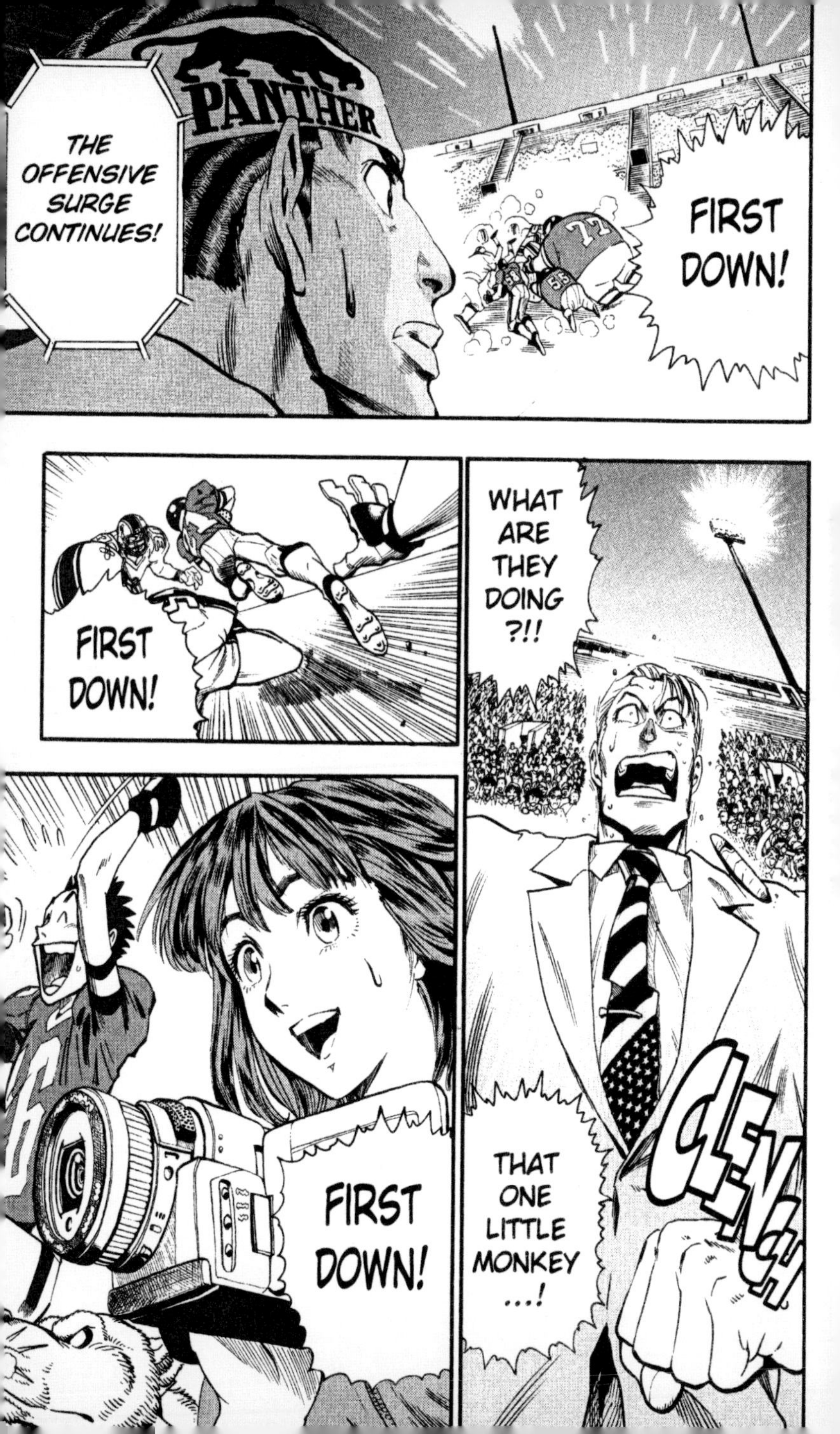
FIRST DOWN!
THE OFFENSIVE SURGE CONTINUES!
WHAT ARE THEY DOING?!!
CLENCH
THAT ONE LITTLE MONKEY...!
FIRST DOWN!
FIRST DOWN!

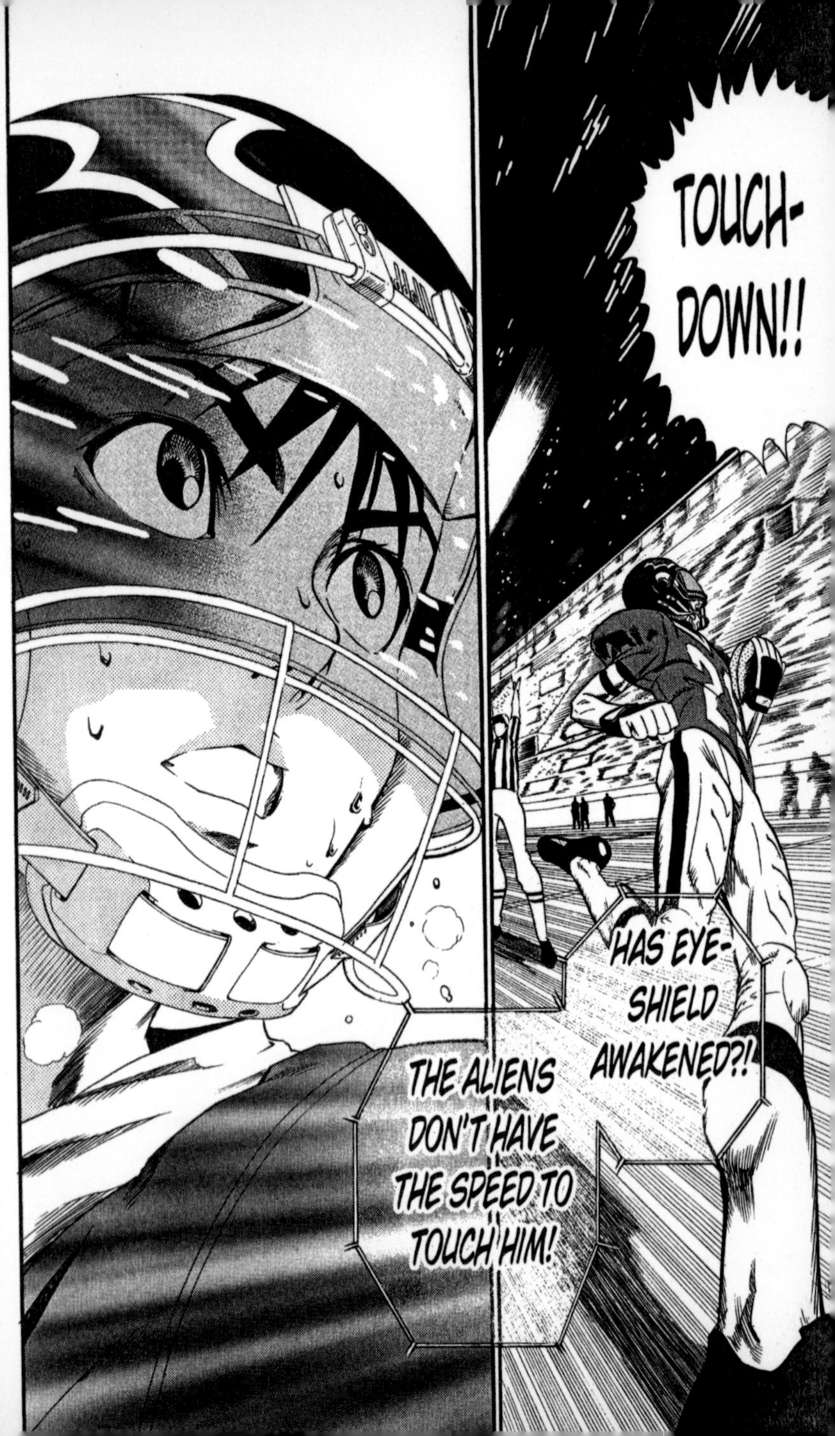
TOUCH-DOWN!!
HAS EYE-SHIELD AWAKENED?!
THE ALIENS DON'T HAVE THE SPEED TO TOUCH HIM!

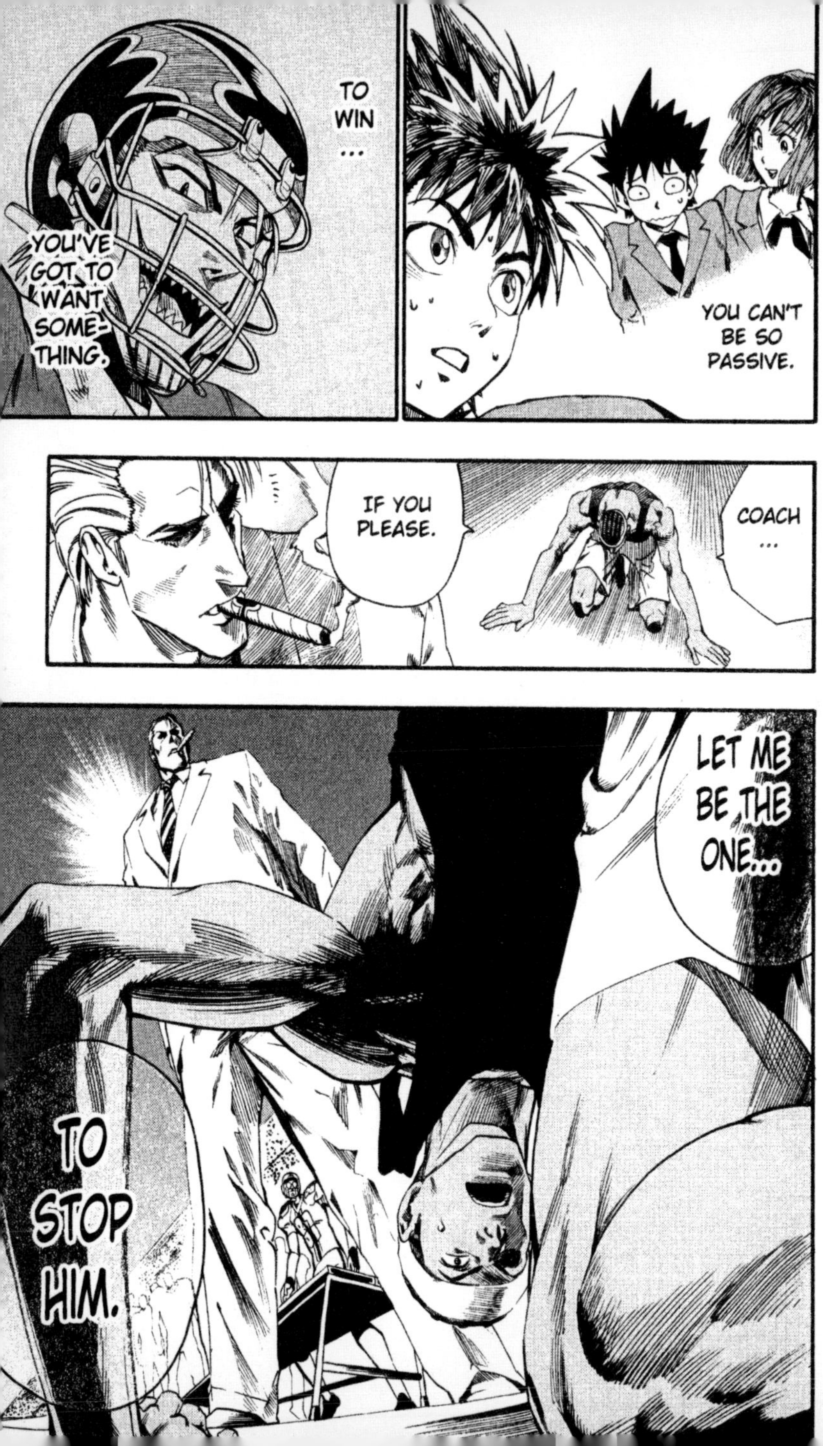
YOU CAN'T BE SO PASSIVE.
TO WIN ...
YOU'VE GOT TO WANT SOME-THING.
COACH ...
IF YOU PLEASE.
LET ME BE THE ONE...
TO STOP HIM.

Eyeshield 21 Survey Corner **Devil Bat 021**

Investigation File #005

Uncover Watt's true nature!!

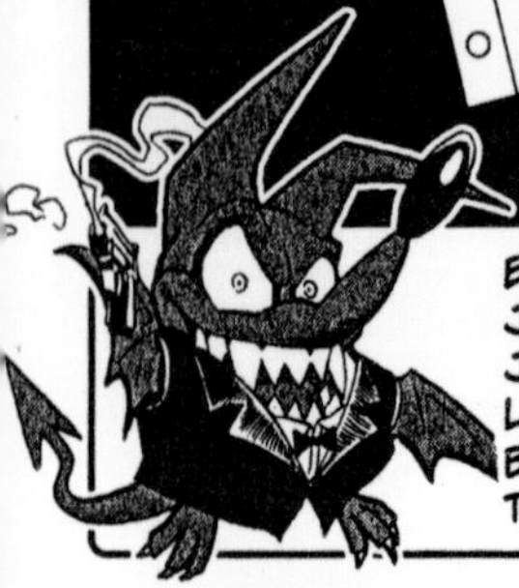

EVEN THOUGH HE'S KNOWN AS A JAPAN SCHOLAR, WHY DOES WATT'S JAPANESE SEEM SO BOGUS?
LIKE, HOW COULD HE LET THEM GET BIG POOP AND LITTLE PISSER TATTOOS...?

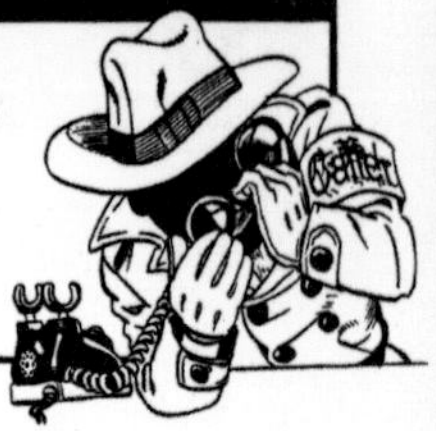

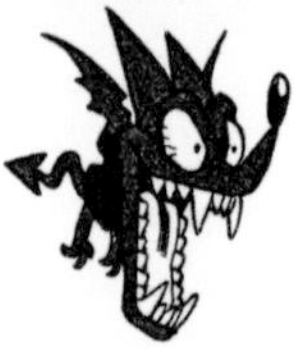

WATT'S A PSEUDO-JAPAN SCHOLAR!!

WHAT, DID YOU THINK HE WAS A WICKED MASTER OF JAPANESE CULTURE?!

CLEVER SPY THAT I AM, I SNUCK A PEEK AT WATT IN PRIVATE!

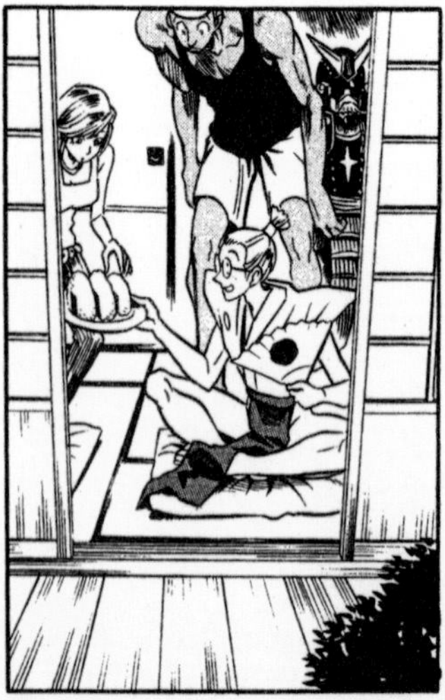

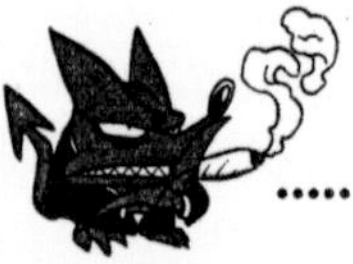

.....

SURVEY REPORT.
WATT IS NOT WICKED.
THAT'S JUST THE WAY THAT HE IS.

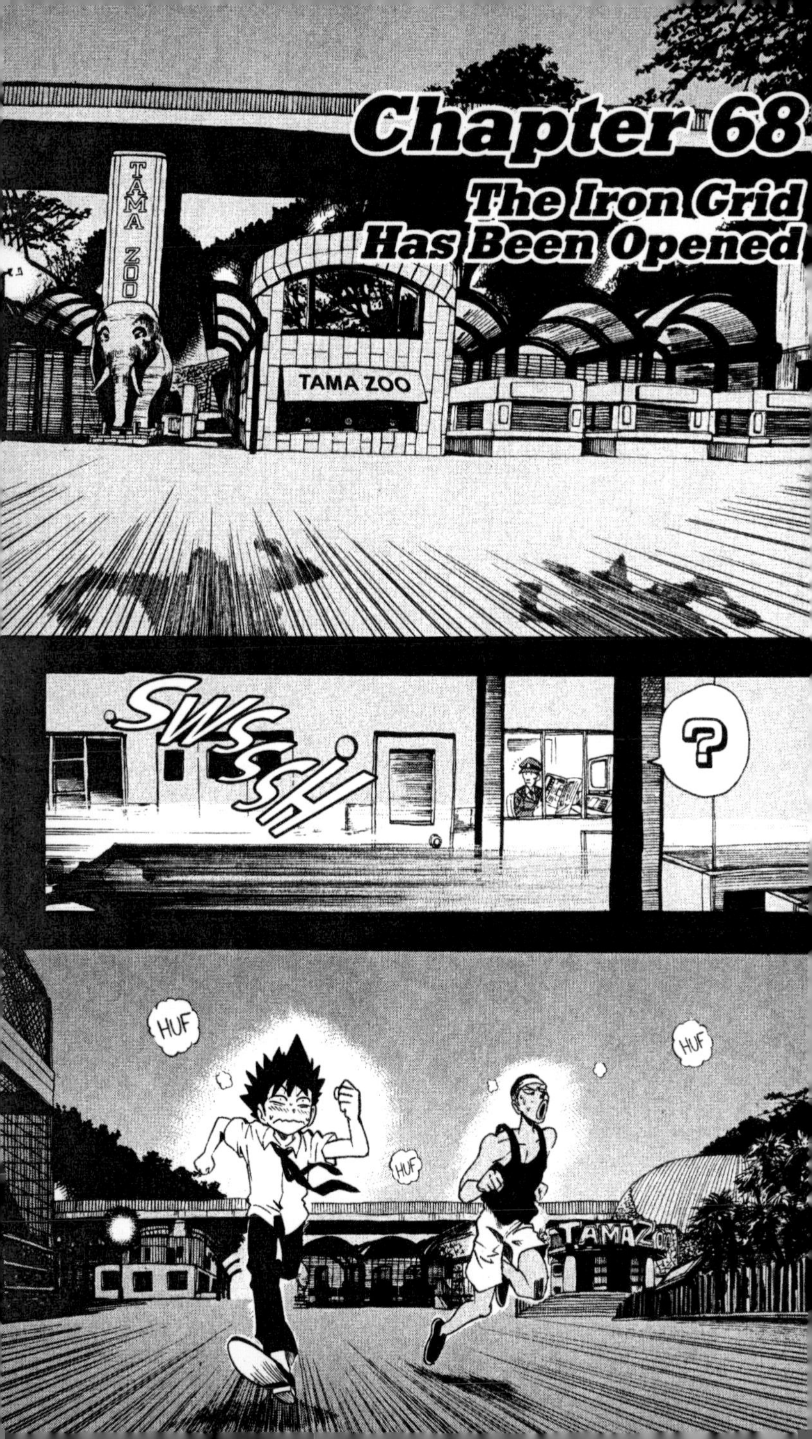

Chapter 68
The Iron Grid Has Been Opened
TAMA ZOO
TAMA ZOO
?
SWSSH
HUF
HUF
HUF
TAMA ZOO

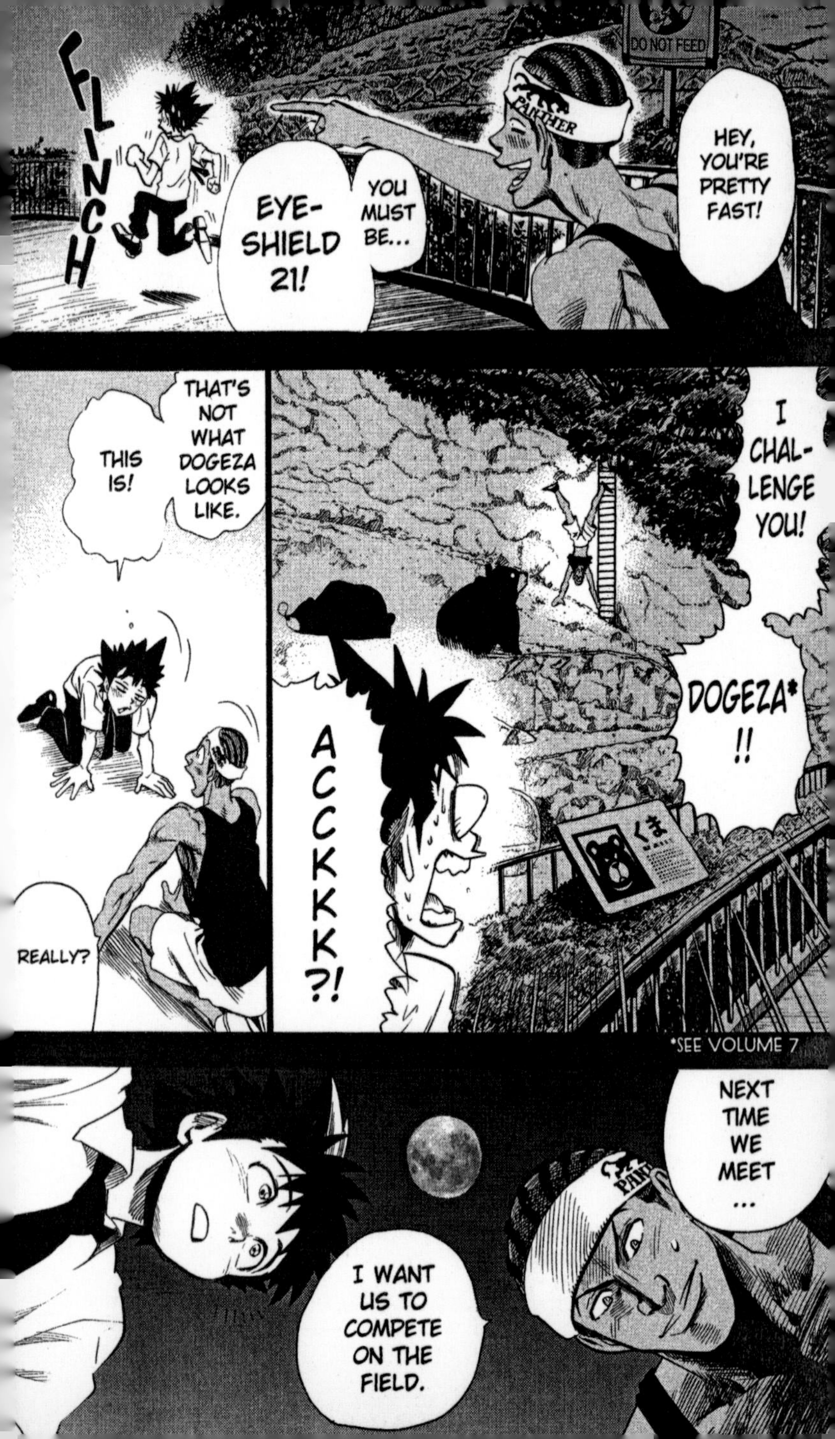
DO NOT FEED
PANTHER
HEY, YOU'RE PRETTY FAST!
YOU MUST BE...
EYE-SHIELD 21!
FLINCH
I CHAL-LENGE YOU!
DOGEZA* !!
くま
ACCKKK?!
THAT'S NOT WHAT DOGEZA LOOKS LIKE.
THIS IS!
REALLY?
*SEE VOLUME 7
NEXT TIME WE MEET ...
I WANT US TO COMPETE ON THE FIELD.

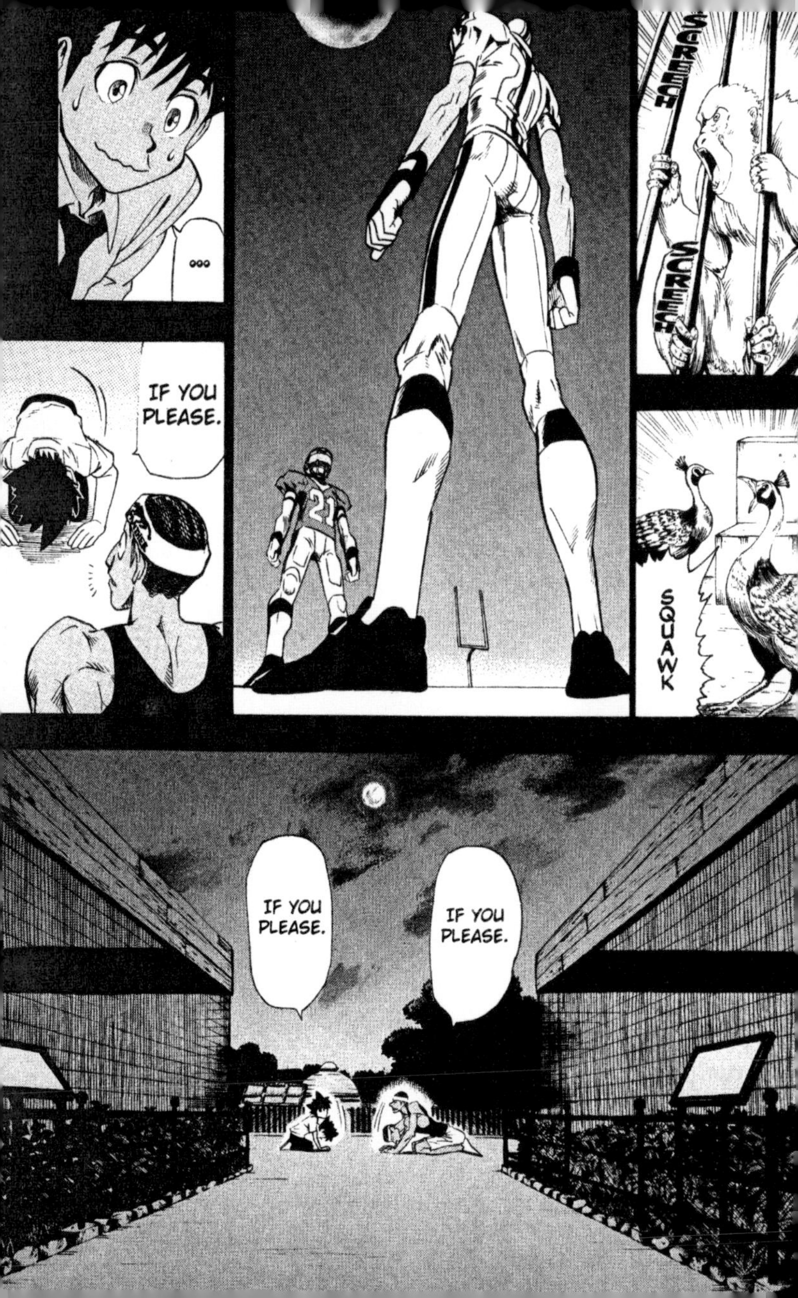
SCREECH
SCREECH
SQUAWK
...
IF YOU PLEASE.
IF YOU PLEASE.
IF YOU PLEASE.

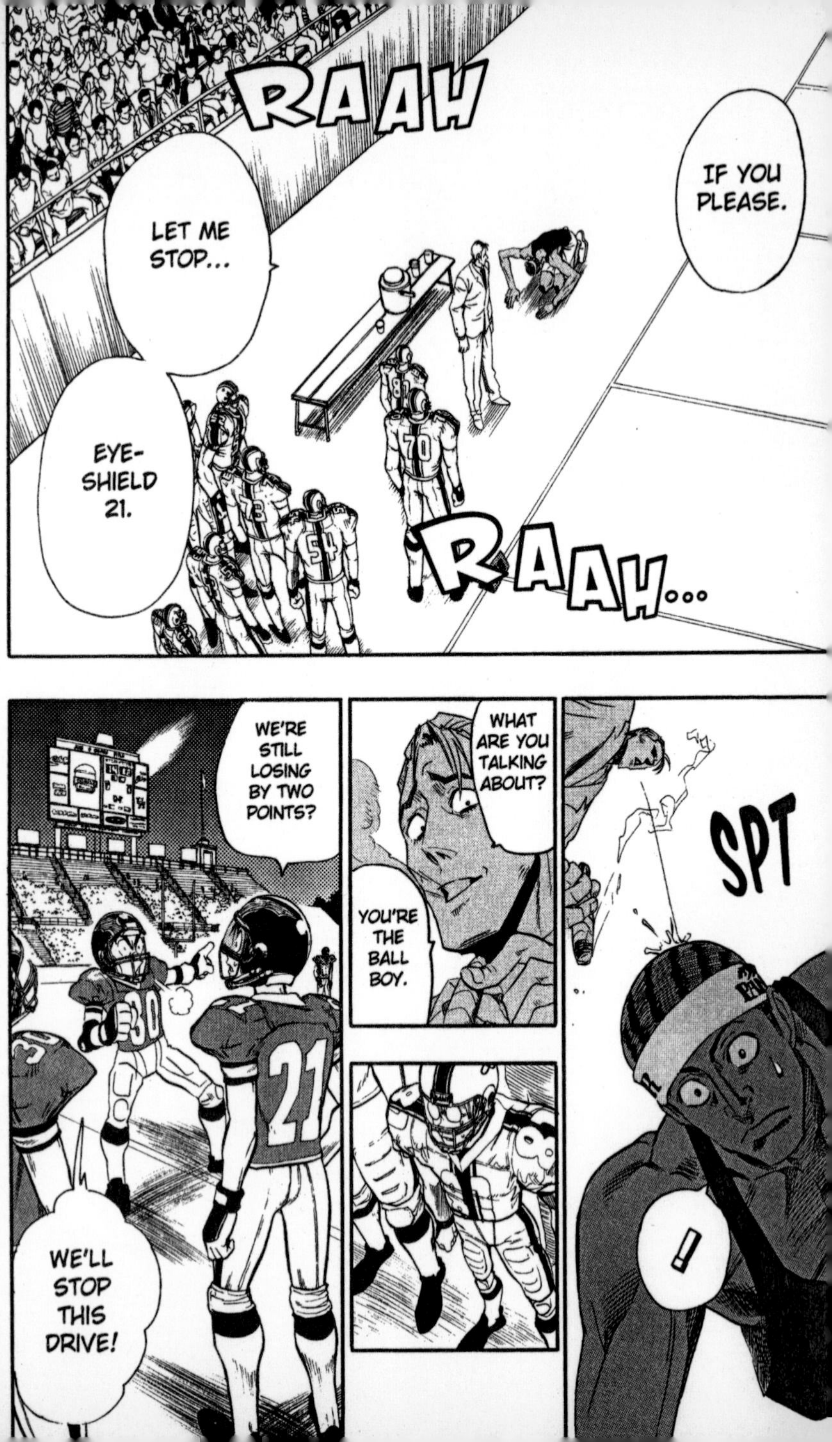
RAAH
IF YOU PLEASE.
LET ME STOP...
EYE-SHIELD 21.
RAAH...
SPT
!
WHAT ARE YOU TALKING ABOUT?
YOU'RE THE BALL BOY.
WE'RE STILL LOSING BY TWO POINTS?
WE'LL STOP THIS DRIVE!

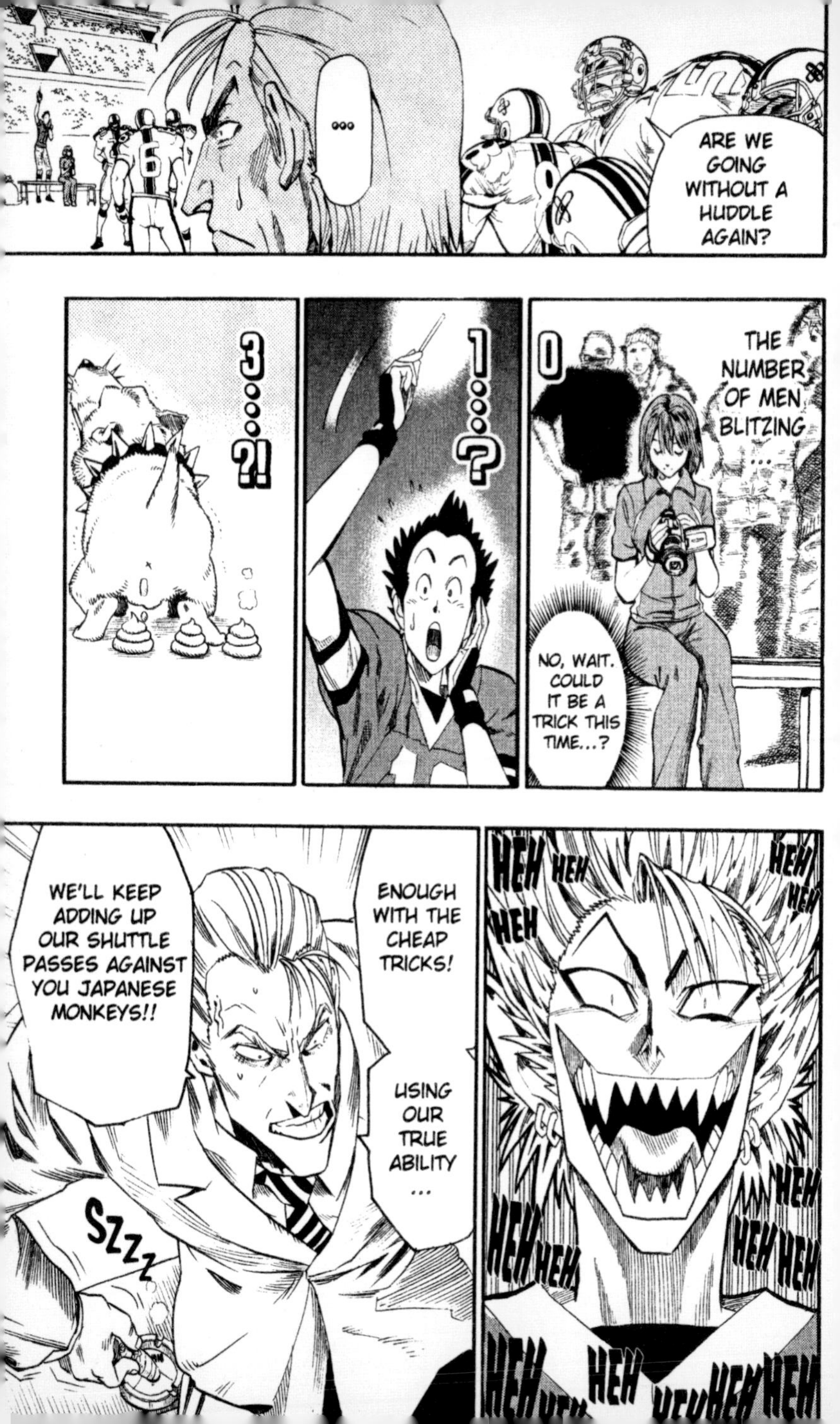
ARE WE GOING WITHOUT A HUDDLE AGAIN?
...
THE NUMBER OF MEN BLITZING ...
0
NO, WAIT. COULD IT BE A TRICK THIS TIME...?
1...?
3...?!
HEH HEH HEH HEH HEH HEH
HEH HEH HEH HEH HEH HEH
HEH HEH HEH HEH HEH HEH
ENOUGH WITH THE CHEAP TRICKS!
USING OUR TRUE ABILITY ...
WE'LL KEEP ADDING UP OUR SHUTTLE PASSES AGAINST YOU JAPANESE MONKEYS!!
SZZZ

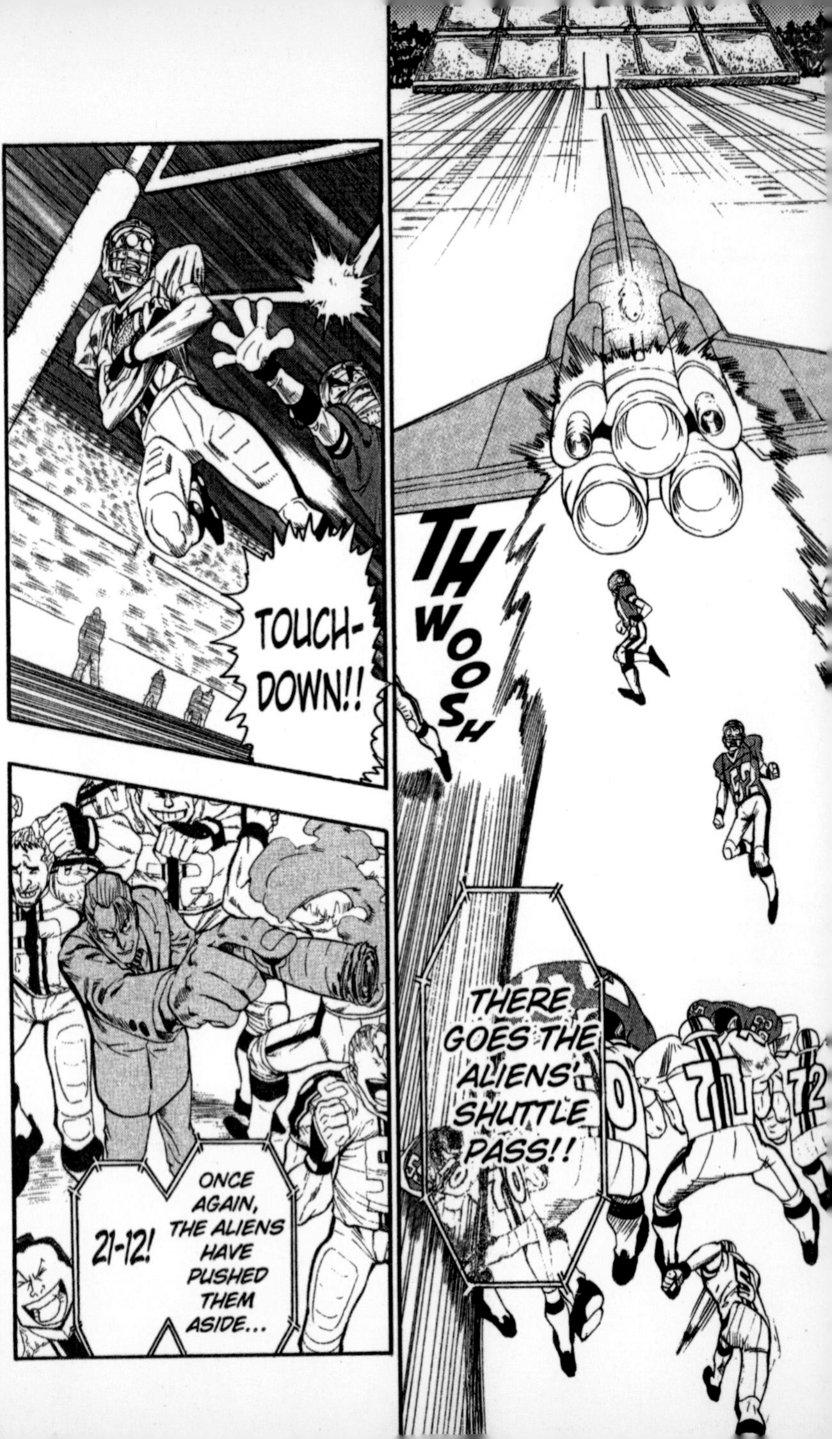
THWOOSH
THERE GOES THE ALIENS' SHUTTLE PASS!!
TOUCH-DOWN!!
ONCE AGAIN, THE ALIENS HAVE PUSHED THEM ASIDE...
21-12!

READ THIS WAY

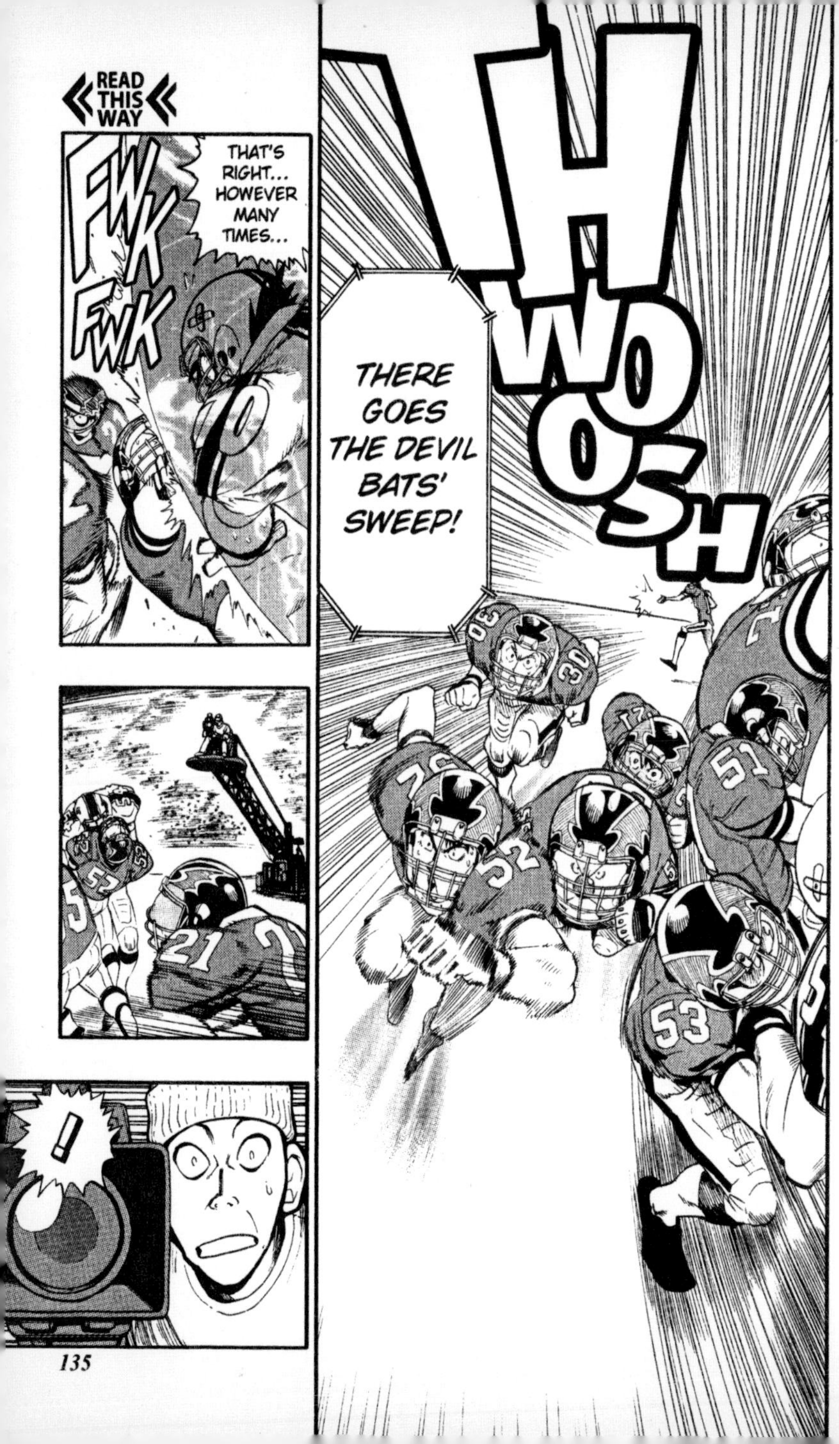
WOOSH
THERE GOES THE DEVIL BATS' SWEEP!
FWK FWK
THAT'S RIGHT... HOWEVER MANY TIMES...
!

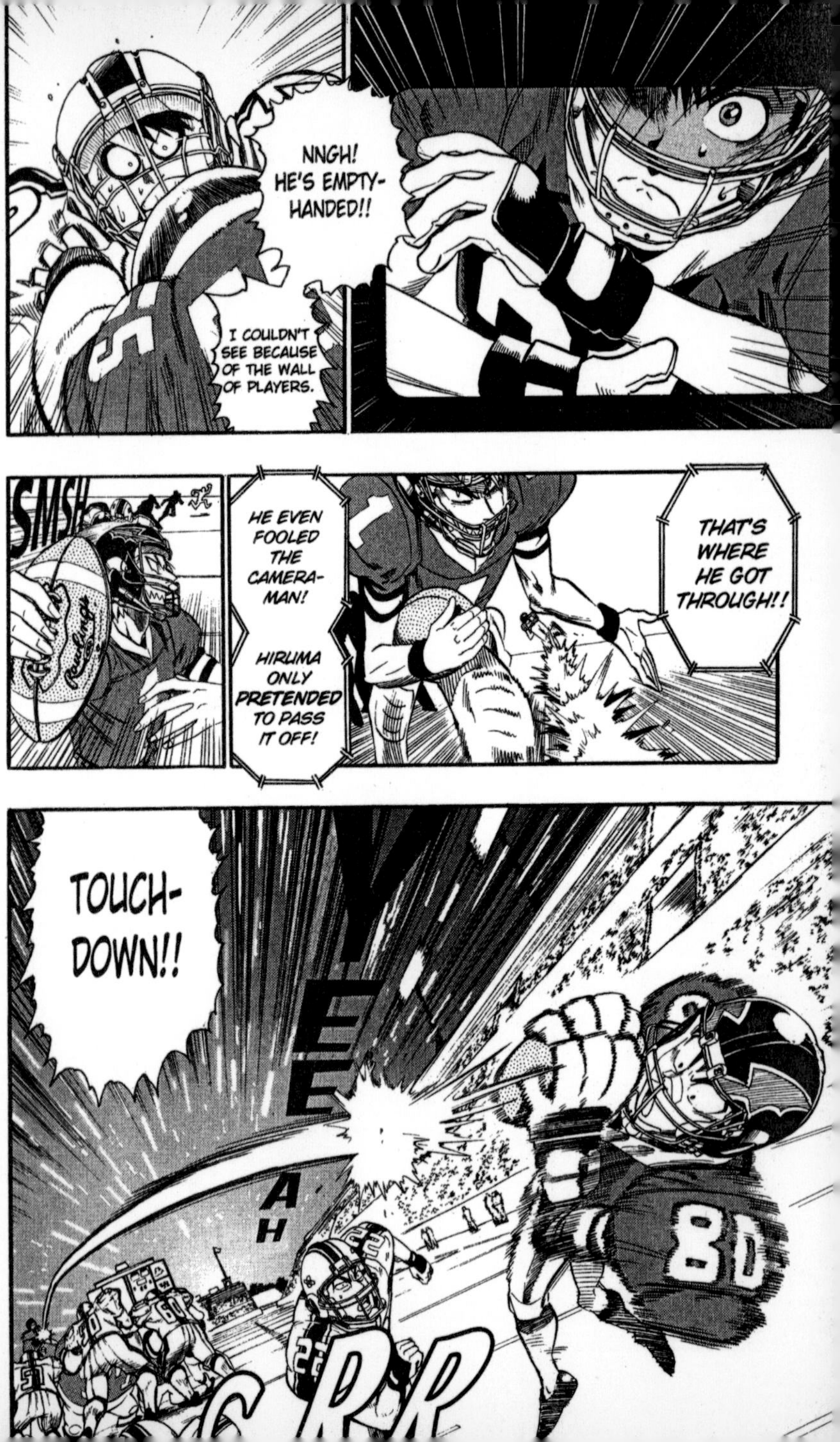
NNGH! HE'S EMPTY-HANDED!!
I COULDN'T SEE BECAUSE OF THE WALL OF PLAYERS.
THAT'S WHERE HE GOT THROUGH!!
HE EVEN FOOLED THE CAMERA-MAN!
HIRUMA ONLY PRETENDED TO PASS IT OFF!
SMSH
TOUCH-DOWN!!

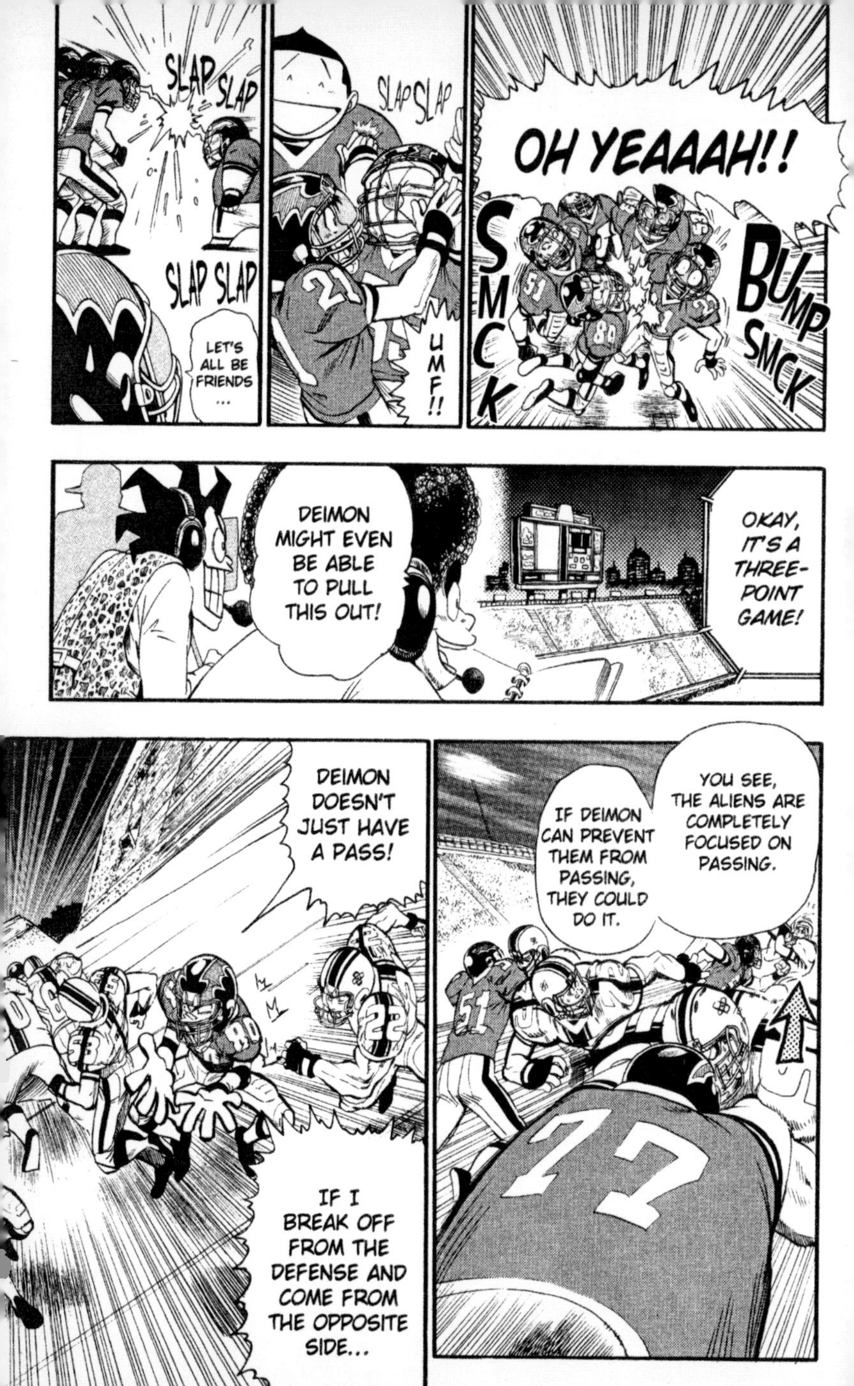
OH YEAAAH!!
SMCK
BUMP
SMCK
SLAP SLAP
UMF!!
SLAP SLAP
SLAP SLAP
LET'S ALL BE FRIENDS ...
OKAY, IT'S A THREE-POINT GAME!
DEIMON MIGHT EVEN BE ABLE TO PULL THIS OUT!
YOU SEE, THE ALIENS ARE COMPLETELY FOCUSED ON PASSING.
IF DEIMON CAN PREVENT THEM FROM PASSING, THEY COULD DO IT.
DEIMON DOESN'T JUST HAVE A PASS!
IF I BREAK OFF FROM THE DEFENSE AND COME FROM THE OPPOSITE SIDE...

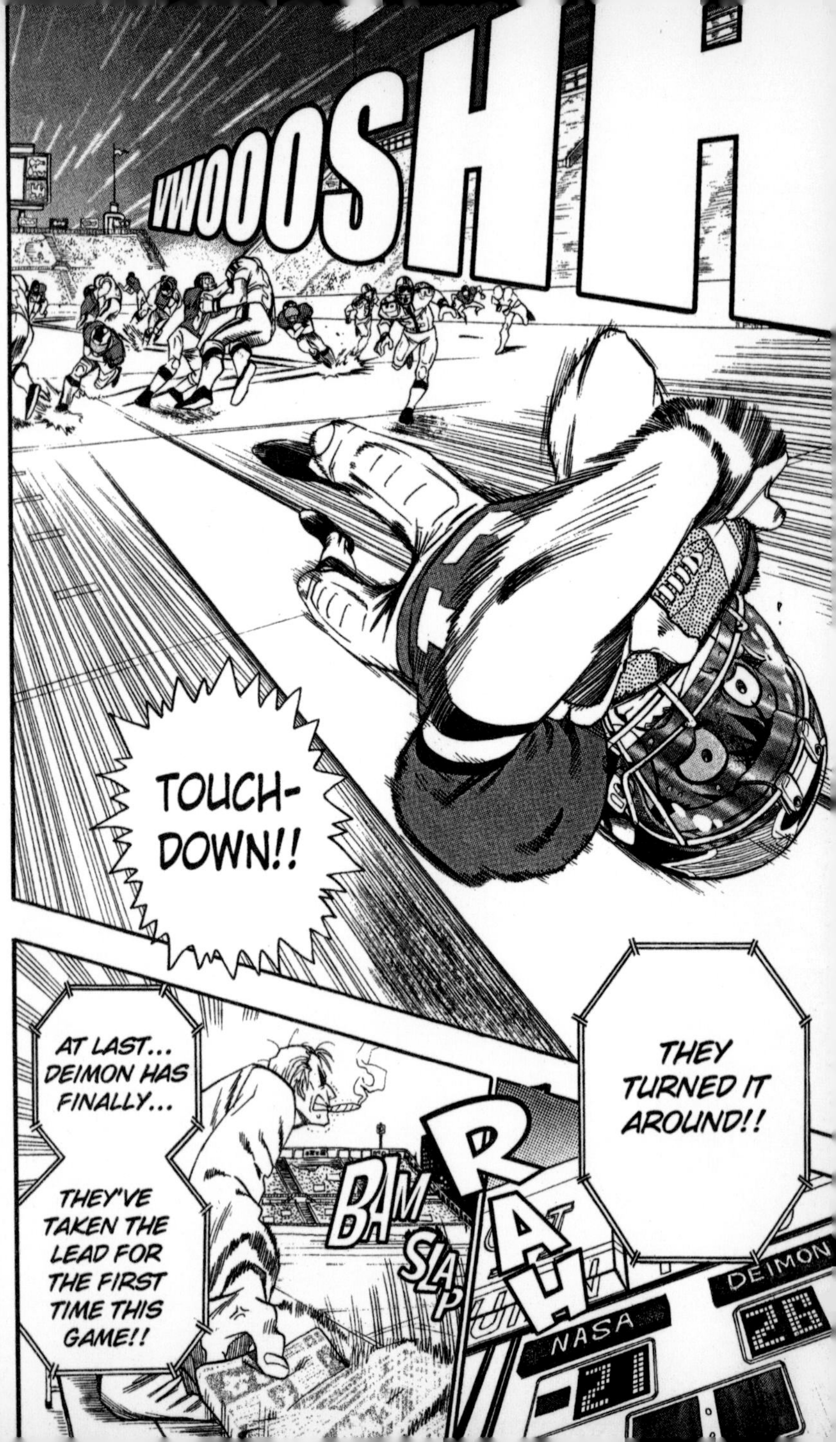
VWOOOSHH
TOUCH-DOWN!!
THEY TURNED IT AROUND!!
BAM
SLAP
RAH
DEIMON
26
NASA
21
AT LAST... DEIMON HAS FINALLY...
THEY'VE TAKEN THE LEAD FOR THE FIRST TIME THIS GAME!!

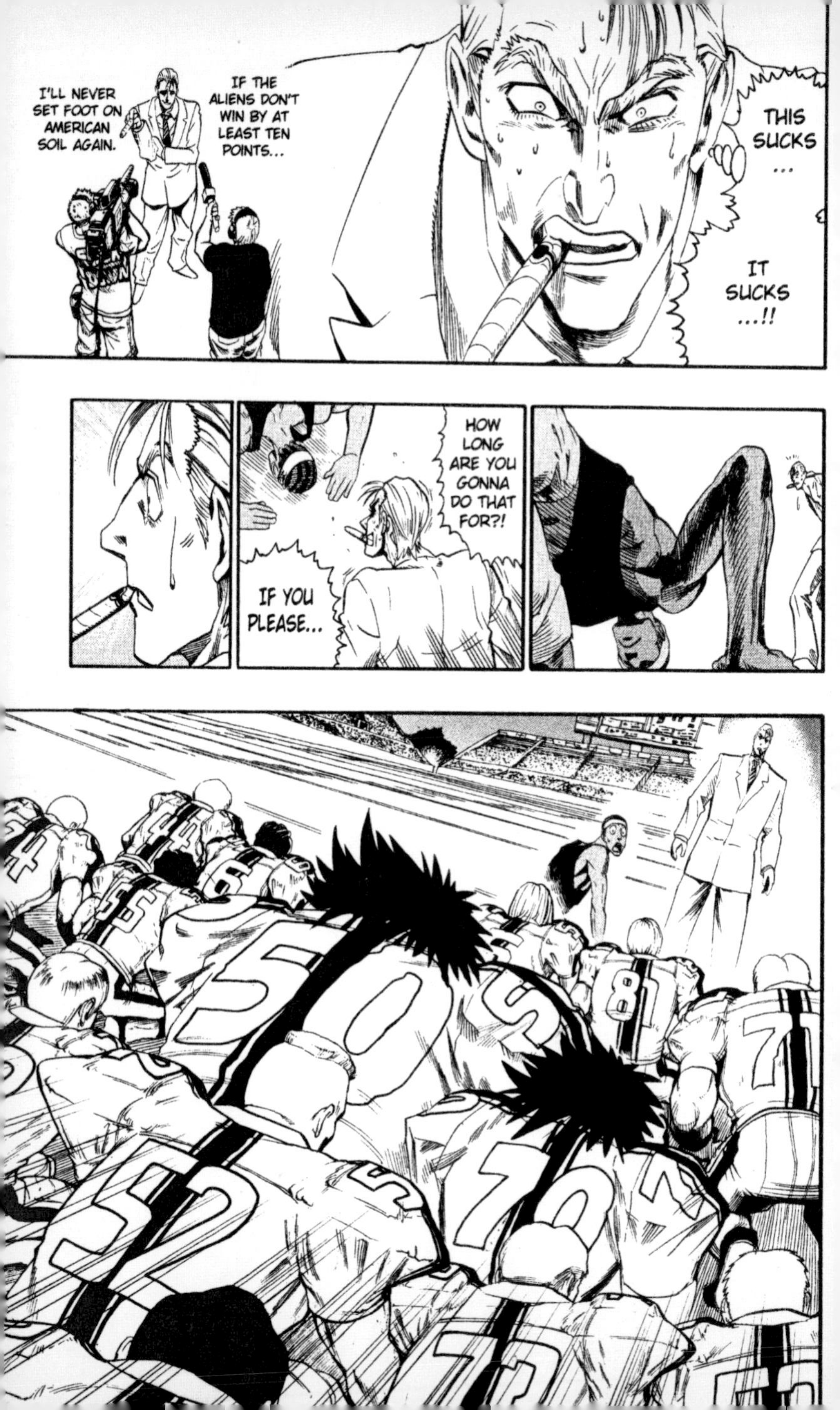
THIS SUCKS...
IT SUCKS...!!
IF THE ALIENS DON'T WIN BY AT LEAST TEN POINTS...
I'LL NEVER SET FOOT ON AMERICAN SOIL AGAIN.
HOW LONG ARE YOU GONNA DO THAT FOR?!
IF YOU PLEASE...

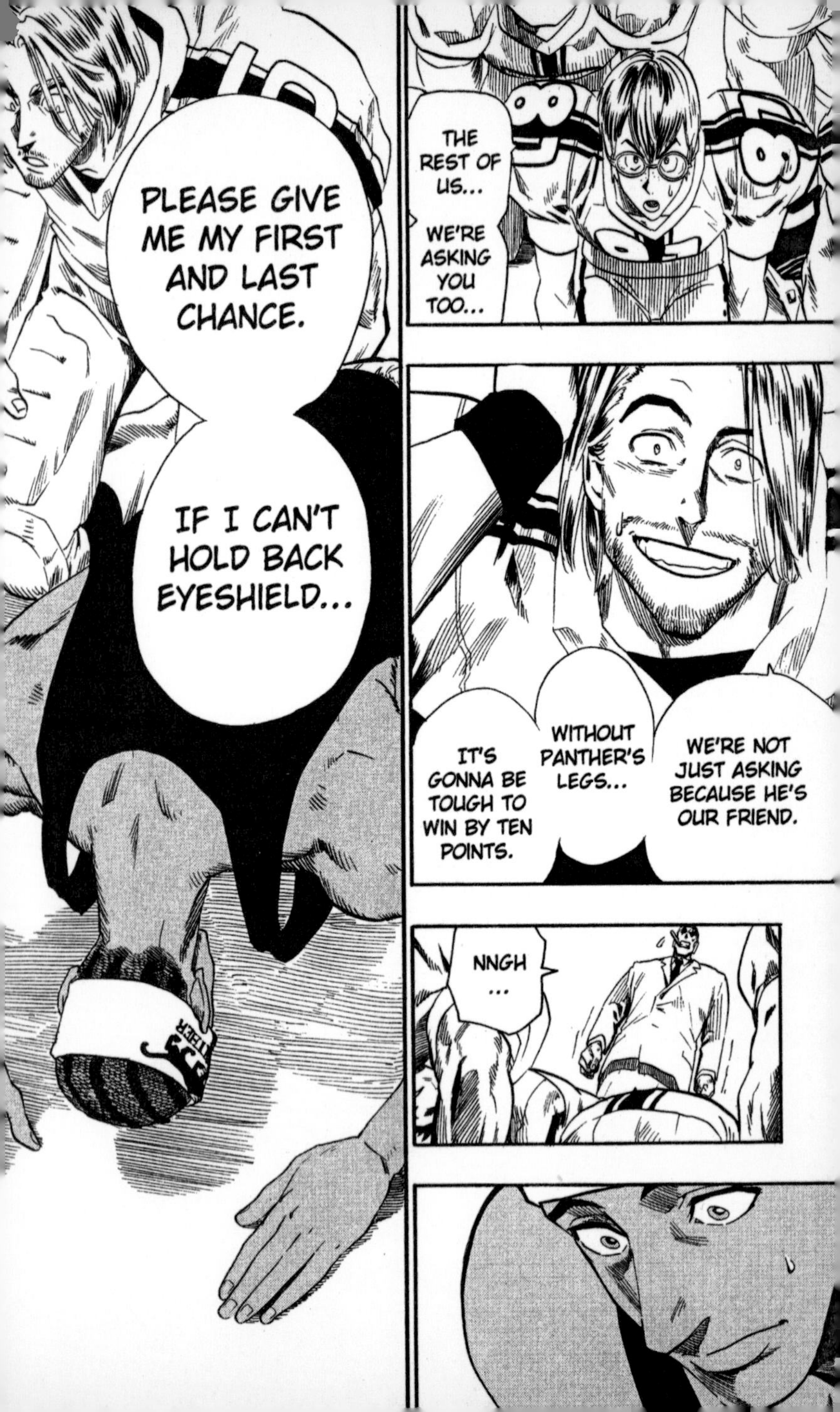
THE REST OF US...
WE'RE ASKING YOU TOO...
WE'RE NOT JUST ASKING BECAUSE HE'S OUR FRIEND.
WITHOUT PANTHER'S LEGS...
IT'S GONNA BE TOUGH TO WIN BY TEN POINTS.
NNGH ...
PLEASE GIVE ME MY FIRST AND LAST CHANCE.
IF I CAN'T HOLD BACK EYESHIELD...

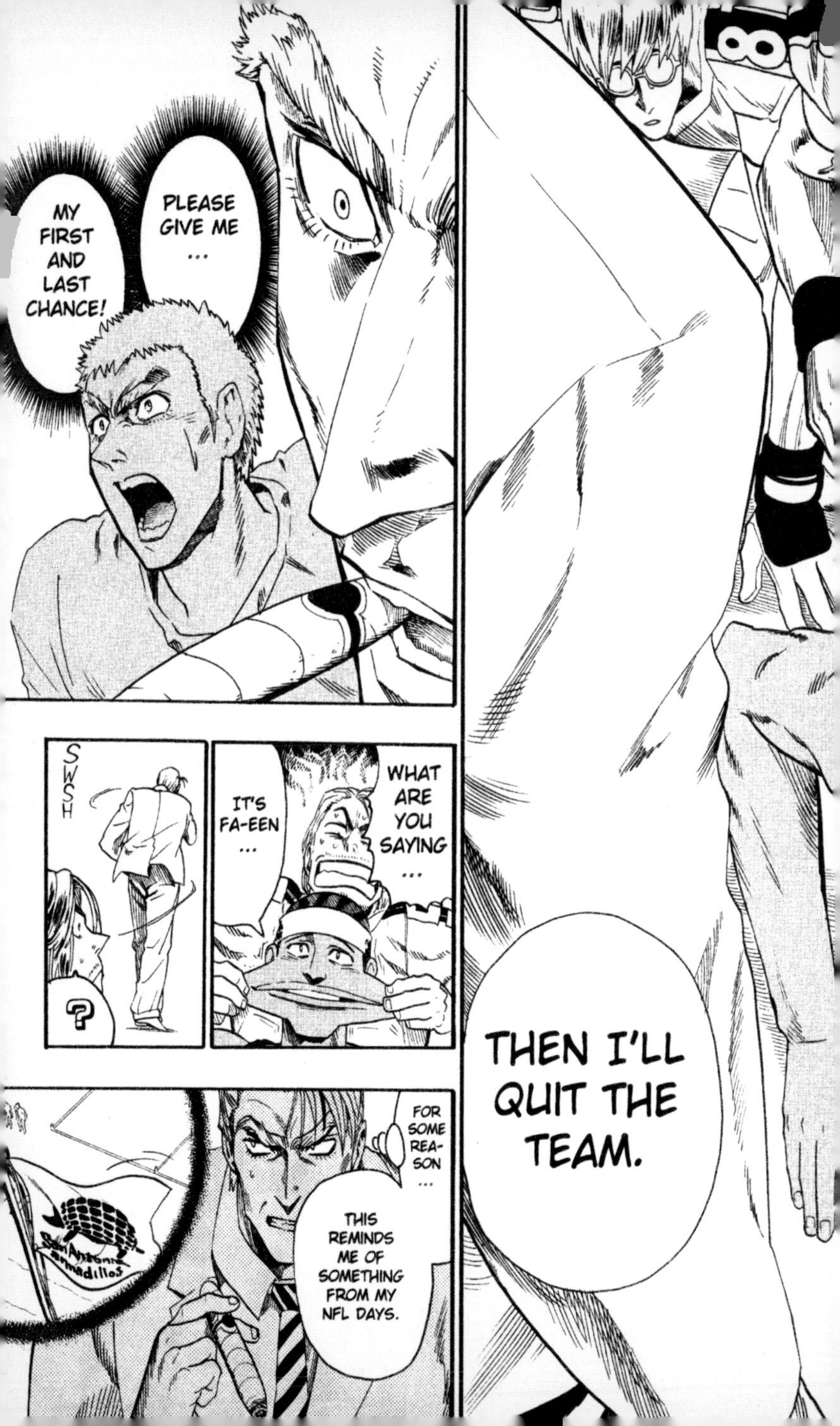
THEN I'LL QUIT THE TEAM.
PLEASE GIVE ME ...
MY FIRST AND LAST CHANCE!
WHAT ARE YOU SAYING ...
IT'S FA-EEN ...
SWSH
?
FOR SOME REA-SON ...
THIS REMINDS ME OF SOMETHING FROM MY NFL DAYS.
San Antonio armadillos

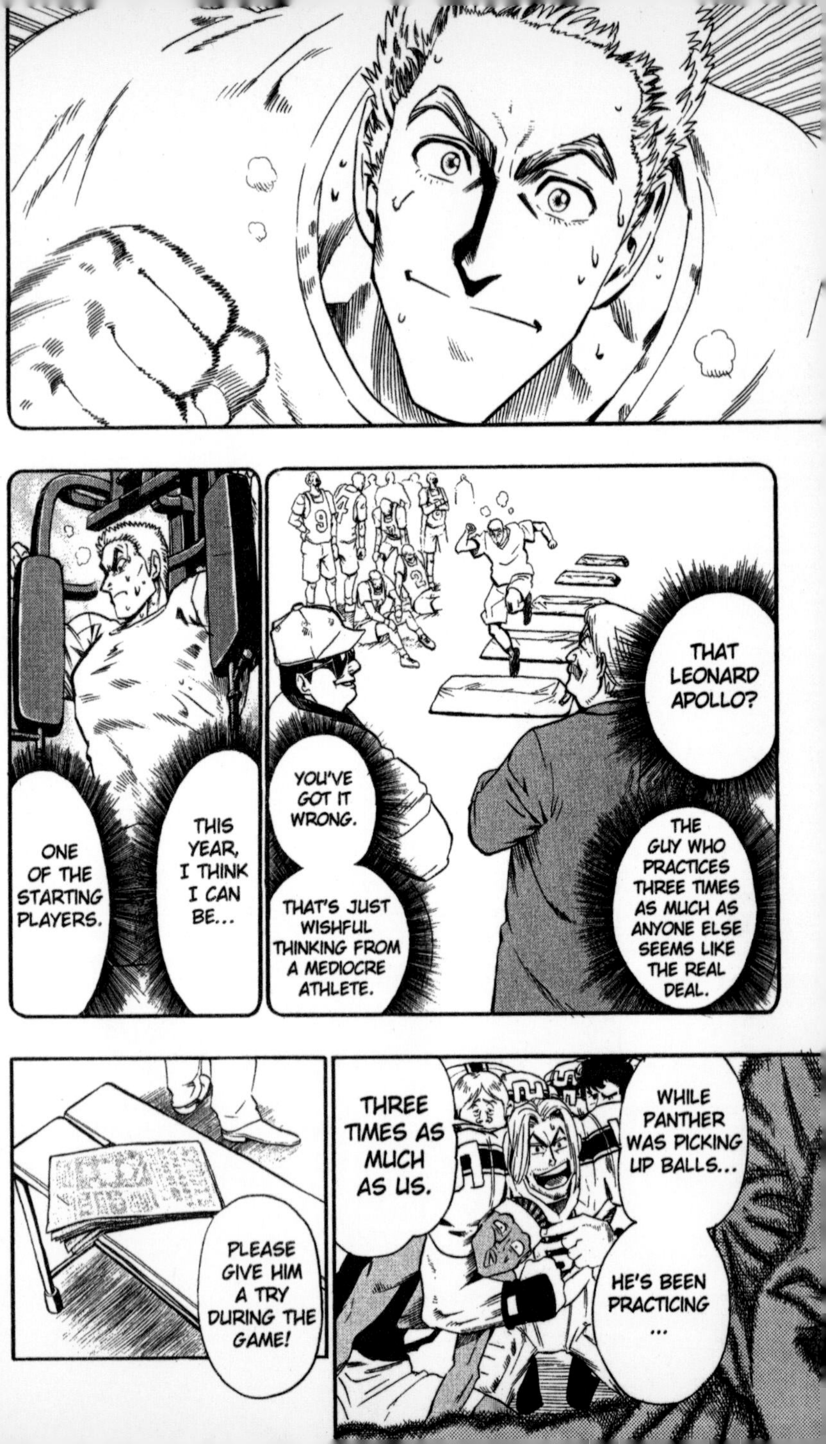
THAT LEONARD APOLLO?
THE GUY WHO PRACTICES THREE TIMES AS MUCH AS ANYONE ELSE SEEMS LIKE THE REAL DEAL.
YOU'VE GOT IT WRONG.
THAT'S JUST WISHFUL THINKING FROM A MEDIOCRE ATHLETE.
THIS YEAR, I THINK I CAN BE...
ONE OF THE STARTING PLAYERS.
WHILE PANTHER WAS PICKING UP BALLS...
HE'S BEEN PRACTICING ...
THREE TIMES AS MUCH AS US.
PLEASE GIVE HIM A TRY DURING THE GAME!

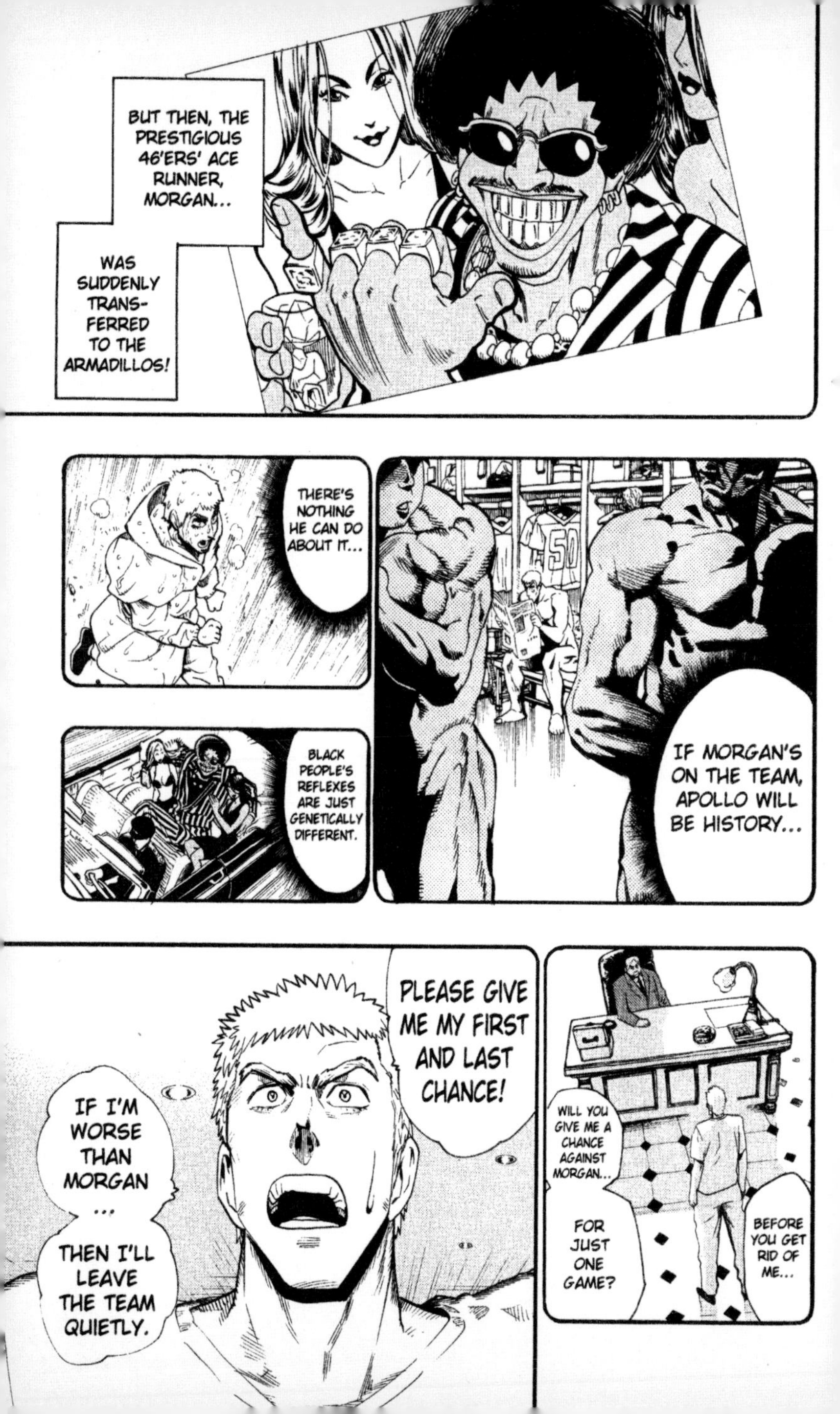
BUT THEN, THE PRESTIGIOUS 46'ERS' ACE RUNNER, MORGAN...
WAS SUDDENLY TRANS-FERRED TO THE ARMADILLOS!
IF MORGAN'S ON THE TEAM, APOLLO WILL BE HISTORY...
THERE'S NOTHING HE CAN DO ABOUT IT...
BLACK PEOPLE'S REFLEXES ARE JUST GENETICALLY DIFFERENT.
WILL YOU GIVE ME A CHANCE AGAINST MORGAN...
BEFORE YOU GET RID OF ME...
FOR JUST ONE GAME?
PLEASE GIVE ME MY FIRST AND LAST CHANCE!
IF I'M WORSE THAN MORGAN...
THEN I'LL LEAVE THE TEAM QUIETLY.

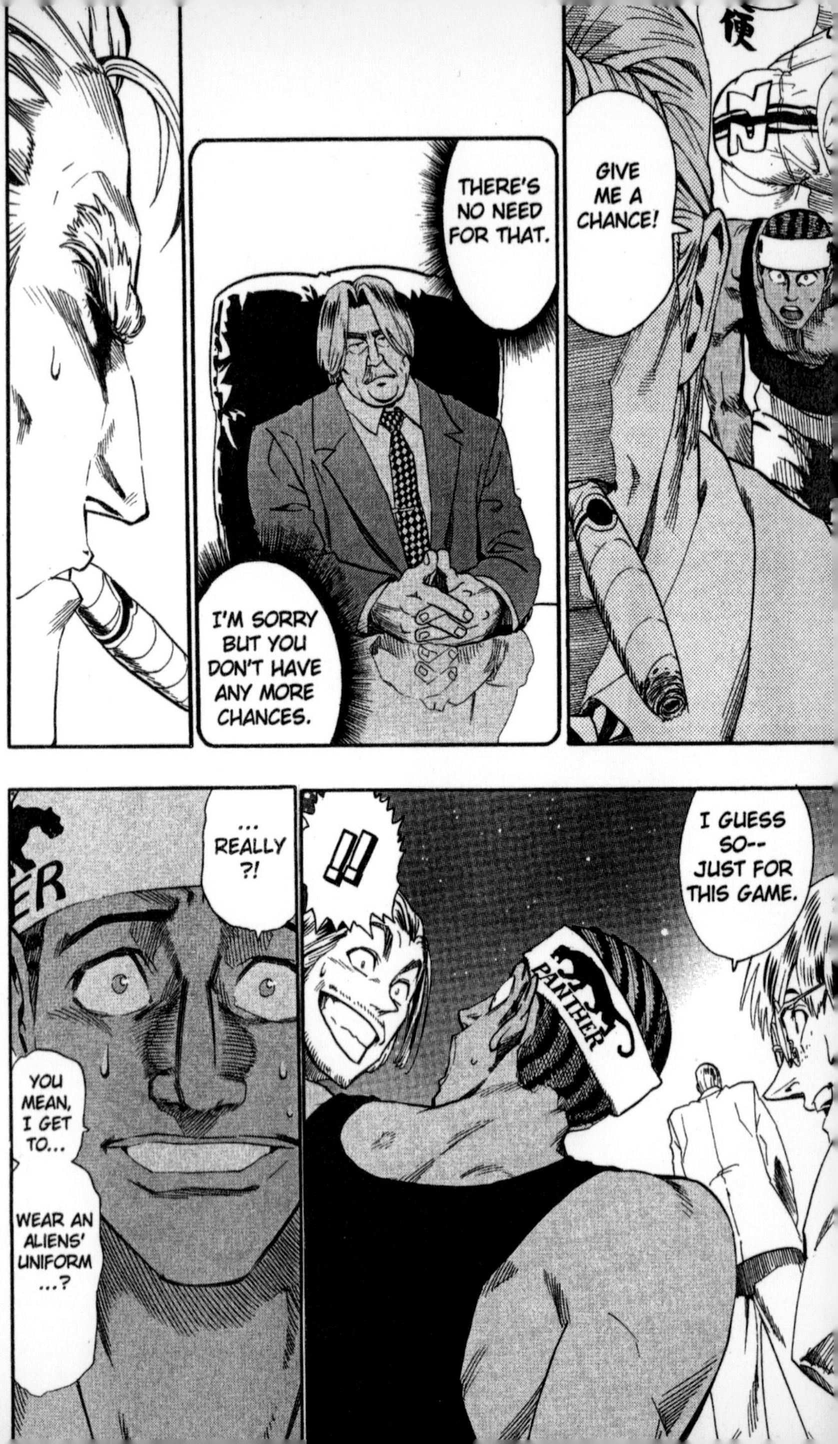
GIVE ME A CHANCE!
THERE'S NO NEED FOR THAT.
I'M SORRY BUT YOU DON'T HAVE ANY MORE CHANCES.
I GUESS SO-- JUST FOR THIS GAME.
!!
PANTHER
... REALLY ?!
YOU MEAN, I GET TO...
WEAR AN ALIENS' UNIFORM ...?

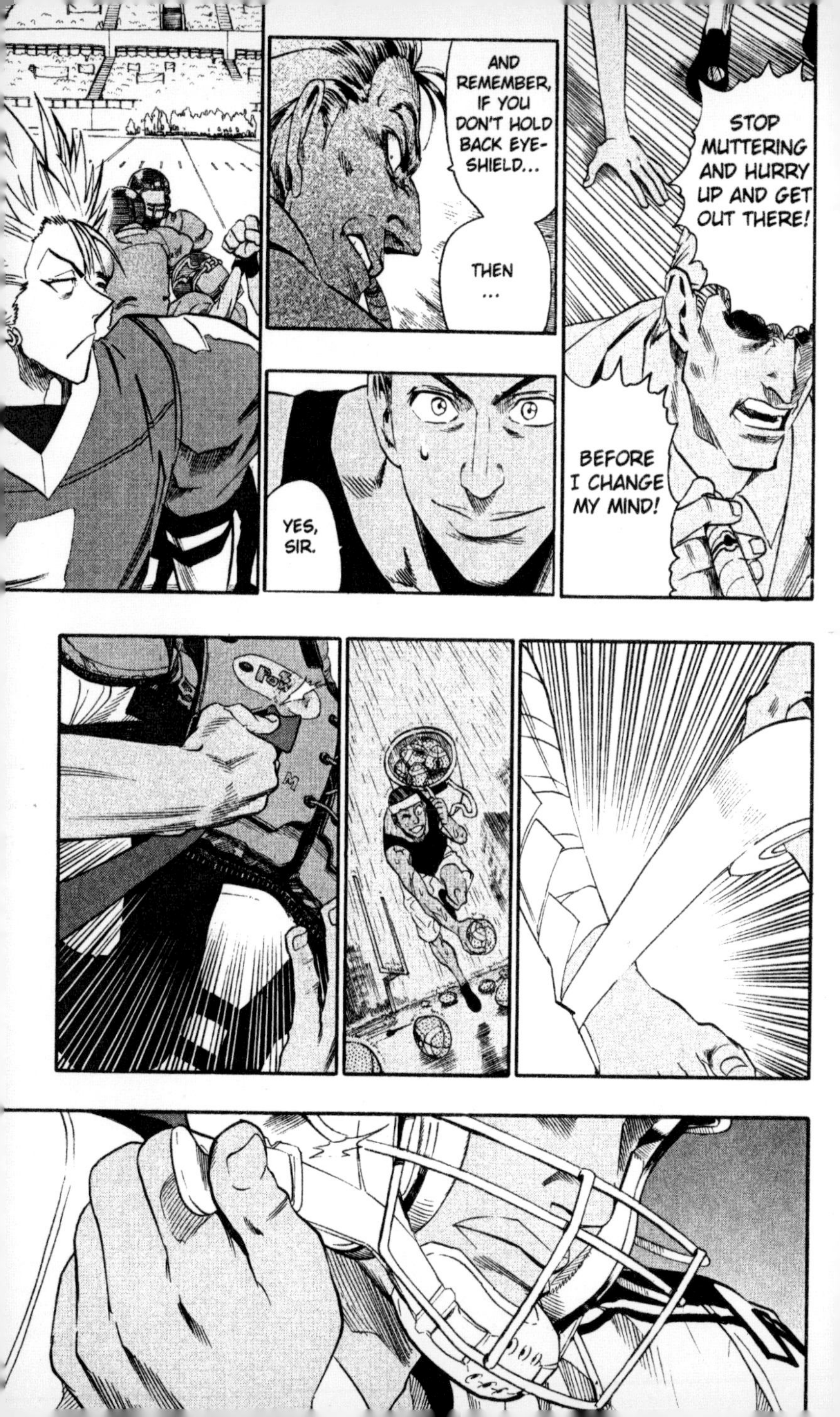
STOP MUTTERING AND HURRY UP AND GET OUT THERE!
BEFORE I CHANGE MY MIND!
AND REMEMBER, IF YOU DON'T HOLD BACK EYE-SHIELD...
THEN ...
YES, SIR.

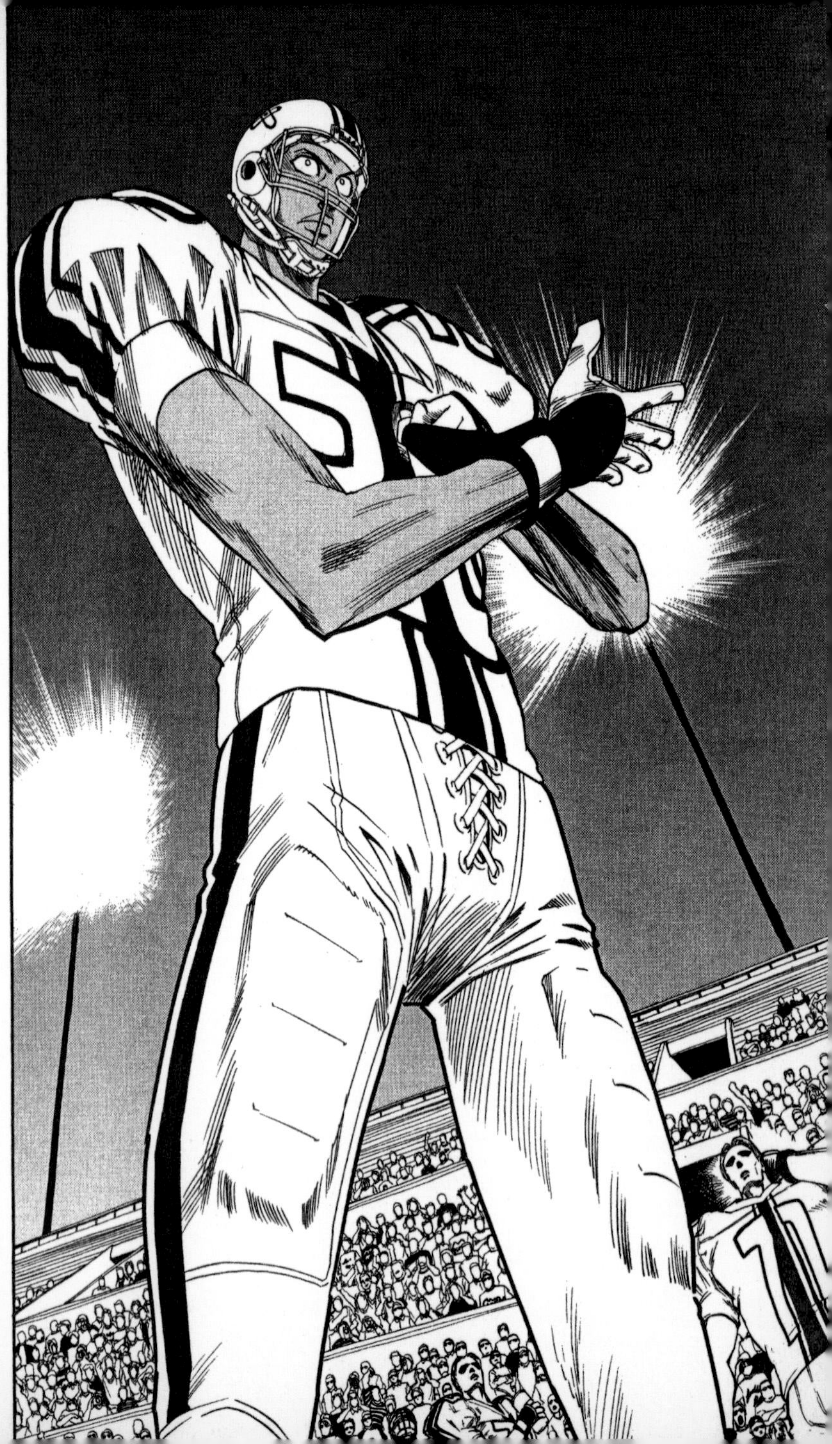

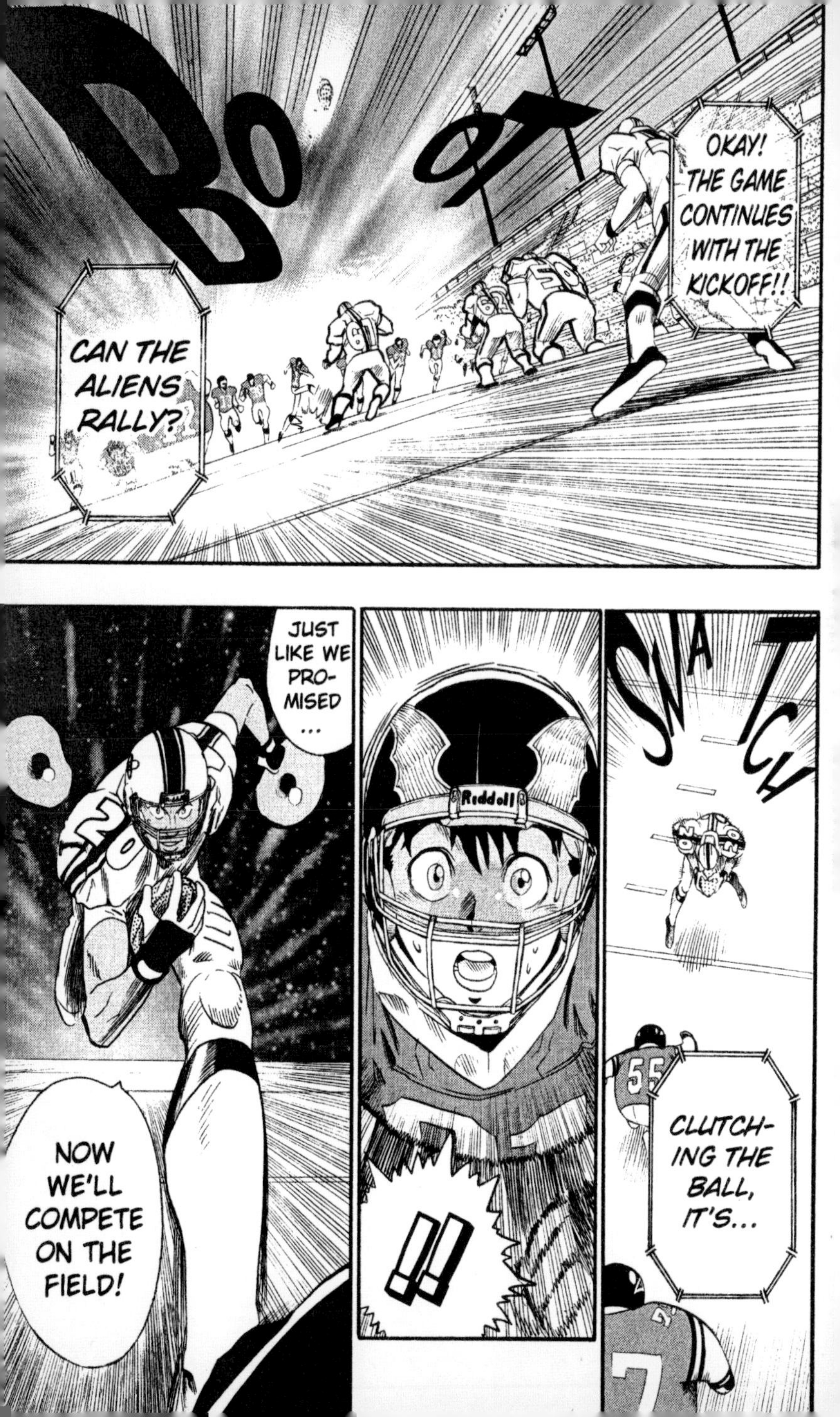
BOOT
OKAY! THE GAME CONTINUES WITH THE KICKOFF!!
CAN THE ALIENS RALLY?
SNATCH
CLUTCHING THE BALL, IT'S...
!!
JUST LIKE WE PROMISED ...
NOW WE'LL COMPETE ON THE FIELD!

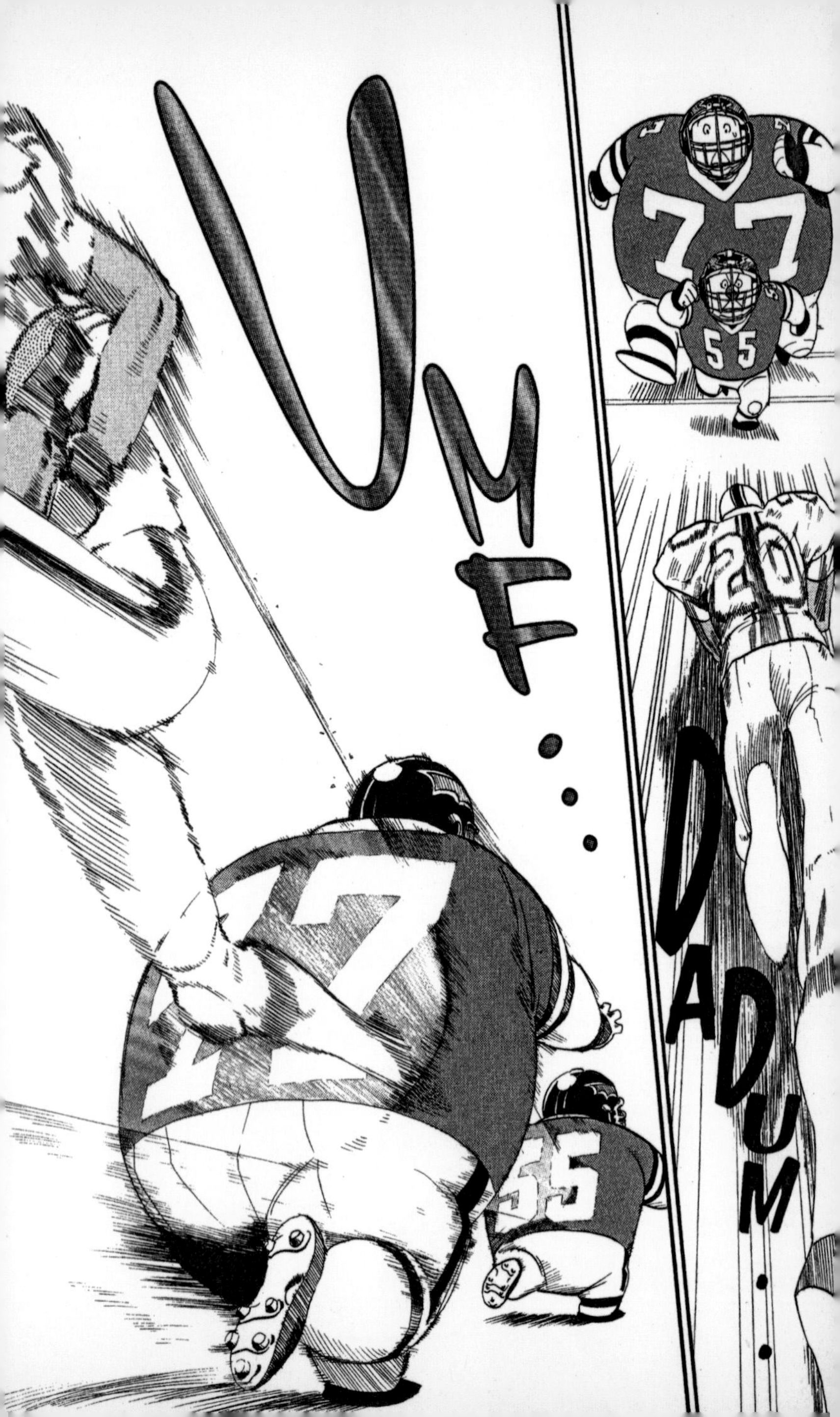
DADUM
UMF...

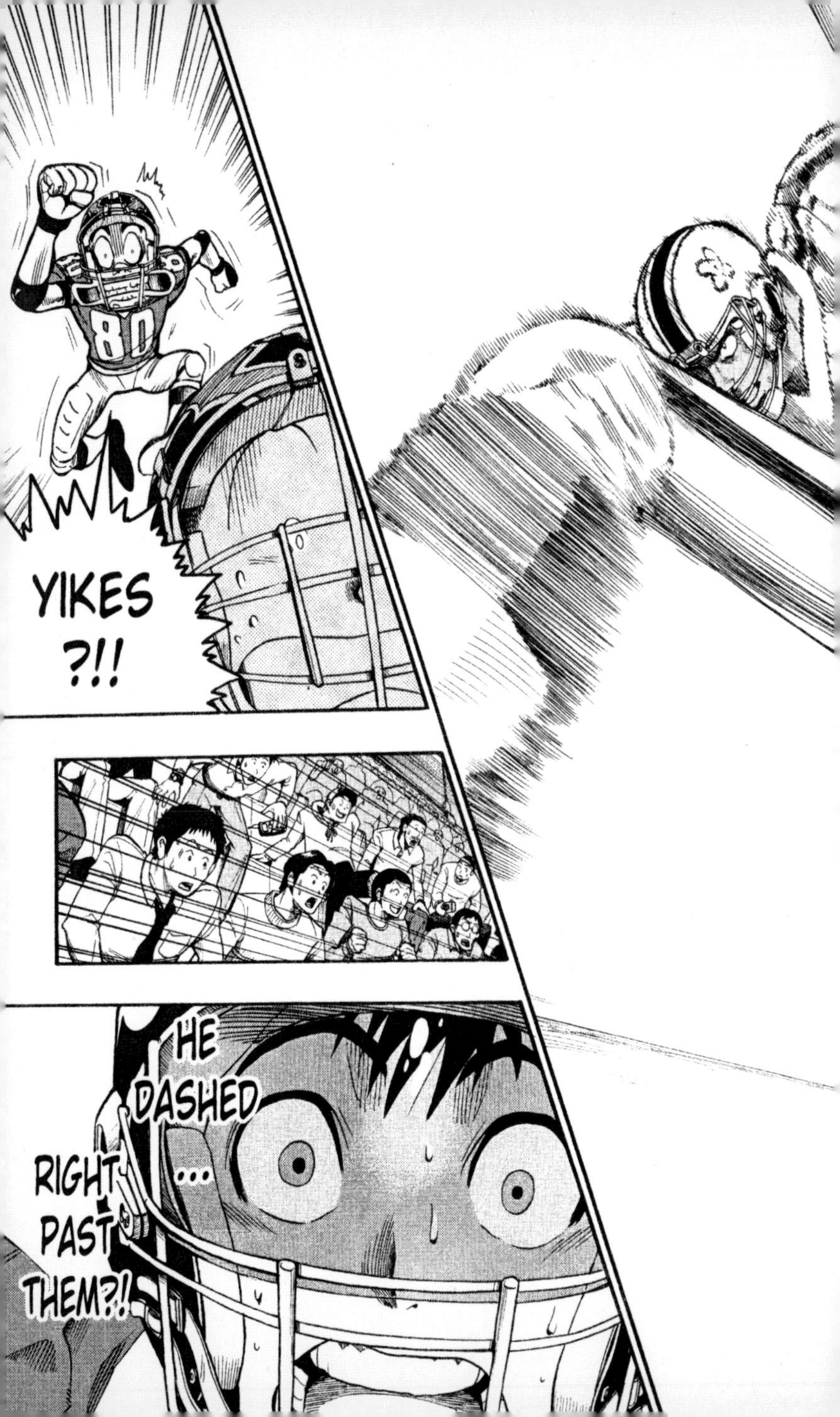
YIKES ?!!
HE DASHED ...
RIGHT PAST THEM?!

Eyeshield 21 Survey Corner **Devil Bat 021**

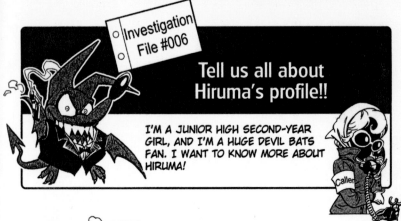

Investigation File #006

Tell us all about Hiruma's profile!!

I'M A JUNIOR HIGH SECOND-YEAR GIRL, AND I'M A HUGE DEVIL BATS FAN. I WANT TO KNOW MORE ABOUT HIRUMA!

Caller

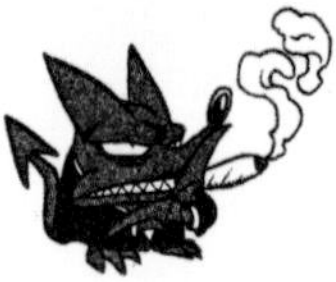

PFFFT...

I KNEW SOMEONE WOULD ASK THIS EVENTUALLY.

IF I'M TOLD TO INVESTIGATE, I HAVE TO INVESTIGATE, EH? NOTHING IS IMPOSSIBLE FOR THE CLEVER DEVIL BAT SPY.

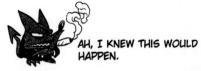

Investigative Report
Hiruma Full Profile

Yoichi Hiruma

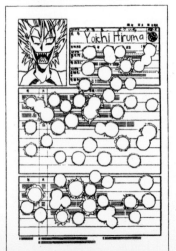

AH, I KNEW THIS WOULD HAPPEN.

GIRLIE, THERE ARE SOME THINGS IN THIS WORLD YOU JUST HAVE TO LET BE.

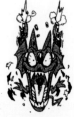

GOT IT?! STOP ASKING ME THESE QUESTIONS!!

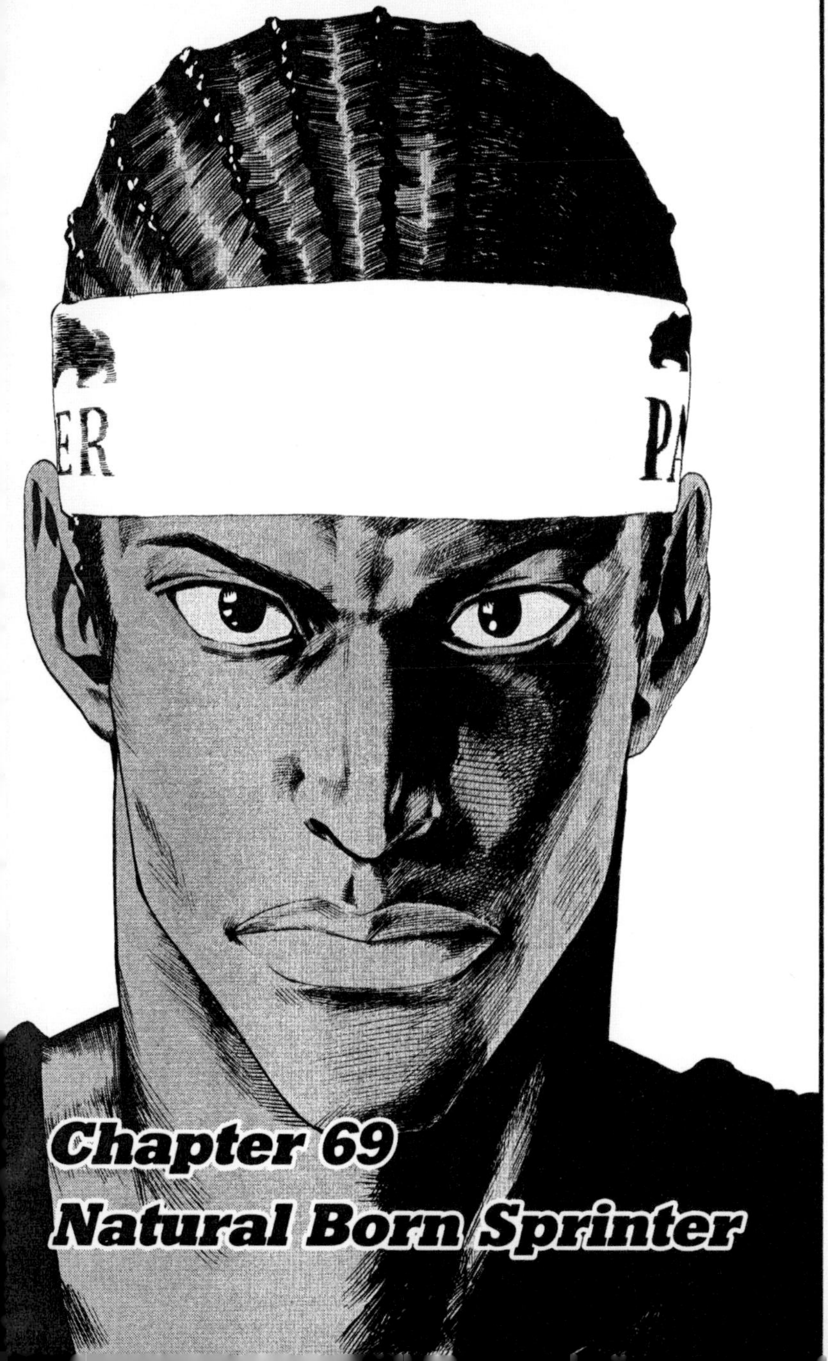
Chapter 69
Natural Born Sprinter

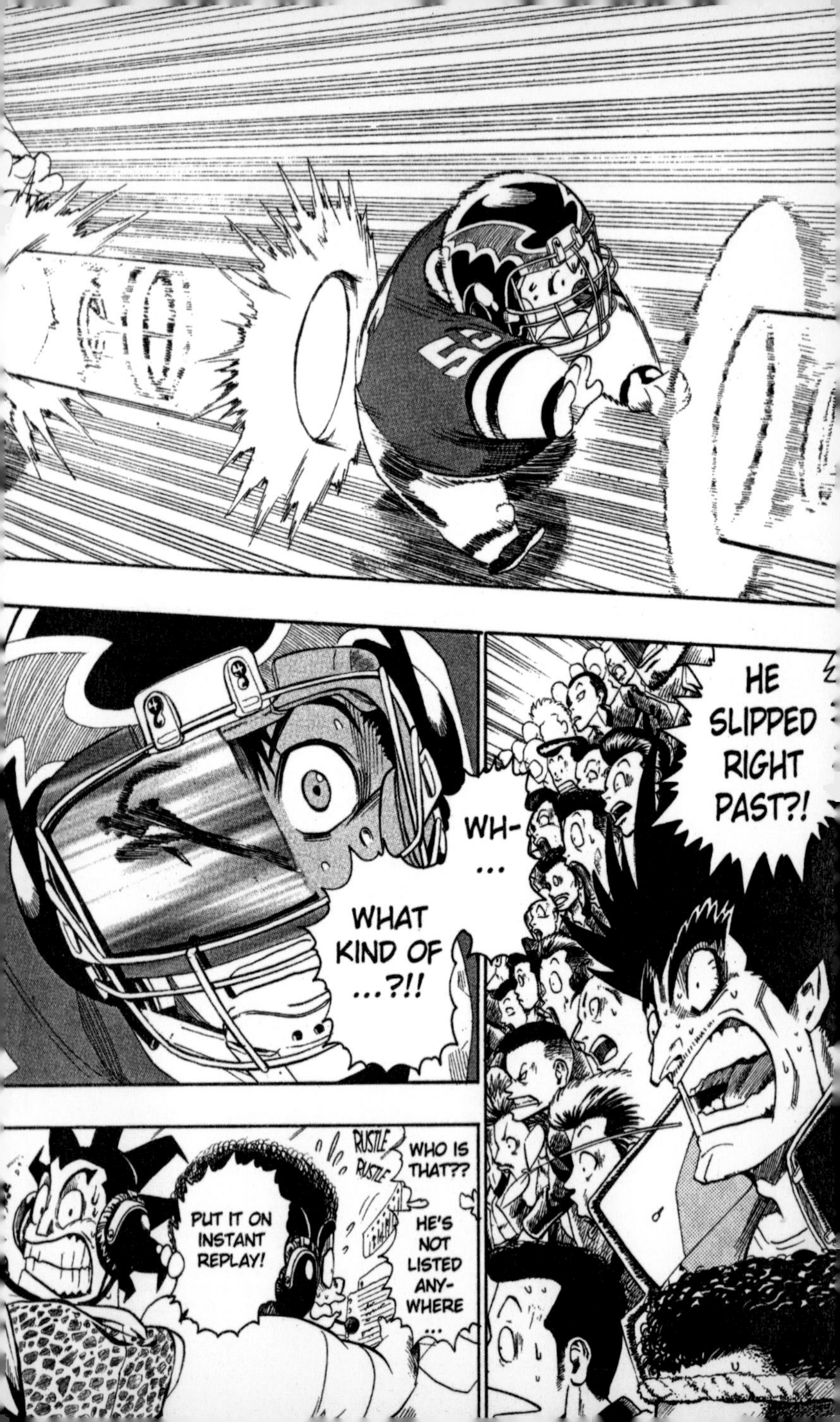
HE SLIPPED RIGHT PAST?!
WH- ...
WHAT KIND OF ...?!!
RUSTLE RUSTLE
WHO IS THAT??
HE'S NOT LISTED ANYWHERE ...
PUT IT ON INSTANT REPLAY!

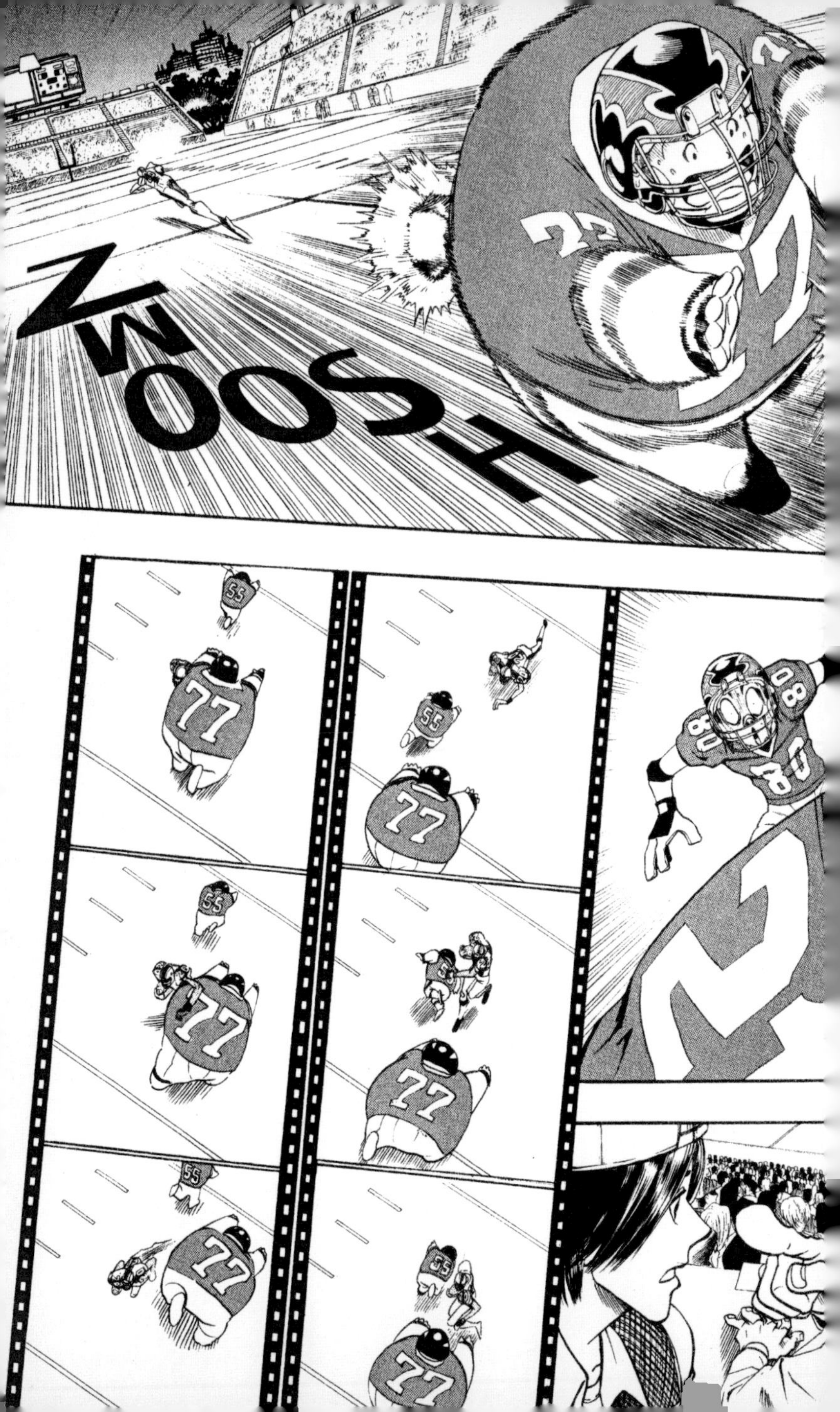
ZWOOSH

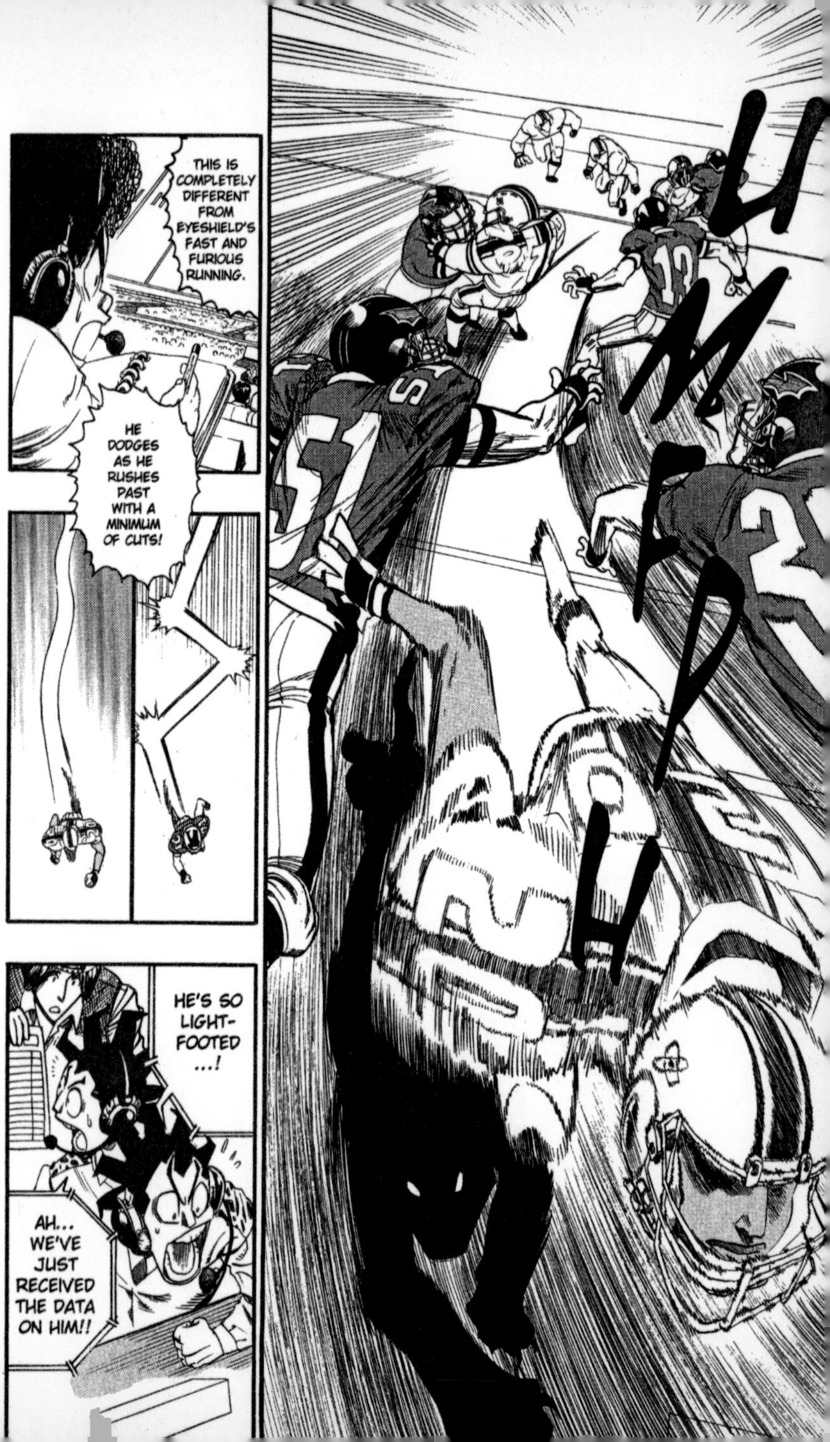
THIS IS COMPLETELY DIFFERENT FROM EYESHIELD'S FAST AND FURIOUS RUNNING.
HE DODGES AS HE RUSHES PAST WITH A MINIMUM OF CUTS!
HE'S SO LIGHT-FOOTED ...!
AH... WE'VE JUST RECEIVED THE DATA ON HIM!!

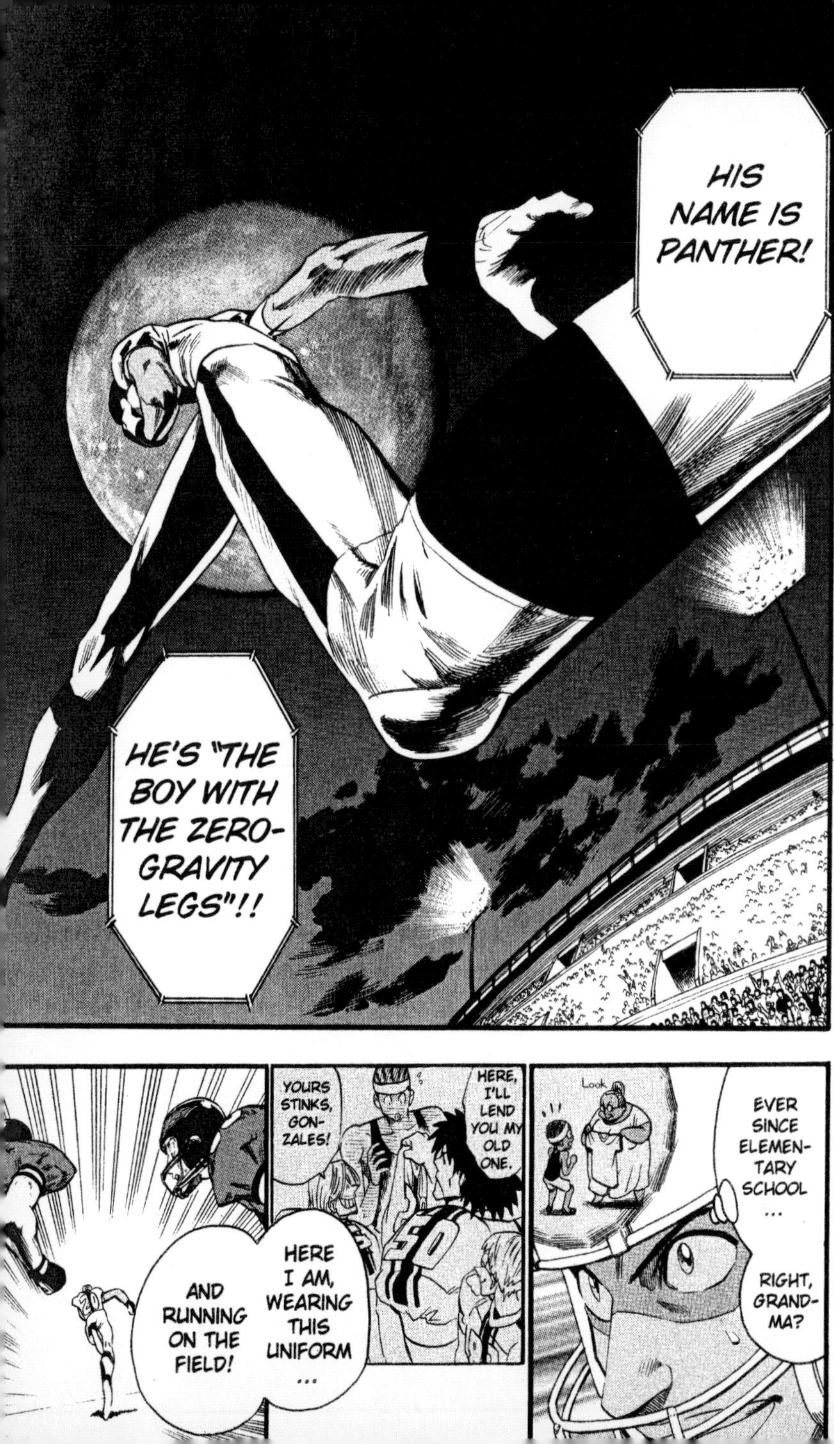
HIS NAME IS PANTHER!
HE'S "THE BOY WITH THE ZERO-GRAVITY LEGS"!!
Look
EVER SINCE ELEMENTARY SCHOOL...
RIGHT, GRANDMA?
HERE, I'LL LEND YOU MY OLD ONE.
YOURS STINKS, GONZALES!
HERE I AM, WEARING THIS UNIFORM...
AND RUNNING ON THE FIELD!

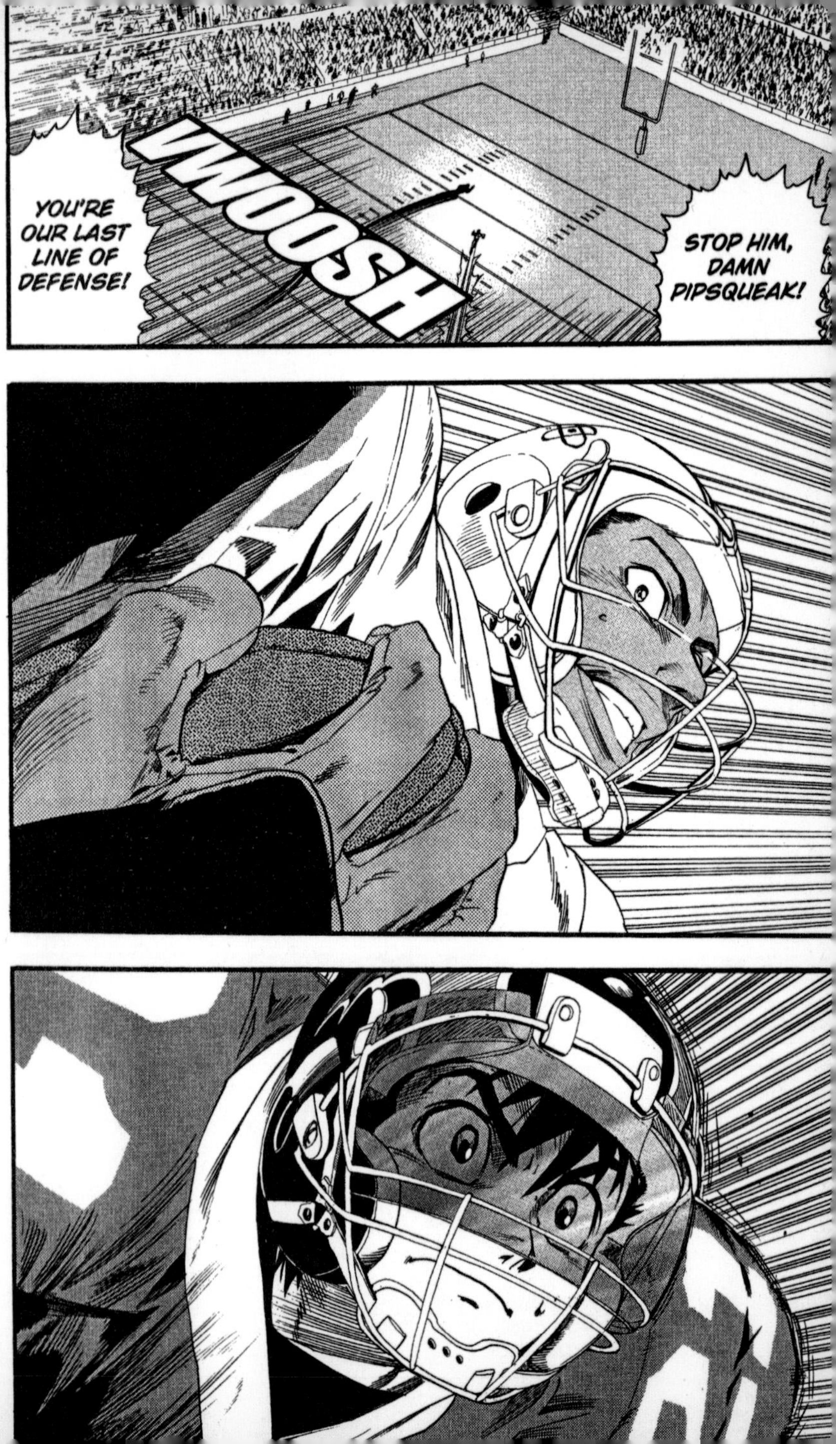
STOP HIM, DAMN PIPSQUEAK!
VWOOSH
YOU'RE OUR LAST LINE OF DEFENSE!

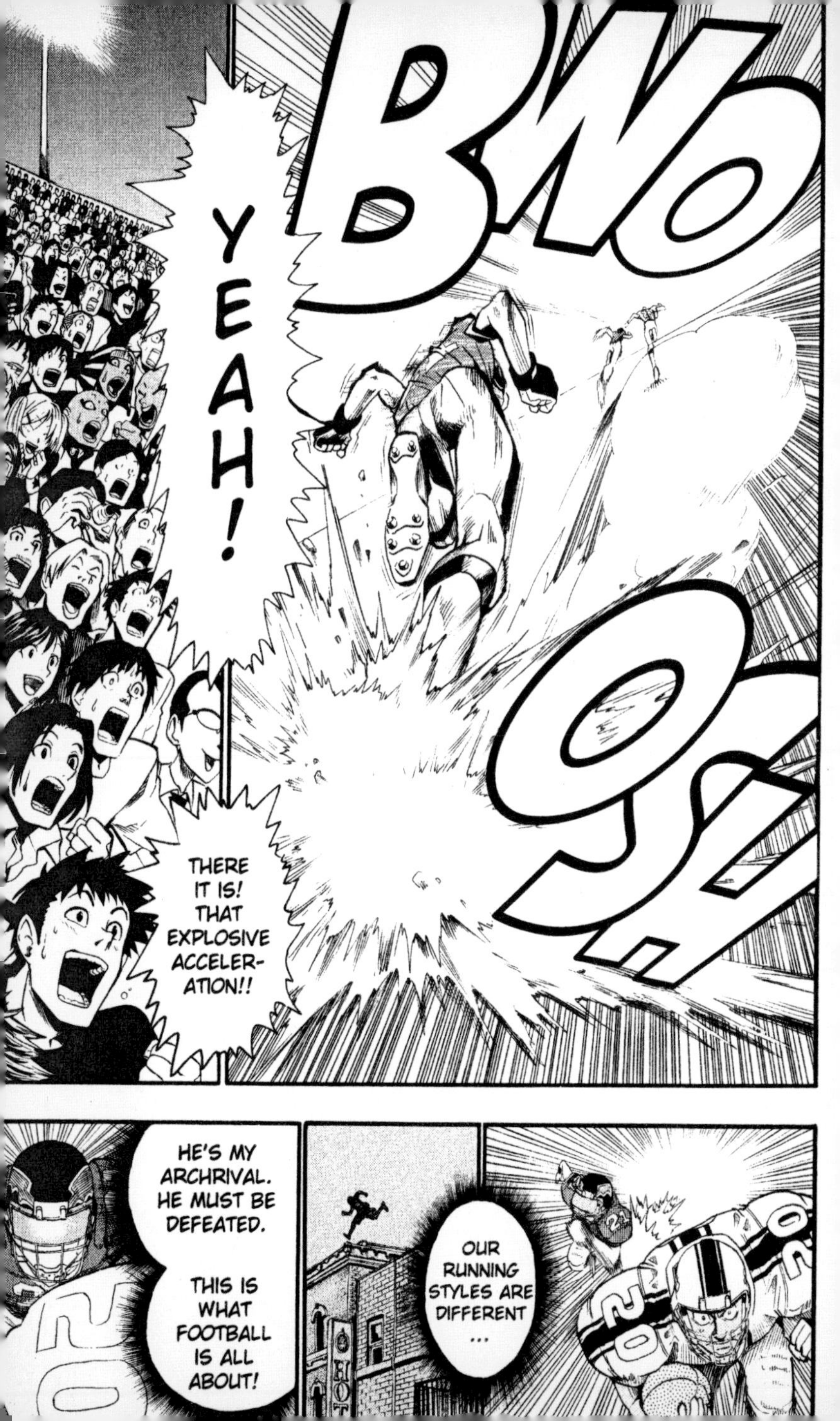
BWOOSH!
YEAH!
THERE IT IS! THAT EXPLOSIVE ACCELER-ATION!!
OUR RUNNING STYLES ARE DIFFERENT ...
HE'S MY ARCHRIVAL. HE MUST BE DEFEATED.
THIS IS WHAT FOOTBALL IS ALL ABOUT!

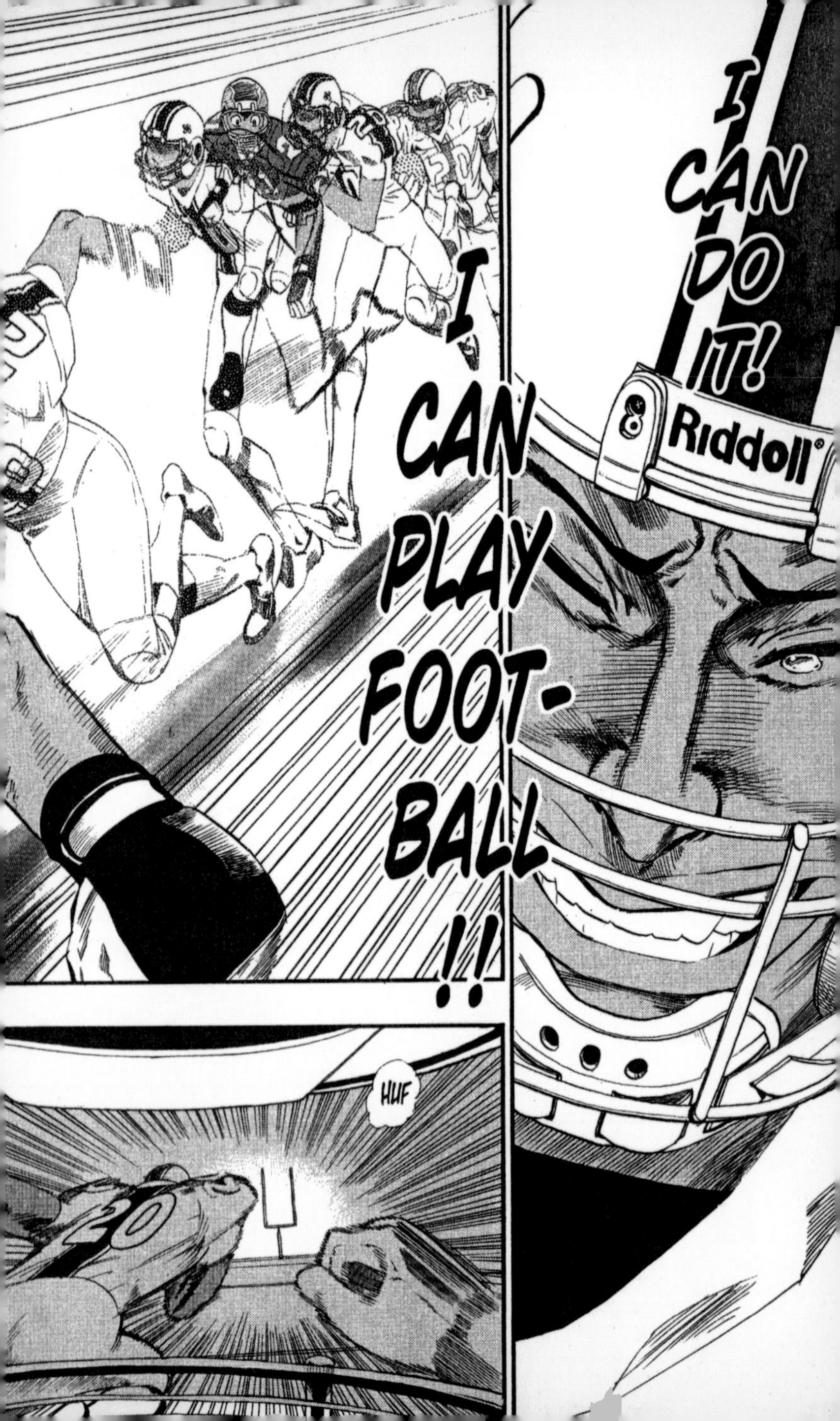

I CAN DO IT!
Riddoll
I CAN PLAY FOOT-BALL!!
HUF

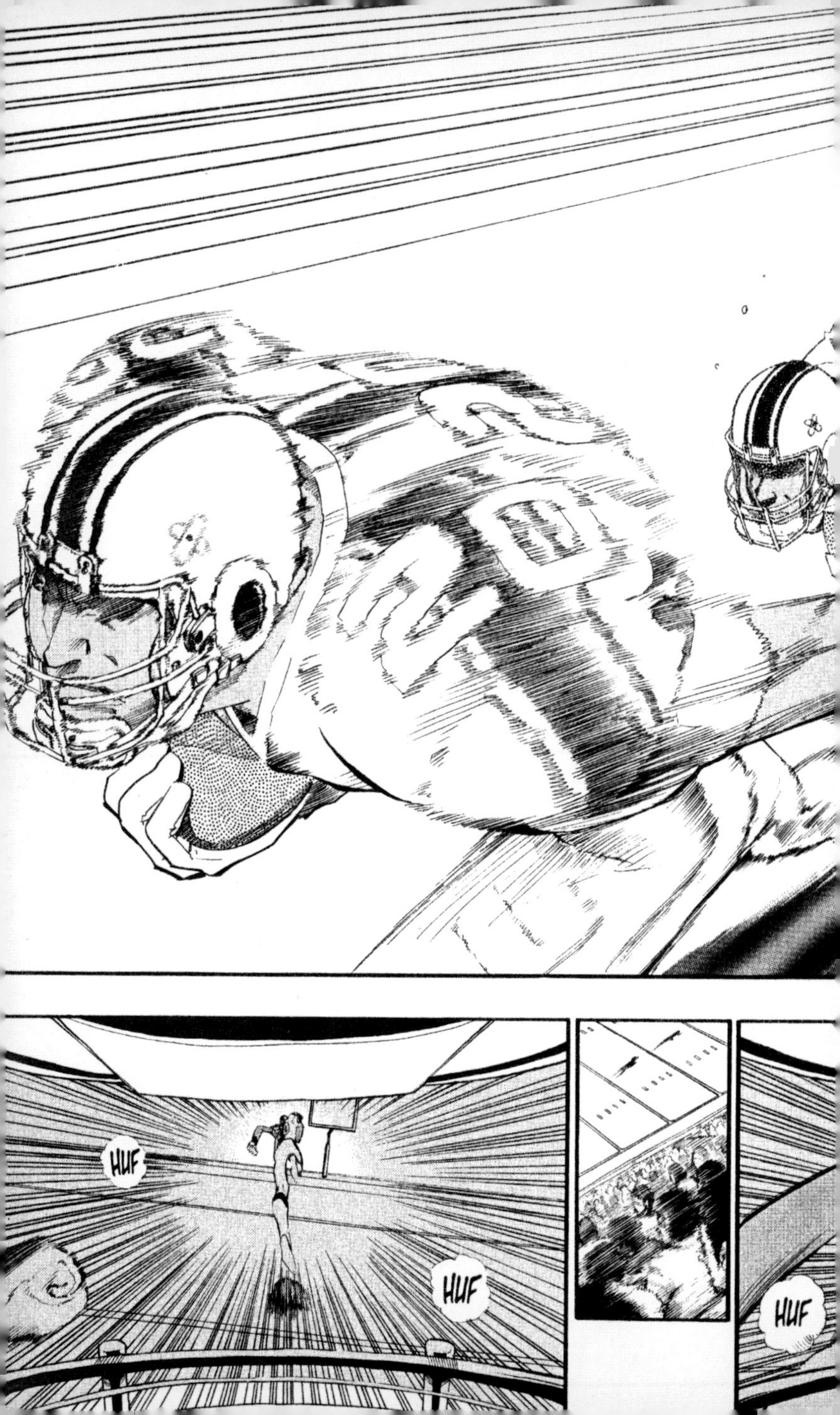
HUF
HUF
HUF

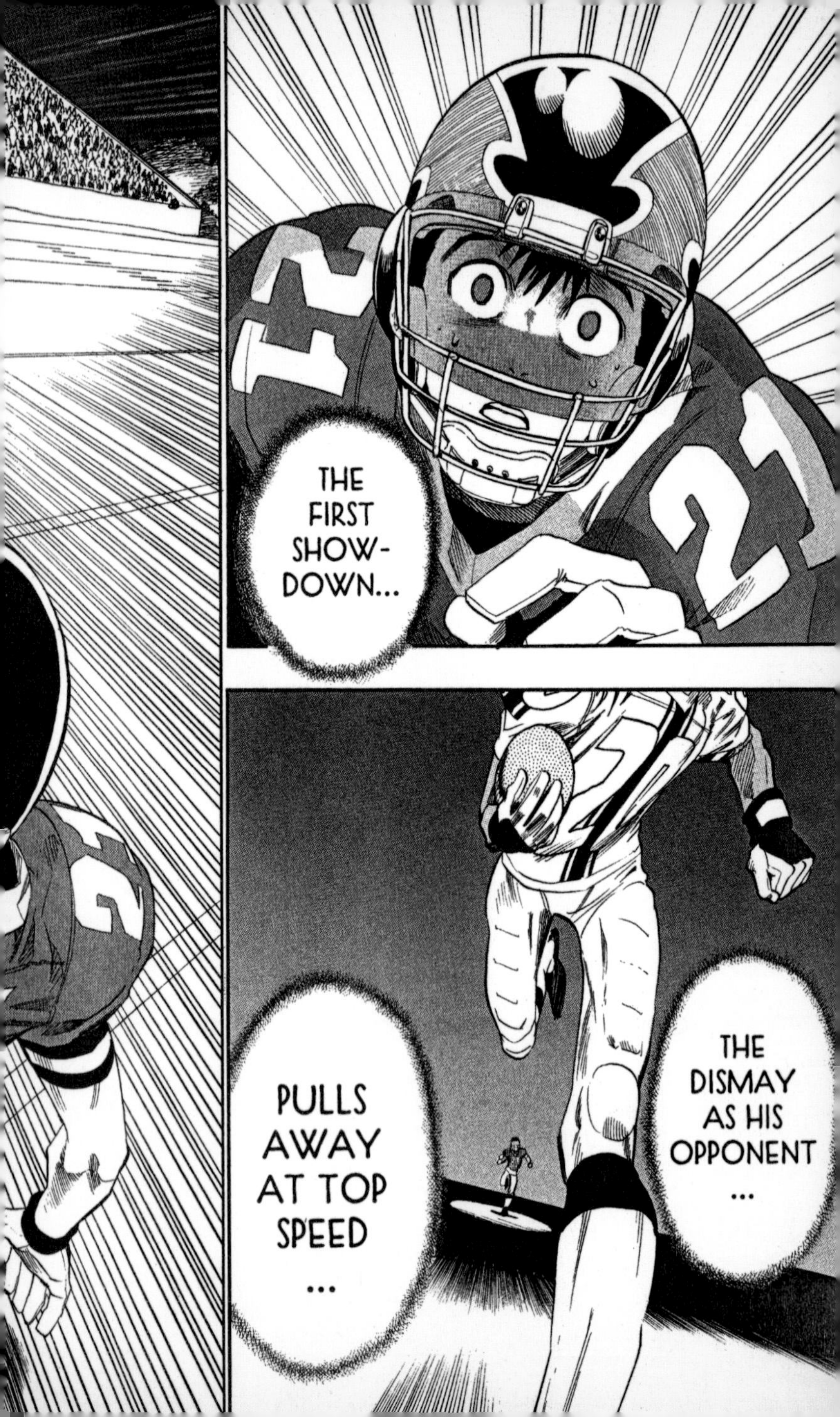
THE FIRST SHOW-DOWN...
THE DISMAY AS HIS OPPONENT ...
PULLS AWAY AT TOP SPEED ...

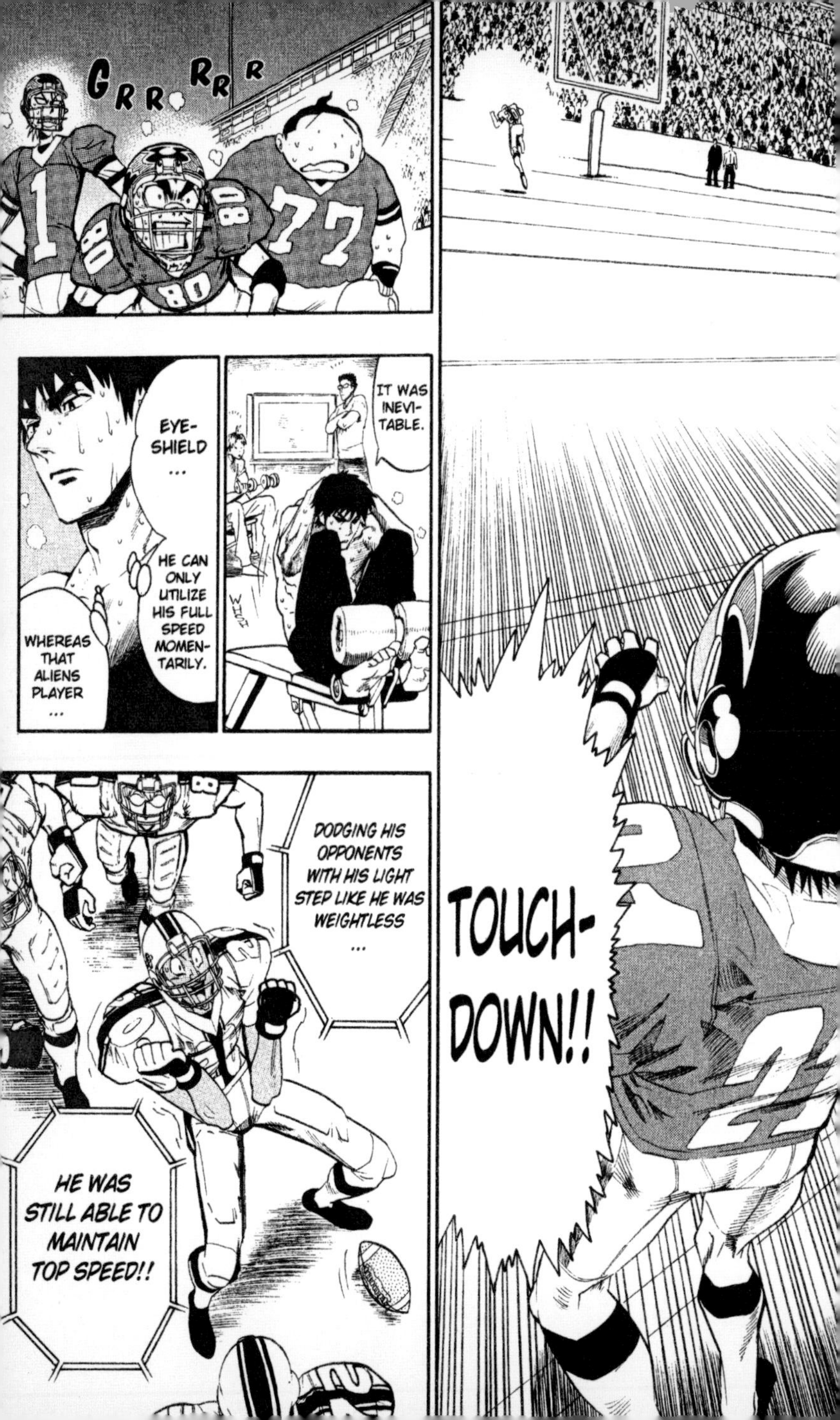
TOUCH-DOWN!!
GRRRRRR
IT WAS INEVITABLE.
WHSH
EYE-SHIELD ...
HE CAN ONLY UTILIZE HIS FULL SPEED MOMENTARILY.
WHEREAS THAT ALIENS PLAYER ...
DODGING HIS OPPONENTS WITH HIS LIGHT STEP LIKE HE WAS WEIGHTLESS ...
HE WAS STILL ABLE TO MAINTAIN TOP SPEED!!

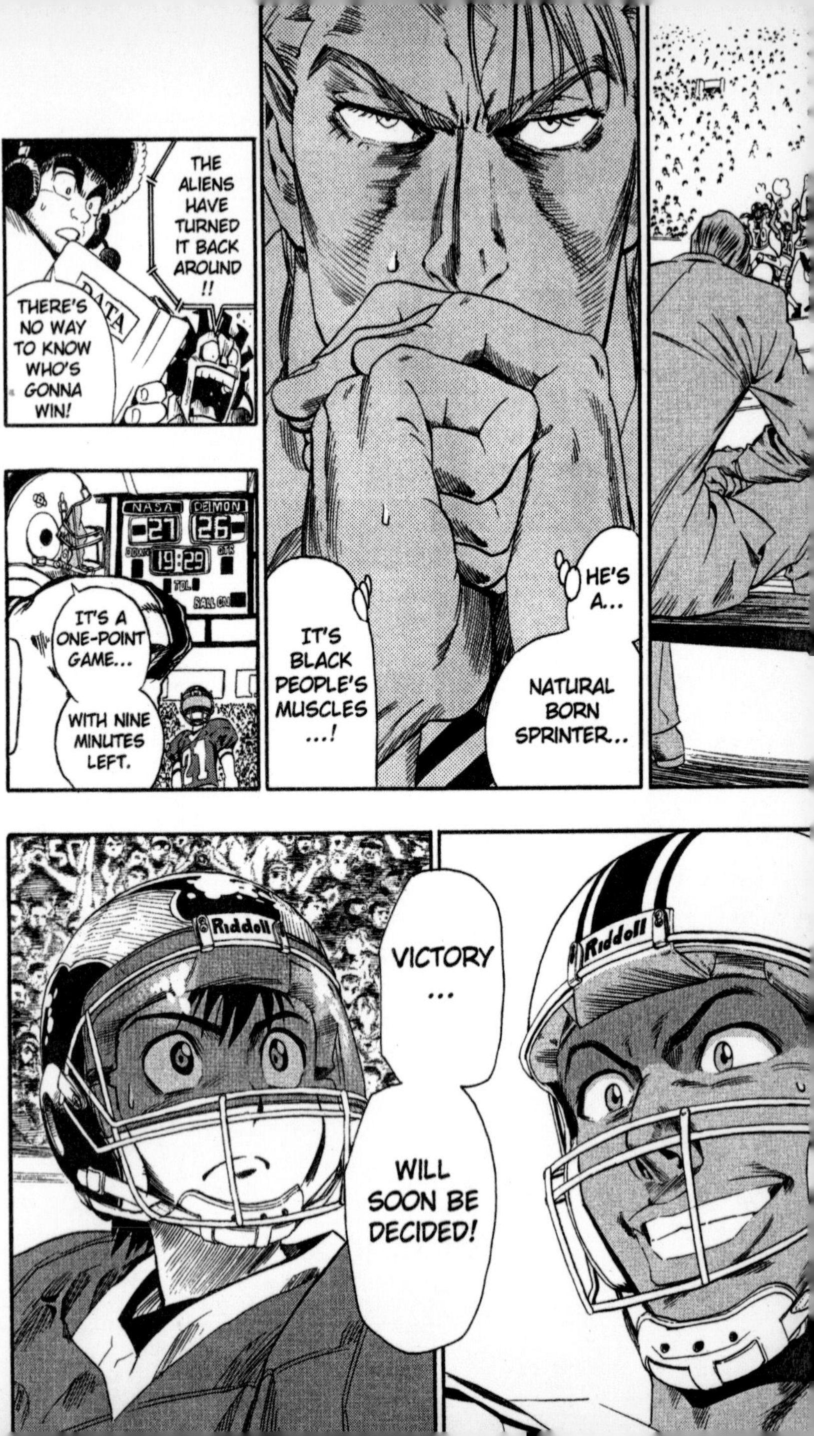
HE'S A...
NATURAL BORN SPRINTER...
IT'S BLACK PEOPLE'S MUSCLES ...!
THE ALIENS HAVE TURNED IT BACK AROUND !!
THERE'S NO WAY TO KNOW WHO'S GONNA WIN!
DATA
NASA
DEMON
27
26
19:29
IT'S A ONE-POINT GAME...
WITH NINE MINUTES LEFT.
Riddoll
VICTORY ...
WILL SOON BE DECIDED!
Riddoll

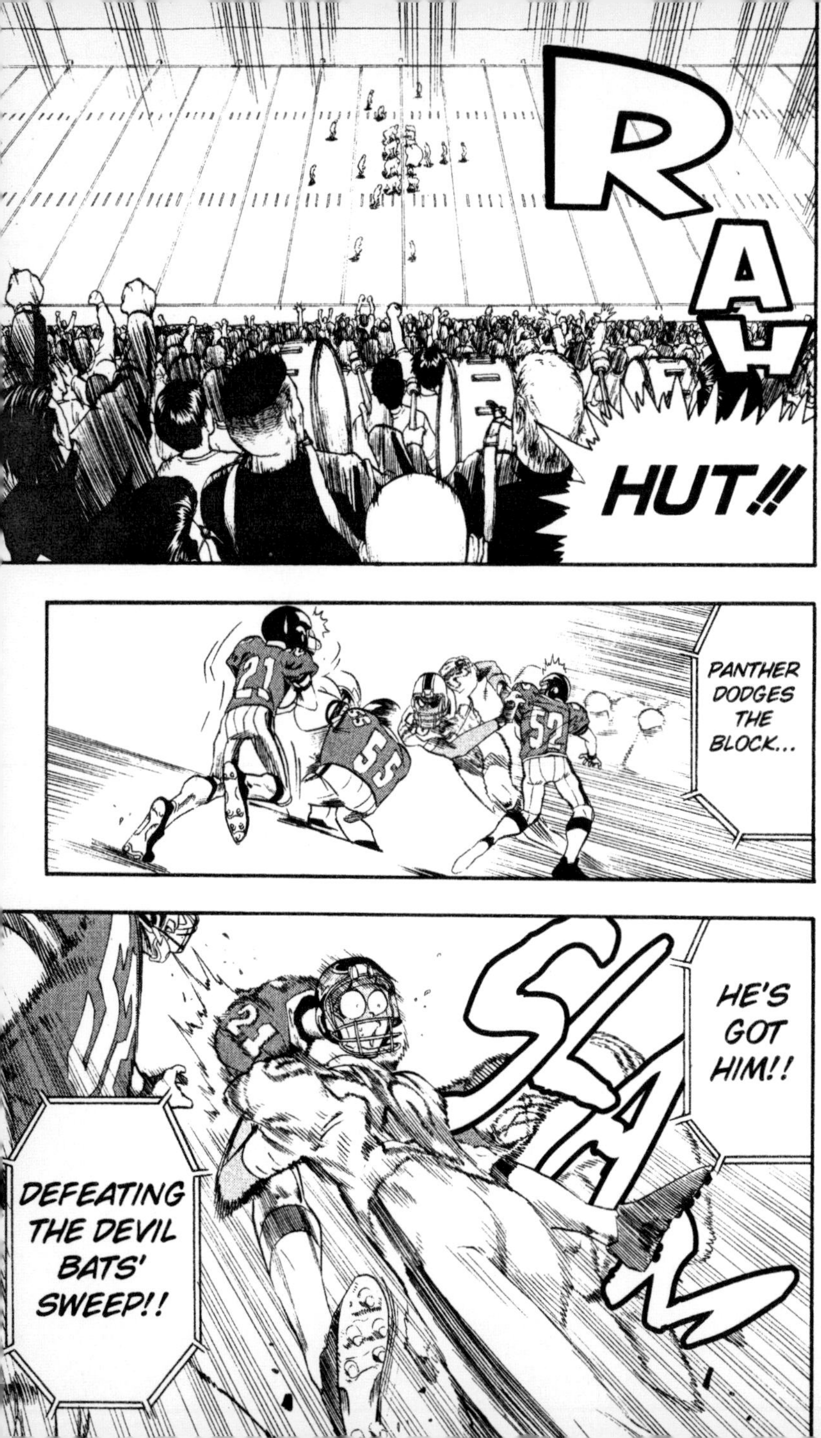
RAH
HUT!!
PANTHER DODGES THE BLOCK...
HE'S GOT HIM!!
SLAM
DEFEATING THE DEVIL BATS' SWEEP!!

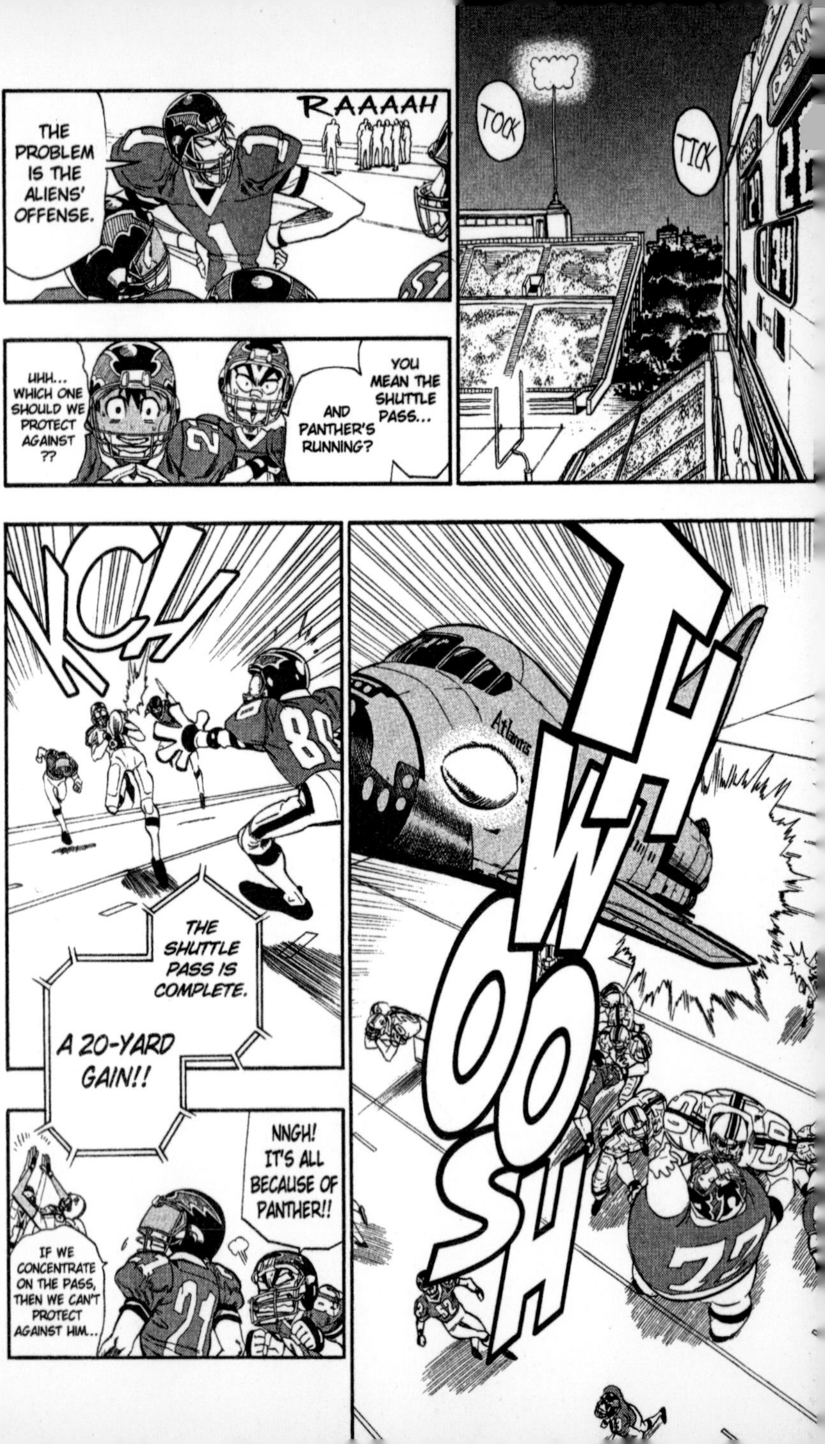
TICK
TOCK
RAAAAH
THE PROBLEM IS THE ALIENS' OFFENSE.
YOU MEAN THE SHUTTLE PASS...
AND PANTHER'S RUNNING?
UHH... WHICH ONE SHOULD WE PROTECT AGAINST ??
THWOOOSH
KCH
THE SHUTTLE PASS IS COMPLETE.
A 20-YARD GAIN!!
NNGH! IT'S ALL BECAUSE OF PANTHER!!
IF WE CONCENTRATE ON THE PASS, THEN WE CAN'T PROTECT AGAINST HIM...

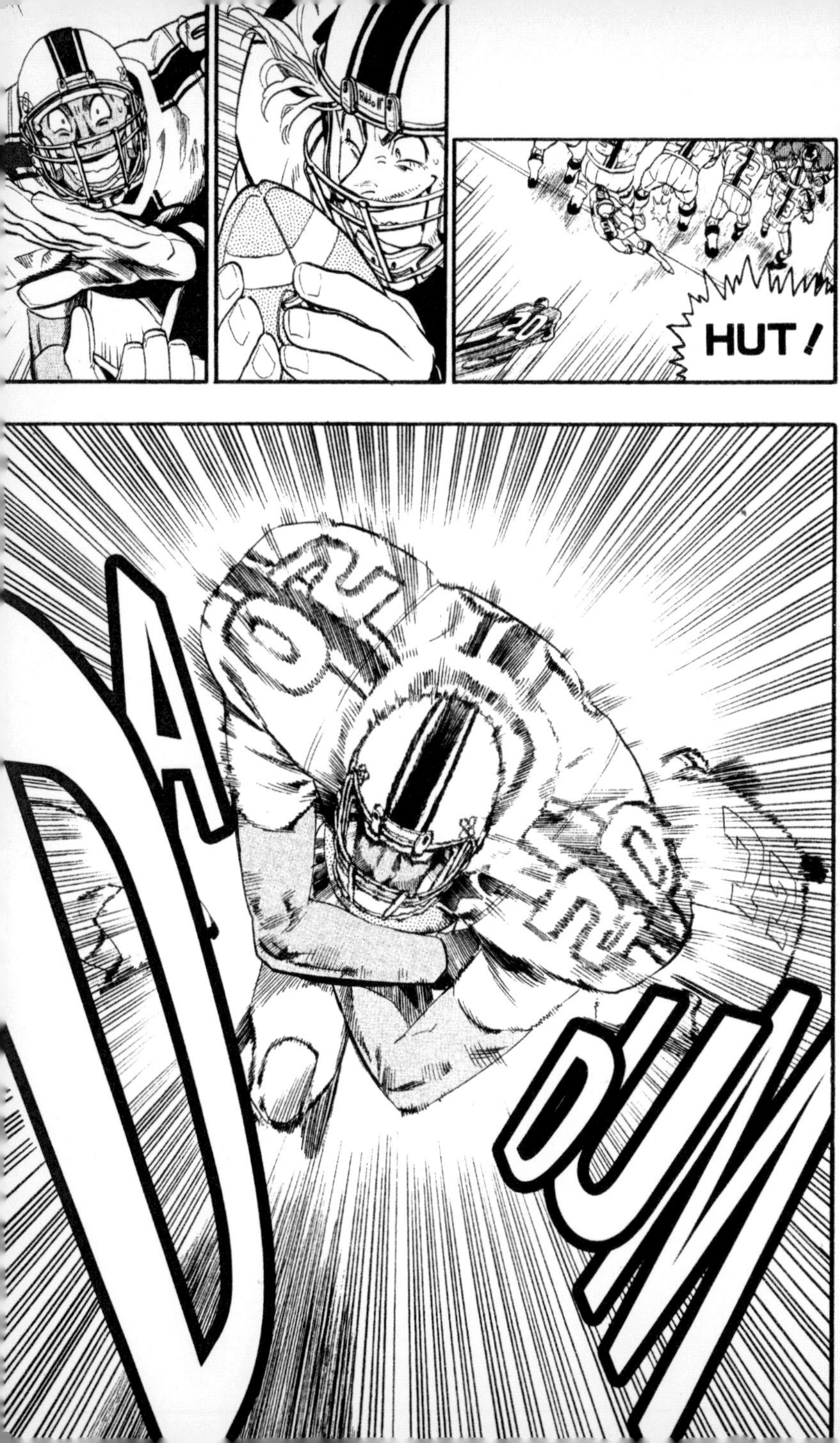
HUT!

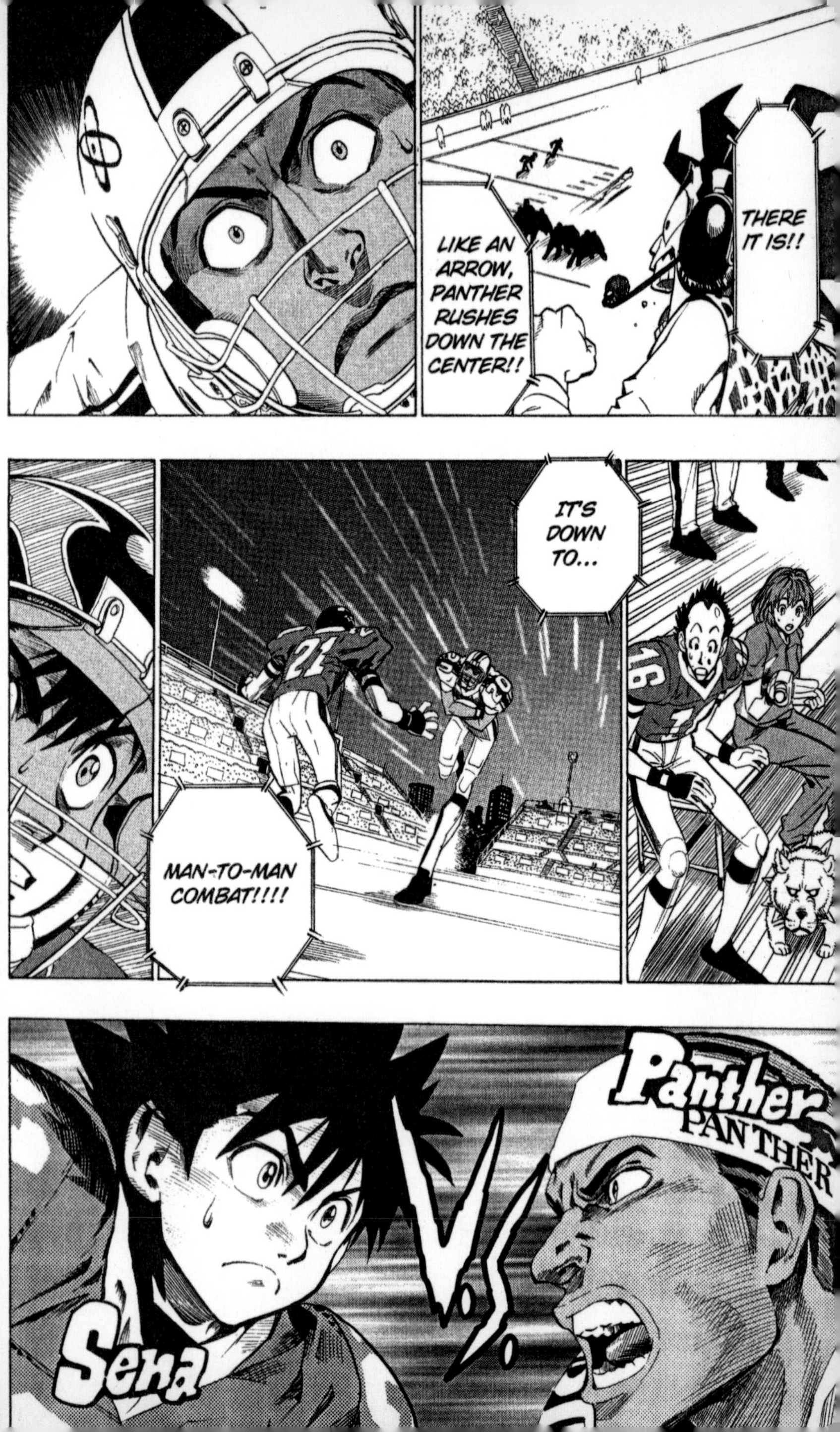
THERE IT IS!!
LIKE AN ARROW, PANTHER RUSHES DOWN THE CENTER!!
IT'S DOWN TO...
MAN-TO-MAN COMBAT!!!!
Panther
PANTHER
V.S.
Sena

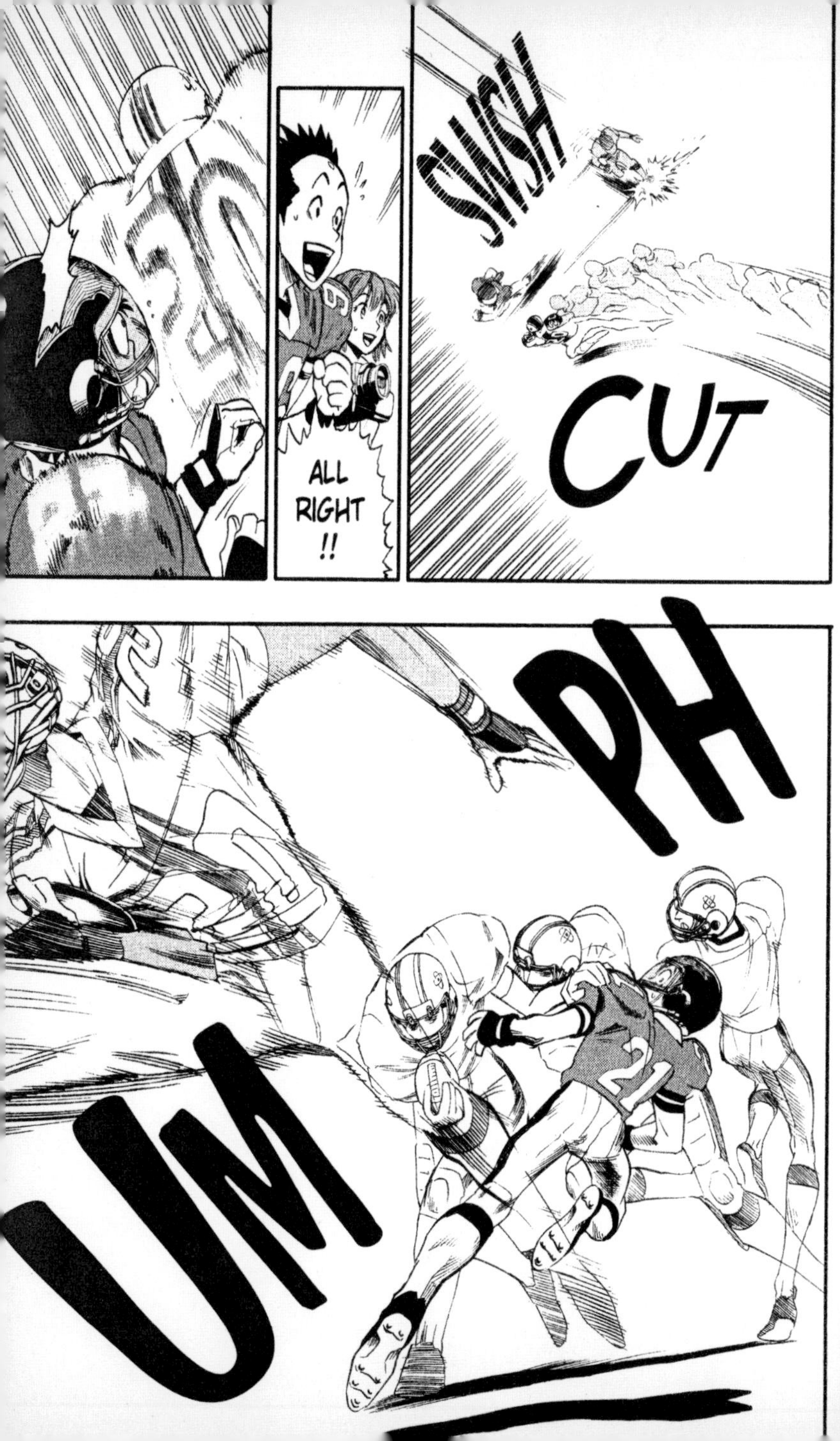
SWISH
CUT
ALL RIGHT !!
UMPH

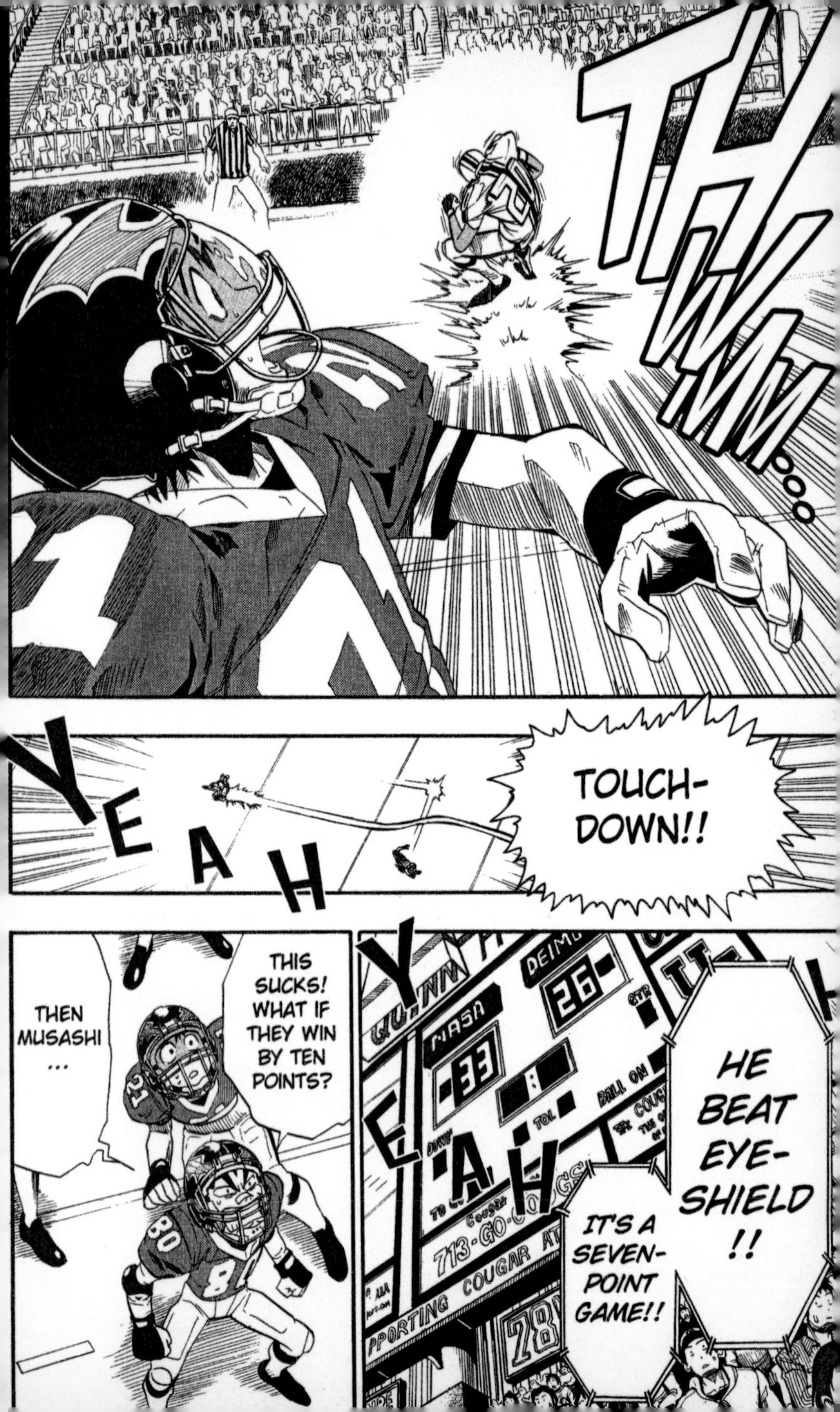
THWMMMooo
TOUCH-DOWN!!
YEAH
HE BEAT EYE-SHIELD!!
IT'S A SEVEN-POINT GAME!!
YEAH
THIS SUCKS! WHAT IF THEY WIN BY TEN POINTS?
THEN MUSASHI ...

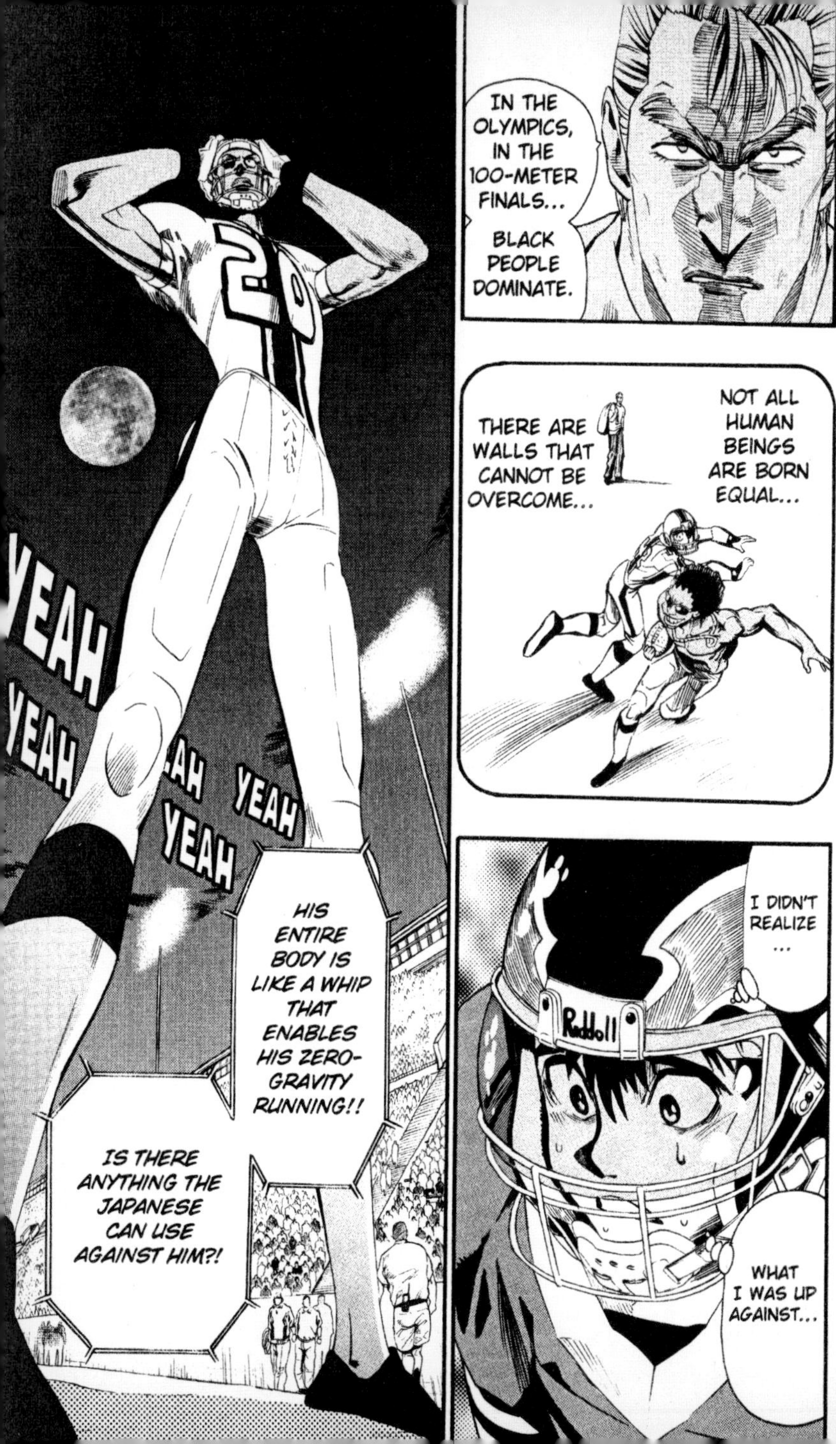
IN THE OLYMPICS, IN THE 100-METER FINALS...
BLACK PEOPLE DOMINATE.
NOT ALL HUMAN BEINGS ARE BORN EQUAL...
THERE ARE WALLS THAT CANNOT BE OVERCOME...
I DIDN'T REALIZE ...
Riddell
WHAT I WAS UP AGAINST...
YEAH
YEAH
YEAH
YEAH
HIS ENTIRE BODY IS LIKE A WHIP THAT ENABLES HIS ZERO-GRAVITY RUNNING!!
IS THERE ANYTHING THE JAPANESE CAN USE AGAINST HIM?!

Eyeshield 21 Survey Corner **Devil Bat 021**

Investigation File #007

Who is stronger, Gonzales or Kurita?!

STRAIGHT UP! WHO IS MORE POWERFUL, BIG POOP GONZALES OR KURITA?!!

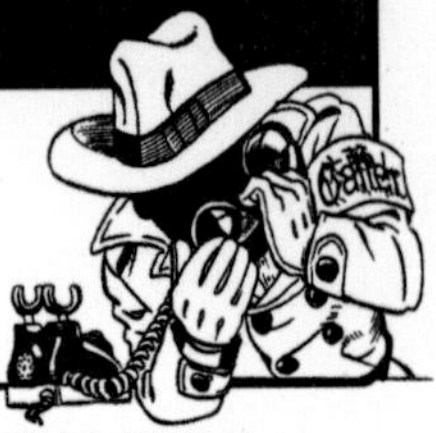

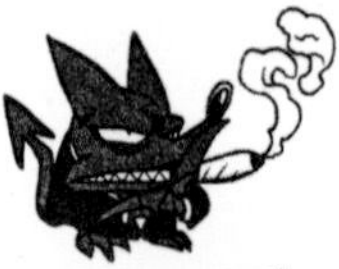

WHEN IT COMES TO POWER, IT'S NOT THAT SIMPLE.

IF YOU MEAN THE DESTRUCTIVE POWER AT THE MOMENT OF IMPACT, THEN IT'S GONZALES WITH HIS MUSCULAR UPPER BODY.

BUT IF IT'S SIMPLY BLOCKING POWER, THEN WOULDN'T IT BE THE FULL FATTY, KURITA?

Investigation File #008

Who is faster, Panther or Shin?!

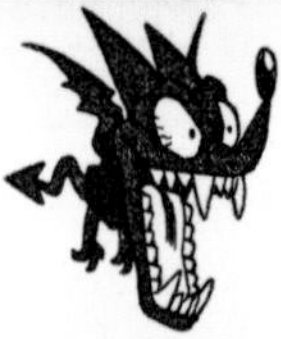

THIS MIGHT BE ANSWERED IN THE NEXT VOLUME OR THE ONE AFTER, GOT IT? STAY TUNED, HEE HEE HEE!!

Send your queries for Devil Bat 021 here!!

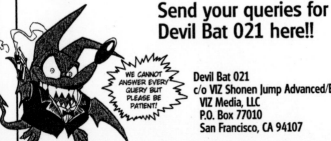

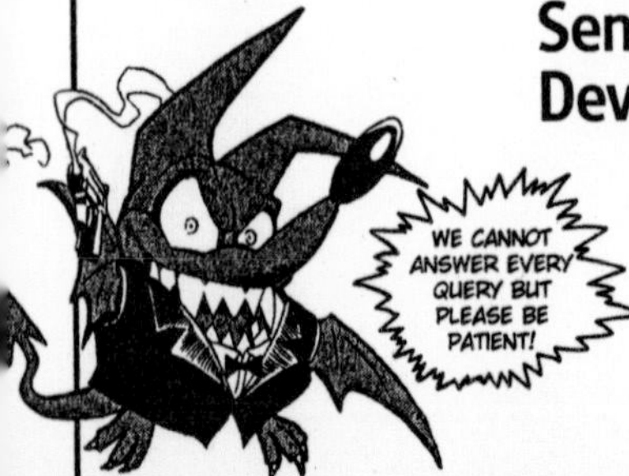
WE CANNOT ANSWER EVERY QUERY BUT PLEASE BE PATIENT!

Devil Bat 021
c/o VIZ Shonen Jump Advanced/Eyeshield 21
VIZ Media, LLC
P.O. Box 77010
San Francisco, CA 94107

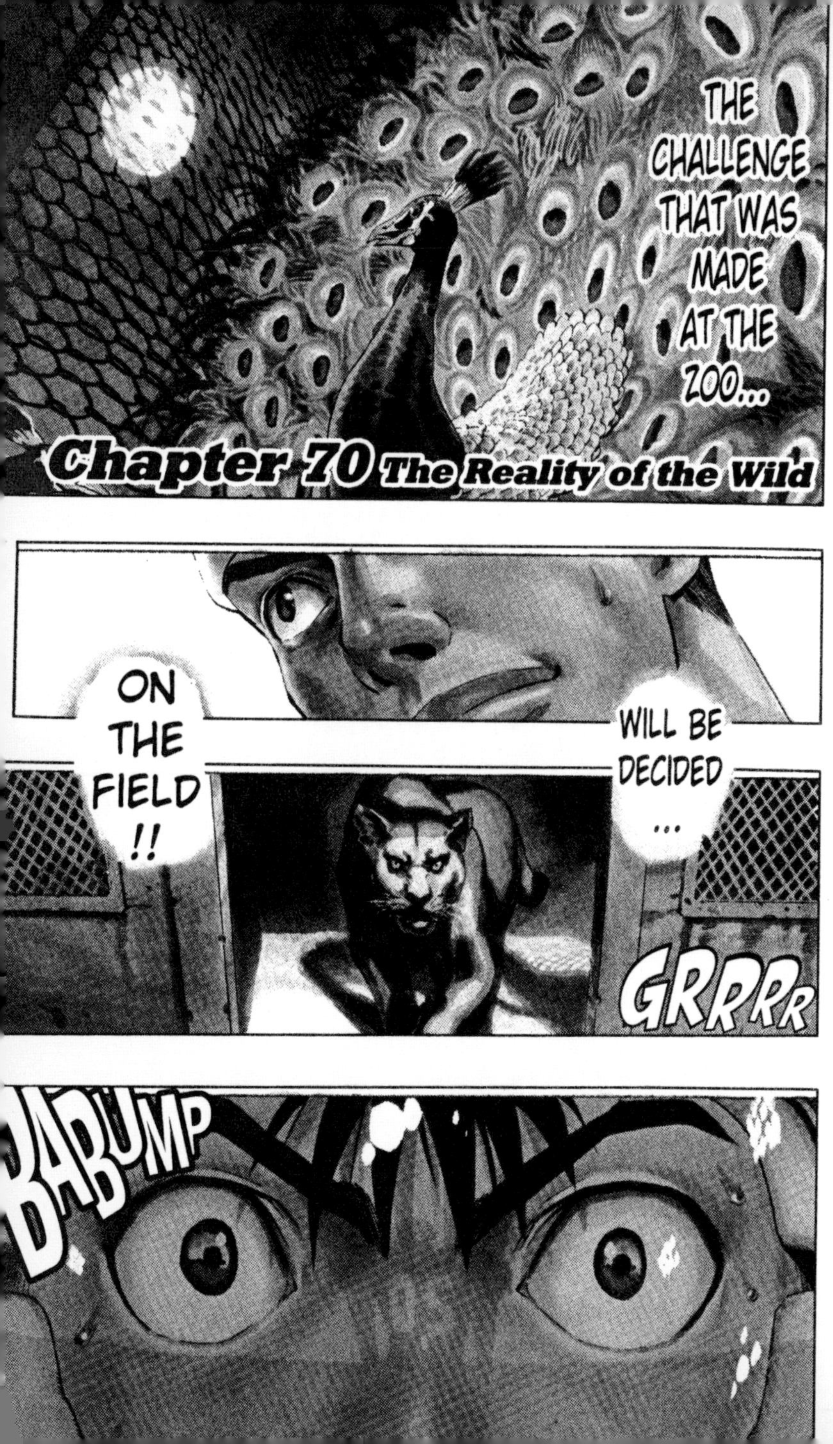
THE CHALLENGE THAT WAS MADE AT THE ZOO...
Chapter 70 The Reality of the Wild
WILL BE DECIDED ...
ON THE FIELD !!
GRRRR
BABUMP

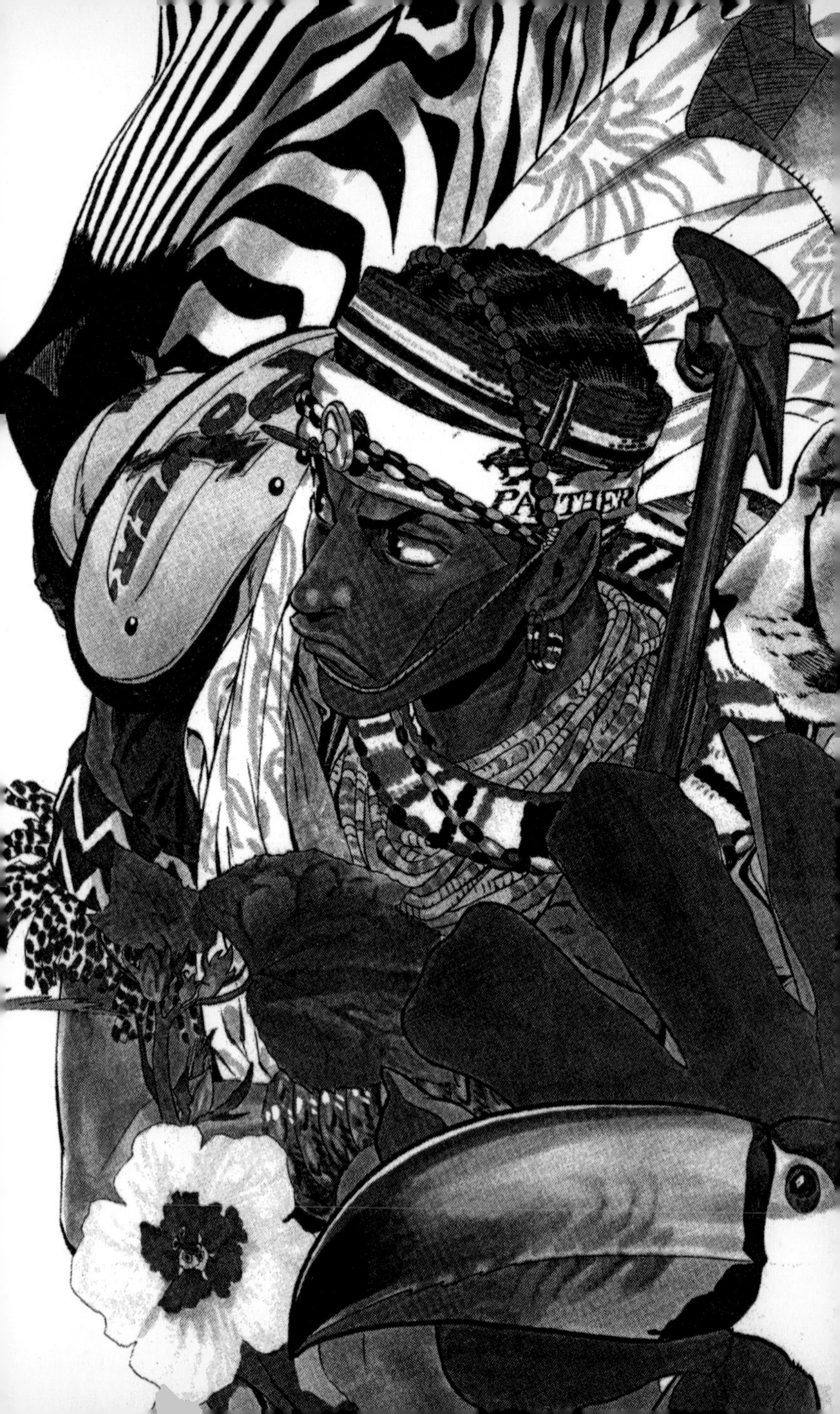

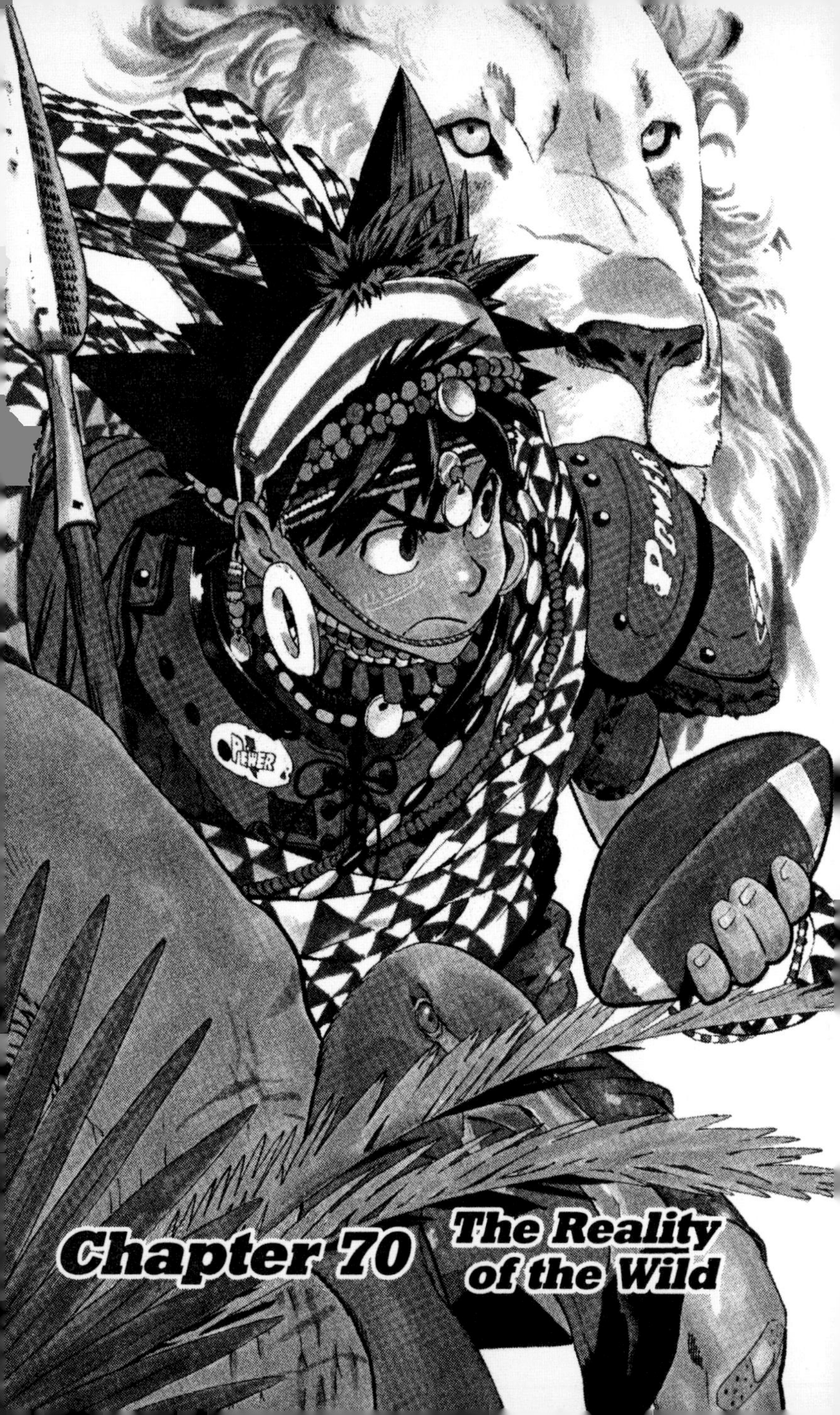
Chapter 70
The Reality of the Wild
POWER
POWER

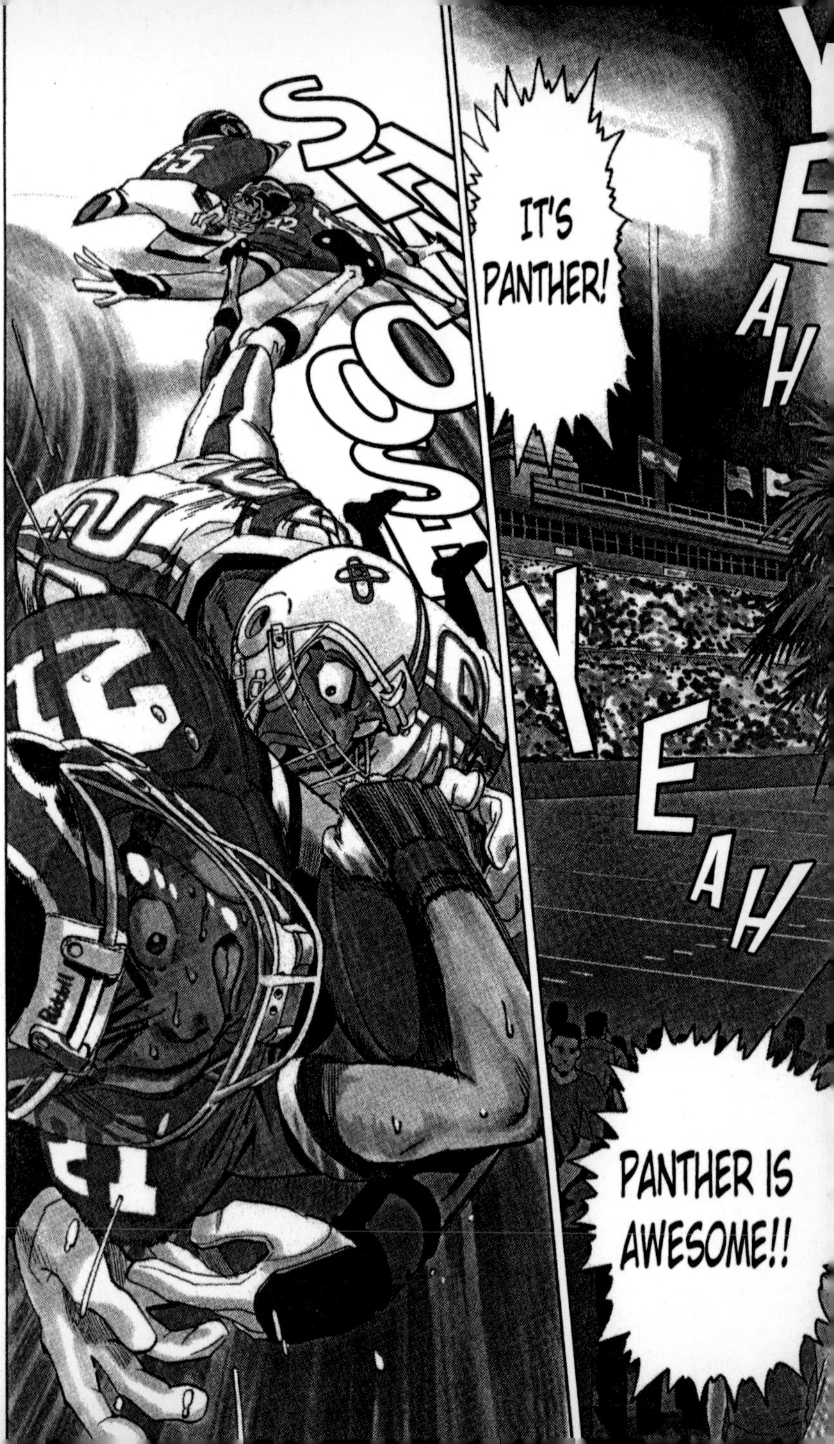
YEAH
IT'S PANTHER!
YEAH
PANTHER IS AWESOME!!

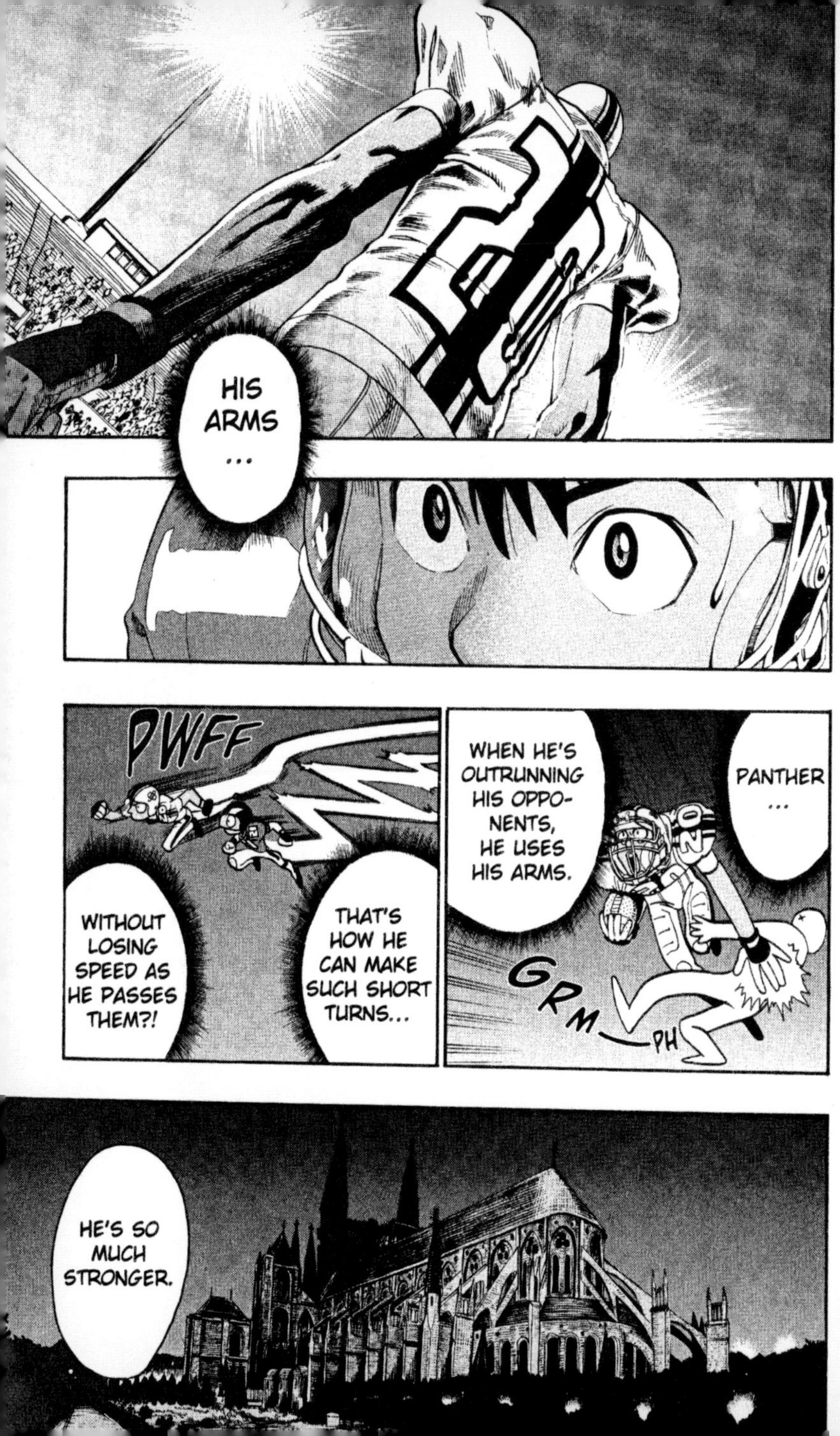
HIS ARMS ...
PANTHER ...
WHEN HE'S OUTRUNNING HIS OPPONENTS, HE USES HIS ARMS.
GRM—PH
PWFF
THAT'S HOW HE CAN MAKE SUCH SHORT TURNS...
WITHOUT LOSING SPEED AS HE PASSES THEM?!
HE'S SO MUCH STRONGER.

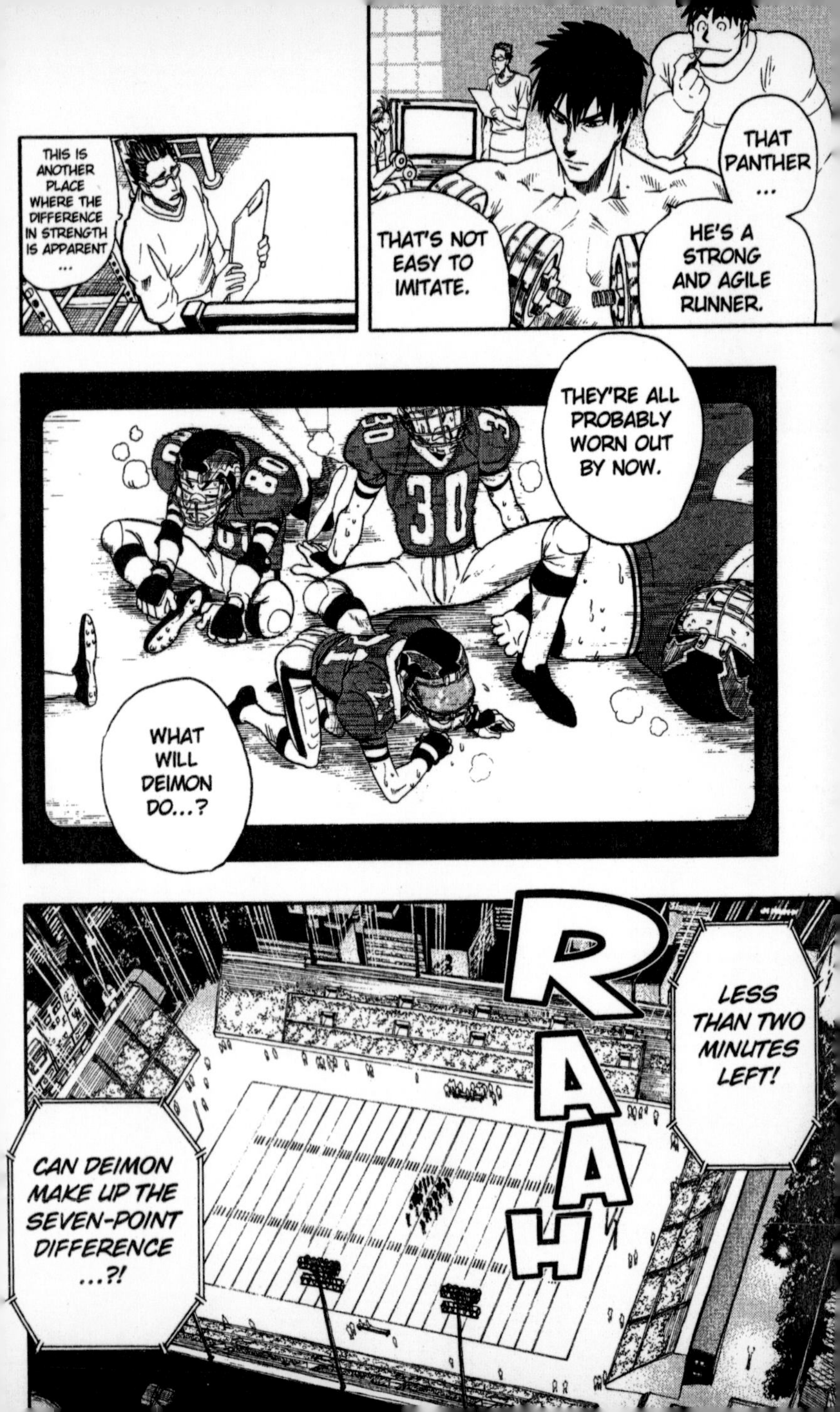
THAT PANTHER ...
HE'S A STRONG AND AGILE RUNNER.
THAT'S NOT EASY TO IMITATE.
THIS IS ANOTHER PLACE WHERE THE DIFFERENCE IN STRENGTH IS APPARENT ...
THEY'RE ALL PROBABLY WORN OUT BY NOW.
WHAT WILL DEIMON DO...?
RAAH
LESS THAN TWO MINUTES LEFT!
CAN DEIMON MAKE UP THE SEVEN-POINT DIFFERENCE ...?!

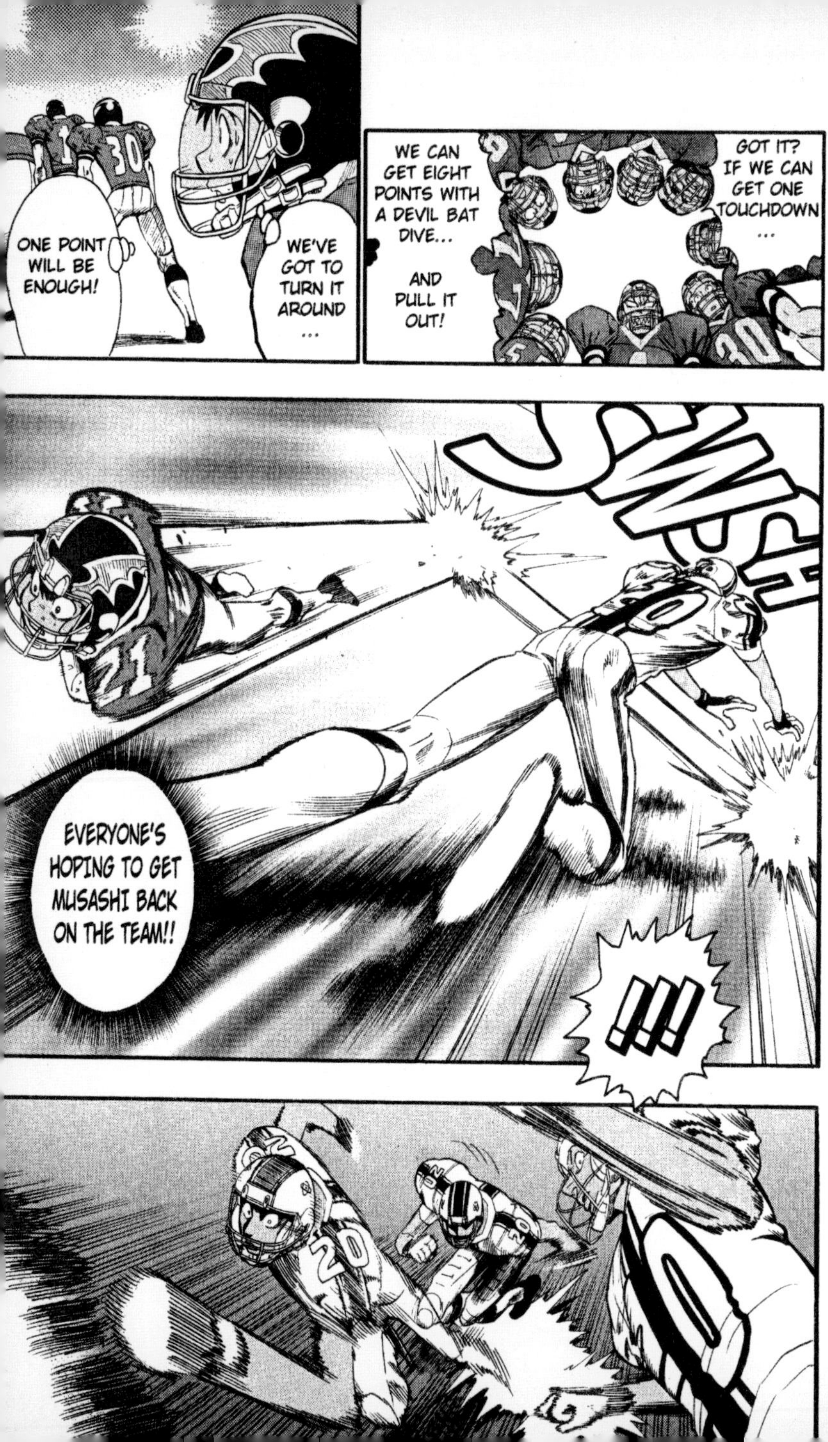
GOT IT? IF WE CAN GET ONE TOUCHDOWN ...
WE CAN GET EIGHT POINTS WITH A DEVIL BAT DIVE...
AND PULL IT OUT!
WE'VE GOT TO TURN IT AROUND ...
ONE POINT WILL BE ENOUGH!
SWISH
EVERYONE'S HOPING TO GET MUSASHI BACK ON THE TEAM!!
!!!!

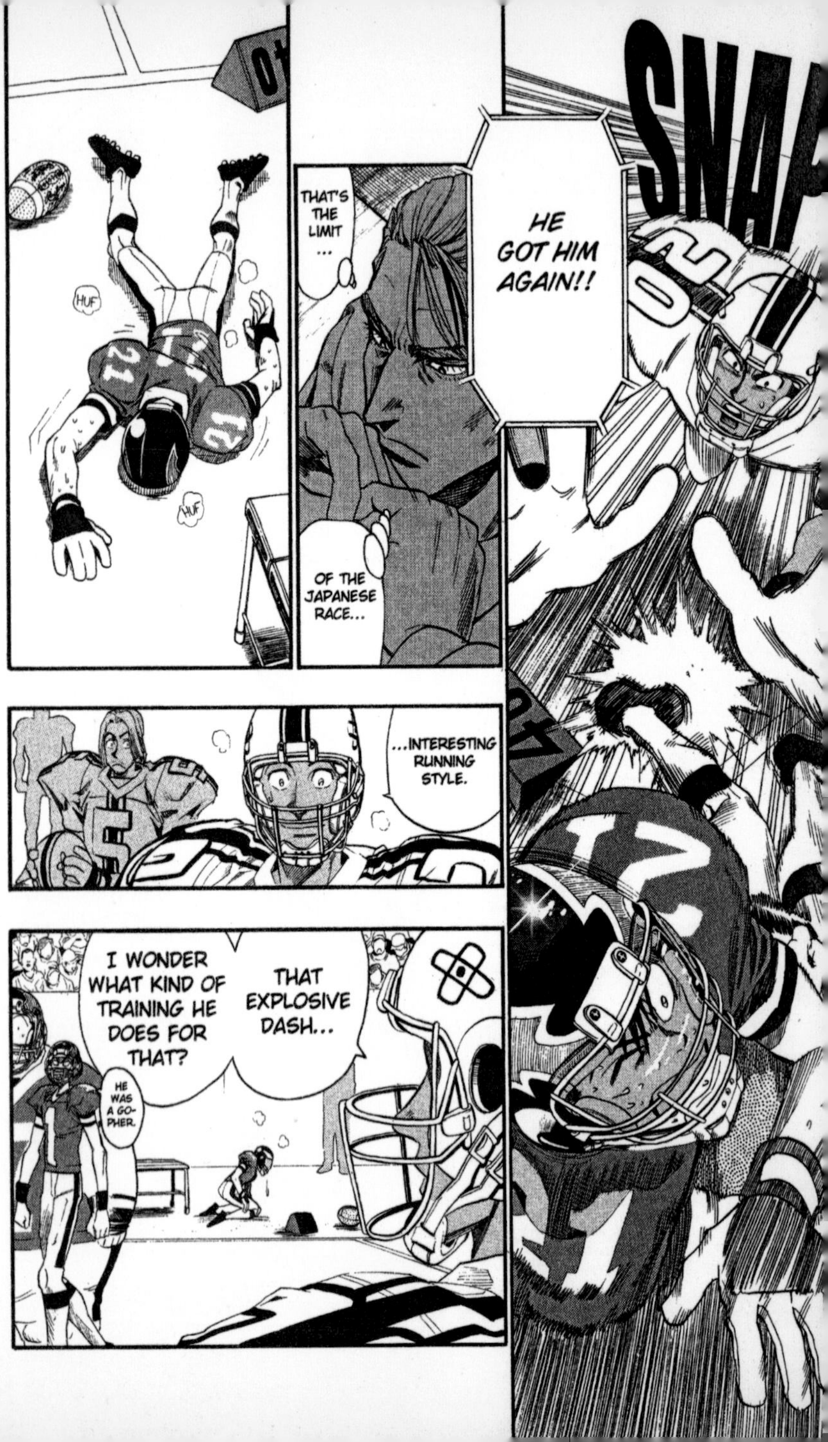

SNAP
HE GOT HIM AGAIN!!
THAT'S THE LIMIT ...
OF THE JAPANESE RACE...
HUF
HUF
...INTERESTING RUNNING STYLE.
THAT EXPLOSIVE DASH...
I WONDER WHAT KIND OF TRAINING HE DOES FOR THAT?
HE WAS A GO-PHER.

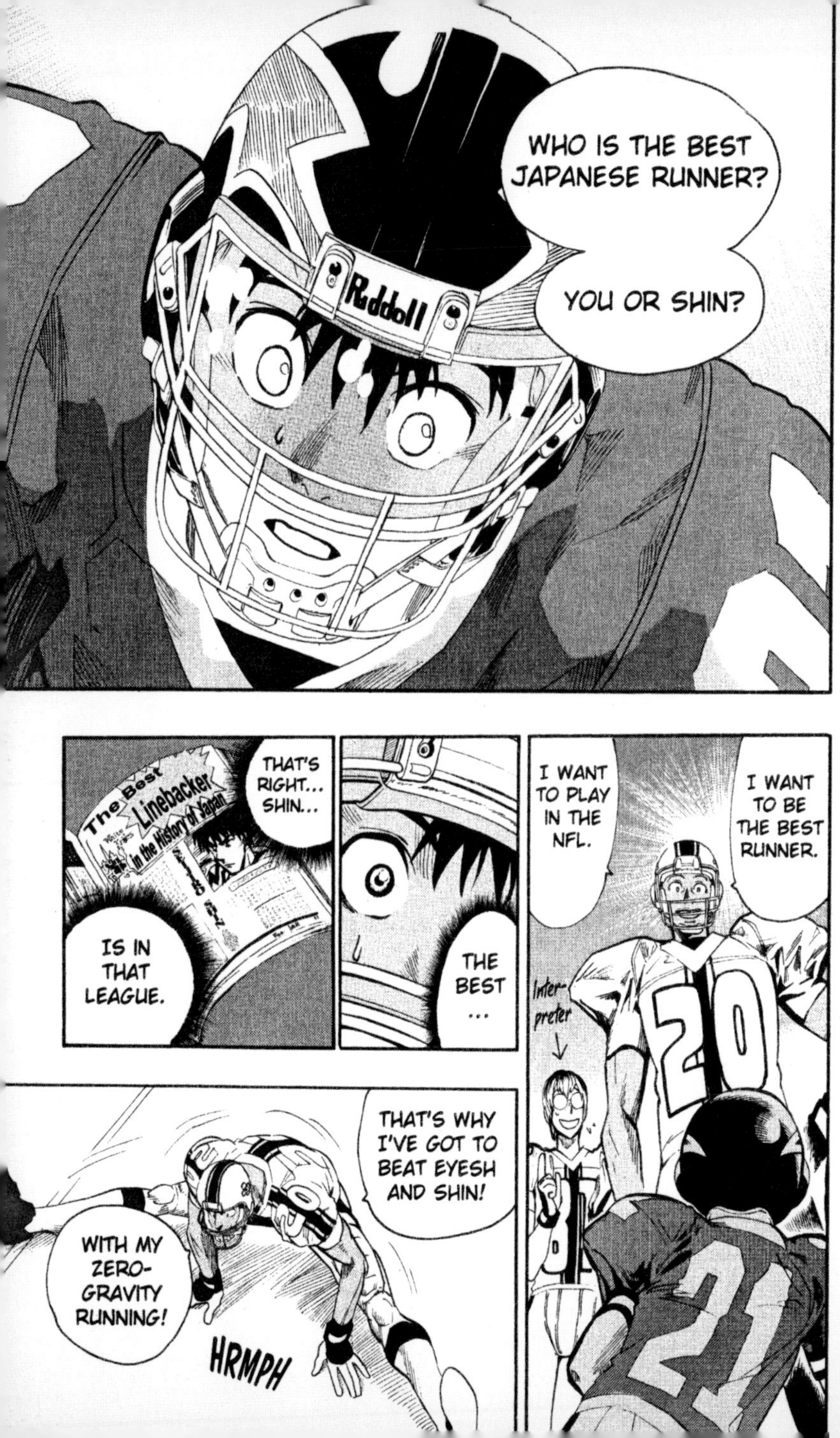
WHO IS THE BEST JAPANESE RUNNER?
YOU OR SHIN?
I WANT TO BE THE BEST RUNNER.
I WANT TO PLAY IN THE NFL.
Inter-preter
THE BEST ...
THAT'S RIGHT... SHIN...
The Best Linebacker in the History of Japan
IS IN THAT LEAGUE.
THAT'S WHY I'VE GOT TO BEAT EYESH AND SHIN!
WITH MY ZERO-GRAVITY RUNNING!
HRMPH

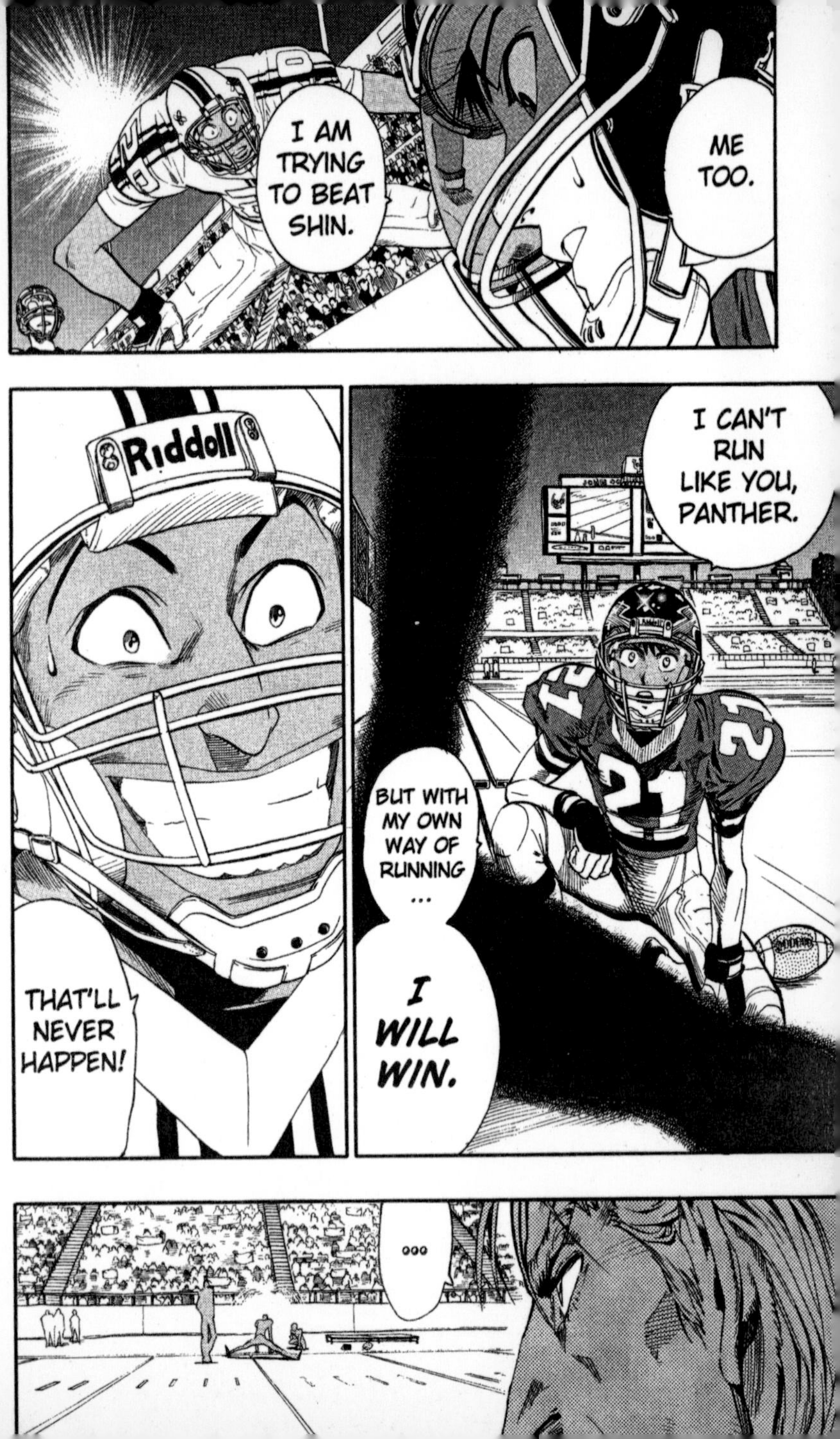

I AM TRYING TO BEAT SHIN.
ME TOO.
I CAN'T RUN LIKE YOU, PANTHER.
BUT WITH MY OWN WAY OF RUNNING ...
I WILL WIN.
Riddell
THAT'LL NEVER HAPPEN!
...

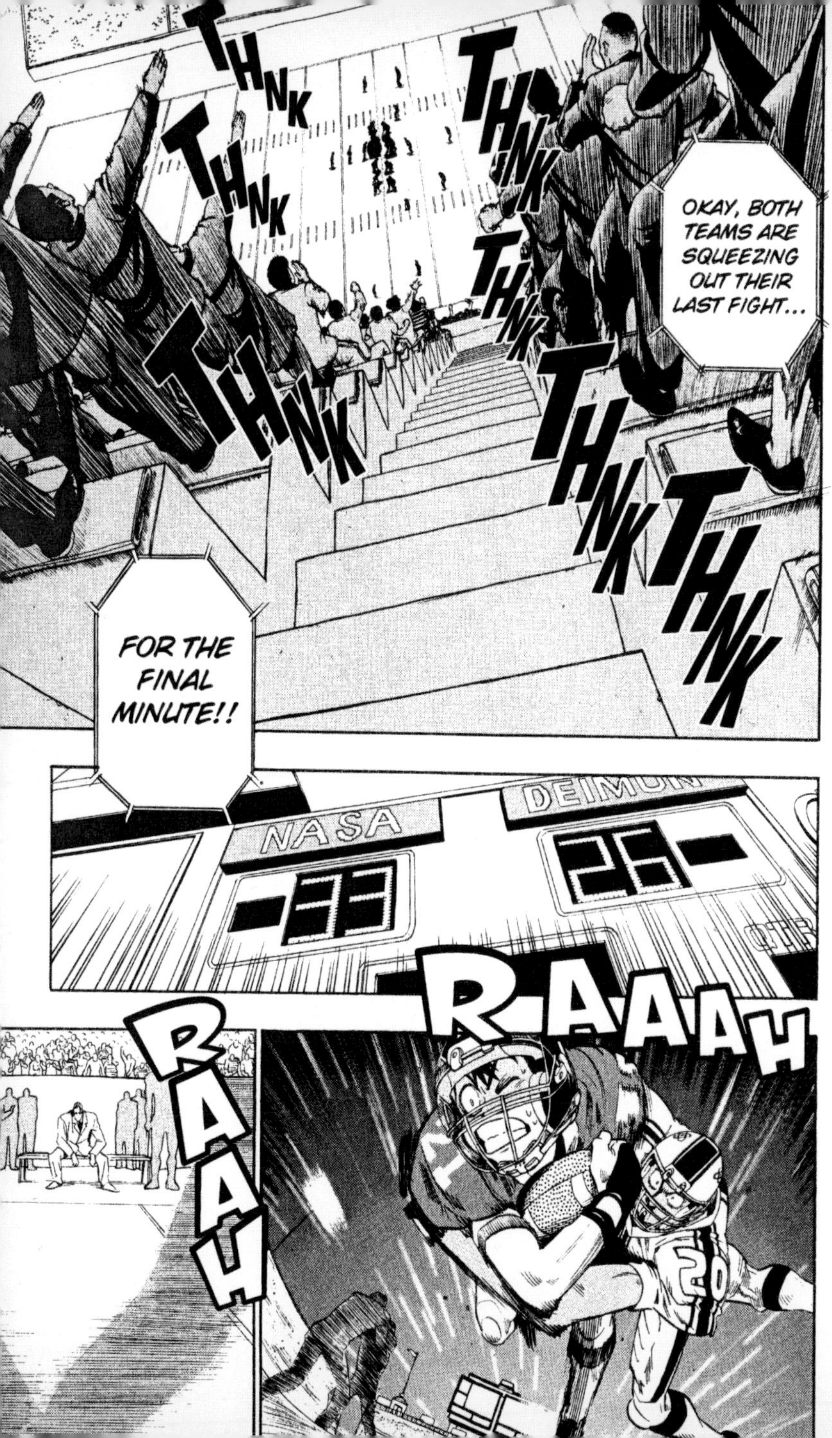
THNK
THNK
THNK
THNK
OKAY, BOTH TEAMS ARE SQUEEZING OUT THEIR LAST FIGHT...
THNK
THNK
THNK
FOR THE FINAL MINUTE!!
DEIMON
26
NASA
33
RAAAAH
RAAAH

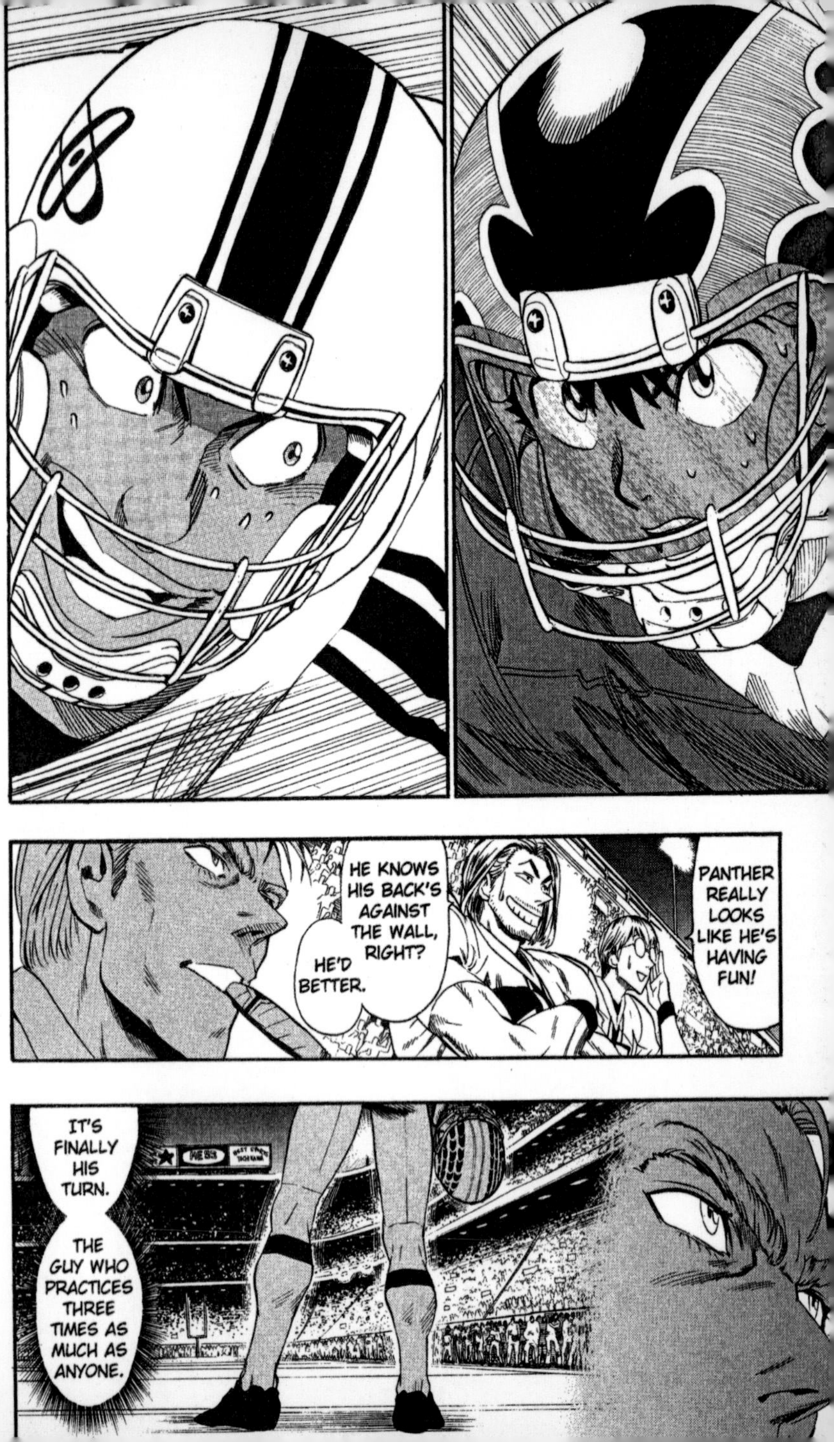
PANTHER REALLY LOOKS LIKE HE'S HAVING FUN!
HE KNOWS HIS BACK'S AGAINST THE WALL, RIGHT?
HE'D BETTER.
IT'S FINALLY HIS TURN.
THE GUY WHO PRACTICES THREE TIMES AS MUCH AS ANYONE.

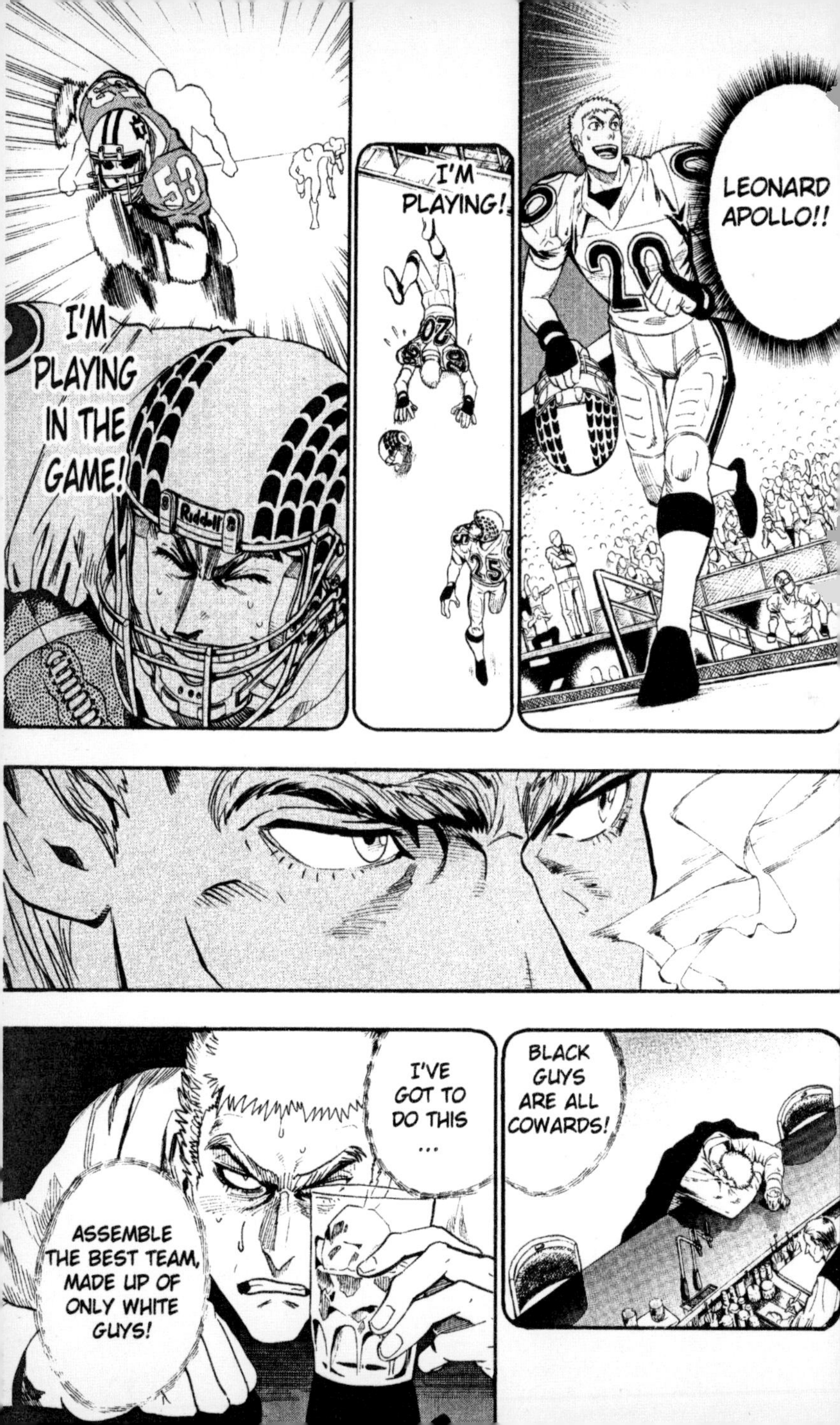
LEONARD APOLLO!!
I'M PLAYING!
I'M PLAYING IN THE GAME!
BLACK GUYS ARE ALL COWARDS!
I'VE GOT TO DO THIS ...
ASSEMBLE THE BEST TEAM, MADE UP OF ONLY WHITE GUYS!

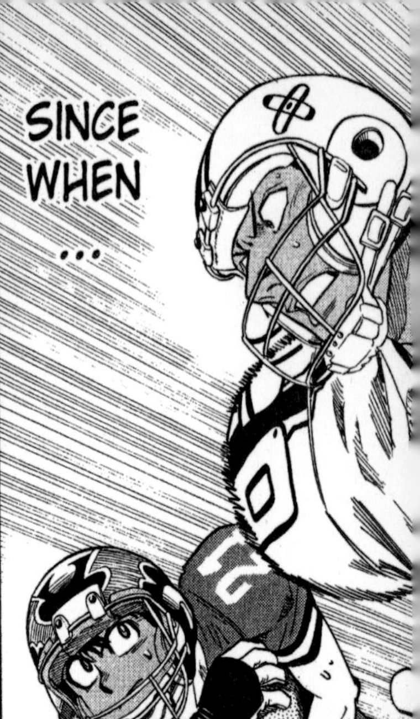
SINCE WHEN ...
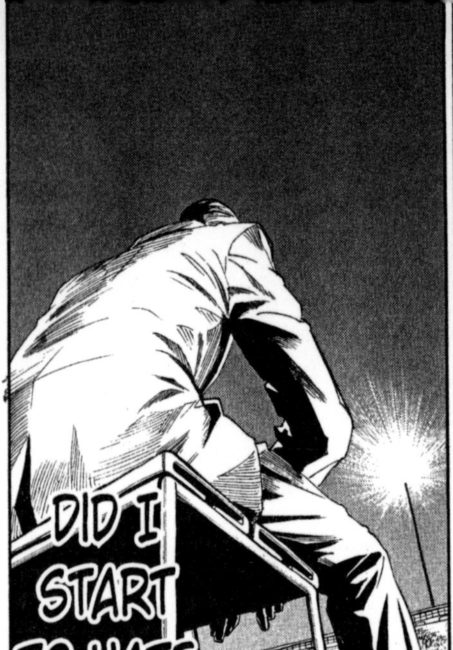
DID I START TO HATE FOOT-BALL ...
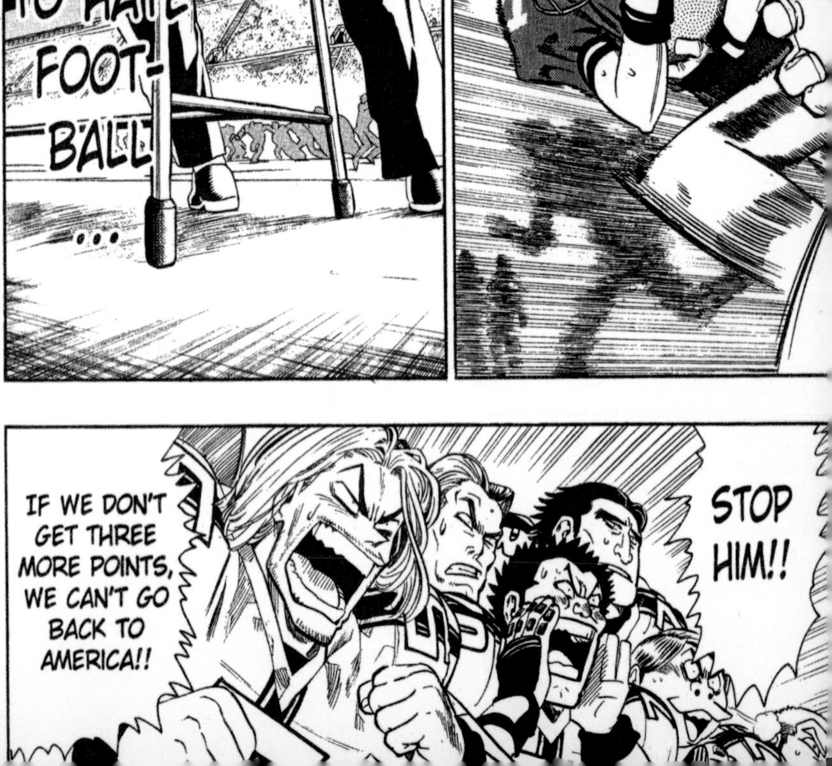
STOP HIM!!
IF WE DON'T GET THREE MORE POINTS, WE CAN'T GO BACK TO AMERICA!!

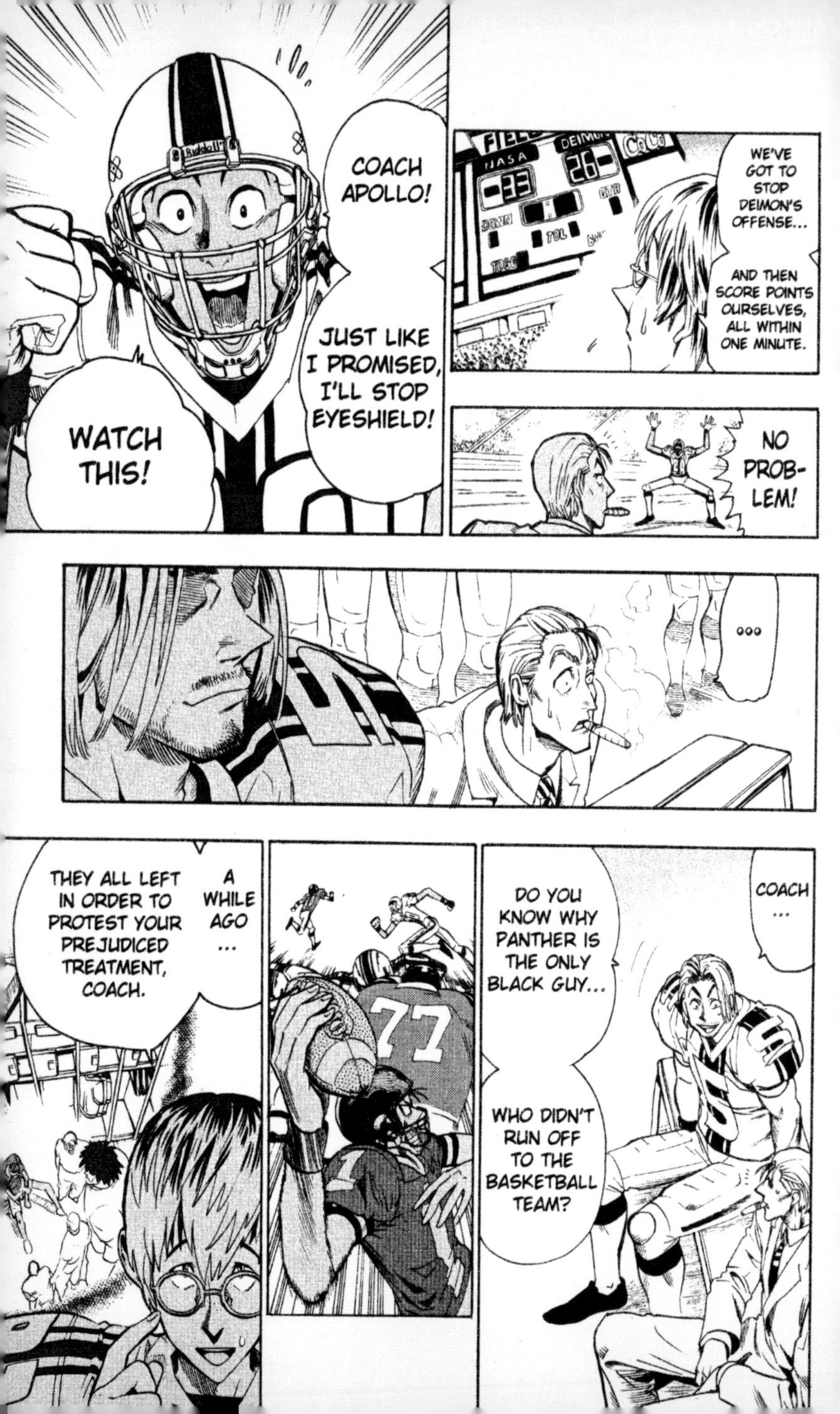
WE'VE GOT TO STOP DEIMON'S OFFENSE...
AND THEN SCORE POINTS OURSELVES, ALL WITHIN ONE MINUTE.
NO PROB-LEM!
COACH APOLLO!
JUST LIKE I PROMISED, I'LL STOP EYESHIELD!
WATCH THIS!
...
COACH ...
DO YOU KNOW WHY PANTHER IS THE ONLY BLACK GUY...
WHO DIDN'T RUN OFF TO THE BASKETBALL TEAM?
A WHILE AGO ...
THEY ALL LEFT IN ORDER TO PROTEST YOUR PREJUDICED TREATMENT, COACH.

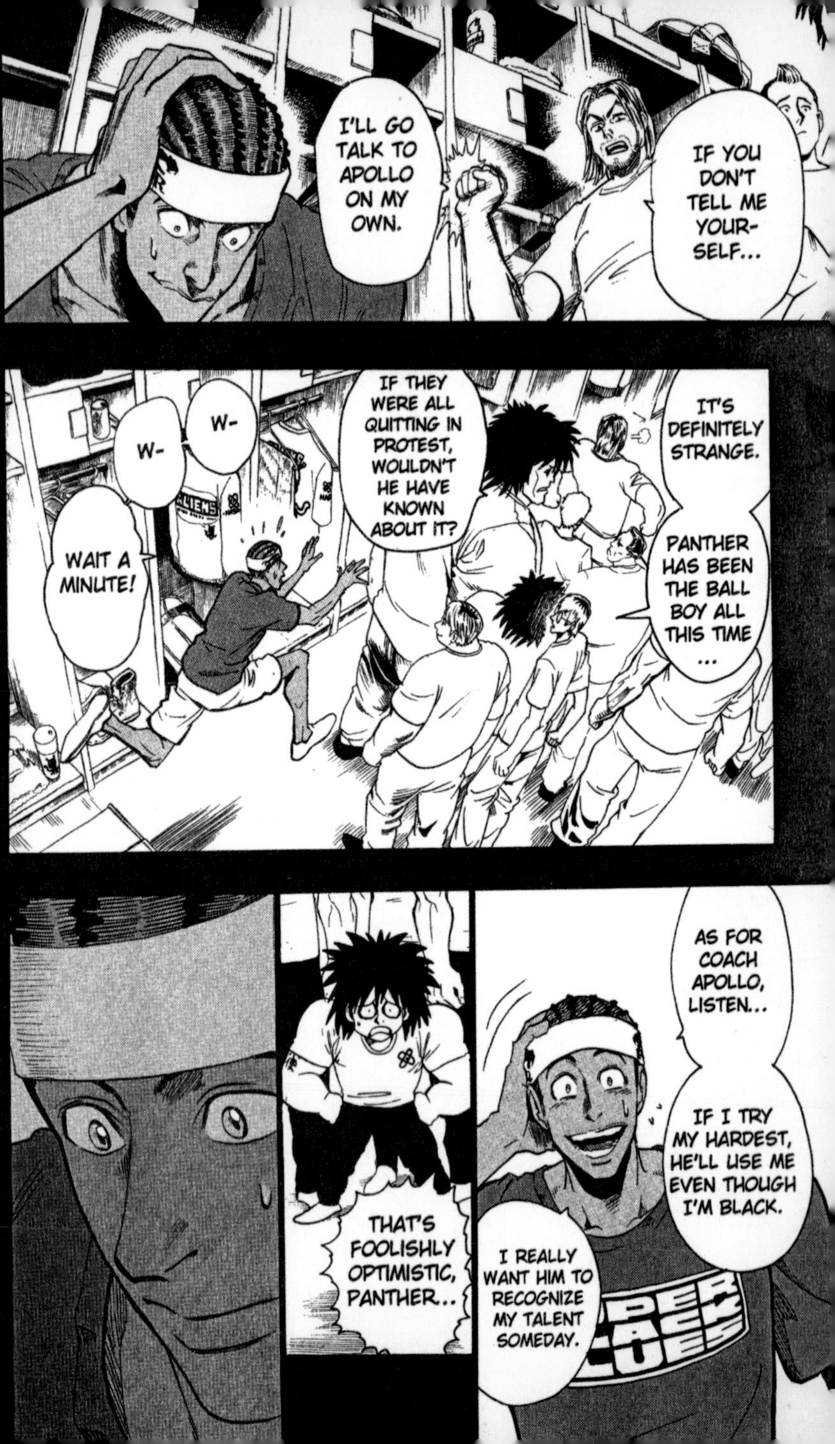
IF YOU DON'T TELL ME YOURSELF...
I'LL GO TALK TO APOLLO ON MY OWN.
IT'S DEFINITELY STRANGE.
PANTHER HAS BEEN THE BALL BOY ALL THIS TIME...
IF THEY WERE ALL QUITTING IN PROTEST, WOULDN'T HE HAVE KNOWN ABOUT IT?
W-
W-
WAIT A MINUTE!
AS FOR COACH APOLLO, LISTEN...
IF I TRY MY HARDEST, HE'LL USE ME EVEN THOUGH I'M BLACK.
I REALLY WANT HIM TO RECOGNIZE MY TALENT SOMEDAY.
THAT'S FOOLISHLY OPTIMISTIC, PANTHER...

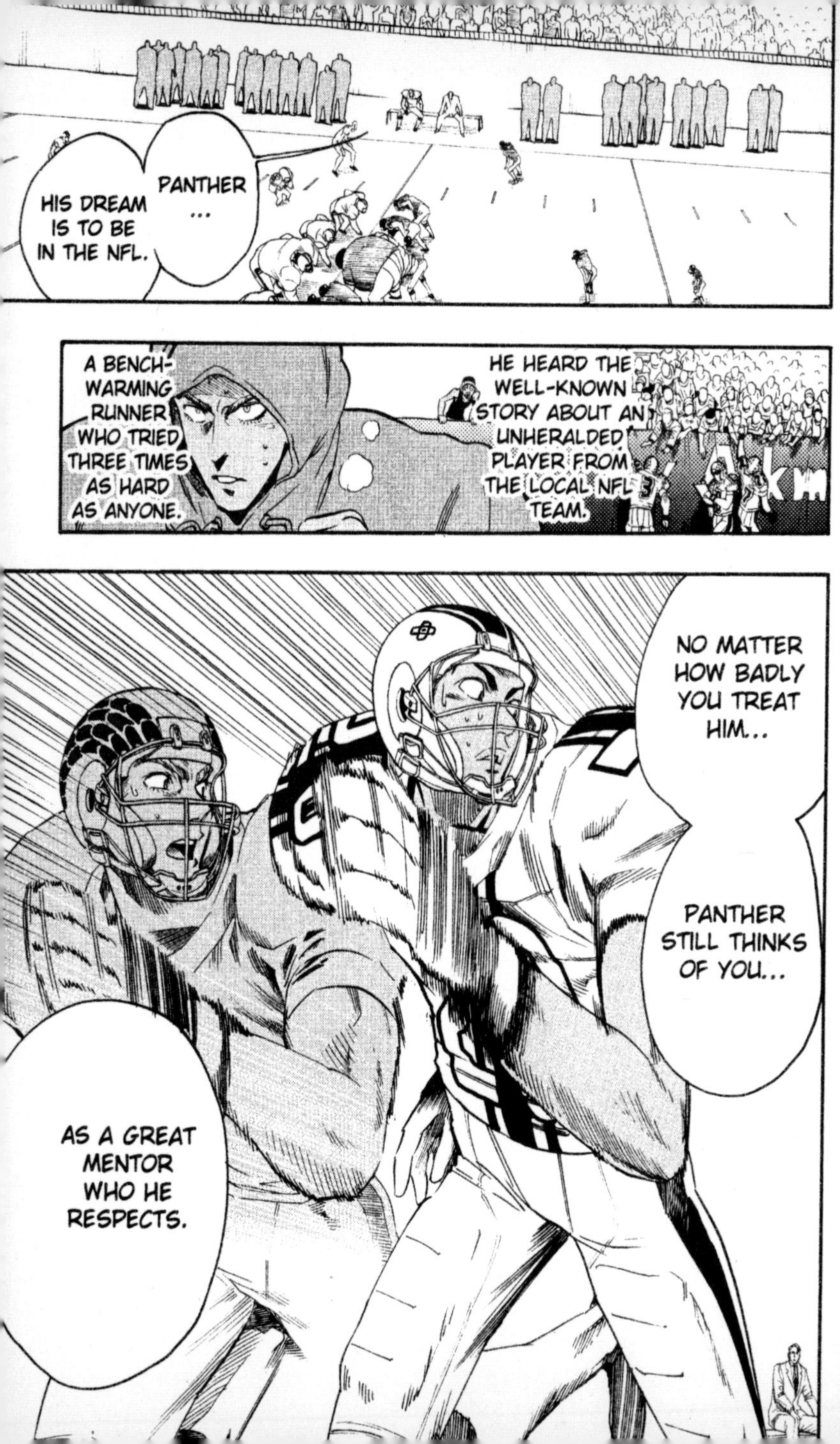
PANTHER...
HIS DREAM IS TO BE IN THE NFL.
HE HEARD THE WELL-KNOWN STORY ABOUT AN UNHERALDED PLAYER FROM THE LOCAL NFL TEAM.
A BENCH-WARMING RUNNER WHO TRIED THREE TIMES AS HARD AS ANYONE.
NO MATTER HOW BADLY YOU TREAT HIM...
PANTHER STILL THINKS OF YOU...
AS A GREAT MENTOR WHO HE RESPECTS.

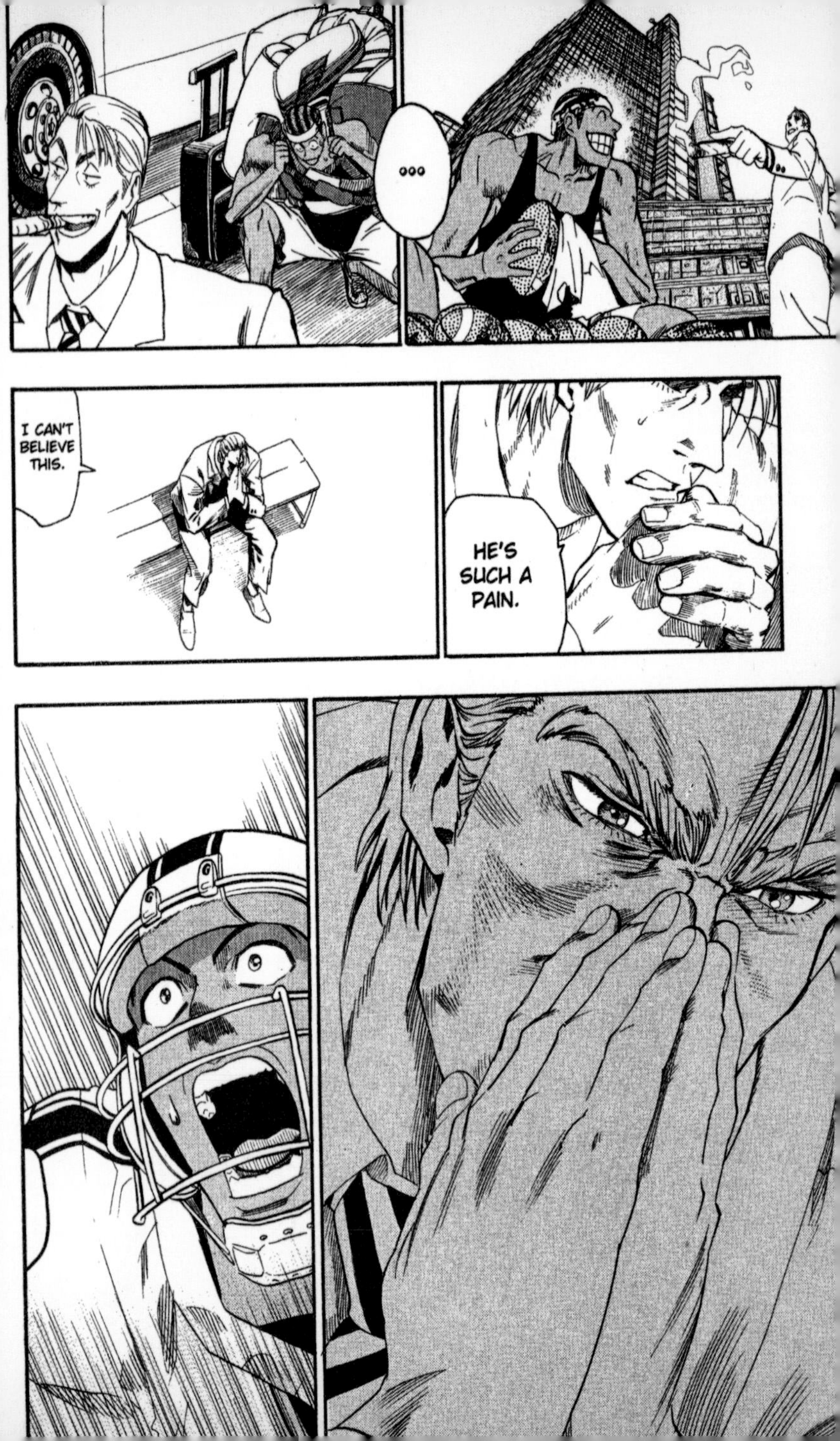
...
HE'S SUCH A PAIN.
I CAN'T BELIEVE THIS.

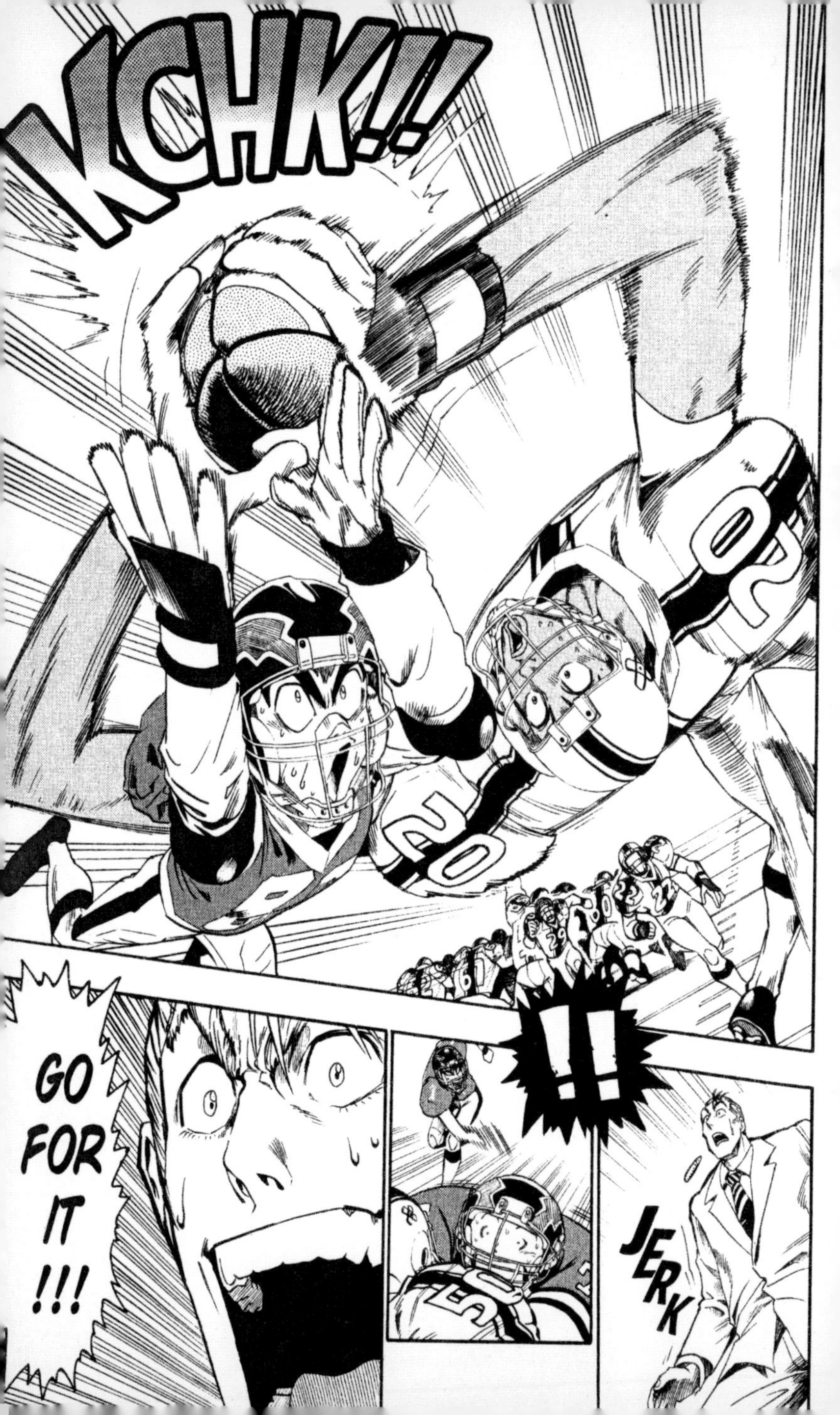
KCHK!!
GO FOR IT!!!
!!
JERK

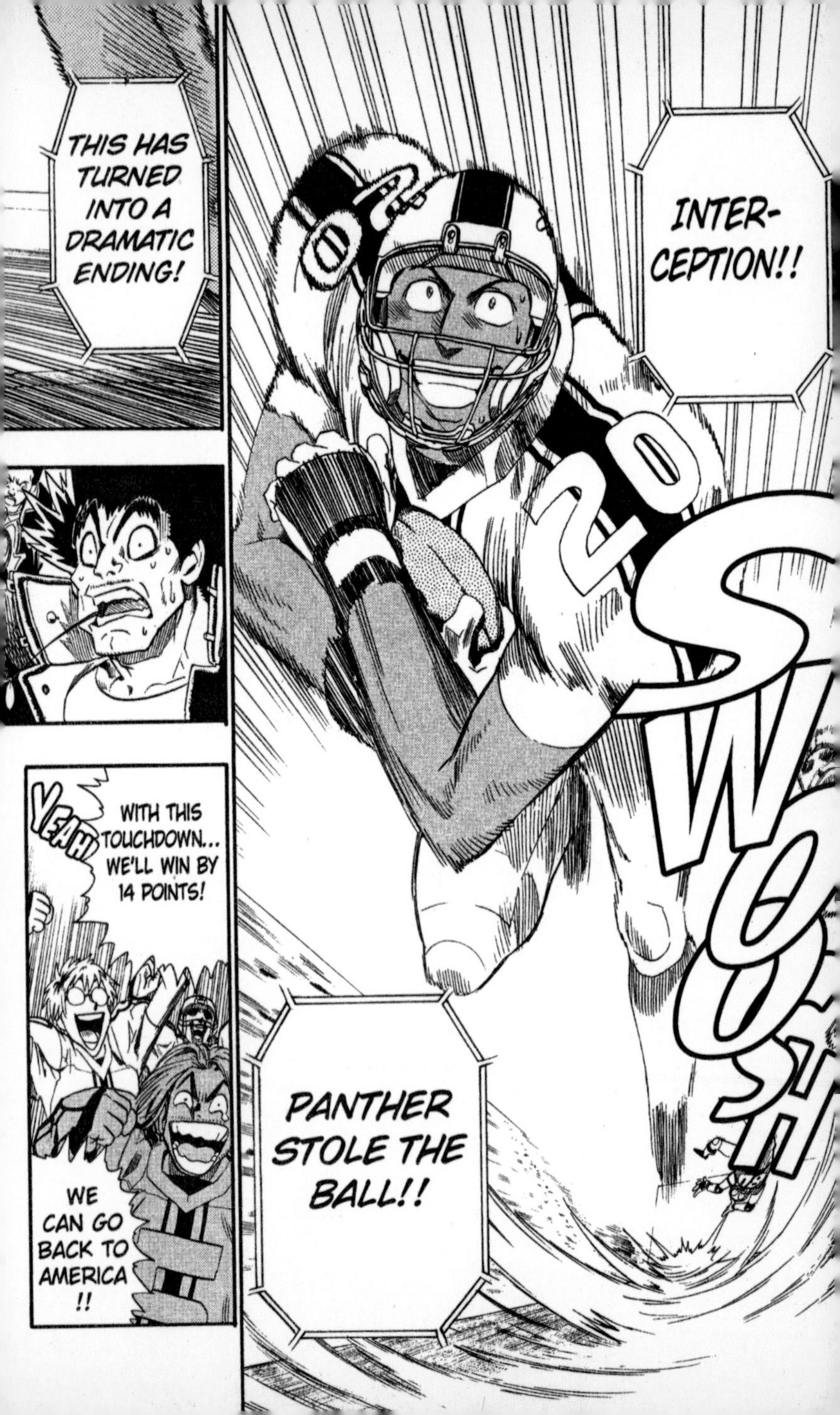
INTER-CEPTION!!
SWOOSH
PANTHER STOLE THE BALL!!
THIS HAS TURNED INTO A DRAMATIC ENDING!
YEAH!
WITH THIS TOUCHDOWN... WE'LL WIN BY 14 POINTS!
WE CAN GO BACK TO AMERICA!!

QUITE A SHIFT FROM DEIMON'S OFFENSE!

PANTHER'S GOING FOR THE TOUCHDOWN!

LOOKS LIKE DEIMON'S PLAYERS DON'T HAVE THE STRENGTH TO GO AFTER HIM!

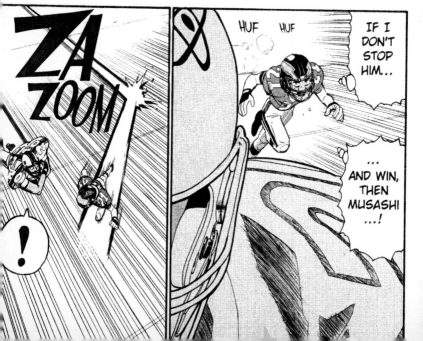

ZA ZOOM!

!

HUF HUF

IF I DON'T STOP HIM..

...AND WIN, THEN MUSASHI...!

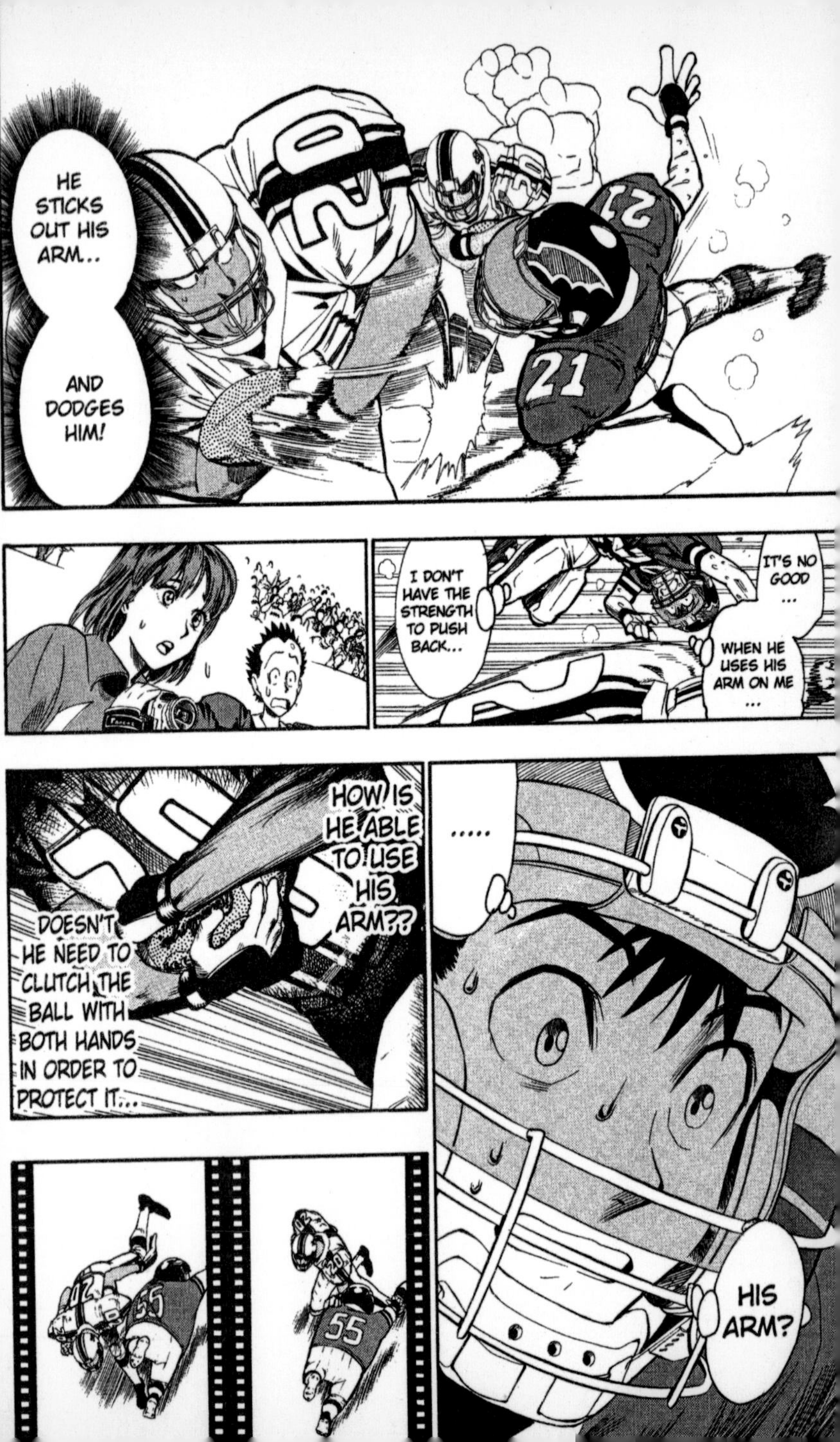
HE STICKS OUT HIS ARM..
AND DODGES HIM!
IT'S NO GOOD ...
WHEN HE USES HIS ARM ON ME ...
I DON'T HAVE THE STRENGTH TO PUSH BACK...
.....
HIS ARM?
HOW IS HE ABLE TO USE HIS ARM??
DOESN'T HE NEED TO CLUTCH THE BALL WITH BOTH HANDS IN ORDER TO PROTECT IT...

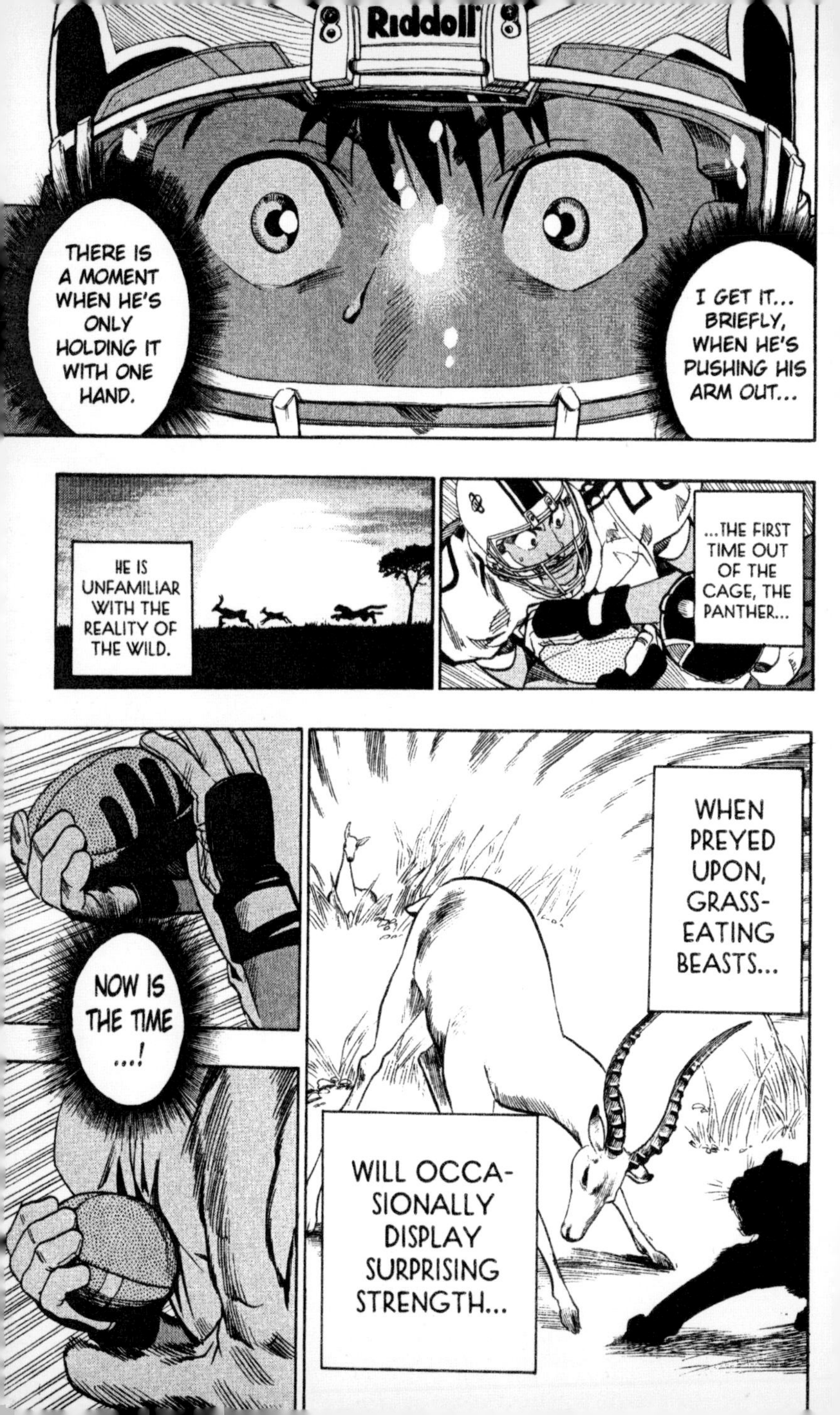
I GET IT... BRIEFLY, WHEN HE'S PUSHING HIS ARM OUT...
THERE IS A MOMENT WHEN HE'S ONLY HOLDING IT WITH ONE HAND.
...THE FIRST TIME OUT OF THE CAGE, THE PANTHER...
HE IS UNFAMILIAR WITH THE REALITY OF THE WILD.
WHEN PREYED UPON, GRASS-EATING BEASTS...
WILL OCCASIONALLY DISPLAY SURPRISING STRENGTH...
NOW IS THE TIME ...!

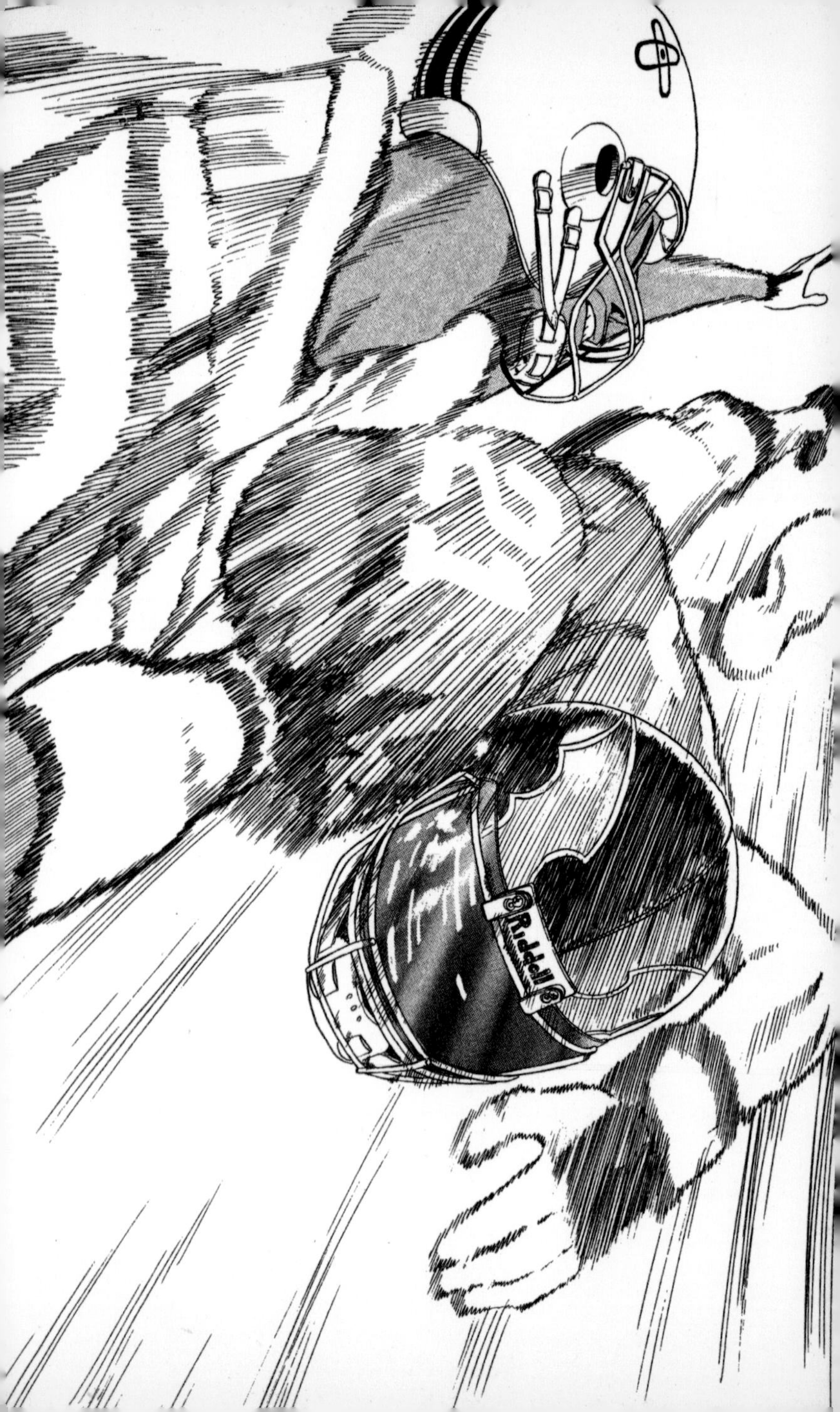
Riddell

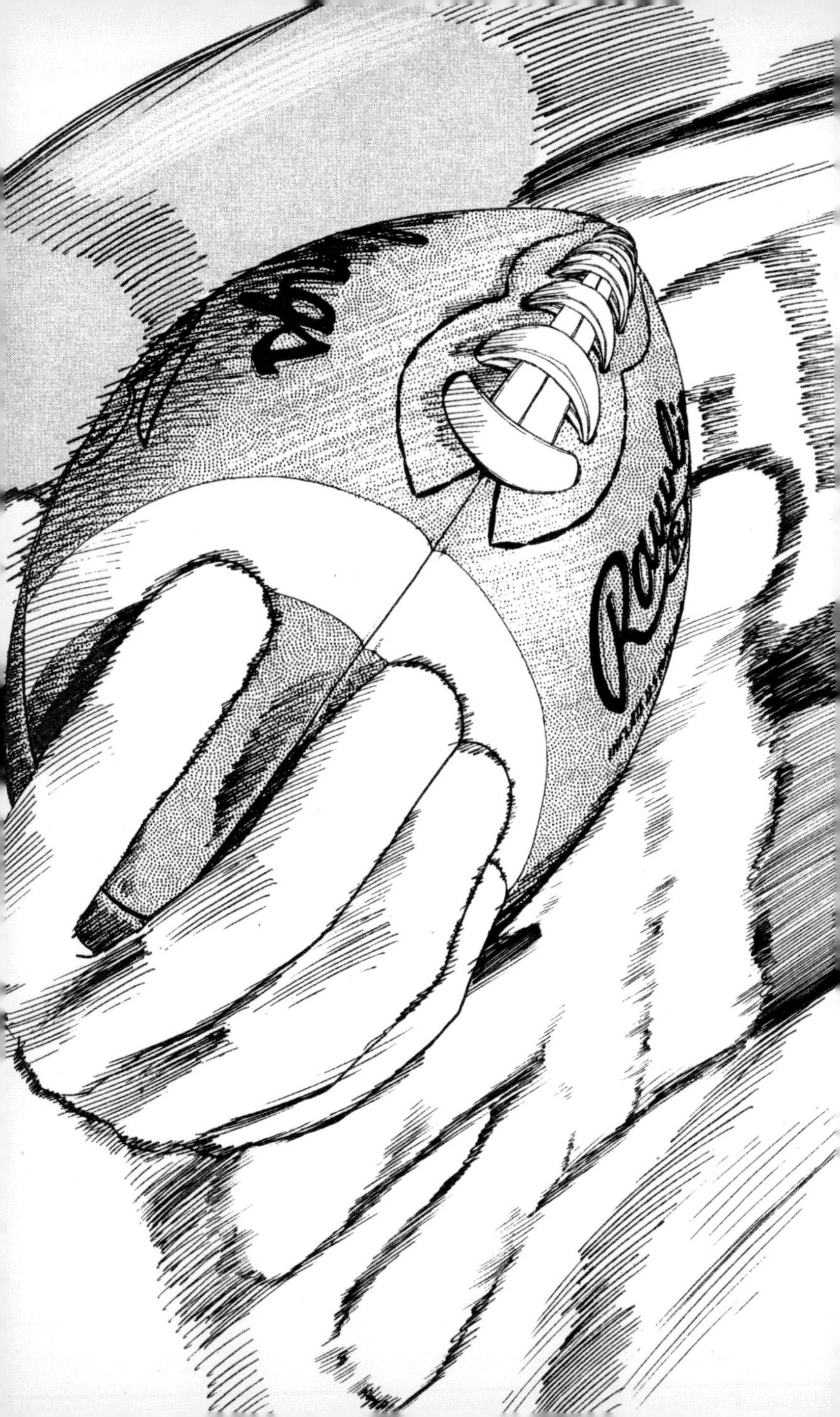

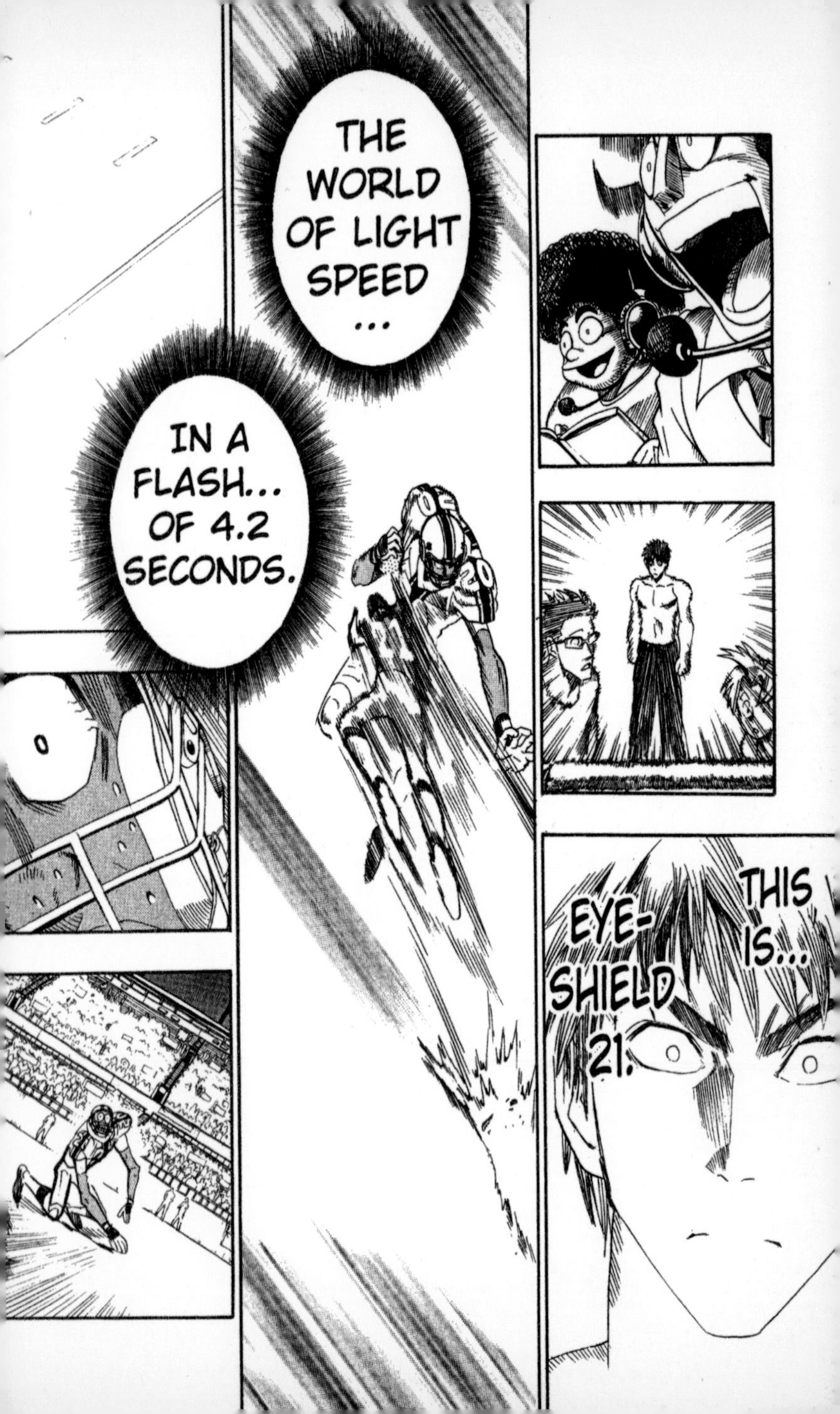
THE WORLD OF LIGHT SPEED ...
IN A FLASH... OF 4.2 SECONDS.
THIS IS...
EYE-SHIELD 21.

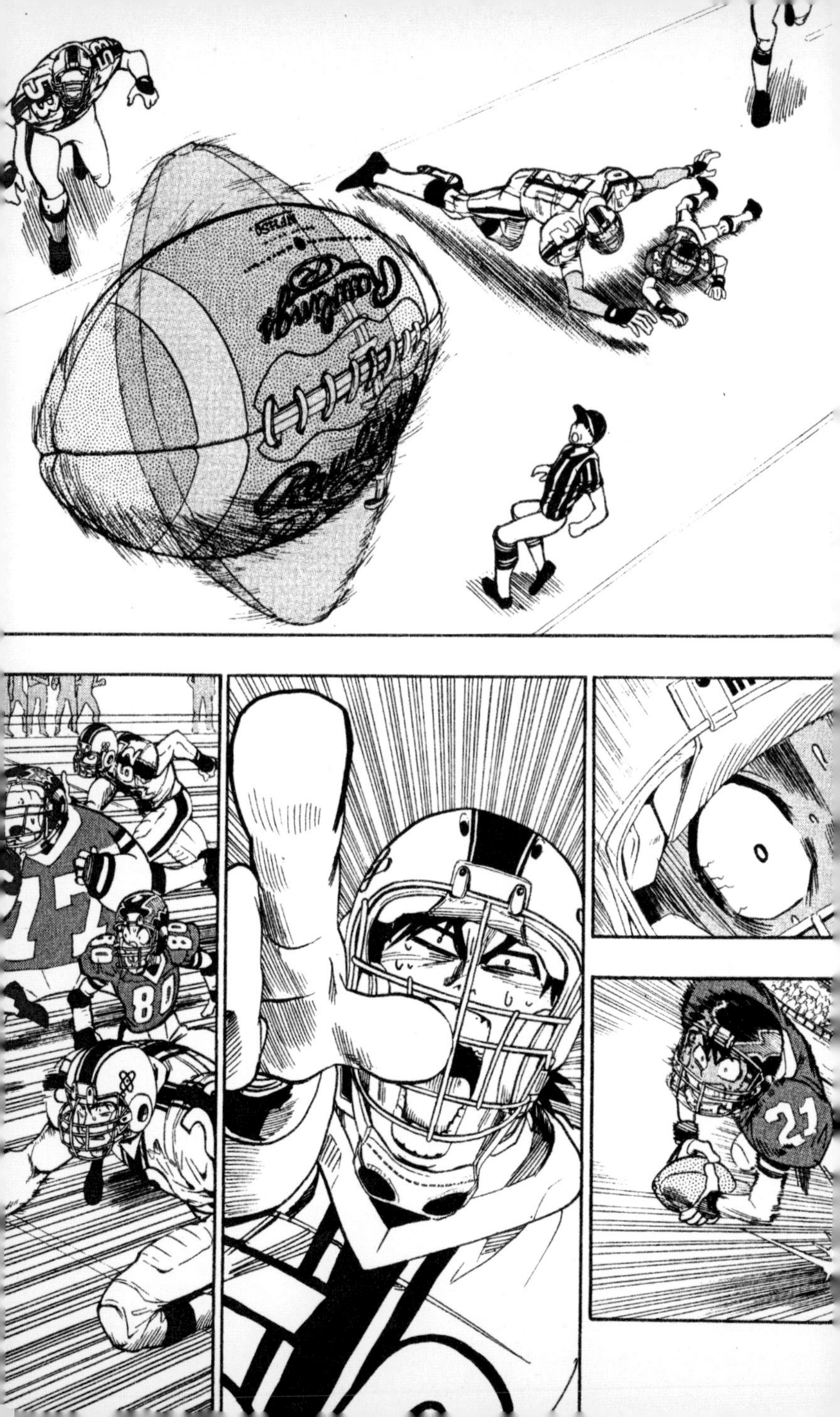

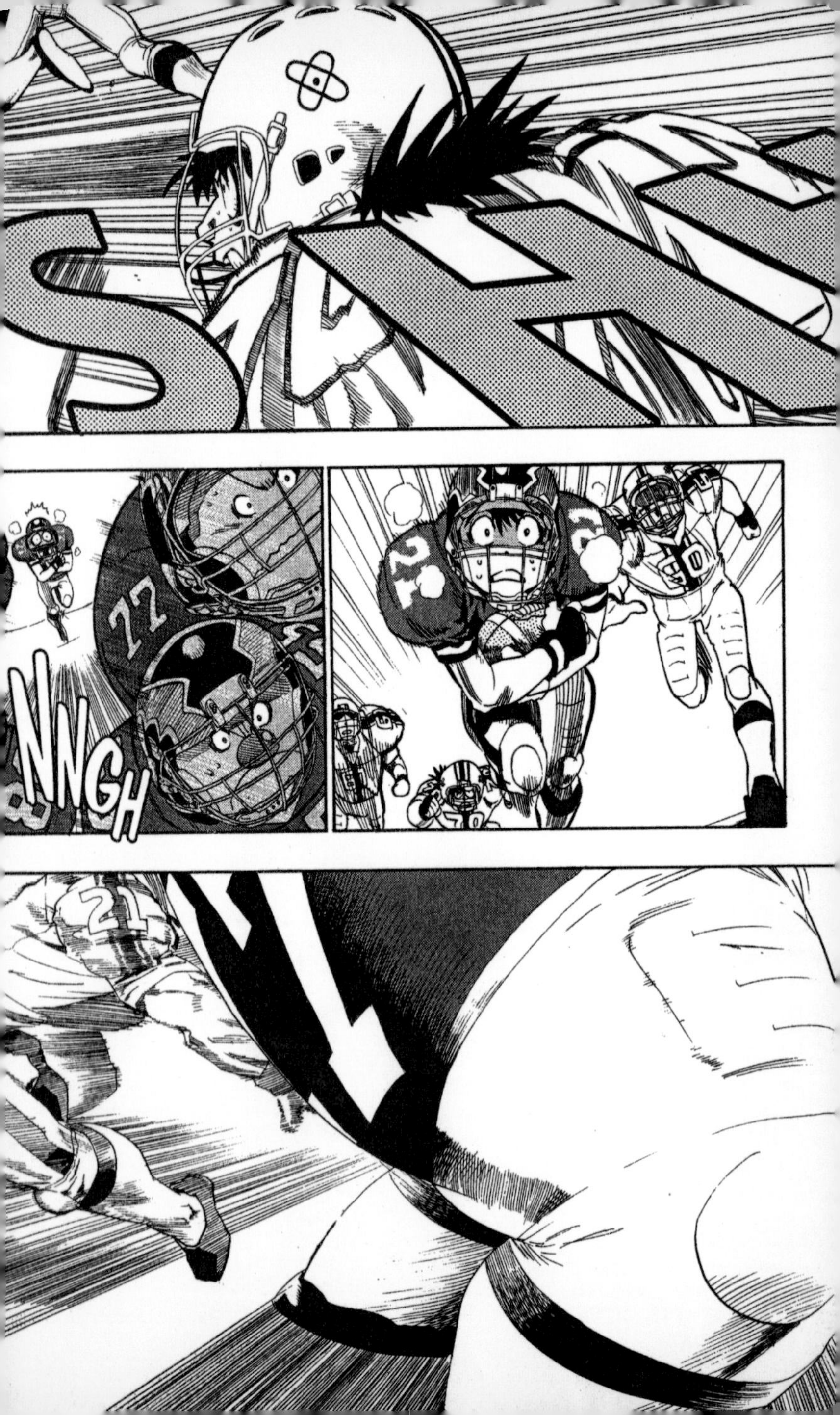
NNGH

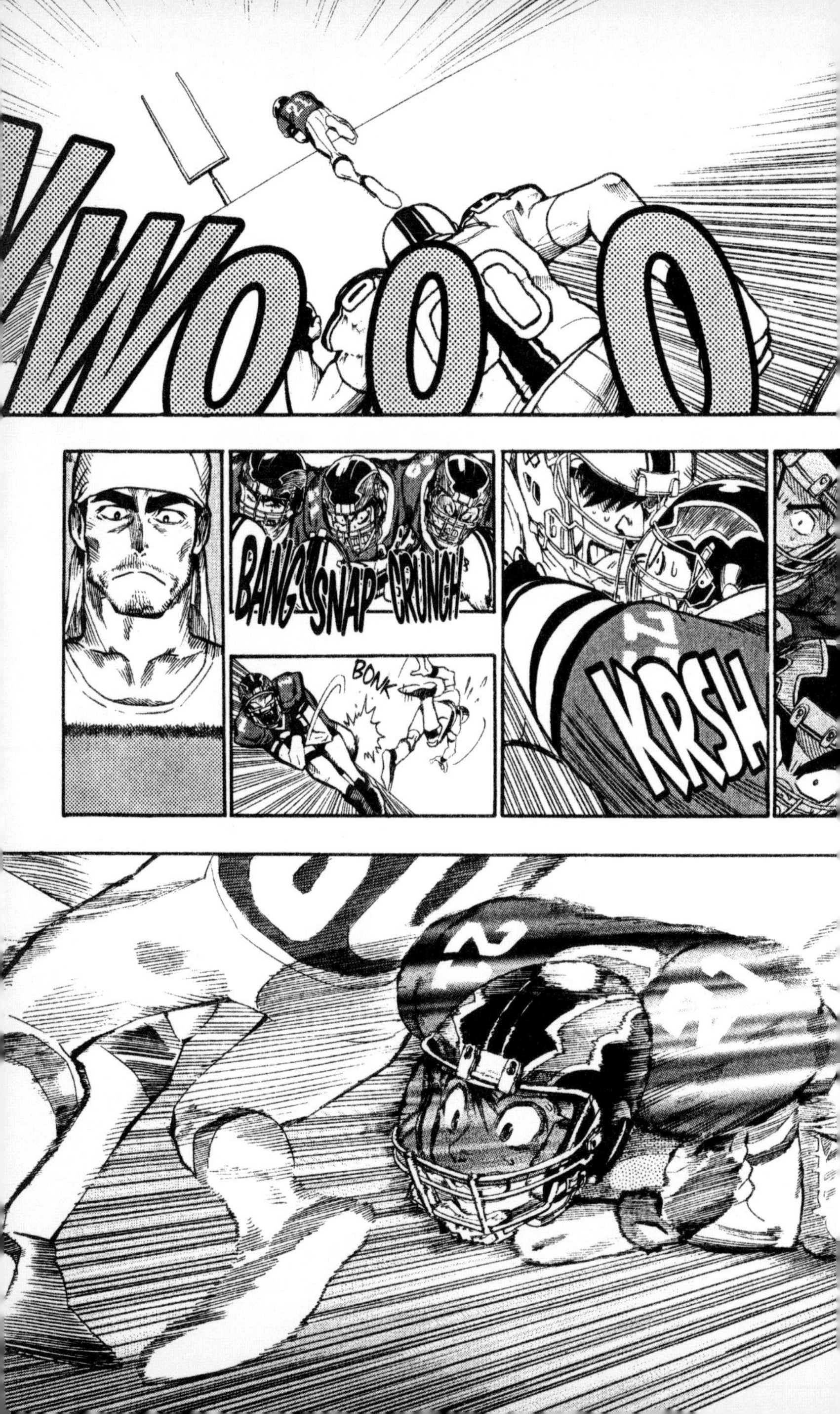
WOOO
KRSH
BANG SNAP CRUNCH
BONK

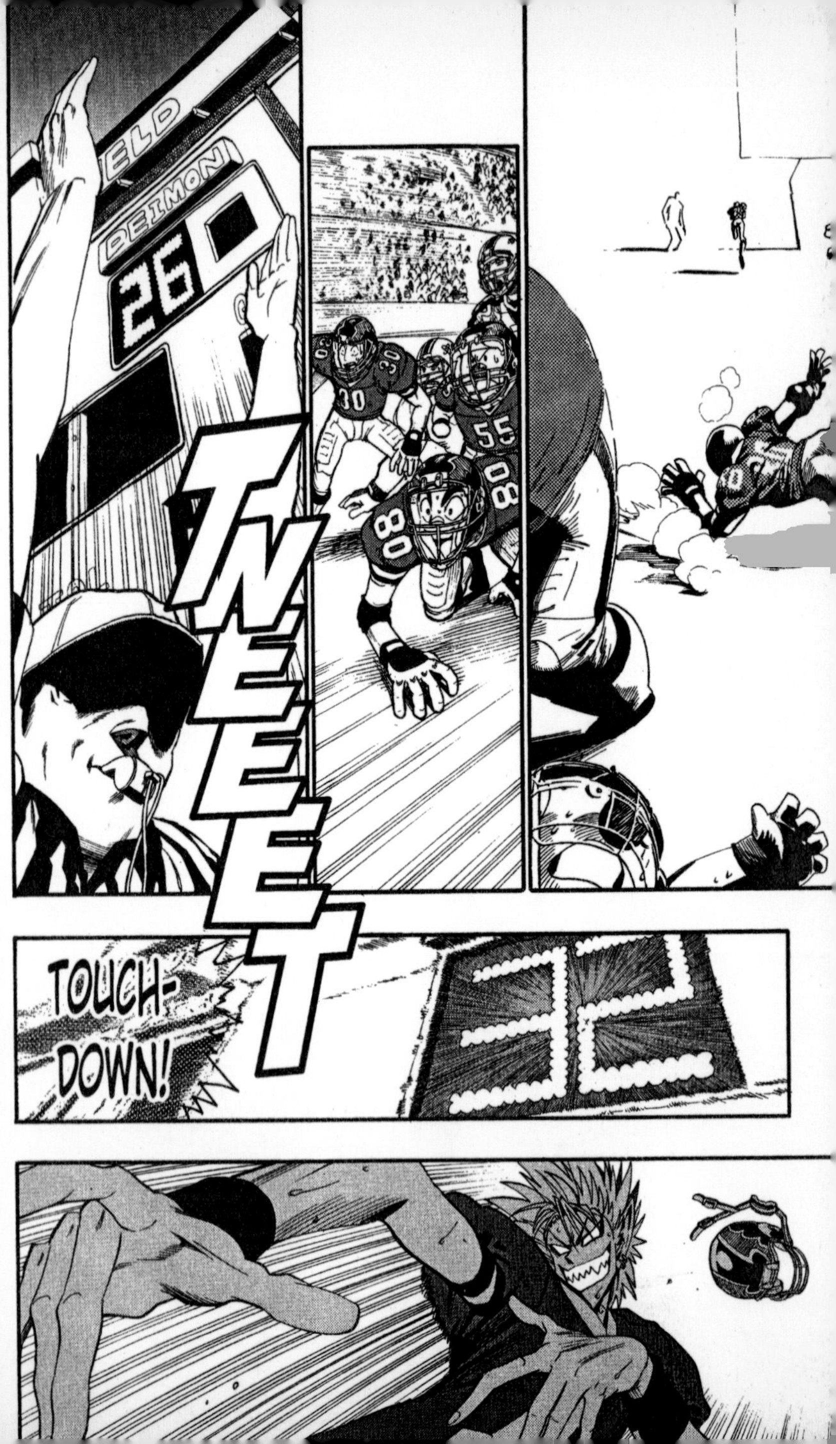
DEIMON
26
TWEEEET
TOUCH-DOWN!
32

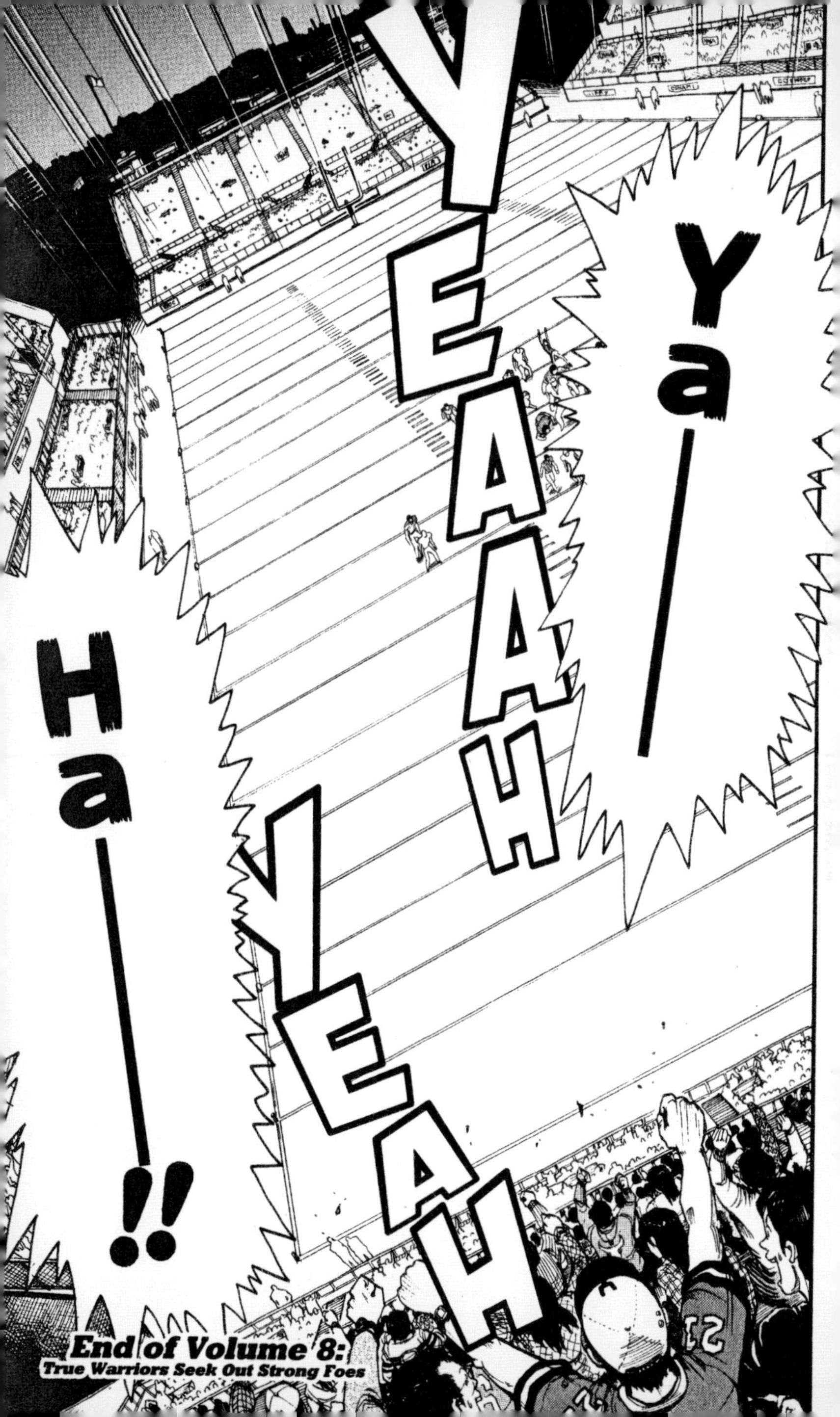
Ya—
YEAAH
YEAH
Ha—!!
End of Volume 8:
True Warriors Seek Out Strong Foes

Deluxe Biographies of the Supporting Cast

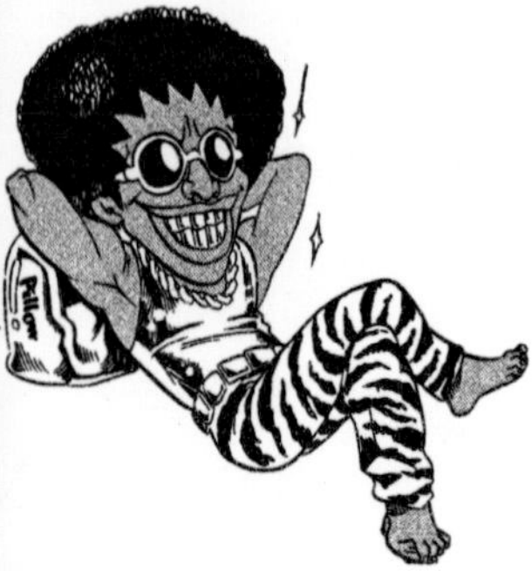
Pillow

Morgan

Being the NFL's star runner has made him a millionaire, earning ¥2 billion ($20 million) a year!

He likes glitter so much, the walls in his home are gold! And the floors! The pillows are gold ingots! Seems like that would be hard to sleep on. The tissues are gold leaf! Seems like that would hard to blow your nose with.

The Muscle Brothers

A legion of big tough guys headed up by Big Poop Gonzales.

Whenever they meet cute girls, they like to tear off their shirts to show off their bulging chests, so they always have to wear new clothes. It's not the best way to pick up girls though...

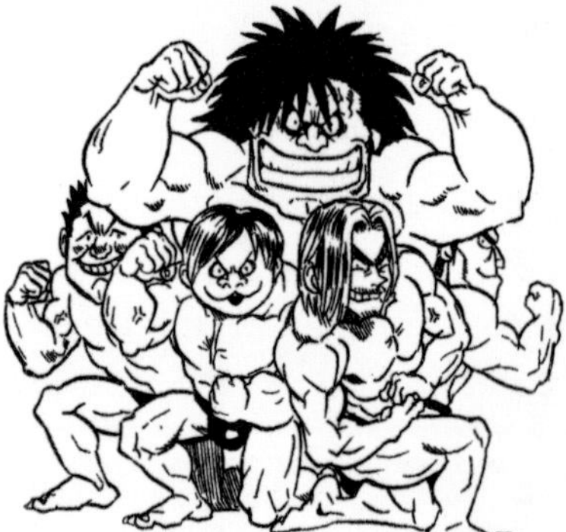

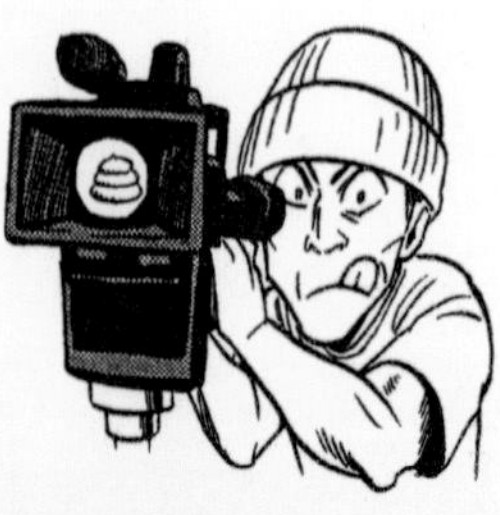

The Cameraman Who Was Fooled By Sena's Moves

He uses his camera to pay them back for being fooled!

He has every moment from the whole game recorded on his camera! He even went as far as taking extra close-ups of Cerberus pooping to show how mad he was. He later got a lot of complaints from viewers.

Tama Zoo

Recently, the monkeys have started doing dogeza when they are begging for food. The animal behavior scientists are concerned about where they could have learned this.

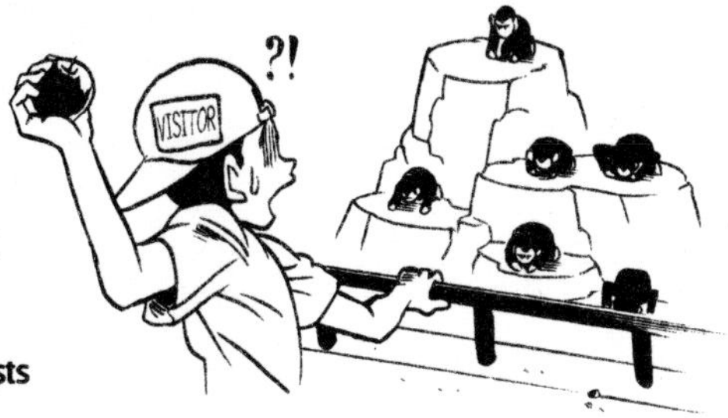
?!
VISITOR

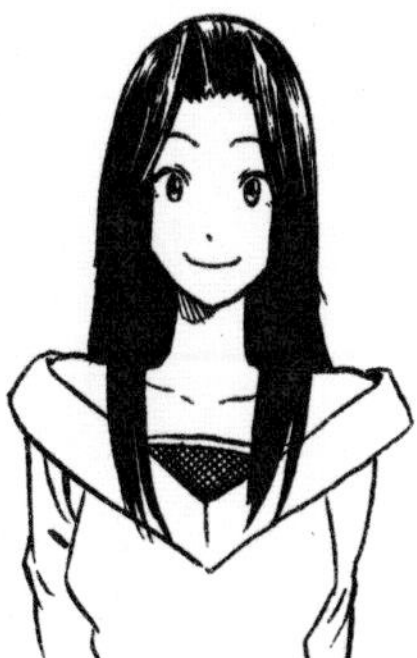

The Girl Who Came Up With the Name "Eyesh"

She likes to give people nicknames. Let's see about the ones she's given to other players:

The guy who has a cross-shaped scar on his cheek — Jumonji

In Japanese, "Ju" means "ten." The kanji "ju" is written as a plus sign. "Monji" = "mark" or "character."

The guy who seems like a little champion — Komusubi

This is a word play on sumo wrestling rankings, with "komusubi" being the lowest of the four rankings. "Yokuzuna" is the highest of the four rankings. The girl thought he was like a "small yokuzuna."

The big guy with a head like a chestnut — Kurita

Kurita is the bigger "yokuzuna." In Japanese, "kuri" means "chestnut" and "ta" means "fat."

The Owner of the Armadillos

Now they say that the origin of the team name is because there are so many armadillos in Texas... but really it has to do with the owner's personality.

Whenever the team loses, he hides away in his office and, like an armadillo, curls himself into a ball and cries. It's really a terrible name for a team...

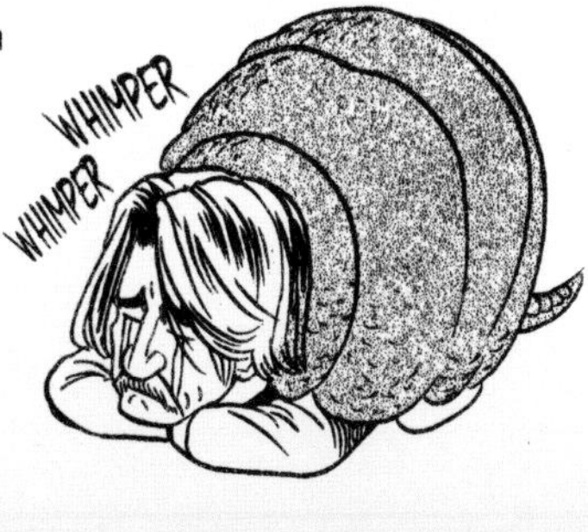
WHIMPER
WHIMPER

Next volume's sneak preview: There are many sudden new developments!! What happens to Eyeshield 21???

○○○○ Story Arc

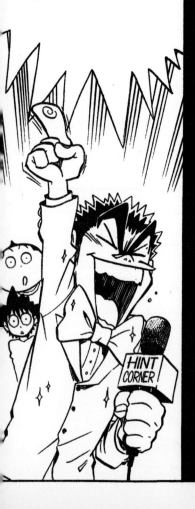

HERE ARE MAXI-HINTS ABOUT WHAT HAPPENS IN THE NEXT VOLUME!!
HINT CORNER

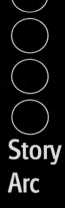

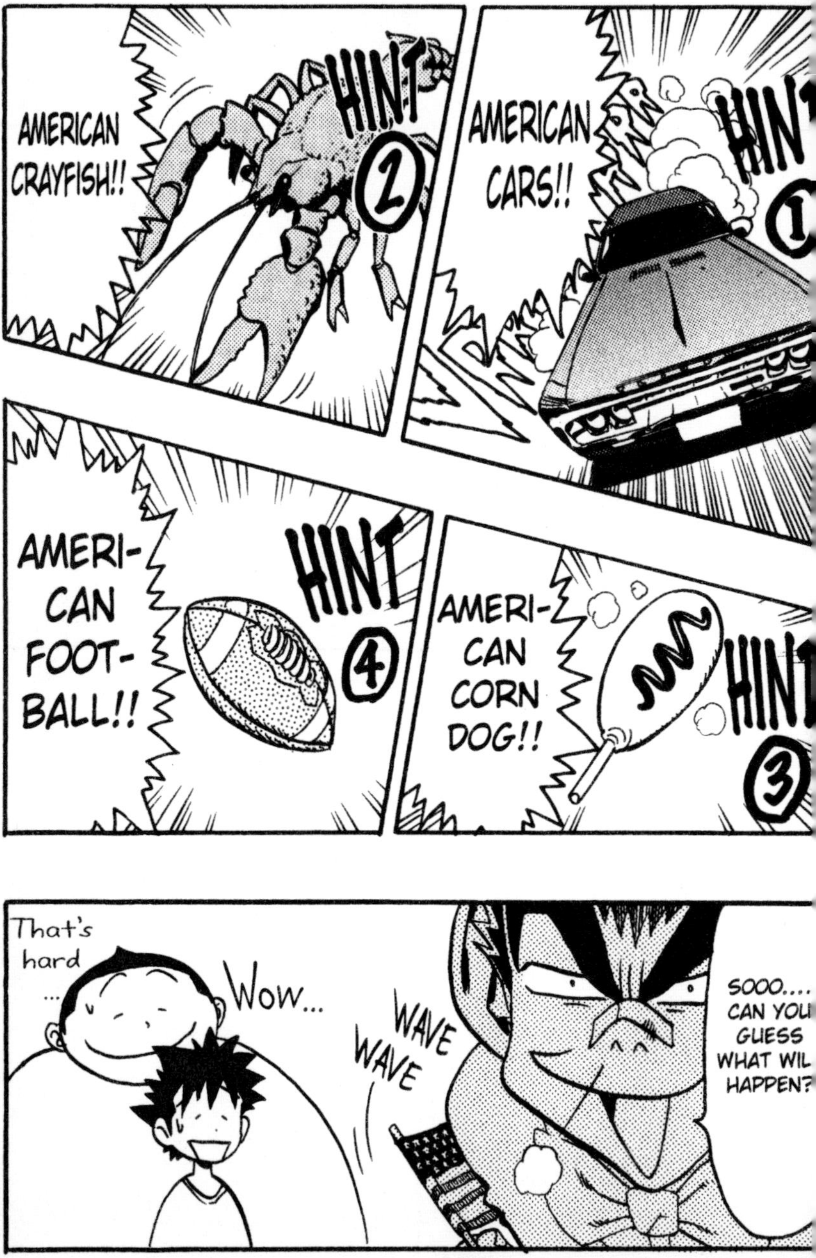

HIN
1
AMERICAN CARS!!
HINT 2
AMERICAN CRAYFISH!!
HINT 3
AMERI-CAN CORN DOG!!
HINT 4
AMERI-CAN FOOT-BALL!!
SOOO.... CAN YOU GUESS WHAT WIL HAPPEN?
WAVE WAVE
Wow...
That's hard ...

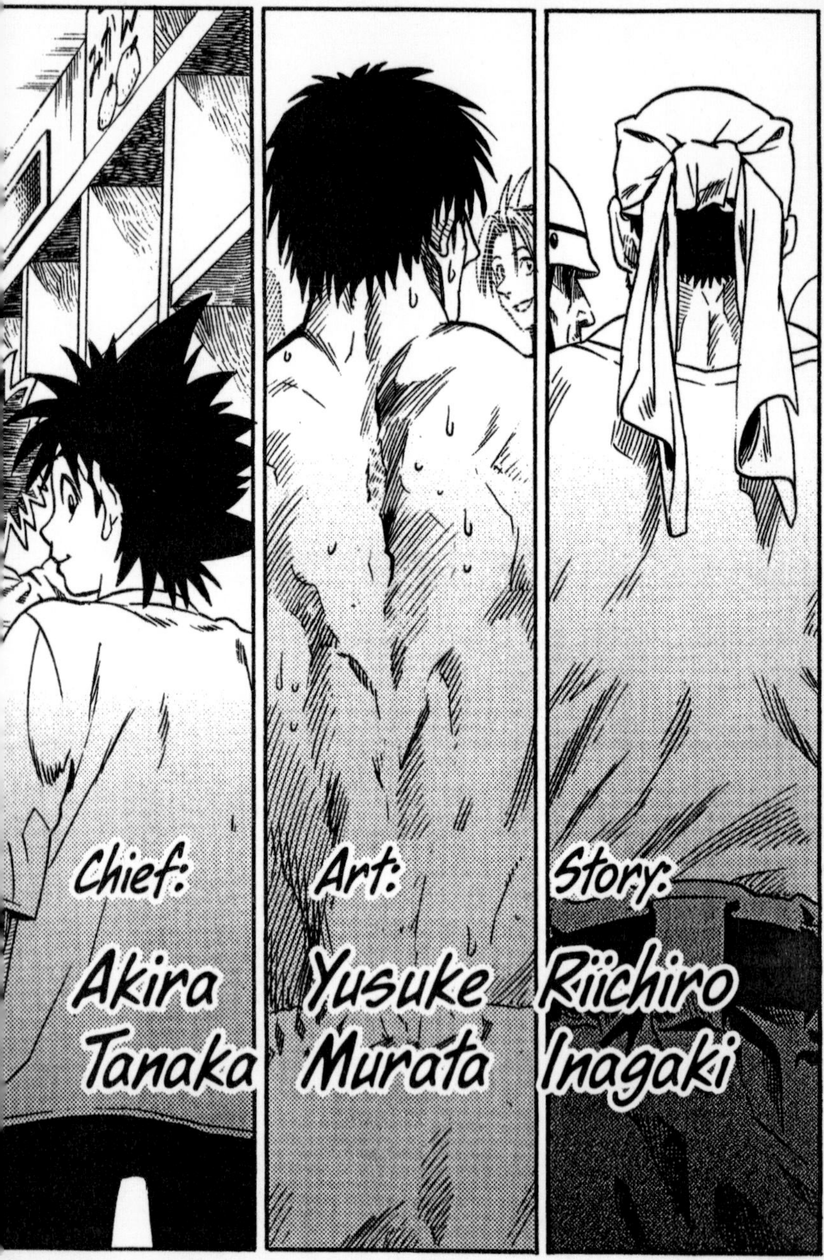
Story:
Riichiro Inagaki
Art:
Yusuke Murata
Chief:
Akira Tanaka

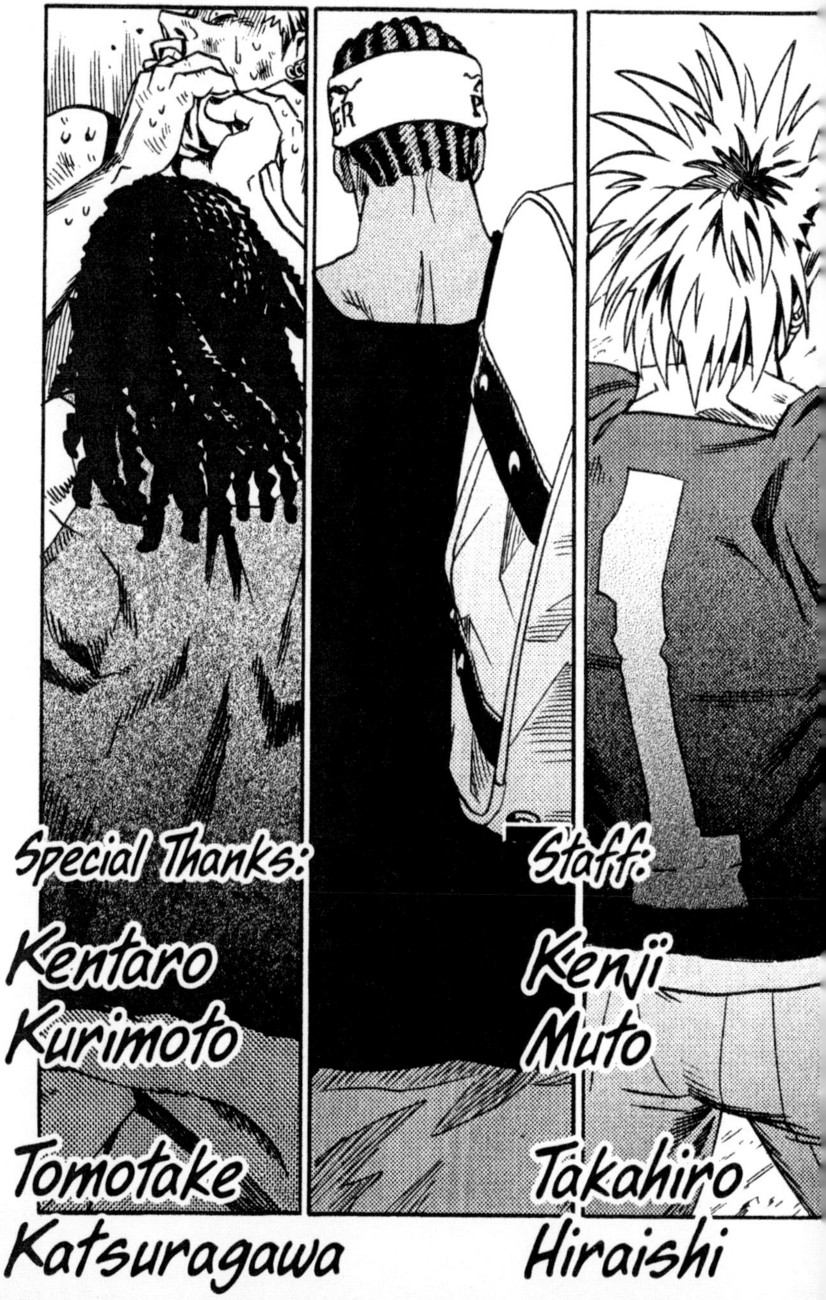

Staff:

Kenji Muto

Takahiro Hiraishi

Special Thanks:

Kentaro Kurimoto

Tomotake Katsuragawa

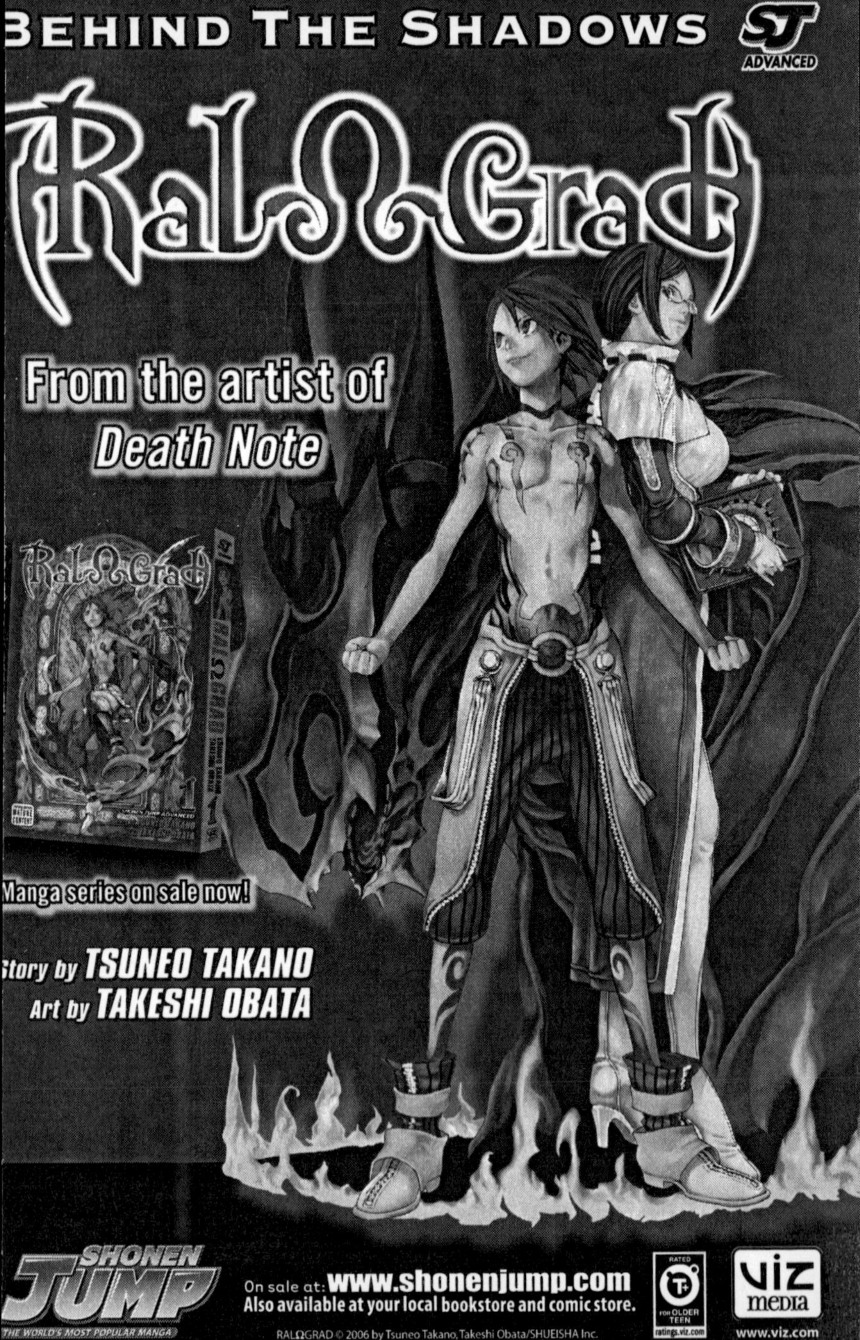
BEHIND THE SHADOWS
SJ ADVANCED
RalΩGrad
From the artist of Death Note
Manga series on sale now!
Story by TSUNEO TAKANO
Art by TAKESHI OBATA
SHONEN JUMP
THE WORLD'S MOST POPULAR MANGA
On sale at: www.shonenjump.com
Also available at your local bookstore and comic store.
RATED T+ FOR OLDER TEEN
ratings.viz.com
VIZ media
www.viz.com
RALΩGRAD © 2006 by Tsuneo Takano, Takeshi Obata/SHUEISHA Inc.

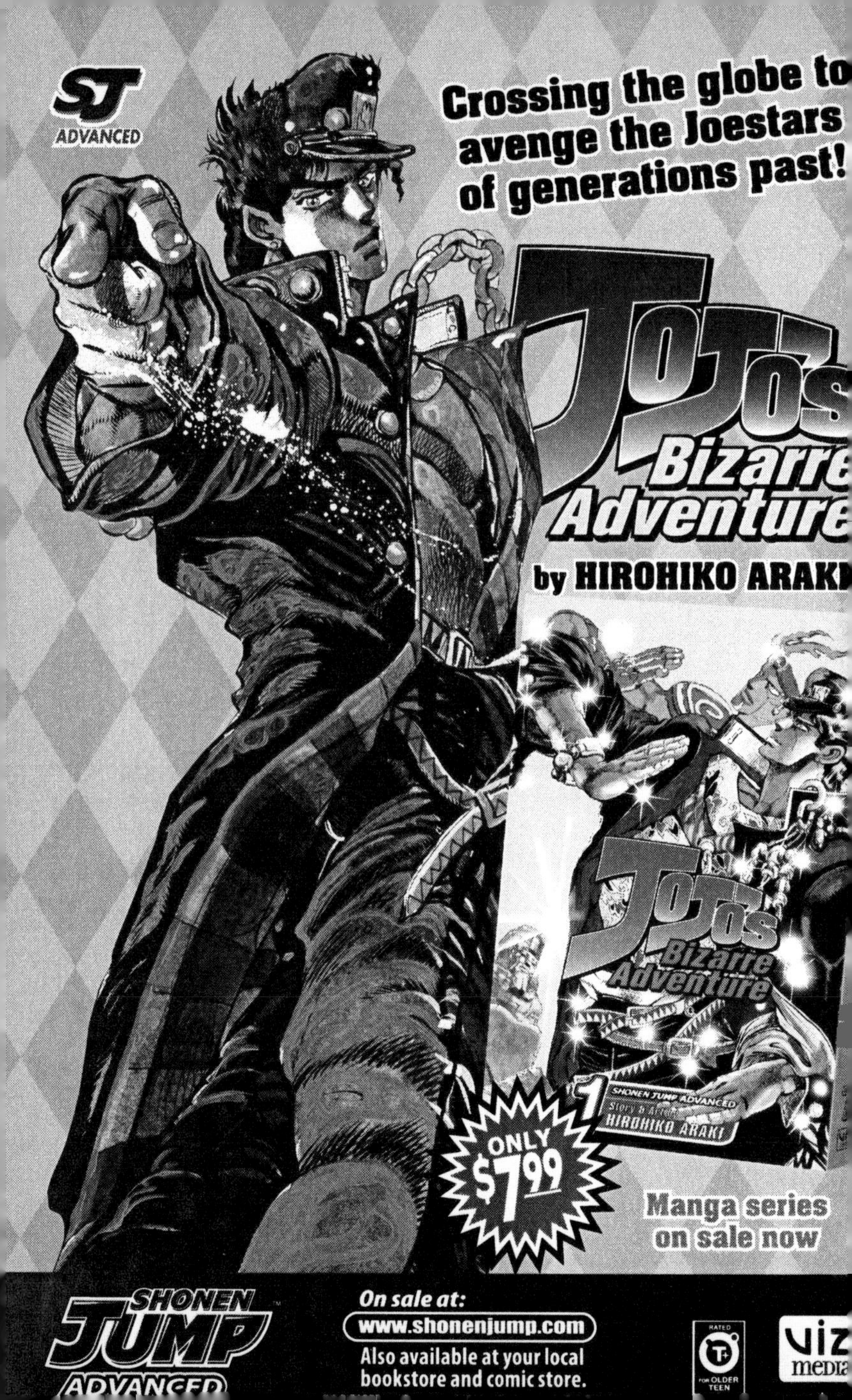
SJ ADVANCED
Crossing the globe to avenge the Joestars of generations past!
JoJo's Bizarre Adventure
by HIROHIKO ARAKI
1 SHONEN JUMP ADVANCED
Story & Art by HIROHIKO ARAKI
ONLY $7.99
Manga series on sale now
SHONEN JUMP ADVANCED
On sale at:
www.shonenjump.com
Also available at your local bookstore and comic store.
RATED T+ FOR OLDER TEEN
viz media

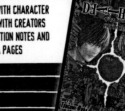

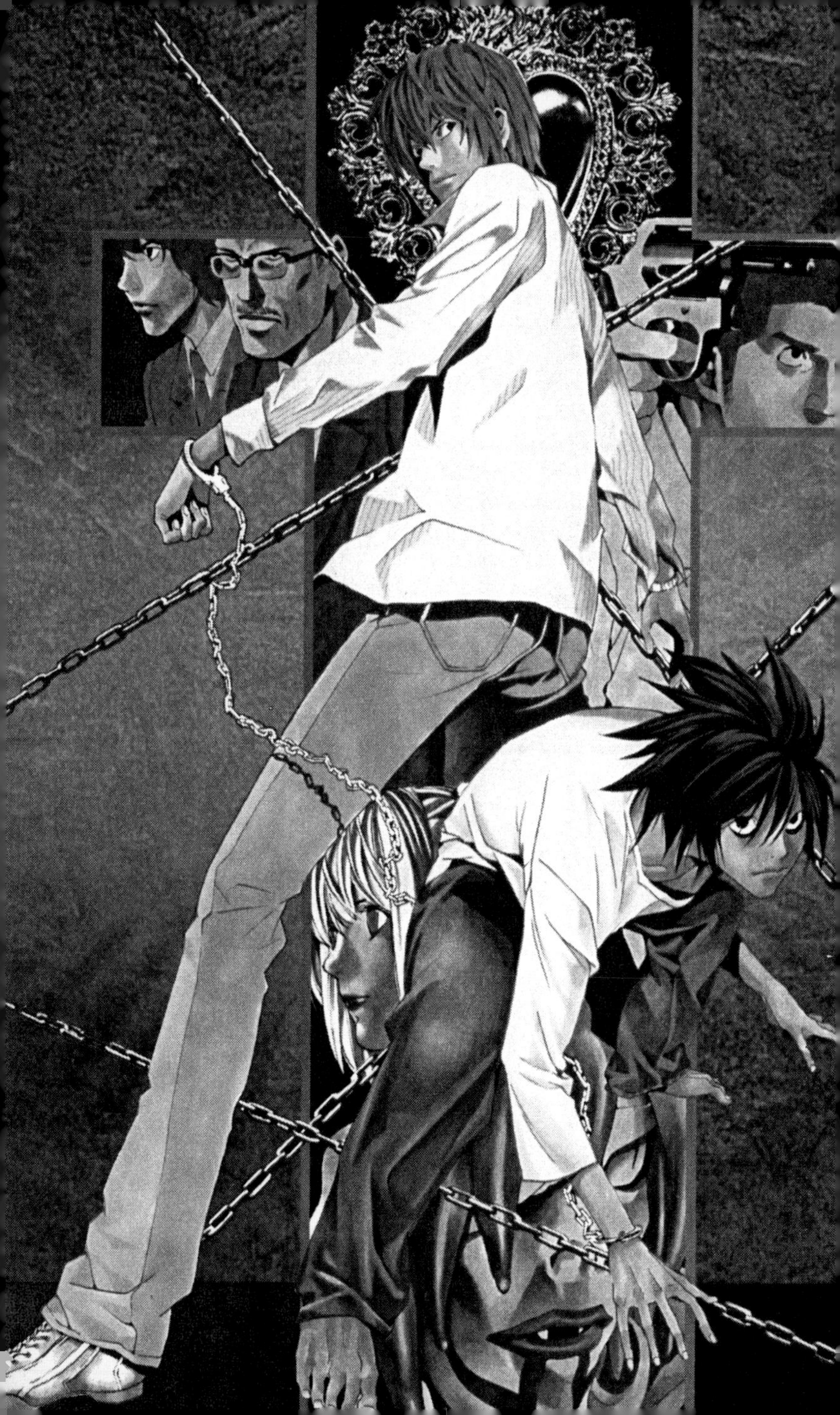

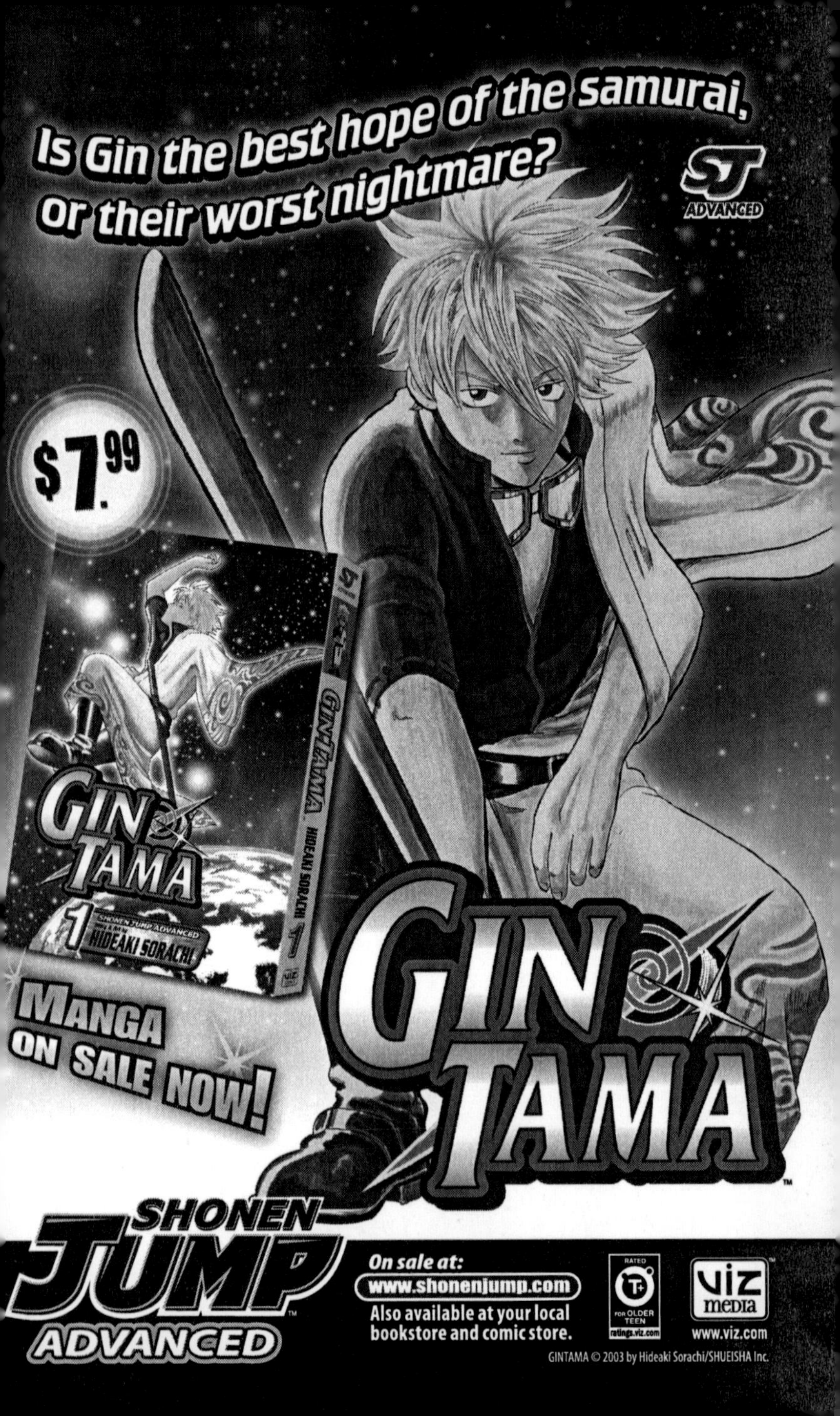
Is Gin the best hope of the samurai, or their worst nightmare?
SJ ADVANCED
$7.99
GIN TAMA
1
SHONEN JUMP ADVANCED
HIDEAKI SORACHI
MANGA ON SALE NOW!
GIN TAMA™
SHONEN JUMP™ ADVANCED
On sale at:
www.shonenjump.com
Also available at your local bookstore and comic store.
RATED T+ FOR OLDER TEEN ratings.viz.com
viz media
www.viz.com
GINTAMA © 2003 by Hideaki Sorachi/SHUEISHA Inc.

Tell us what you think about SHONEN JUMP manga!

ViZ media